Praise for *The Sewing Girl's Tale*

New York Times *Editors' Choice*
Winner of the Bancroft Prize
Francis Parkman Prize Winner
Winner of the Gotham Book Prize
New York Society Library's NYC Book Award Winner
Journal of the American Revolution *Book of the Year*

"Fascinating . . . An excellent and absorbing work of social and cultural history." —*The New York Times Book Review*

"A vividly intimate portrait of American life as the nation was coming into being. Mr. Sweet has given us a masterpiece of splendidly readable social history." —*The Wall Street Journal*

"*The Sewing Girl's Tale* is an extraordinary achievement, combining enthralling narration and impressive historical detective work. When in 1793 Lanah Sawyer, a naïve young seamstress, is raped in a brothel by a wealthy man-about-town, she refuses to remain silent and sets off a major scandal, enveloping her family and his, criminal and civil courts, an outraged mob, debtors' prison, forged letters, Alexander Hamilton,

and more. Readers will not be able to put this book down!"
—Mary Beth Norton, author of
In the Devil's Snare: The Salem Witchcraft Crisis of 1692

"Sweet draws on a dizzying array of archives and sources to pick up the traces of Sawyer's world, one long gone from the Manhattan of today.... Sweet makes us care about her, about her pursuit of justice, and how she made it through."
—*The Times* (UK)

"In 1793, in New York City, in a fifteen-hour rape trial followed by fifteen minutes of jury deliberations, six powerful attorneys representing a man of privilege did all they could to turn seventeen-year-old Lanah Sawyer into someone who didn't matter. In *The Sewing Girl's Tale*, historian John Wood Sweet provides a masterful counter. In a brilliant reconstruction of one of the most telling criminal cases in American history, he brings to life not only Sawyer but all the malevolent forces aligned against her, including one Alexander Hamilton. Lanah Sawyer and her story mattered—then, and now."
—Ken Armstrong, Pulitzer Prize–winning reporter and coauthor of *Unbelievable*

"In this incisive historical investigation, Sweet ... reconstructs a memorable story that reveals the virulent anti-feminism embedded in American democracy.... This carefully researched

book will appeal to historians, feminist scholars, and anyone with an interest in narratives that chronicle female erasure in a social system created by and for the benefit of (White) men."
—***Kirkus Reviews***

"*The Sewing Girl's Tale* is a masterful narrative history, featuring a remarkable combination of riveting drama and world-class scholarship. *The Sewing Girl's Tale* is a mystery, a true crime tale, a courtroom drama, and a scathing analysis of a society stacked against young women. John Wood Sweet has written a story of sex and power that is both vividly historic and ripped from the headlines."—**Debby Applegate, Pulitzer Prize–winning author of *Madam* and *The Most Famous Man in America***

"A masterful and sweeping account of life in 1790s America, where the tensions between classes, the role of the men who enslaved people in determining justice and the enforcement of patriarchal gender roles would each play a part in Sawyer and Bedlow's fates."
—***Star Tribune*** (Minneapolis)

"John Wood Sweet's dazzling book transforms a modest sewing-girl's story of date rape by a rich libertine into a fully realized, near novel-like treatment of the sexual morals of the 1790s. Historians familiar with Lanah Sawyer's rape case will be awed by his stunning research finds, while general readers will marvel at his astute psychological renderings of all his characters. By close analysis of Sawyer's options, actions, and words, Sweet fleshes her out from a near-voiceless victim to a young woman intent on getting justice in a legal system stacked by class and gender." **—Patricia Cline Cohen, author of** *The Murder of Helen Jewett*

"Sweet paints an evocative portrait of 18th-century New York. The result is a vivid addition to the history of sexual politics in America." *—Publishers Weekly*

"Sweet's narrative combines meticulous research with his extensive historical expertise. . . . A fascinating dive into history while restoring Lanah's place in her own narrative." *—The Atlanta Journal-Constitution*

"An incredibly immersive, highly readable exploration of an important moment in American history, perfect for readers of true crime, history, women's history, and narrative nonfiction alike." *—Booklist*

"In all good histories a heart lies beating, if the historian is patient and attuned enough to hear it. John Wood Sweet, in a dazzling investigative turn, has restored a bright corporeality to eighteenth-century New York, which here feels as alive as it did the day Lanah Sawyer asked the courts to believe a woman. Urgent and resonant, this book is a reminder that history persists in all our bodies." **—Katy Simpson Smith, author of** *The Story of Land and Sea*

The
Sewing Girl's
TALE

The *Sewing Girl's* TALE

A Story of Crime and Consequences

in Revolutionary America

JOHN WOOD SWEET

A HOLT PAPERBACK

HENRY HOLT AND COMPANY

NEW YORK

Holt Paperbacks
Henry Holt and Company
Publishers since 1866
120 Broadway
New York, New York 10271
www.henryholt.com

The Library of Congress has cataloged the hardcover edition as follows:

Names: Sweet, John Wood, 1966– author.
Title: The sewing girl's tale : a story of crime and consequences in
   revolutionary America / John Wood Sweet.
Description: First edition. | New York : Henry Holt and Company, 2022. |
   Includes bibliographical references and index.
Identifiers: LCCN 2021060806 (print) | LCCN 2021060807 (ebook) |
   ISBN 9781250761965 (hardcover) | ISBN 9781250761972 (ebook)
Subjects: LCSH: Bedlow, Henry—Trials, litigation, etc. | Trials
   (Rape)—New York (State)—New York—History—18th century | Sawyer,
   Lanah, approximately 1776– | Rape—Social aspects—New York (State)—New
   York—History—18th century.
Classification: LCC KF223.B43 S94 2022 (print) | LCC KF223.B43 (ebook) |
   DDC 345.73/02532—dc23/eng/20220430
LC record available at https://lccn.loc.gov/2021060806
LC ebook record available at https://lccn.loc.gov/2021060807

ISBN 9781250871480 (trade paperback)

Our books may be purchased in bulk for promotional, educational, or business use. Please contact
your local bookseller or the Macmillan Corporate and Premium Sales Department at (800) 221-7945,
extension 5442, or by e-mail at MacmillanSpecialMarkets@macmillan.com.

Originally published in hardcover in 2022 by Henry Holt and Company

First Holt Paperbacks Edition 2023

Designed by Meryl Sussman Levavi

Printed in the United States of America

D 3 5 7 9 10 8 6 4

For

Elizabeth Wood Sweet

1936–2018

who taught me to sew and a thing or two about resilience.

Contents

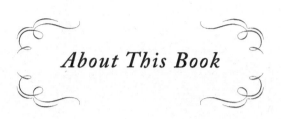

About This Book

Although written as narrative, *The Sewing Girl's Tale* is a work of history. I follow the conventions of traditional scholarship—with a few nods to readability.

Dialogue: Direct quotes are presented in the conventional way, as are paraphrases. Much of William Wyche's *Report of the Trial of Henry Bedlow, for Committing a Rape on Lanah Sawyer* (New York, 1793) consists of testimony rendered in the third person. In passages where I could transpose third-person testimony into direct dialogue with only minor changes to verbs and pronouns, I have done so and presented the result without quotation marks and set off in italics.

Quotes: Original spellings, punctuation, and capitalization have been retained—with a few exceptions, indicated in the notes.

Names: In Wyche's *Report*, a number of proper names are garbled or confused. I have used the manuscript trial minutes and other sources to accurately identify individuals. Corrections to Wyche's *Report* are made silently in the text and documented in the notes.

Addresses: Since 1793, New York's street numbers, street names, and block configurations have changed repeatedly, but most of the locations referred to in this story can be identified with precision. For clarity, I generally refer to locations by their modern street addresses.

The
Sewing Girl's
TALE

Lanah Sawyer's New York

Circa 1793

HUDSON RIVER

FRESH WATER POND

Paulus Hook Ferry

Modern Shoreline

Columbia College

Debtors' Prison

The Fields

St. Paul's Chapel

PARK ROW

Robert Towt

Bathing house

BROAD WAY

Mother Carey

BEEKMAN ST.

Samuel Hone

Miss Steddiford

ANN ST.

Lanah Sawyer

Evertson & Riggs

BROAD WAY

JOHN ST.

GOLD ST.

Lucretia Harper

GREENWICH ST.

Trinity Church

BROAD ST.

Mayor Varick

PEARL ST.

Corré Hotel

Federal Hall

WALL ST.

Mrs. Bruce

FRONT ST.

Alexander Anderson

BROAD ST.

DOCK ST.

MOORE ST.

The Battery

EAST

Map by Gene Thorp

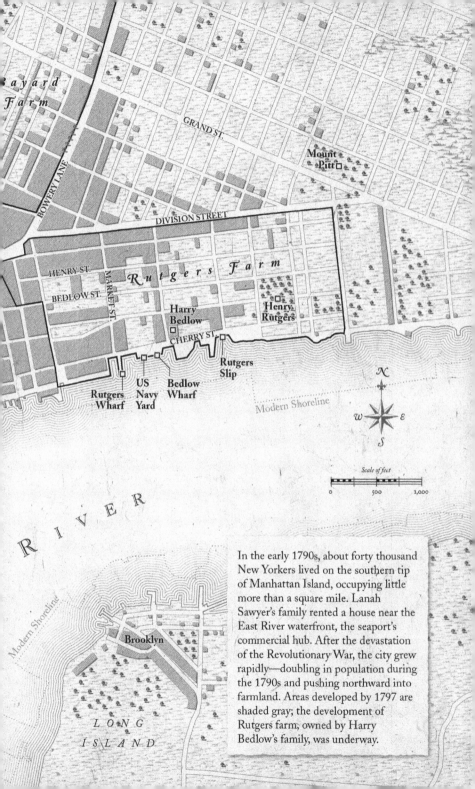

BAYARD FARM

GRAND ST.

BOWERY LANE

Mount Pitt

DIVISION STREET

HENRY ST.

BEDLOW ST.

MARKET ST.

Rutgers Farm

Harry Bedlow

CHERRY ST.

Henry Rutgers

Rutgers Slip

Rutgers Wharf

US Navy Yard

Bedlow Wharf

Modern Shoreline

N
W E
S

Scale of feet
0   500   1,000

R I V E R

Modern Shoreline

Brooklyn

L O N G
I S L A N D.

In the early 1790s, about forty thousand New Yorkers lived on the southern tip of Manhattan Island, occupying little more than a square mile. Lanah Sawyer's family rented a house near the East River waterfront, the seaport's commercial hub. After the devastation of the Revolutionary War, the city grew rapidly—doubling in population during the 1790s and pushing northward into farmland. Areas developed by 1797 are shaded gray; the development of Rutgers farm, owned by Harry Bedlow's family, was underway.

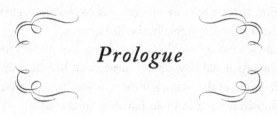

Prologue

The sun that rose for the rest of the world that morning was not the one that rose for Lanah Sawyer. At daybreak, the dark void of the new moon began to block the sun as it crept up over the horizon, casting a shadow over the city. By six o'clock, the eclipse was over—the sun broke free, the moon disappeared, and raking light illuminated the city pretty much the way it did on any other late-summer morning. But even then, all Lanah could see was darkness.

Light suddenly filled the room two hours later, when Harry Bedlow rose from the bed and opened the window shutter. After hours disoriented by the dark, Lanah Sawyer could see that it was broad daylight. This was her first chance to get a good look at her surroundings, but by this point she knew all too well where she was: in a crudely built room at the back of a brothel. Until late the night before, she had been flattered by the attentions of the twenty-six-year-old gentleman. To a seventeen-year-old sewing girl, he had seemed like an unexpectedly fine beau. It wasn't until they had been less than a block away—now, peering out into the alley, she could almost see the spot where, walking together up Broadway, they had reached the dark, narrow entrance of Ann Street—that she had realized who he really was, where he was trying to take her, and the trouble she was in.

If she had slept at all, it had been fitfully. During the long, moonless night, the darkness had been complete. Several times, she had climbed out of the bed and tried to find a way to escape. But she could see nothing. Feeling her way around the room, her fingers brushing along the rough plank walls, she had found the window. But the shutters were closed, and she couldn't pry them open. She found the door, too, but it was locked, and she couldn't figure out how to release the mechanism. Not that she had much time to try. Each time she got up, Harry noticed, got up too, and forced her back to bed. Eventually, she had given up.

Sometime around eight o'clock, Mrs. Carey had opened the door and fetched a three-year-old boy who, it turned out, had slept all night in a boarded-off corner of the room. For them, it was breakfast time.

Harry dressed himself and told Lanah to do the same.

Make haste, he added. *I suppose Mrs. Carey wishes us to be gone.*

Then he walked out and closed the door. The thin walls of the house did little to muffle the sound of his footsteps, the click of his walking stick, the opening and closing of the door as he stepped out into the street. There were other sounds, too, as Mother Carey, the little boy, the two women who worked in the house, and a young Black servant all went about their business at the start of another day.

It was now shortly after eight. Throughout the night, the small, dark room had been Lanah's prison. But now that she could leave, now that she was alone, it had become a kind of refuge.

For Harry Bedlow, leaving Mother Carey's had been easy. Untroubled by concern about Lanah, he could step out into the street without a care. Who was going to think twice about a somewhat disheveled gentleman leaving a bawdy house in the morning? At home were his parents. However pious they were, they had had plenty of time over the years to accustom themselves to his debauchery. Even if people knew precisely what Harry Bedlow had been up to the night before, there was little reason for him to worry about repercussions.

For Lanah, things were different.

Alone, tired, disoriented, unwelcome, Lanah took stock. Her loose, flowing linen shift, which served as underwear, was stained with blood from between her legs. There was nothing she could do about that, and it wouldn't show. Over it, there were petticoats tied around her waist and stays laced snug. Taking up her calico gown, Lanah assessed the damage: it was torn in a few places, and two or three of the strings that held it together had been ripped off. In that condition, she could not wear it in the street with any decency.

But that was a problem she could solve. Lanah was skilled with a needle and thread, which she carried in a reticule dangling from her wrist or a pocket hidden under her skirts. She worked as a seamstress to help her family make ends meet. As she stitched the gown back together, Lanah took her time. Almost two hours passed.

Finally, she pulled the gown on over her shoulders, tied the strings, and fastened the bodice with straight pins—a reminder that she didn't have the means to pay for manufactured hooks and eyes. She pulled a broad-brimmed hat onto her head and gloves onto her hands, leaving no skin exposed from her toes to her neck.

Then, she opened the door and ventured into the narrow passageway. One direction led toward the front door, which opened onto Beekman Street. The other direction led toward the back door, through a gated yard, and to the alley that opened out onto Ann Street.

Right there in front of her stood the brothel keeper.

"Deary"—Mother Carey said with jarring familiarity; she had been anticipating the young woman's departure with an eye toward discretion—"you may go out the back or the front door, as I have looked out and there is nobody in the street."

A flash of anger overcame Lanah. She responded to the older woman with startling defiance.

Suddenly, it was clear that Lanah Sawyer was not going to let her story end the way either Harry Bedlow or Mother Carey had expected.

1

Rescue

Lanah didn't understand their language, but when the foreign men started tossing out catcalls, their meaning struck home. Eleven days before she ended up in Mother Carey's back room, Lanah had stepped out into the wet city streets after a long day of rain. It was chilly for late summer; the air felt raw. The seventeen-year-old seamstress was walking alone, but she wasn't the only one who had ventured out.

Sunday evening was a popular time for leisurely strolls, social calls, spiritual lectures, and errands. Lanah may have been visiting an aged aunt who lived on the Bowling Green, picking up sewing jobs, or making a delivery as she headed into Broadway. Newly regraded to improve drainage, the roadbed had been paved with cobblestones, lined with gutters to channel storm water and clear away filth, and edged with wide, raised sidewalks. Under her feet, the wet stone slabs glittered in the gathering darkness and the glow of new whale-oil streetlamps.

As she made her way along Broadway, Lanah caught the attention of a group of Frenchmen. They began to offer up what she later described as "insults." Standard fare included abrupt propositions, outlandish compliments, and demands that she endure the abuse with a smile: *Mademoiselle, voulez vouz donnez moi votre coeur? . . . Voulez vous donnez moi un baiser? . . . Voulez vous couchez avec moi ce soir? . . . Vous êtes une belle ange! . . . Je crois que je mourrai si vouz ne mariez avec moi! . . . Vouz etes chagrinée?*

Young miss, would you give me your heart? . . . Or a kiss? . . . Or sleep with me tonight? . . . You are a beautiful angel! . . . I believe I will die if you won't marry me! . . . Why so sad?

These "Frenchmen" were most likely gentlemen recently arrived from

Saint-Domingue, where a bloody revolution had plunged the richest and most brutal colony in the world into turmoil. Over the summer, refugees—mostly planters, colonial officials, their families, and some enslaved domestic workers—had crowded into American seaports, driving up the prices of food and shelter and exciting calls for charitable contributions and government support. Several hundred of them were reportedly crammed into a single house on Vesey Street, just to the west of Broadway, near St. Paul's Chapel.

Meanwhile, the French Revolution had brought other Frenchmen into the city—including boisterous sailors on merchant vessels and men-of-war, aristocrats fleeing the Terror, and the French minister Citizen Genêt, who had just arrived in the city, determined to drag America into his country's war against Britain. The turmoil stirred up by Genêt threatened to undermine the authority of President Washington, inflamed conflicts between conservative Federalists and radical republicans, and provoked a series of violent street fights. Adding to the tension was the epidemic of yellow fever that was spreading up the Atlantic coast. Already, it had reached Philadelphia, where it would soon kill one person in ten. Now, New York was under threat. As the storm that day raged, some prayed that it would wash away whatever was causing the dreadful disease.

Lanah had no doubt dealt with harassment on the street before. Indeed, the problem was one of the reasons given in support of the recent street improvements. A letter published in the *New-York Journal* several years earlier had pointed out that Broadway was some eighty feet wide, but that without sidewalks there was no protection for foot passengers. "Waggons, carts, carriages, horse and foot are promiscuously and dangerously intermixed," complained the anonymous author. "Let a woman be dressed as neat as a Quaker, she is exposed to the mercy of drivers of every sort, and the disposition to insults of this kind is too prevailing." Improving the city's streets had not solved the problem of insolent rogues. And, as a snobbish letter published in the summer of 1793 pointed out, these "scoundrels" were not just poor boys and workingmen; some of them had surprisingly respectable connections.

Some men liked to imagine that women relished such attention. Royall Tyler opened his play *The Contrast* with a flirtatious young woman describing how, while walking on the Battery, she had contrived to flip up her skirts for the benefit of a group of male onlookers, who enthusiastically voiced their appreciation. "*Ha!*" said one, commenting on her well-turned ankle. "*Demme,*" cried another, "*what a delicate foot!*"

The problem of street harassment was particularly acute for young women of Lanah's station, genteel enough to value a reputation as modest, respectable, and sexually innocent yet obliged by necessity to work to help support her family financially. A working-class girl could hardly afford the luxury of a chaperone every time she had business to transact—or simply wanted to escape from the confines of a small, crowded home. Navigating her way through the streets of the growing city often required navigating the threat of sexual aggression.

On this blustery evening, however, something unexpected happened. Lanah caught the attention not only of the lewd Frenchmen but also of another man: a bystander who chose to intervene. This time, Lanah would not have to defend herself alone.

The stranger "came up," as she later put it, and "rescued her."

It was easy for her to see that this good Samaritan was a gentleman. His skin was pale; his white-powdered hair was fashionably coiffed. He favored elegant clothes, tailored from expensive fabric and designed to make it clear that he didn't do any kind of physical labor. He carried a walking stick, a badge of status that men of a certain rank carried not because they were afraid of losing their balance but because they could. The city's poor and working men, or its many enslaved and free Blacks, would cause alarm if they were seen in the streets brandishing staves or clubs. But gentlemen carried walking sticks and were not always reluctant to use them on insolent street urchins, pigs that strayed into the street, or even vulgar foreigners.

The gallant gentleman also had bright blue eyes, rosy red lips, and a sly smile.

To the object of his concern, his attractions were only increased by his polite attentions. He even offered to escort her home, which was a short walk away. She agreed, and he "attended her home to her father's house in Gold-Street."

Before taking his leave and disappearing into the night, he introduced himself with flattering courtliness. He did not presume to the familiarity of mentioning his first name; he offered only an occupation and a last name.

I am, he told her, "lawyer Smith."

SUNDAY, SEPTEMBER I, 1793.

The following Sunday, Lanah once again ventured out into the city. And once again, she was alone. But the weather could not have been more different: it was a classic late-summer day, the skies clear, the air cleansed by overnight rain, and the temperature at midday a balmy 82 degrees. Somehow, though, the young seamstress ended up back where she had been on that chilly, stormy evening a week earlier: standing in the street, face to face with the charming young lawyer Mr. Smith.

Perhaps it was just a happy coincidence. Or perhaps she had found her feet retracing their steps along Broadway that evening, enjoying the summer air against her cheeks, idly hoping that she might run into lawyer Smith again. She wouldn't have been the only young person to return to the scene of a chance encounter, hoping to catch another sight of an alluring figure.

Since the previous week, Lanah had had plenty of opportunities to reflect on the events of that evening and the feelings they evoked—to relive the insults of the Frenchmen, her fear, her relief when the mysterious gentleman stepped in to rescue her. Perhaps she had indulged herself by turning idle fantasies over in her mind: Had she been imagining things in the confusion of the moment, or had she really felt a spark of romance pass between them? If lawyer Smith claimed a place in her imagination that week, it was no doubt largely because he seemed so different from the kind of man she typically encountered, because the way of life he represented was so different from the one she seemed destined to live.

At seventeen, Lanah was old enough to be thinking seriously about the prospect of marriage. In her social circle, women often married in their late teens. The men they married were typically somewhat older, in their twenties: old enough to get established in their occupations and start their own households. In the years to come, Lanah's two sisters would marry at ages seventeen and eighteen. Her brother married a seventeen-year-old when he was twenty-one, fresh out of his apprenticeship. Lanah's cousin Lucretia Harper, who lived down the street, had married for the first time when she was all of fifteen.

The older women in her life—her mother, her cousin, the elderly aunt who lived by the Bowling Green, and their friends—were, no doubt, curious about potential suitors. They may even have been tempted to suggest suitable candidates. A young man in her stepfather's company of branch pilots, perhaps, or the well-behaved son of a barrel maker down the street.

Matronly meddling aside, the pressure to marry was strong. Above all, marriage in working families was an economic necessity. Women simply could not earn high enough wages in any respectable occupation to support themselves independently—though widows who inherited a profitable shop or had enough capital to open a boardinghouse almost never remarried. Marriage was also an economic necessity for working men. Craftsmen, artisans, and "mechanics" earned much higher wages than their sisters—but not high enough that they could afford to pay for all of the domestic labor required to keep a household running: buying, preparing, and cooking food; sewing, repairing, and washing clothes; tending fires, fetching water, and cleaning.

Lanah's own parents were a case in point. Her mother, Jane Outen Bogert, came from a respectable family of modest means. None of Lanah's grandparents had been rich, but her grandparents on both sides had owned property near the spot on Gold Street where Lanah's family now lived. Before the war, when her grandfather Bogert died, his widow inherited two houses and didn't feel the need to remarry. When Jane was seventeen, she married Francis Sawyer, a skilled twenty-eight-year-old artisan who made carriages and wheels. Their first surviving child, Lanah, was born in 1776. But Francis died around the time she was seven, just as the war was ending. Lanah herself was old enough to remember the strain her mother felt, faced with the impossible task of supporting herself and four small children. Luckily, the widow Jane Sawyer found a new husband quickly. Within a year, she married another man a few years older than herself, John Callanan, who as one of the busy seaport's official branch pilots earned a decent living.

The model of marriage Lanah witnessed as she came of age was not particularly glamorous. Her stepfather was a good example of the kind of man who it would have seemed appropriate for her to marry: a man who did skilled but nonetheless physical work, who earned enough to support a large household but not in much comfort. He rented a modest house in a modest neighborhood. Theirs was a crowded household. That summer, there were at least nine family members living there: Lanah's mother and stepfather, her two sisters, and four half siblings, including a seven-month-old baby. Missing from the house was Lanah's brother, Peter, who had been apprenticed to one of her stepfather's fellow branch pilots who lived around the corner. At the time, boys were generally considered economic liabilities. But, in working families, girls were assets.

As the eldest daughter, Lanah was likely responsible for a large share of the domestic labor, including caring for her young half siblings. She also worked as a seamstress to supplement the household's income, taking in small jobs from other households or piecework from tailors and completing them at home in moments when she wasn't needed for anything else.

So it would hardly be surprising if Lanah were intrigued by the gentleman who had rescued her the previous week. By seventeen, she was all too familiar with the endless work that was the lot of a wife in a working-class household—and the even worse lot that befell a working-class woman without a husband. A lawyer like Mr. Smith represented another kind of man, another kind of life.

When Lanah Sawyer and lawyer Smith encountered each other on the street a second time, it was entirely possible that they had both been out looking for each other.

Sawyer made a point of not being forward. Whether because she was too modest, too anxious, or simply too punctilious to speak to him, she waited to see if he would notice her. Gratifyingly, he did. Describing the encounter later, she specified that he was the one who "accosted" her.

Then, "they entered into a conversation"—a conversation that took an unmistakably flirtatious turn.

At one point, he asked if she would join him the next evening for a walk on the Battery.

It was a romantic gesture. On evenings that summer, dozens of genteel couples could be seen promenading along the Battery, enjoying the cool breezes, the sound of the water, and each other's company. On a clear day, the views extended in all directions: across the Hudson River to New Jersey, across the East River to Brooklyn, and down along the city's vast natural harbor to the islands of the inner bay and, beyond them, the opening of the Narrows. That July, one proud New Yorker exclaimed, "Our Battery has now become one of the most delightful walks, perhaps, in the world."

Over the previous several years, the city had transformed the Battery into its first public park. Lanah was old enough to remember it at the end of the war: the rubble of the ruined fort, the barracks, and other military structures. Now, all of that had been swept away, the landscape regraded and expanded into the water, charming walkways constructed, and a large flagpole raised on the flat roof of an octagonal tower. The tower was intended as a kind of romantic folly, evoking the image of a bygone castle, but to most New Yorkers it was more reminiscent of an oversized butter churn. Still, it had its uses: couples often climbed up its narrow staircase and crowded onto its roof to enjoy the views and exhibit themselves to those below. Two rows of young elm trees, intended to shade the walkways from the summer sun, had just been planted, their slender trunks still encased in boxes to protect them from marauding pigs and goats, which not infrequently escaped from backyard pens.

Just off the Battery, the dashing English horseman John Bill Ricketts had recently opened his equestrian circus, in which he displayed feats like riding two horses at one time, standing with one foot on each and, balanced precariously on his shoulder, a "flying" boy with both arms and one of his legs outstretched.

As exciting as lawyer Smith's invitation may have seemed, Lanah demurred.

I am engaged on Monday evening, she told him.

She had good reason to hesitate. Why would a man like him be interested in a girl like her? Lawyers and other gentlemen did not marry the daughters of branch pilots. And without a prospect of marriage, a walk on the Battery could lead to nothing but trouble. The rules of female decorum were not as rigid among working people as they were among the city's genteel elite, but any young woman who allowed her respectability to come into question could easily find herself ruined.

The publications of the day were full of accounts of young women seduced by gentlemen, enticed into giving up their innocence, and then abandoned to the harsh fate of fallen women. The most popular novel of the era, Susanna Rowson's *Charlotte Temple: A Tale of Truth* (1791), was set during Lanah's childhood in Revolutionary New York and was supposedly based on real events. Fifteen-year-old Charlotte was enticed into eloping with a dashing officer, only to find herself abandoned, scorned by respectable folk, and pregnant. She died giving birth in a miserable hovel, the home of a lowly servant who, alone among New Yorkers, recognized her inner virtue. In the city, the fictional heroine took on a surreal afterlife. At some point, in the hallowed cemetery surrounding Trinity

Church on Broadway appeared a gravestone bearing her name, which, ever since, romantics have visited with flowers and tears. Meanwhile, a series of old houses vied for the distinction of being the scene of the tragic heroine's death. According to an 1826 newspaper report, when a shopkeeper at 22 Bowery Lane "discovered" that he occupied the "very house in which Charlotte Temple died," swarms of visitors came to inspect the "venerable edifice."

Yet those weren't the only stories that would have reached Lanah's ears. There were also romantic stories about the overwhelming force of true love—stories like Johann Wolfgang von Goethe's *The Sorrows of Young Werther* (1774), about a young gentleman who could not go on living without the woman he loved. His romantic death inspired a rash of copycat suicides, a phenomenon still known as the Werther effect. There were also happier tales in which love conquered all obstacles—including such impediments to marriage with a rich, respectable man as a young woman's lack of social rank or fortune. Indeed, during Lanah's lifetime it had become increasingly common for young couples to insist on marrying for love, even when that caused conflicts with their families.

Such stories offered Lanah, and young women like her, a vision of an alternate world. They described a kind of man very different from those she knew. They lionized a model of marriage very different from the one she had observed growing up.

Such stories may also have encouraged Lanah to imagine that a young lawyer really might be interested in *her*.

Lawyer Smith was not put off when Lanah told him she was busy Monday evening.

How about Tuesday evening? he replied.

I am "also engaged" then.

"Surely, you are not engaged on every evening," he protested. With self-confident charm, he pressed on: "you can certainly go Wednesday."

"I am not engaged then," she allowed, a bit coyly.

He "conveyed her home" and departed—as a family friend looked on from across the street.

61 GOLD STREET. MONDAY, SEPTEMBER 2, 1793. MORNING.

The next morning, Samuel Hone, a young baker who lived across the street, was anxious to speak with Lanah. He had seen her arrive home the evening before, had recognized the gentleman accompanying her, and was concerned. Soon, he got his chance.

Hone and his wife were close friends with Lanah's parents and fairly typical of the working families who predominated in the neighborhood. At twenty-seven, Hone had been married for seven years and had a growing family. Neither particularly affluent nor desperately poor, Hone rented one half of a long, skinny parcel (owned by Lanah's aunt) that stretched along Gold Street. Facing Beekman Street was a house occupied by a grocer; toward Ann Street was a modest bake house where Hone and his family lived and worked. That summer it was described as well suited for "extensive" business producing "ship bread" and other aspects of the baking business. Ship bread was one of the staples that supported the bustling seaport: hard, dry loaves designed to be stored in the hold of a ship for long periods. Living with the Hones were several white youths (probably apprentices) and one enslaved person.

Hone was about ten years younger than Lanah's mother and stepfather, who were in their late thirties, but he was old enough to see the seventeen-year-old through the eyes of an older brother. And, like Lanah's mother, both of the Hones had deep roots in the neighborhood. Hone's parents lived around the corner on Ann Street. Before the war, the families of both Lanah's mother and Hone's wife, Hannah Quereau, had owned houses on the same stretch of Gold Street, just a block away.

Hone caught Lanah's attention.

What a smart Beau you have got, Hone observed. It was less a tribute to her powers of attraction than an expression of paternalistic concern, calling attention to the class difference between people like them and the man she had been with.

He is a lawyer Smith, Lanah offered, ignoring Hone's innuendo.

No, it was not, Hone insisted, "for it was *Harry Bedlow*."

Lanah knew the name. And she recognized her neighbor's implicit warning.

Harry Bedlow was a man whose reputation preceded him. At the time, the city was really just a small town, only about forty thousand people, living within less than a mile of each other on the southern tip of Manhattan. Lanah did not know Harry Bedlow by sight, but she had heard enough about him to know that he was bad news. He was, she knew, "a very great rake."

A rake, at the time, was a very specific kind of man: an elite sexual predator. For Lanah, the term was no doubt familiar both from word of mouth and also from novels and other published writing. The term was shorthand for what you would end up with if you raked through the coals of hell. Several variations of the word—"Rakehell, *n.* a very debauched fellow, a wretch" and "Rakish, *a.* loose, debauched, lewd, thoughtless"—appeared in America's first dictionary, published by Noah Webster, who, as it happened, moved to New York City just days before Lanah first met the intriguing lawyer. In the cultural imagination, a rake was a gentleman who made a habit of seducing naïve young women. Another entry in Webster's dictionary read: "Seduce, *v. t.* to lead astray by arts, entice from duty, debauch."

In the seduction stories of the day, the "rake" was a far cry from the reformable bad boys of modern romance novels. He was more like Satan: his characteristic mode was to target a virtuous young woman, win her trust under false pretenses, lead her into temptation, and leave her morally ruined. Sometimes, as in *Charlotte Temple*, the rake ended up regretting the damage he caused—but only after it was too late. Often, as in the French novel *Les liaisons dangereuses* (1782), the rake took sadistic pleasure in his victim's suffering.

The figure of the rake haunted parents. Toward the end of the war, Abigail Adams warned a young cousin about the supposedly "reformed Rake" Royall Tyler—only to have him start courting her own daughter. John Adams's objection to the match was vindicated a few years later when Tyler published *The Contrast*, a play that suggested that he had not really outgrown his moral dissipation. Staged in 1787 at the John Street Theatre (just behind the home of Lanah's friend Miss Steddiford), it was the first American play to be professionally produced. Set in New York, *The Contrast* mocked the prudery of New England bumpkins and celebrated the dissipations of urban sophisticates—including loveless marriages of convenience, adulterous affairs, and an array of duplicitous arts used by men to take advantage of women.

The danger represented by a rake was very different from that posed by the lewd Frenchmen who had harassed Lanah on Broadway the previous week. Their menace was overt. Their threat, at its most extreme, was an imminent assault. The rake represented a hidden danger: he operated by stealth, unobtrusively selecting his target, dissembling his true motives, professing false regard, using his arts to engender trust and render his victim emotionally vulnerable.

Lanah rejected Hone's suggestion that the man who had rescued her from the Frenchmen was actually the notorious rake Harry Bedlow. Nothing in lawyer Smith's behavior so far had done anything to disrupt her image of him as a gallant gentleman whose attentions were as flattering as they were unexpected.

That could not be, Lanah protested. *He had said his name was lawyer Smith.*

Reading the character of a stranger is always a challenge—and one that was especially acute in emerging modern cities like New York. Since the war, the city's population had doubled, and it would double again and again in the coming decades as immigrants from near and far sought out new opportunities and, sometimes, new identities. The philosopher Adam Smith embraced this future, speculating in his *Theory of Moral Sentiments* (1759) that, compared with old worlds of intimate, local, and personal relationships, new worlds of strangers would encourage people to act with more restraint, discipline, and propriety. We want strangers to see us as we see ourselves, he reasoned. But not everyone used the power of anonymity to embrace their better nature. And for a young woman like Lanah Sawyer evaluating a new acquaintance like "lawyer Smith," the stakes could be high.

When one of Margaret Livingston's sons left the family manor up the Hudson River Valley in 1795, she reminded him to send back reports about the people he would encounter in the city: "I hope you will write often as you can with convenience to your self—you are now in the center of business and dissipation—many new characters to investigate—virtues to contemplate and vices to detest." It would amuse those left behind, she indicated, to relive his efforts to "read" the characters of strangers.

The amusement offered by novels was much the same. The proliferation of fictional stories centered on heroines, heroes, and villains encouraged readers of all ranks to think of themselves—and others—as characters, as protagonists with coherent, though often obscure, personalities. The most enduringly famous novel written during this period, Jane Austen's *Pride and Prejudice*, originally drafted in the mid-1790s, focuses precisely on the danger of misreading strangers. Initial snap judgments almost thwart the romance that eventually develops between Elizabeth Bennet and Fitzwilliam Darcy. Meanwhile, the alluring figure of George Wickham is a classic example of how a rake, posing as a gallant officer, could threaten the welfare of an entire family by seducing a susceptible sixteen-year-old. That's why Austen initially called the book *First Impressions*.

It was an implicit warning—one that was necessary because, for young women like Lanah Sawyer, the lure of love could so easily push caution aside.

62 GOLD STREET. WEDNESDAY, SEPTEMBER 4, 1793, EVENING.

Lanah had not exactly agreed to go for a walk with lawyer Smith on Wednesday evening.

Over the previous several days, there had been plenty of time for her to reflect on the possibility that the man presenting himself as lawyer Smith might actually be a notorious rake. The stakes were high. Nothing good could come of an acquaintance with a man like Harry Bedlow. And the bad outcomes were very bad indeed. But lawyer Smith had seemed gallant and attentive—not crude like the Frenchmen—and interested in striking up a romance. Did the seventeen-year-old sewing girl feel a frisson of excitement about the prospect of such a "fine beau"? He had rescued her from an ugly incident in the street. Maybe that chance encounter would lead to another kind of rescue: maybe he would end up marrying her and freeing her from the drudgery, the anxiety that seemed to be a working-class woman's destiny. Who could say? With love in the air, anything was possible.

As the appointed time drew near, Lanah set about preparing for her rendezvous with lawyer Smith. The sultry, late-summer weather had been interrupted the night before by a cold snap, and the temperature that afternoon had barely risen past 65 degrees. The dry air felt brisk against her skin as Lanah contemplated what would be appropriate to wear for a walk on the Battery with a gentleman.

It wasn't like she had a lot of options. Even though she could sew her own clothes, the cost of the materials meant that she didn't have many dresses. Ironically, fabric was so expensive that Lanah's skill with a needle and thread was most often hidden from view: on the loose linen shift that served as underwear and on the laced corset that kept her posture upright. These undergarments featured dense rows of fine stitching to fortify them against the rigors of heavy wear and endless washing. Over them, Lanah wore petticoats, tied around her waist with stout strings.

Then she took up what was, no doubt, her best dress: a "calico gown made with a drawn frill round the neck." Calico, a thin cotton cloth imported from India, had been widely valued for its intricate color prints.

But recently, a craze for loosely draped, high-waisted gowns, modeled after ancient marble statuary, had begun to bring plain white into vogue. As a young woman visiting the city a few years earlier observed, the wardrobe of young "ladies" reflected lives largely devoted to leisure and social calls and freedom from the kind of domestic drudgery that would ruin expensive, hard-to-clean fabrics: "Each of them had one silk dress for parties, one white muslin for afternoons, and one calico for morning dress." But Lanah was not one of those ladies. The kind of garment that elite women considered humble and utilitarian, Lanah might well have prized as her finest.

Lanah would have constructed the dress with long, looping stitches so that it could be taken apart and refashioned in the future—as she grew or as styles changed. Indeed, she may have bought or been given a used gown, taken it apart for the fabric, and refashioned it to her liking. Lanah's tight budget was reflected in the absence of expensive manufactured fasteners on the dress, like hooks and eyes.

Lanah pulled the gown over her shoulders and tied and pinned the bodice in place. At her waist, Lanah wore a cloth bag, either a pocket tied under her gown or an ornamental reticule, in which she could discreetly carry whatever small items she might need: a handkerchief, a needle and thread, and, perhaps, a few coins.

A respectable woman in public had to keep her entire body covered—from her neck right down to her toes. So Lanah drew on gloves that would have reached up to the bottom of her gown's sleeves. Even her hair was to be kept at least partially covered with a hat. Since she was going out, it was no homey mobcap but rather some formal, dramatic, broad-brimmed affair. Even in the evening, when no fair complexion was endangered by the sun, fashion favored big hats surmounted with billowy poufs of fabric or wide, flat hats sporting long feathers.

Then, she slipped out the front door. Lanah's home, like many of the city's older houses, had a Dutch front door. Sometimes, she could be seen standing inside, looking out over the bottom half of the door into the street. But this evening, she went outside and sat down. Many houses had a small bench built into the stoop, a perch for someone looking to watch the world go by—or to wait, shielded from the prying eyes of those inside.

If the seventeen-year-old Lanah had wanted to introduce her "beau" to her family—or if she had wanted him to see the inside of her modest home—she would have simply waited inside for him to knock. But there were plenty of reasons not to. She may have been concerned about what lawyer Smith would think of her family and their modest circumstances. Certainly, she would not have been the first teenager to be embarrassed by her parents. And, to a man of fashion, her house would no doubt seem cramped, crowded, and crude. Her mother did own some Sawyer family furniture, which she later took pains to dole out in her will, as well as a few pieces of silver, which included a set of cups engraved with her and her second husband's intertwined initials. But the bulk of their furnishings were cheap, old-fashioned, and utilitarian. At the same time, Lanah had good reason for wanting to slip away from home without attracting too much attention. Surely, her parents would have had questions about a "fine beau" like lawyer Smith, a man so conspicuously above their station in life.

And so, Lanah was sitting on the front stoop of her stepfather's house when lawyer Smith approached. He was dressed in a coat and waistcoat and carrying that classic symbol of genteel status, a walking stick. He came up to her and asked if she would take a walk.

Perhaps reading ambivalence in her expression, lawyer Smith reassured Lanah that they would not be going out alone. They would be joined by a Miss Steddiford—whom, he recalled, Lanah had previously mentioned as "a young lady of her acquaintance"—and another gentleman.

The Steddifords were an eminently respectable family, among the more prominent people Sawyer knew. Gerard Steddiford had served as a high-ranking officer in the Continental Army, was a member of the Society of the Cincinnati, and operated an auction house on Wall Street. Lanah's friend was probably the Steddifords' eldest daughter, Hannah, who was about eighteen. Had Lanah dropped her friend's name while chatting with laywer Smith on one of the two occasions he had walked her home? Had he pried the name out of her while trying to discover whether their social circles overlapped?

Lanah agreed to walk with him to her friend's home. It was not far—only a block south down Gold Street and a few more blocks west on John Street. The Steddifords rented a house on the north side of the street, near the theater, about half a block from Broadway.

For "lawyer Smith," calling at the Steddiford house was a risk. He clearly wanted to reassure Lanah that their walk together would be safe and respectable. But how did he know what to expect when they knocked on the door and asked for Lanah's friend? If he really were well enough acquainted with the family to know young Hannah Steddiford's social calendar, how could he expect to call at their house without having someone blow his cover and reveal his true identity? Conceivably, even if he didn't know the family he might have arranged for a friend of his to ask her out that evening—for a walk, perhaps, or to the circus, a religious meeting, or the theater. But that would have required a remarkable coincidence and additional risk. And what would have happened if Lanah's friend actually was at home? How would he explain where he got the impression that she had plans for a walk that evening? So, it was with a considerable bravado—and confidence in his ability to improvise—that "lawyer Smith" presented himself at Mr. Steddiford's home.

As it happened, whoever answered the front door said that Mr. Steddiford's daughter was out.

They must have gone ahead to the Battery, lawyer Smith suggested.

Accordingly, Lanah continued with him in that direction—half a block farther to the corner of Broadway and then down along its wide stone sidewalk. The east side of the street was lined with a mature assemblage of mostly brick town houses—including some of the most valuable properties in the city, such as Mayor Richard Varick's imposing compound on the corner of Broadway and Pine Street, with coal and wood vaults under the sidewalk and various outbuildings, including an office, a privy, and a coach house at the rear. At some point, Lanah and her companion crossed to the west side of the street, where the structures were all new. Everything between lower Broadway and the Hudson River had been laid waste by fires during the war—about the oldest things on that side of the street were stone markers in the graveyard surrounding the recently rebuilt Trinity Church. Despite a frenzy of construction, even some of the desirable lots along lower Broadway remained vacant. Many of Lanah's parents' friends and their families were buried in the Trinity churchyard—as would be her baby half brother Owen Callanan when he died a few years later.

Just past Trinity Church was a hotel where the celebrated French chef Joseph Corré purveyed a variety of confections, including some of America's first ice cream. It was a rare and expensive indulgence. When the federal government was headquartered in the city, President George Washington had spent large sums having Corré's ice cream catered for his guests. His extravagance had not gone unappreciated: when Abigail

Adams, the vice president's wife, attended a formal event at the president's home, she was struck by his "grace ease & dignity"—and by the fact that the refreshments included ice cream.

Lanah and her companion stopped for a glass. Evidently, the temptation to taste this exotic treat won out over whatever urgency she felt about catching up with Miss Steddiford. The scene inside the hotel was a reminder for Lanah that lawyer Smith inhabited a world of luxury and leisure far removed from her ordinary experience. When a young medical student was looking for a way to indulge his mother one evening, he proposed a walk to Corré's to "take a glass of ice cream by way of experiment." Happily, at a cost of 1 shilling per glass, it proved to be "a very delicious refreshment for warm weather." As they ate, a group of French officers "came capering in on the same errand."

Lanah and her companion lingered over glasses of melting ice cream, eating, talking, and people watching, for about an hour and a half. Finally, they stepped back out into Broadway and headed down to the Battery.

At the base of Broadway, Lanah and her beau passed the Bowling Green, entered the Battery through a gate, and enjoyed a long, leisurely stroll. The cool evening air carried the gentle murmur of waves and the creaking of innumerable wooden ships at anchor.

On evenings that summer, dozens of ladies and gentlemen could be seen strolling through the park—mostly in couples, walking side by side. The ladies sported big, exuberant hats, hair flowing down to their shoulders, and tight-waisted gowns with long, full skirts. The gentlemen wore their hair long, pulled back, and surmounted by broad-brimmed hats. Most were in traditional knee breeches and stockings, but a few had adopted the fashion for long trousers and the new, knit fabrics that allowed a thigh-hugging fit. In an image sketched that summer, some pause to chat or lean against the railing along the water; some raise up a hand to hail an acquaintance or point out a view. Others crowd on top of the "churn," appreciating the vistas and the opportunity to exhibit themselves to those below. A few couples stroll hand in hand. Some stand close enough that his arm might be around her waist. At the center of the open lawn one couple stands facing each other, their bodies close; they hold each other's hands and seem to be lost in each other's eyes.

As Lanah and her beau strolled and idled, time seemed suspended. Later, she would remember walking around the park twice—but it must have been more than that. Presumably, along the way they spent a lot of time doing the kinds of things other couples did there: pausing to take in the night air, walking hand in hand or even with his arm around her waist, enjoying each other's company. They were there for hours and never did run into Miss Steddiford.

Suddenly, Lanah's romantic reverie was interrupted by the sound of church bells ringing the hour. That evening, it had been easy to lose track of the time. The sun had set around six thirty, the glow of twilight had mostly faded by seven, and no moon had risen to brighten the darkness or mark the passage of time with its movement across the night sky.

Lanah counted twelve chimes reverberating across the city—and began to panic.

It was midnight. She should have been home hours ago. How could she have so completely lost track of time?

Lanah was "alarmed," as she later recalled. Like any teenager out too late at night, she was facing more than just the practical inconvenience of being locked out of her home. If she couldn't simply slip in, she would have to face her parents—anxious, annoyed, disapproving, and, likely, irate. She shared her "fears" with her companion.

Lawyer Smith did his best "to quiet" her anxiety.

It is only ten, he reassured her. She must have miscounted.

Ten was not exceptionally late. That summer one city resident, concerned about "scoundrels" harassing respectable folk enjoying an evening stroll on the Battery, had suggested that the city should post a watchman there until ten o'clock. Fashionable dinner parties often ran later. And, though the night was dark, the city's major streets were illuminated by whale-oil lamps. But for people like Lanah's parents, the cost of candles and lamp oil was a significant expense, so they didn't generally stay up long past nightfall.

Lanah, with her companion, headed homeward—but they did not rush. It took an hour for them to pass back out of the Battery into the base of Broadway. There they encountered three of the city's night watchmen, known as "leatherheads" because of their distinctive headgear.

What time is it? Lawyer Smith asked.

It is one o'clock, the watchmen replied.

This, presumably, revived Lanah's alarm—and her dread about the reception she would meet with at home.

After the city watchmen, Lanah saw nobody else in the streets that night.

She and her companion continued up Broadway in the direction of her home.

When they got down to the corner of John Street, Lanah later recalled, "she was going to turn down," but her companion "kept his arm around her" and nudged her farther northward along Broadway. That was the way they had come, but there were other cross streets that would serve just as well. Indeed, the next corner was Fulton Street, which offered a slightly more efficient route to her parents' house on Gold Street.

But they continued past Fulton.

Soon, Lanah found herself standing at the apex of what is now City Hall Park but then was known as "the Fields." Across Broadway, St. Paul's Chapel and its churchyard marked an area notorious for its streetwalkers and brothels and known, wryly, as the "Holy Ground."

At this point, Lanah's companion indicated that he wanted to turn right. She resisted.

Her home was only a few blocks away, at the other end of Ann Street. But this stretch of the crooked street—which had been cut through the block only a few years earlier—had already acquired a terrible reputation.

Lanah "knew there were vacant lots there" and she "had heard the street was filled with bad people." She thought it would be "improper for a young girl to go down there."

Her impressions were well founded. That block of Ann Street was indeed a den of vice, filled with brothels and disorderly taverns.

But her companion insisted.

Keeping a "tight hold of her," he began to force her down the dark, narrow street.

Suddenly, Lanah knew, something was wrong—everything was wrong.

Her neighbor had been right. She had been deceived. The man she was with was not lawyer Smith.

All of her thoughts and feelings about him now appeared in an ominous new light—his gallantry, his persistence, his charm, his arm around her.

Too late, she realized "he was really Harry Bedlow." Too late, she recognized his true intentions.

Lanah Sawyer opened her mouth to scream.

A hand flew up to stifle it.

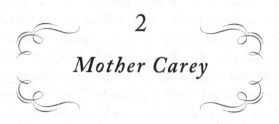

2

Mother Carey

Mother Carey was sound asleep when the silence of the dark night was pierced by the sharp rap of a gentleman's walking stick against her front door. Whoever was there, he was persistent. Rousing herself from bed, she made her way to the window, swung open the shutter, and peered out into the street. With no moon, it was almost as dark outside as it was inside. She couldn't see much. But she could see enough.

At the door was a young gentleman. She knew who he was, no doubt. It was hard to succeed as the keeper of a bawdy house without a knack for remembering names and faces. The city was small. People talked. And Harry Bedlow, at twenty-six, had already acquired a reputation. He was just the kind of man who kept women like Ann Carey in business.

And he had been to Mother Carey's before. Later, one of his lawyers allowed that "he was probably well known" there. Other bawdy houses operated down the street, around the corner, a short walk away. He could have knocked on any number of doors, but he had chosen hers. Perhaps, on a previous occasion, he had enjoyed the company of one of her girls. Perhaps he had been there with a streetwalker who couldn't bring him back to her own lodgings. Perhaps he had rented a room for some other kind of private tryst. Evidently, Mother Carey had done her job well—and he had left comforted by the sense that he and the old bawd shared a kind of bond, that she didn't judge him the way his parents did, that whatever he did in her house would stay in her house.

Harry demanded to be let in.

Mother Carey hesitated.

The young man himself wasn't much of a problem. Mother Carey had grown old selling sex to men with more money than morals. Day in and day out, men in the city made the transition from the world of family life and business affairs to the world of illicit sex—and back—without incident. Not all of them were quite as arrogant and inconsiderate as Bedlow, who had, after all, woken her up in the middle of the night not to beg her pardon and crave indulgence but rather to demand service. Still, humoring the whims and flattering the vanity of overentitled men was part of the job. If he had been alone, there would have been no problem at all; at that moment, Mother Carey had two women asleep in the house who could have been put to work. Nor would it have been a problem if he had showed up with a streetwalker ready to get down to business with him and share part of her fee with Carey.

But he was not alone. And the woman he was with was not some disreputable hussy. Mother Carey may very well have recognized the young woman out in the street; they had lived for years just two blocks apart. (It would turn out that at least one member of Carey's circle did know Lanah Sawyer by sight.) Or, perhaps, Mother Carey saw enough of her clothing in the dark to determine that it wasn't the kind of outré outfit that marked a woman of ill repute. In the end, she remembered only one detail about Lanah's gown: that it had a "frill round the neck." Mother Carey was a woman with a professional interest in cleavage.

Lanah Sawyer was, in fact, just the kind of woman who could get a bawd like Mother Carey into trouble.

In the popular imagination, it was the other way around.

Stories about older women conniving at the seduction of innocent maidens were everywhere—from sentimental seduction stories and lugubrious poems to ribald cartoons and explicit pornography. Even the term "bawd" itself had ugly connotations—derived as it was from old French terms for "indecent" and "shameless," with none of the exoticism and courtesy evoked by the much later term "madam."

It was commonly imagined that the women who worked in brothels and walked the streets had started out as respectable, modest girls, too innocent and unwary for their own good—and had been reduced to prostitution after being seduced and ruined by some man, often with the assistance of some nefarious old procuress. In the more moralistic stories, the seducer, like the devil, pursues a conquest that is not just physical but also moral: he strives to persuade his victim, at the last minute, to consent to sex—to become the agent of her own destruction. The ideal of feminine innocence went hand in hand with a sadistic fetish for ruining virgins.

For seventeen-year-old Lanah Sawyer, or any young woman with pretensions to respectability, to set foot in a brothel—with a man, after midnight—was to enter a world of scandal and shame from which she might never emerge.

Strange to say, Mother Carey, too, had a reputation to protect. As a woman running a business in the shadow of the law, she had to be careful. Running a bawdy house was technically illegal. But law enforcement was notoriously lax—unless a pimp or madam attracted scandal or raised the ire of their neighbors. Over the years, Carey had managed to stay out of trouble by choosing a propitious location, screening her clients, managing the women who worked for her, and convincing those who lived nearby that her establishment, as establishments like hers went, was relatively decent.

As a business matter, the question was not so much the young woman's demeanor—whether she was eager, demure, distraught, or even fighting tooth and nail. Mother Carey was in the business of pleasing men, not women. But the late hour and the ruckus in the street only increased the odds of public notice. What if a neighbor had woken up and looked out to see what was happening? And then there was the question of how the young woman would react in the morning—would she cause trouble?

Mother Carey told Harry that she would not let him in.

My doors are locked, she added, softening the blow, *and my husband is away from home.*

This much was true. Her doors no doubt were locked, and her husband was not there that night. At that moment, her challenge was to persuade the young gentleman to go away without wounding his pride or provoking a scene.

As for what she said next, memories differed in the weeks to come.

"*I cannot open them*" was what Lanah heard. A white lie, perhaps, since Carey was in fact quite capable of doing so.

But what Mother Carey remembered saying has a ring of truth: *I am afraid of opening the doors.*

She was right to be afraid.

Harry Bedlow had been there before. He knew there was another way in. And he wasn't one to take no for an answer.

Although Mother Carey's business was illegal, it operated as an open secret—one small corner of the city's vast underground market in illicit sex. Street walkers and bawdy houses were so prevalent that most New Yorkers hardly gave them a second thought. Sometimes, indeed, getting a little attention took a bit of work. One chilly afternoon in early 1793, one of Mother Carey's girls wanted to drum up business without heading out into the streets, so she did what she could from the comfort of the front room.

At that moment, a young medical student and a couple of friends were heading home from the college after a lecture on, as it happened, the anatomy of the human heart. As they passed between the Brick Church on Beekman and Mother Carey's house, they got an unexpected eyeful: "a Prostitute, gaily dress'd, appear'd at the Window and displayed her Breast to our view, with a most artful smile." The brief peep through Mother Carey's front window didn't succeed in procuring the young man's patronage, but it seems to have altered the way he saw the world, at least for a time.

As he approached his eighteenth birthday, Alexander Anderson saw himself as something of a romantic. When a respectable young woman caught his eye that spring, he cheerfully, if somewhat nervously, observed the conventions of genteel courtship: he walked her home (all the while worrying that he might ruin her gown by stepping on its train); he called on her at home and sat with her family in their parlor (wondering if they were all a bit too proud of her beauty); he endured joshing from his friends about being "up to his eyes in love." But in the months after the peep show at Mother Carey's, he was painfully aware that all around him was depravity. He was "very much" surprised when a man sought treatment for gonorrhea and observed that it was his eighth bout with the disorder. A fellow apprentice persisted in harassing a servant woman, provoking her to strike out in anger and ultimately lose her position. And everywhere he turned, it seemed, there was another prostitute. One afternoon, he hiked up to the Bowery only to find "the rural prospect" destroyed by the appearance of "three young girls who by their wanton behavior sufficiently declar'd their profession." One evening, on his way to an evening French class, he stopped to relieve himself against a wall only to be approached by "a mulatto wench . . . in a very familiar manner."

In the 1790s, more than a century before the invention of modern dating culture, an underground sexual economy flourished on a scale almost unimaginable today. Men, whether they were married or not, enjoyed wide sexual latitude: they could often pursue an active sexual double life without incident. Women, on the other hand, faced a stark contrast between sexual respectability and social ruin. Young Alexander Anderson, who often attended three worship meetings on Sundays, was not alone in regarding respectable maidens with reverence and their fallen counterparts with disgust. This obsession with female innocence constrained men's access to casual sex—and, perversely, fueled demand for prostitution. Even poor women carefully guarded their reputations. Consequently, men paid one group of women to provide the services that their respectable counterparts would not.

Even the worldly French refugee Médéric Louis Élie Moreau de Méry—who fled Paris shortly after the execution of Marie Antoinette in the fall of 1793—was surprised by the scale and prevalence of New York's sexual underground. In a city "so recently sprung into being," Moreau had expected a certain innocence. Instead, he discovered, "women of every color can be found in the streets, particularly after ten o'clock at night, soliciting men and proudly flaunting their licentiousness in the most shameless manner." If prostitution seemed to be everywhere, in some places there seemed to be little else. "In many parts of the city, whole sections of the streets are given over to street-walkers for the plying of their profession." A man could enjoy a quick tryst with a streetwalker almost anywhere—in an alley or the back room of a tavern, in a vacant lot or a graveyard. Or he could take advantage of the comforts and services offered by the city's "houses of debauchery." At the time, the city's "Holy Ground" at the base of the old city commons was the most notorious sex district in the city—and, indeed, in the new nation. It was there that Mother Carey had built her business, competing successfully over the years against a host of rivals.

Mrs. Carey followed a time-honored business model: she rented a modest house on a side street and employed only about two live-in women. Prostitution was primarily a women's business, as it had long been; taverns and inns were typically run by men, brothels and boardinghouses by women. About two-thirds of all bawdy houses were run by single women, widows, and married women acting on their own. To make ends meet, such small operations offered a variety of services. Carey might charge men who came to her house for time with one of her live-in girls. Or, if business were slow, she might send one of her girls out into the streets (or to the front window) to bring in men. When necessary, she would send out for other girls. Moreau described this process in salacious detail: If a man visits a "procuress" and she has no suitable girl at hand, "she is asked to use her influence to obtain a friend who is free"; the bawd suggests a "desirable companion" and sends out to discover "if there is any hope"; if the woman is available, she comes to the brothel. The brothel keeper typically took one-third of the woman's fee, which was higher, Moreau noted, if "one's desires run to a beautiful person of high rank, or one more difficult to persuade"—or even that most desirable commodity, a virgin. Other times, a brothel might function like a modern no-tell motel. A streetwalker might come in with a trick in tow, offering to split her fee in exchange for the use of a room. Similarly, a man with sex on his mind and a wife at home—or, in Harry Bedlow's case, parents at home—might rent a room at a brothel for a discreet tryst.

At the time, prostitution itself was not illegal. As late as 1914, New York law didn't prohibit the buying and selling of sex; it only regulated where such transactions could take place: private homes and hotels were acceptable, streets and tenements were not. In the new American republic, as in England, streetwalkers did run the risk of being arrested under laws against vagrancy. Among those prosecuted in the 1790s were women who sported names like Kitty Kane and Sally Nice. Hauled into an informal magistrate's court and denied the chance to mount an effective defense, such women were almost always convicted and punished for being "common prostitutes," even though that was not, in itself, a crime. Technically they were guilty only of lacking a legitimate means of support. Soliciting sex in the streets was specifically outlawed in the nineteenth century—but only, in the words of an 1860 statute, if done "to the annoyance of inhabitants or passersby." In Mother Carey's day, what was illegal was running a bawdy house.

In the eyes of the law, a person who ran a brothel was guilty of "keeping a disorderly house." This was a catchall criminal charge that applied to any commercial establishment that allowed disreputable people, including enslaved people and sometimes simply "negroes," to gather for the purposes of drinking, gambling, generally "misbehaving themselves," or "whoring." The offense of disorderly house keeping was based on the patriarchal notion that the household was the lowest level of government and that the head of a household, generally assumed to be a man, was responsible for keeping his wife, children, servants, employees, enslaved workers, and anyone else living under his roof under control. Like streetwalkers, disorderly-house keepers were only sporadically prosecuted, and convictions for disorderly house keeping, compared to other crimes, were rare. In practice, a house became "disorderly" in the eyes of the law only when it became a nuisance in the eyes of its neighbors.

The consequences of drawing the wrong kind of attention could be swift and severe. In late 1767, newspapers reported that a man died after a brawl in the new brick Broadway house of the celebrated bawd Caty Crow. Within a month, she was prosecuted in New York's highest court for keeping a bawdy house, fined a whopping £100, and sentenced to a year in prison. Instead, she put her house up for sale and skipped town.

To stay in business, Mother Carey relied on her good instincts, her financial savvy, and a broad series of strategies: she put on a plausible public face, avoided legal trouble, chose a suitable location, outfitted her house strategically, screened clients effectively, and kept everything that happened in her house discreet, maintaining good relations with her neighbors.

In the fall of 1793, Mother Carey was fifty-four—which, in the eyes of her contemporaries, made her seem "old" or "aged." Life expectancies were short; few, at the time, made it past sixty. Carey's origins, like those of many women on the margins of eighteenth-century society, are obscure. Certainly, she had long experience with the business of prostitution, and may very well have grown up in the business. It was a common enough story. At a time when the working life of prostitutes was notoriously brief, those who grew old in the profession were often those who developed the skills and the wherewithal to become managers. The celebrated English bawd Charlotte Hayes was suckled at the bosom of her mother's brothel.

So was her fictional American counterpart Moll Placket-Hole, whose name referred to the slit in a woman's skirt that provided access to an interior pocket. Her ribald, supposedly true *Adventures* (1765) depicted her as a lusty girl whose exposure to the depravity of her mother's brothel destroyed her virtue and warmed her blood. When Moll was twelve, her mother responded to a business setback by selling her virginity—for the "Trifling Consideration" of ten pounds. Initially, Moll was kept by her purchaser, but he soon lost interest and abandoned her to the fate of a fallen woman. "Virtue lost and good Reputation (if she ever had it) gone," Moll accepted the life of a common prostitute. During her teens, she experienced all of the "common" professional hazards: repeated bouts of venereal disease and unpleasant treatments, unwanted pregnancies, and spells in the public house of correction. By the time she turned twenty, Moll's body was so broken down that she could no longer earn her living by it.

In most stories about fallen women, this is where the narrative turns to poverty and death. Moll, in contrast, reinvented herself as the keeper of her own bawdy house, drawing on her long experience in the trade. She prospered. Eventually, she acquired a husband. For some real bawds, like Charlotte Hayes, marriage helped secure access to the capital they needed to outfit their businesses. For Moll Placket-Hole, the man she passed off as her husband served a different business purpose: "It was necessary that a Man should live with her, that they might appear to the Public, as *honest* Housekeepers."

Mother Carey was married at least twice. Most recently, on a Tuesday in late April 1783, the "widow" Ann Glover and the self-described "innkeeper" James Carey, both of the city of New York, had posted a civil marriage bond to certify that their marriage would be legitimate and then stood before the Reverend Benjamin Moore of the Anglican parish, who solemnized their vows. Most likely, both Careys had been in the city for some time. Although the war was effectively over, the city was still occupied by the British; those who had evacuated at the start of the war hadn't yet returned. Quite possibly, the widow Ann Glover and the "innkeeper" James Carey had spent the war years catering to the demand for prostitutes generated by the presence in the city of thousands of military men. Before the war, one visitor put the number of "ladies of pleasure" lodging in the Holy Ground at "above 500"—or almost one in ten women in the city. By 1780, when the number of British military men in the city had swelled, it was said that there were some 2,000 prostitutes among a total civilian population of about 12,000.

In the war's aftermath, the Careys adopted a series of plausible guises to obscure the true nature of their operation. During the 1780s, James Carey repeatedly described himself as the keeper of some legitimate business in the hospitality line—as an "innkeeper" at the time of his marriage, as a "lodging-house" keeper in the city's first published directory in 1786, as a "tavern" keeper a year later. But whatever they were up to, it was not operating a legal inn or tavern. Such businesses were strictly regulated by the city and required a license from the mayor. Obtaining a license involved paying a fee; promising not to allow gambling, card playing, shuffleboards, billiards, or, of course, "whoring"; and posting a substantial bond, signed by two other individuals. In the ten years before 1793, the city issued such licenses to hundreds of New Yorkers—but not to the Careys. Years later, when a boy who grew up in the neighborhood recorded what he knew about Mother Carey, he described her first as the keeper of a "boarding house for sailors" and then, more frankly, as the keeper of a "brothel."

Despite her marriage, Ann Carey was firmly in charge of the business. Around 1790, "Mrs. Carey," not her husband, appeared on a list of their landlady's tenants. By that time, her husband had started identifying himself in other lines of work—as a humble "laborer" in 1791, and, vaguely, as a "trader" in 1792 and 1793. Like other married women, Mother Carey was legally "covered" by her husband's identity: he was the one listed in the city directories, in tax assessments, and in census rolls. And her authority to conduct business on her own was restricted. Nonetheless, it was common for women with absent husbands (and widows with sufficient capital) to operate independent businesses—often boarding, lodging, and bawdy houses. A case in point was Mother Carey's neighbor Hannah Gould, who used the house leased by her husband Peter, a "mariner," to operate what she described as a "boarding house."

During all this time, Mother Carey successfully skirted the law. Since the end of the war, the city had prosecuted hundreds of licensed tavern keepers and innkeepers for violating the terms of their licenses. For example, Joseph Corré, who by 1793 was famous for the ice cream served at his new "hotel" on Broadway, was prosecuted in 1791 for keeping a "billiards table" in the tavern he had operated down by the Battery. Others were prosecuted for operating taverns and inns without licenses. And hundreds more New Yorkers were prosecuted for maintaining houses that for various reasons were considered "disorderly"; a few surviving indictments specifically cite the offense as "whoring." But no prosecution ever targeted Ann Carey or her husband.

She kept herself out of trouble in part through her choice of an auspicious base of operations. By 1793, she had been operating for the better part of a decade out of the same house at what would now be 3 Beekman Street, which at the time was still on the northern fringe of the city's development. At the time of their marriage in 1783, James Carey had been operating his "inn" in the house next door. For a time in the mid-1780s, they had moved a few blocks south to a house on the east side of Broadway. But as the fire-ravaged area on the western side of town was rebuilt, Broadway reclaimed its status as a prestigious thoroughfare, and gentrification made the neighborhood less comfortable for the Careys. So, in 1787, they moved back to their earlier haunt.

It was a good spot for an illegal business. The Carey house was on the northern edge of a large, irregular parcel known as the Vineyard (earlier in the century it had been so far north of the city's commercial and residential districts that it may literally have been used to grow grapes). In the 1750s, the several-acre tract had been cut up into dozens of urban lots—the Careys' was fairly typical at twenty-five feet wide and seventy-five feet deep—and let out on long-term leases. Since before the war, the Vineyard had been a favored location for taverns and bawdy houses. Around the corner from the Carey property lay the old city commons, which was just being refurbished as a park. Over the previous year, the city had ordered the planting of shade trees and the construction of a fence to keep out the cows that provided milk for the Almshouse. On the far side of the new park was the notorious "Holy Ground." Much of the land between that stretch of Broadway and the Hudson River was owned by Trinity Church, which was famously untroubled about renting its properties to disorderly-house keepers. And the widow Ann White, who had inherited the Vineyard from her Loyalist husband at the end of the war, adopted a similar attitude. Effectively, the tract became an extension of the Holy Ground.

By 1793, Mother Carey's block housed tavern keepers, washerwomen, grocers, and tradesmen—all operating cheek by jowl with at least six bawdy houses. Such a dense concentration of vice had practical advantages. Neighbors were less likely to take offense and complain to the authorities; some, indeed, saw the large numbers of streetwalkers and bawdy houses as good for business. As one moral reformer lamented, "the neighbours are pleased to have it so, because the resort of sailors and others to them, brings money to the taverns and dram shops."

Mother Carey's house was a modest two-story wood-frame structure that probably extended across the full width of the twenty-five-foot lot. It was far more substantial than some of the crude one-story hovels on other parts of the block but far less grand than the city's finer town houses. It had been built around 1767 as an accessory to the tavern on the corner of

*Mother Carey's house (on the right, numbered 3), drawn in later life
by the son of George Washington's dentist.*

Beekman and Park Row. The first floor had originally been taken up by a
large room, twenty-eight feet deep, "designed for dancing." Either Carey
or a previous tenant had reconfigured the space with crude board parti-
tions, built like barn stalls. Now, there was a parlor in front and two private bedrooms, separated by a narrow passageway, in back. Mother Carey
evidently didn't think it was worth the expense to install lath-and-plaster
walls, which were quite common even in modest houses—and would
have offered more privacy and soundproofing. On the second floor there
were three bedrooms and, above them, a large garret. Very likely there
was a cellar as well, housing a kitchen and storerooms. In back was an
overgrown yard, cluttered with piles of discarded clam shells, guarded
by loud dogs, and surrounded by a high fence, with a gate opening onto
an alley that led through the interior of the block back to Ann Street. It
was an unusual feature: relatively few houses in the city had a completely
separate back exit.

Although content with a roughly built structure, Mother Carey outfitted the interior of her house with some expensive luxuries, presumably
to put her more refined guests, like Harry Bedlow, at ease. To help ensure
their comfort in bed, she invested in costly feather mattresses. She also
acquired elegant mahogany furniture and at least one looking glass, which
she most likely deployed in her front room, or parlor—which, in a brothel,

provided a crucial space for receiving visitors, entertaining those who were waiting, and negotiating business.

Keeping the wrong people out of her house was another way in which Mother Carey, like other bawdy-house keepers, avoided trouble. It wasn't just strangers, thieves, and thugs that she had to keep at bay. Pushy young-bloods, rowdy sailors, or belligerent drunks could cause trouble if one gave them an opening. Others might show up at a brothel with the explicit purpose of raising a ruckus: an outraged wife, looking for her wayward husband, might show up to make a scene. Or a husband might appear, looking for his wife. God forbid that a bawdy-house keeper should have to deal with an outraged parent looking for a no-longer-so-innocent daughter.

When screening potential clients, a bawd like Mother Carey relied on her ability to quickly read the character of strangers. One elaborate procedure was described by Moreau. "Women, usually well along in age, are known to be procuresses," he reported, and a newcomer to the city might get detailed descriptions of particular brothels from a local acquaintance. But a first-time visitor needed a "reliable friend" to make a personal introduction, which could involve sitting in the parlor to get acquainted. After they established a rapport, the visitor would then ask the procuress for permission to return on his own.

Trust was necessary because bawds and clients were the keepers of each other's secrets. For most men, their time in a brothel or with a streetwalker was a kind of double life that they wanted to keep separate from their other relationships. A newspaper in Boston jokingly suggested that the government should require separate establishments for older and younger men—to avoid awkward encounters between fathers and sons. One outrageous gentleman, it was said, flaunted his debauchery by leaving his distinctive horse tied up in front when he visited houses of ill fame. But most men wanted to control knowledge of their illicit encounters. Moreau reported the exasperating experience of a "French gentleman" who found himself effectively blackmailed in one of New York's brothels: even after they had settled on a fee, the woman he was with kept demanding more and more money, warning him that without it the bawd who ran the house could not be relied upon to keep quiet.

It was with this concern in mind that the *Adventures of Moll Placket-Hole* described a well-run brothel as like a "Port of Trade" in which all the customs duties were paid immediately, in cash, so that its keeper did not need to employ clerks or keep records. Consequently, the bawd "could not remember all who *entered*, and *unloaded their freights* there." As Mother Carey and Harry Bedlow no doubt knew all too well, bawds and their clients depended upon a kind of mutually assured discretion.

Over the years, Mother Carey deftly navigated the line between notoriety and neighborliness. That is what struck a boy who grew up around the corner, the son of the dentist who crafted some of George Washington's best dentures. He drew a sketch of her house as it appeared in his mind's eye: a low, two-story clapboard structure with a large vitrine on the first floor (see p. 33). In front of the house, he drew a single figure: a stout woman in a mobcap, sweeping the stoop. If Mother Carey ran a dirty business, at least she kept it clean.

Looking back through a veil of Victorian prudery, he saw Mother Carey as a nostalgic reminder of a bygone era when a procuress like her could play the role of a good neighbor to a rich, respectable family like his. He told a story about how, on the occasion of his sister's baptism in 1789, Mother Carey had saved the day. When his family and the Presbyterian pastor gathered in the Brick Church to perform the rite, they discovered to their consternation that there was no baptismal font at hand and no other vessel to hold the water. Someone was dispatched to find one—and his search ended across the street at Mother Carey's. She had just the thing. The three-week-old baby was baptized in the old bawd's punchbowl.

3 BEEKMAN STREET. THURSDAY, SEPTEMBER 5, 1793. AROUND 2:00 A.M.

Some time later, Mother Carey was back in bed. Having dealt with the problem of the importunate gentleman at her front door, she had nodded off "into a doze of sleep." But her peace of mind did not last long. Soon, she was roused by the sound of dogs barking and a noise at her back door. She got up again, this time "greatly alarmed." It sounded like thieves were trying to break in.

She told the woman who was sharing her bed, Mary Franklin, to get up, too, and come with her. Dressed only in her shift, Carey made her way through the dark house.

At the back door, she paused.

Who is there? Carey inquired.

"A friend," came the reply through the door.

Recognizing the voice as Harry Bedlow's, Mother Carey unlocked the door and opened it.

In the inky darkness, there he stood, along with the same young woman. Once again, Harry asked if he could come in.

Once again, Mother Carey faced a fateful decision.

It was the same question she had considered before, but now her state of mind was different. An overzealous customer was a better problem to face in the middle of the night than a violent burglar. But whatever relief she may have felt was tempered by the fact that she had underestimated Harry Bedlow's persistence. He had traveled all the way around the block to Ann Street, up the narrow alleyway that cut through the block to the rear of her property, and through the gate in her seven-foot-tall fence. He could have tried his luck at a number of other nearby brothels—several of which he had no doubt passed. But he was fixated on getting into hers.

Perhaps Mother Carey figured that it was better to face the consequences of letting him in than to risk whatever he might do next if she refused. Perhaps she felt that it was less of a problem letting him in through the back door than the front—it was, after all, much more private and shielded from view. Or, perhaps, standing at her back door in the middle of the night, roused from sleep for the second time, Mother Carey simply felt worn down.

"There is a room," she said.

Mother Carey ushered them through the door and closed it.

Inside, the darkness was absolute. Any light from the moonless night sky was blocked by the heavy wooden doors and window shutters. And Mother Carey wasn't even carrying a candle. In her rush to investigate the alarm at the back door, she hadn't bothered to light one.

She led Harry and the young woman down a narrow hallway—only three feet wide, it wasn't difficult to navigate in the dark—and into one of her small back rooms.

As she made her way back to bed, Harry called out once again.

He wanted a candle.

Mother Carey ordered Mary Franklin to fetch one and hurriedly pulled on some clothes.

A few moments later, Carey returned to the back room, "shoved the candle in at the door, and went away."

In the glow of the candle, Lanah could make out the contours of the small, crudely built room, the door, the shuttered window, the chair, the bed, and Harry pulling off his coat and then his waistcoat.

❧

As Mother Carey shut the door to the back room and returned to bed, Harry was approaching the consummation of a very specific kind of desire. He had gone to considerable effort to strike up an acquaintance with a naïve young woman; to mislead, charm, and entice her; to get her out alone with him; and to get her into that room. Now, he was looking to take his pleasure in the comfort of a feather bed, by the light of a candle, at his leisure.

Even if Lanah had been eager for the encounter, what Harry had in mind would leave her gravely compromised, at risk of social ruin. For some men, the harm such a woman would suffer was almost irrelevant. For others, in the age of the Marquis de Sade, it was part of the pleasure.

For Mother Carey, it was a potential problem. Having agreed to let Harry and Lanah into her back room, Mother Carey found herself enacting the era's most scandalous image of a bawd: conniving with an ill-intentioned gentleman to ruin a naïve young woman.

The iconic version of this story was presented in the English painter William Hogarth's six-part series *A Harlot's Progress* (1731–1732), with his characteristic combination of moralism and humor. The first plate focuses on a pretty young woman, dressed in maidenly white, standing at a literal crossroads. Dangling from her wrist are a pair of scissors and a pincushion: she intends to make her way in the world as a sewing girl. An old woman, her face spotted with black syphilis sores, accosts the young woman—hoping to entice her into an illicit encounter. In the background, the old woman's client gropes himself in anticipation. At that moment, the fate of the young innocent hangs in the balance.

Subsequent scenes show the now-fallen woman as the (unfaithful) mistress of a Jewish merchant, as a common prostitute, as an inmate in the city's workhouse, and, finally, dying a miserable death from syphilis. Her life-changing seduction—or rape—is never shown. For Hogarth, the distinction between enticement and coercion doesn't seem to matter. He leaves us to assume that the gentleman in the first scene took his pleasure and left the young woman ruined, but all he shows is the procuress

A procuress targets a young woman in Hogarth's A Harlot's Progress.

earning her fee. In Hogarth's vision, the active agent of the young woman's ruin is the old bawd.

In the popular imagination, a woman like Mother Carey could make good money by satisfying men's fetish for having sex with a virgin. According to published accounts, Charlotte Hayes could earn huge sums by satisfying requests to procure specific maidens. Salacious exposés of life in urban brothels detailed all manner of ingenious ploys used by bawds and pimps to inveigle unwary girls. One gambit involved posting a fake advertisement for a domestic servant and directing applicants to come to a rented apartment where the girl chosen for the position could be held and, one way or another, seduced. At the same time, a certain cynicism about women's innocence prevailed. Moreau noted that New York bawds could charge a premium for a woman "supposed to be a novice at love." For her part, Charlotte Hayes reportedly viewed virginity as a renewable resource—no more difficult to restore than it was to make a dessert. "As to maidenheads," she boasted, it was her opinion that "a woman might lose hers a hundred times, and be as good a Virgin as ever."

This, according to popular lore, was the other motivation bawds and pimps had in ruining young women: the prospect of turning their victims into profitable employees. After tricking or coercing a respectable girl into losing her virginity, a bawd might then be able to turn her "ruined" victim into a compliant worker by persuading her that, after what had happened, her only option was to accept her fate—to take the only kind of refuge and the only kind of work still available to her.

So-called seduction stories and their more ribald and pornographic counterparts, which typically began with deception and often ended with coercion, frequently amounted to rape fantasies.

The object of desire was precisely the kind of woman who had to be tricked into a compromising position: a fresh-faced country girl, a virtuous young woman from a genteel family—in short, a woman who would not ordinarily consent to casual sex or willingly enter a life of prostitution. Capitalizing on this fetish, guidebooks to London prostitutes during the 1790s weren't above advertising specific girls as so innocent that they had entered the life only through deception or force.

In reality, bawds like Mother Carey did face the challenge of recruiting workers. Turnover is always a challenge for employers, and in prostitution, new faces were always in demand. Moreover, prostitution, as a line of work, had a variety of drawbacks: it could be unpleasant, it could be emotionally draining, and, even in the best of circumstances, it was dangerous. Published accounts emphasized the devastating effects of venereal diseases like syphilis—which was treated with mercury, a poison that did nothing to ameliorate the disease but did cause excessive salivation, madness, and death. The world of prostitution was also violent. In the city's court records, men and women who appeared in cases involving prostitution and disorderly houses often turned up again in cases involving violent assaults, robberies, and attempted murder.

Nonetheless, the basic methods brothel keepers like Mother Carey used to attract and retain workers bore little resemblance to published accounts of seduction and ruin. The allure of maidenly innocence notwithstanding, the tastes of men and the availability of women varied. In a city where a tenth of the population was Black, sex across the color line was common. Women of color worked the streets and in bawdy houses—and ran a good number of them. One woman named Dinah Sheffee was prosecuted in 1798 for running a brothel in the Holy Ground, at 51 Warren

Street, that attracted Black and white patrons. A few years later, a white grocer who lived around the corner, at 83 Chambers Street, complained that a tenant was operating a brothel out of his basement apartment. Entering the premises one day, he found one "White Man in the very fact of Committing adultery with a Black Woman"—and another "White Man undressed and in bed with two Black Women."

Hundreds, if not thousands, of women would hardly have flocked into New York's brothels or filled its streets late at night if it were not for the fact that prostitution, as a line of work, also had compelling attractions.

Most important, prostitution offered high wages. At the time, women's earnings were typically punishingly low. A widow might carry on a family business; a woman with sufficient capital might find operating a boardinghouse a good way to make ends meet. But other kinds of work available to women generally paid less than even the basic requirements of subsistence. Women with respectable jobs—laundresses and seamstresses, for example—were typically dependent upon either their parents or their husbands for a large part of their subsistence. A single woman looking to support herself independently had two basic options. She could turn to a job as a live-in domestic servant, though both demand and wages were driven down by the large number of enslaved women in the city, like the three Black women who labored in the Bedlow household. Alternatively, a young woman could turn to prostitution, which offered much better pay. A prostitute might charge three dollars for a typical encounter—well more than the daily wages of a sailor or workman and four times those of a laundress or ironing woman, even after the bawd took her one-dollar cut.

Prostitution could also offer women a kind of autonomy and emotional support that many valued. In the 1790s, when bawdy houses were relatively small and most often managed by women, working conditions were comparatively good. Despite sensational accounts in the popular press, brothel keepers at the time enjoyed little coercive power. The figure of the modern pimp—dominating the business, exploiting prostitutes financially, and controlling their options—would not emerge until about a century after Mother Carey's day; only after the politics of urban vice shifted decisively and concerted policing forced prostitution underground did the business come to be dominated by male protection rackets. Until then, many women found a certain camaraderie and emotional support in brothels, working alongside women who didn't judge them. Having sex with men for a living could even be a way for a woman to free herself from male control. A woman who wanted to escape an abusive or underemployed husband—and who didn't have a comfortable family or a profitable trade to fall back on—often faced a choice between prostitution and abject poverty. One unhappily married woman threatened her husband that if he didn't let her do as she pleased, she would move out. Anticipating the obvious retort—"And where will you go?"—she declared that she would "become a common Whore." And that is exactly what she did. Five years later, according to his divorce complaint, she was managing her own bawdy house.

Of course, a brothel keeper like Mother Carey also faced plenty of competition. A woman working for her might be lured to a competing house or decide to take her chances renting her own lodgings and working the streets.

To keep women under their control, brothel keepers developed a variety of coercive tactics, including forms of debt peonage. A woman might go to live and work in a bawdy house—only to find that whatever she earned from turning tricks was never quite sufficient to pay what she was being charged for room and board. Or a young woman might be encouraged to try on some of the bawd's finery, only to be hit with an exorbitant rental fee—or, if she tried to escape, prosecuted for theft.

A real-life example of this ploy appears in a lawsuit from the mid-1790s that involves a woman just a year older than Lanah Sawyer. Eliza Bowen was born in Providence, Rhode Island. Her mother, just fourteen at the time, raised her in a bawdy house run by a Black woman who had only recently escaped from slavery. When Eliza was seven, rioters attempting to clean up the neighborhood destroyed the brothel. The town fathers incarcerated Eliza's mother and bound Eliza herself out as a domestic servant. In 1795, having recently become free from her indenture, Eliza went to a local shop and bought yards and yards of shiny green silk and other finery on credit. Soon, the shopkeeper slapped her with a suit for debt. Why would a girl like her buy a gaudy, expensive, and impractical outfit she couldn't afford? Presumably it had something to do with the man who settled the debt on her behalf: he was not related to her, but he was later prosecuted for running a bawdy house. Within a few years, Bowen did make her break. She moved to New York and took up work in the new Park Theatre, around the corner from the site of Mother

Carey's house, a notorious cruising ground for young women looking to turn tricks.

According to the books and magazines favored by middling and elite women, once a maiden was "ruined" she had no alternative but to accept a life of prostitution and an early death (if she hadn't already succumbed to despair and committed suicide). But, for a large segment of the population in a city like New York, a young woman's "ruin" was not nearly so absolute. Just as there were many routes that led into the life of prostitution, there were also some routes that led back out again. A woman might go back and forth between selling sex and other occupations. A woman who had worked as a prostitute might even be able to open up a respectable new chapter in her life by getting married.

In New York, the most celebrated example of such a marriage was Eliza Bowen's. In 1803, while working at the new theater on Park Row, she met the wealthy Haitian refugee Stephen Jumel, struck up a relationship, and eventually married him. She became a celebrated socialite, whom Aaron Burr in later life married for her money, and whose house, the Morris-Jumel Mansion, stands today as one of the city's only surviving eighteenth-century landmarks.

In truth, such Cinderella stories were rare. For manipulative men with economic power, the fantasy had its uses: holding out the promise of marriage could encourage a woman to exert herself to be pleasing without any actual legal or financial commitment on his part. Such stories reflect disturbing elements of the culture of romance: they lionize men's superior social and economic power, cast "slut-shamed" women as in need of redemption, and suggest that the one thing that can lead men to set aside their base motivations is the transcendent power of romantic love.

Women working as prostitutes might well get married, but generally not to any kind of Prince Charming. More typical was the story of Mary Burties, who was living in a brothel in the vicinity of Mother Carey's house in the years before the revolution. In early 1773, Burties dazzled a new arrival to the city, presumably one of her customers. He was an immigrant from Ireland who had run away from servitude in Maryland, escaped to New York, and found work as a gunsmith. "I knew she had followed a loose way of life," he later remarked, but "I loved her." They got married in early April. She gave up her job and moved in with him. But he almost immediately fell sick, and when she went back to work, he grew jealous. One night in mid-May, he followed her to the brothel in the Holy Ground where she was working, waited outside, and watched through a window until she left the house with two men, leaving the door unlocked. He stole the bar that should have been securing the door, crept up behind them in front of St. Paul's Chapel (where Park Row and Ann Street converge on Broadway), and dealt one of the men a fatal blow to the head. At least, that is the story he told to a local printer who hawked copies to the thousands of spectators who gathered to witness his execution on the Chinese Chippendale–style gallows that stood at the head of the old city commons, a stone's throw from Mother Carey's house. For Mary Burties, six months of marriage had done nothing to change her lot in life—except involve her in scandal and expose her working life to public view.

"Fallen" women like Mary Burties might not have been welcomed in the city's more refined parlors, but neither were they utter social outcasts.

Mother Carey herself participated in the same kinds of social connections and sacred rituals as New Yorkers of all ranks. In early 1790, for example, she stood in Trinity Church and assumed the role of godmother to the newborn baby Thomas Glover. Carey (whose first husband had been a Glover) was evidently related to the boy's father, James Glover, who was vaguely identified in city directories as a "workman" and died soon after the baptism. The baby's mother, a "washer" who lived around the corner from Mother Carey, remarried quickly. Her new husband, a house carpenter, moved into her house but evidently didn't want his stepson underfoot. So, Mother Carey, who may not have expected that the role of godmother would involve any actual responsibility, took him in. By the fall of 1793, the three-and-a-half-year-old boy had spent most of his life in a brothel. It may not have been the worst arrangement: certainly, there were plenty of women in the house with time on their hands during the day, part of which they might have spent keeping a toddler out of trouble.

The actual working lives of the city's bawds and prostitutes were thus a far cry from the stories of seduction and ruin repeated with endless variation in newspapers, magazines, pamphlets, and books. Most prostitutes were women from poor families; they chose prostitution because it seemed better than the alternatives into which they were born.

The situation of a woman like Lanah Sawyer, from a respectable working family and poised for a marriage that would solidify her status, was very different. She had much less to gain from prostitution and much more to lose.

The danger Lanah faced raised the stakes for Mother Carey, too.

In the end, Moll Placket-Hole suffered the fate all brothel keepers feared: public attack and ruin. At the cold, dark heart of her *Adventures* were the outrageous schemes she devised to inveigle "unwary girls." One time, she lured a "handsome" country girl back to her house and summoned a client. After spending what he considered "Time enough in *Civility*," the gentleman "began to treat her *rudely*" and dismissed her protests. On the verge of rape, however, the gentleman realized that he knew her father. Horrified, he stopped what he was doing and escorted the girl to safety. But such evil schemes were not, in themselves, what got Placket-Hole into trouble. It was her pride and public defiance that upset her neighbors and eventually prompted the city to announce a crackdown. Moll Placket-Hole managed to avoid legal trouble, but she failed to learn her lesson. Instead, she returned even more flagrant in her behavior than before. Eventually, the city folk, "tired out with her Insolence," took matters into their own hands: they raised a mob, pulled down her house, and destroyed her belongings.

Writing about New York in the mid-1790s, Moreau tells a strikingly similar story about procurement that ended very differently for all concerned. According to Moreau, a "French gentleman" gained access to an exclusive brothel (by pretending not to be French), and the bawd promised to procure him a "tender beauty" on the condition that he keep the transaction secret. At the last minute, he recognized the "young innocent" as the daughter of a business acquaintance. "What was he to do?" Moreau asks, setting aside any concern about the young woman, her state of mind, or the consequences that might befall her. "Already the matter had gone too far to retreat; and so the final step was taken and happiness put a seal upon his lips." For Moreau, the incident raised no problem—for the gentleman or for the bawd, and perhaps even for the young woman—that couldn't be solved simply by keeping it quiet.

Late in the summer of 1793, Mother Carey had good reason to keep her business discreet. Just weeks earlier, the city had pressed charges against two other nearby bawdy-house keepers. Bridget Parks, who kept a house on what is now Park Row, was found guilty of keeping a disorderly house and fined £12. The other woman simply disappeared. In real life, as in

Moll Placket-Hole's fictional world, a routine police action could end up driving a bawd out of business—at least temporarily. And riots targeting brothels were becoming more common in the 1790s as moral reformers joined forces with local residents looking to "clean up" specific corners of the city. These rioters were almost always men; the brothels they attacked were almost always those run by women.

Over the years, Mother Carey had fashioned a life for herself by building a business that played a small role in a vast sexual system. In a culture that idealized the sexual innocence of some women, disparaged the availability of others, and granted broad impunity to men, prostitution was big business. The narrative of the bawd as a procuress dramatized and personified the culture's obsession with separating respectable and ruined women, the fetish and the anxiety provoked by the idea of imperiled virtue, and, more broadly, the shame of illicit sex and double lives. As a face for uglier aspects of a patriarchal sexual system rooted in double standards and double lives, the bawd had her attractions: her image intensified the chasm between respectable and ruined women and shielded men from responsibility. But the same system that kept women like Mother Carey in business also disparaged and blamed them—and made them vulnerable.

Of course, like the bawd in Moreau's story about the French gentleman and his business colleague's daughter, the problem Mother Carey faced was not exactly what was going on in her back room that night. The problem was what might happen if it were exposed to public view.

3 BEEKMAN STREET. THURSDAY, SEPTEMBER 5, 1793. ABOUT 8:00 A.M.

In the morning, Mother Carey waited for the occupants of her back room to get up and get out. By eight o'clock in the morning, most of the working people in the city had been up for hours and were getting ready to stop for breakfast. Across the street, workmen were busy constructing the soaring wooden steeple of the Brick Church—a project that had prompted a similar endeavor at St. Paul's Chapel around the corner and given rise to knowing jokes about the rival institutions' anxiety over the relative size of their protuberances.

Mother Carey was ready for breakfast, too.

She made her way down the narrow passageway, opened the door, and roused her godson. The toddler had slept soundly all night in a boarded-off space in a corner of the room—or at least had given no outward sign that he had been disturbed by what had gone on in the bed a few feet away. He emerged from his nook, made his way around the bed, and went out through the door. Mother Carey swung the door back into its jamb.

But she left it open a crack. In a house of shame and secrets, it was a discomfiting violation of privacy—a not-too-subtle signal that it was time for Harry and the young woman to leave. Mother Carey was ready to be done with the business of the previous night and get on with the new day.

Harry pulled on his clothes and told Lanah to make haste, that Mother Carey would want her gone. Then he emerged from the back room, closed the door, and presumably settled up with Mother Carey before heading off into the city.

But Lanah was not ready to be rushed. She remained in the back room, alone, mending her torn dress and taking stock of what had happened, for the better part of two more hours.

Meanwhile, Mother Carey and the motley assemblage she liked to think of as "the family" ate breakfast. It was an invented family, one that may have existed primarily in her imagination, a group brought together by a confluence of circumstance, necessity, and compassion. No one who lived in Carey's house was actually related to her by blood: not the woman who spent the night in one of the back rooms ("alone," she later insisted), not the "negro wench" who likely slept in the kitchen or in a garret. Not the woman who had shared Mother Carey's bed—nor, of course, her husband, who had not. Even her godson was only a tangential relation. All of them had faced upheaval in their lives—family ties severed, personal connections broken, and then, around Mother Carey's hearth, forged anew.

In the midst of that routine domestic scene, none of them had any way to know that their world was about to be turned upside down once again. The events Thomas Glover had slept through the night before would soon disrupt any sanctuary he had found in his godmother's house. The same was true of the others.

But Mother Carey, with her long experience and reliable instincts, may have had an inkling that something might be wrong.

The problem wasn't with the young gentleman. Mother Carey had no cause for concern as he emerged from the back room, took his leave, and ventured out into the street. He left her house the same man he had been when he entered. He knew the way the game was played, and it wasn't in his interest to make waves.

But what about the young woman? Even Mother Carey's most self-serving version of what had happened in that back room the night before—that the young woman had been seduced—had the potential to transform the young woman's life. She had entered Carey's house a modest girl from a respectable, working family. She would leave facing the prospect of ruin. For Mother Carey, this itself was not a problem. To her, it may even have seemed like part of the solution.

For a woman like Mother Carey, the "ruin" a woman like Lanah Sawyer faced was not just a shameful turn of fate; it was also a weapon. It could be used to disarm the danger such a woman posed—the possibility that she might run to her family, or friends, or to local magistrates, and proclaim what had happened the night before and the bawd's role in it—by shaming her into silence. And, if convinced of the inevitability of her own ruin, a woman in such position might even be turned to a brothel keeper's advantage—and become a compliant worker.

By the time Lanah finally emerged from the back room, it was about ten o'clock.

Mother Carey greeted her in the passageway and offered to help her slip out of the house. Lanah could go out the back, Mother Carey offered, or out the front—she had looked, and there was no one to see.

This, she soon realized, was a mistake.

Carey's instincts had served her well over the years. But now it seemed that they might be failing her. Maybe she should have adopted a more aggressive approach, greeting the young woman with a warning or a threat? Maybe she had simply misjudged the young woman's character.

Lanah did not respond with gratitude, desperation, or tears. The old bawd's familiarity and solicitude only inflamed her anger.

I will go out the front door, and do not care if the first man I meet with is my father, or some relation or acquaintance, Lanah retorted.

It was an ominous portent. Mother Carey's first instinct the night before had been right: she should never have let Harry Bedlow bring that young woman into her house.

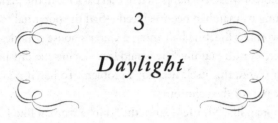

3

Daylight

By the time Mother Carey's front door swung shut and Lanah breathed in the mild morning air, her bravado had evaporated.

What now?

From Mother Carey's stoop there were only two directions she could go: right or left. Straight ahead was the Brick Church, humming with activity as builders worked on its towering steeple. And stretching out from the church on either side was a wrought-iron fence enclosing the entire block in a puddle of overgrown grass, punctuated by gravestones and shaded by a craggy old buttonwood tree. Nothing for her there.

To the right was home, only about two blocks away. From Mother Carey's house, she could see the spot where Gold Street crossed Beekman, the corner of her block. She could be there in just a few minutes.

But she wasn't ready for that. She no doubt longed for the comfort of her family, of her sisters and, especially, her mother. But the prospect of returning home also filled her with dread. Going home would mean dealing with her parents and figuring out what to tell them. She couldn't do that until she herself had begun to make sense of all that had happened.

The crisis Lanah Sawyer faced was not just about emotional anguish—about whatever shame, anger, violation, regret, disappointment, and self-doubt she felt as a result of the night before. Of course, there was always the possibility that she might end up pregnant. That would create its own problems.

The crisis Lanah Sawyer faced was also about how her parents would respond.

By ten in the morning, there was no hope that she could simply slip back home unnoticed. It would be obvious to her parents, and her sisters, that she had not spent the night there, that she had been gone since the evening before. They would no doubt be worried about her—wondering what had happened to keep her away, hoping that she was safe.

But Lanah Sawyer knew her parents well enough to know that when she finally showed her face, they would not simply be relieved—they would also be angry. They would be angry at her disobedience in slipping out the previous evening. They would be angry about her failure to return at a reasonable time. They would be angry because whatever had kept their unmarried, teenaged daughter away overnight would also create a problem for them.

They, too, had a stake in her sexual reputation. If anything tarnished her reputation, it would reflect badly on Sawyer's mother, on her failure to impart to her daughter an adequate moral compass—oriented toward appropriate modesty, prudence, and obedience. For her stepfather, it would be a matter of his authority as a patriarch: his ability to control the women in his household and to defend them from other men. Whatever had happened to her would reflect upon his masculine honor.

Lanah Sawyer wasn't ready for that inevitable moment of truth.

So, stepping down from Mother Carey's stoop, she turned left, away from her parents' house, down the path of avoidance and delay.

Within moments she had reached the end of the short block and faced another turning point. Ahead of her was the Fields, recently fenced to keep out the cows and planted with shade trees, refashioned as a little park. It was, in a sense, the end of the city. To the right she could walk past the prison, the almshouse, the hospital and lose herself among the rolling hills and fields and swamps and ponds and elegant country seats that stretched northward to the tip of the island.

Sawyer headed left again, down Park Row, toward Broadway, into the city. Ahead rose the elegant brownstone bulk of St. Paul's Chapel. To her left was a jumble of small, irregular wooden structures housing carpenters and washerwomen, tailors, grocers, cobblers—as well as the keepers of several taverns and brothels. At the corner, Polly Frazier's bawdy house occupied a ramshackle hovel so squat that Lanah Sawyer, walking past, could reach up and run her hand along its roof.

But then the block ended, and Lanah Sawyer faced the intersection where Park Row and Broadway converged at the tip of the Fields, where

Ann Street, dark and narrow, opened up on the left. This was the spot where, in the dark of the night before, she had, too late, realized that her fond dreams about lawyer Smith had, in fact, been dangerous illusions.

Just as Sawyer approached that fateful juncture, a figure caught her attention. Passing by her was Harry Bedlow.

Jarred by the sight of him, what did she feel?

Lanah had just left Mother Carey's behind. Now she was confronted with Bedlow on the street—a visceral reminder of what had happened the night before, of the happy hopes she had harbored for "lawyer Smith," of the terrible predicament she now faced. He might be able to go about his business—unruffled, oblivious to her, as though nothing had happened the night before. She could not. She was not going to be able to leave him and what he had done to her behind. He wasn't going away. She would have to live with that. She would be haunted by the specter of his presence in the city—even when he wasn't right there in front of her, he would be in her mind.

Did she feel a need to just get out of the streets, to escape from people, to be alone with herself? Did she feel dirty, feel a need to cleanse herself, as though washing her body could wash away what had happened, the betrayal and violation, the shame and the anger?

Later, recounting these events, all she said was that she felt "much distressed and fearful." At the time, her worries turned to another man: her stepfather. She was afraid "lest her father should beat her before he heard her story."

She knew she would have to get to her mother first. This was what most young women did when facing potentially scandalous or shameful problems. A mother might be more understanding and more forgiving; a mother might be an ally, a moderating influence. Lanah Sawyer had particular reasons to get to her mother first: her stepfather had a hot temper and a propensity for violence.

At this point, she was still just a few blocks from home. She might have looked down to her left—to see if she could spot the block where her parents lived. But Ann Street was too narrow and too crooked; that sight line was blocked. In any case, she still wasn't ready to see her parents.

She kept moving.

In the hours to come, Lanah Sawyer struggled with competing impulses: her need to rest, to take time, to settle her emotions, and her need to return home; her fear of disclosing what had happened—fear that she would not be believed, fear that she would be punished, rejected, even disowned—and her urge to reveal all, to seek sympathy and support, to tell her story.

As time passed, the stakes rose. The longer it took her to go home and face her parents, the more likely it was that others outside the family would learn that she had gone missing. As long as the matter could be contained within the family, the issue would stay between Lanah and her parents. Their options would include sweeping the whole thing under the rug. But, as news that there was a problem became more public, the pressures on her parents would shift. The more people who learned that Lanah was in trouble, the more likely it would be that their sense of honor would require some kind of public reckoning. If it came to that, they would have to decide who to blame.

THE BATHING HOUSE AT THE FOOT OF LIBERTY STREET. THURSDAY, SEPTEMBER 5, 1793. LATE MORNING.

Where Lanah Sawyer headed at this point suggests something of her state of mind. She walked several blocks down Broadway, turned right into a side street, and proceeded to Greenwich Street. There, a full block of open land stretched along the banks of the Hudson River from the slip at the end of Liberty Street to the Paulus Hook ferry "stairs" at the foot of Cortlandt Street. There, amidst the bustling wharves and slips, was a quiet refuge. There was the city's first, and only, commercial bathing house.

Since the final years of the British occupation, it had been operated there by a carpenter-turned–lumber merchant, Henry Ludlam. "To the Ladies," read an advertisement in the *Royal Gazette* in August 1782, announcing that Ludlam had recently erected a bathing house on the Hudson River, near the Paulus Hook ferry: "Price for Bathing Four Shillings each time." At a time when indoor plumbing was unheard of in private residences, washing at home involved fetching water from a well, heating it on a fire (if one was lucky), and using rags to give oneself a kind of sponge bath. Every few years, Ludlam—responding to complaints, or trying to head off competition—somewhat defensively announced "improvements." In 1784, he advertised that there was enough water that ladies and gentlemen could bathe at any time of day; in 1787, that warm baths were available on one hour's notice; in 1790, that hot water could be had within thirty minutes.

A visit to the bathing house was a luxury. The four-shilling fee amounted to more than half the daily wages of a laundress, an unskilled workman, or a sailor. This would have been an unusual expense for a seamstress like Lanah Sawyer—but it would also have been about the only place in the city where she could clean up unobtrusively.

At some level, Sawyer's turn to the bathing house suggests a sense that she needed to cleanse herself. For survivors of sexual assaults, this is a common response: a feeling of disgust, an urge to try to wash away the violation, the trauma.

This feeling of being made dirty, of course, might also have been precipitated if she had had sex voluntarily. Hers was a culture that prized female virginity, associated it with feminine purity, and held it up as a hallmark of respectability. To have lost her virginity was to have lost her claim to cultural value. If the fact became public, she stood to lose much more.

The sense of being dirty could also speak to an emotion allied to fear and regret: shame. Modern psychological studies have shown that the emotional responses of rape survivors vary widely and can be shaped by the dynamics of the assault. Survivors of what researchers called "blitz" attacks—now typically called "stranger rapes"—often respond with anger. Their outrage is focused on their attackers, not themselves. Psychologically, anger can be empowering—it encourages women to tell others about what happened, to report the matter to law enforcement, to seek redress. In contrast, survivors of what we would call "acquaintance rapes" often do not feel this kind of anger; they tend to respond with shame. In a sense, they feel responsible for their assailant's behavior; their anger is directed inward, toward themselves, not outward toward others. This is not rational, nor is it a sign that they deserve blame. But it can be debilitating. It promotes a desire for secrecy, silence, inaction; it promotes depression.

This seems to have been closer to Lanah Sawyer's state of mind that summer day. Overwhelmed by despair, "she sat down by the riverside."

Her mind in turmoil, she had sought out a tranquil, relatively private spot.

By midday, the temperature was comfortable, just over 72 degrees. Boats small and large passed up and down the Hudson River. A ferry periodically crossed back and forth from New Jersey to a spot just to the north of where she was sitting. At one o'clock that afternoon, the two-horse mail stage boarded the ferry for the mile-and-a-quarter journey across the river and, then, toward Philadelphia, traveling all night until its arrival.

But the busy seaport's hub of activity was on the other side of the island, where wharves and slips bristled out from Water Street into the East River, whose roiling tidal waters were safer than the Hudson River, where ice flowing downriver in the winter or early spring could crack the hulls of fragile wooden ships. Late in summer, the sun sparkled off the clear water, the waves lapped gently, and the river flowed calmly, steadily by.

Sawyer looked so miserable, sitting there on the riverbank, that she attracted the notice of a gentleman who was out walking with two little boys. He came up and spoke to her.

Why, he asked with evident concern, "do you look so dejected?"

She refused to tell him.

The gentleman importuned her again and met with a like refusal.

Lanah Sawyer found herself living out a real-life version of a scene familiar from countless fictional accounts in newspapers and magazines and books: a well-intentioned gentleman, arrested by the sight of a distressed woman on the street, pauses to ask her what is wrong; she responds by disclosing a sorrowful tale of seduction and ruin. In such stories, the gentleman comes off well: compassionate, benevolent, and sensitive, he is a model of male virtue—the opposite of the heartless rake who would wreak such destruction. But the young woman is always doomed.

One example, set in New York, featured a gentleman, walking home, who stumbles upon a young woman "weeping." What is the matter? he asks. She responds with the story of her life: she had grown up in a country village where she had enjoyed innocent amusements like "evening walks" and "reading some well-chosen book," but then an aunt in the city fell ill, and she had gone for a visit that proved her ruin. Her aunt convinced her to stay in the city and introduced her to a man who took her virginity and her "virtuous" nature. Now a prostitute, she wants to renounce her trade and longs to return home. But that is a hopeless dream. A woman who disclosed the story of her ruin to a stranger might experience some kind of spiritual redemption through the act of confession, but in this world all that was left for her was death. An often-used title for such stories was "The Dying Prostitute."

To the gentleman importuning Lanah Sawyer on that riverbank, death seemed like a plausible danger. Having failed to get her to respond to his earlier entreaties, he tried to guess the nature of her troubles.

Have you lost your lover? he asked. As she slumped on the bank of the busy river, he imagined the source of her despair as a thwarted romance—a romance thwarted by the impersonal demands of maritime commerce.

Has he gone to sea? he pressed.

Neither this reminder of her stepfather's occupation nor the gentleman's misjudged speculation about the source of her sorrow did anything to relax her guard.

Again and again, she refused to answer.

There is sometimes a sense of safety, a sense of anonymity, in speaking with a stranger that can result in free confessions or startling disclosures. Yet Lanah Sawyer's silence is not hard to understand. Her fear of disclosure was realistic. She was no doubt well aware of the electric power of scandal; any hint of her sexual distress could easily spread and have catastrophic consequences. And even if she hadn't crossed paths with this gentleman before, there was no guarantee that she wouldn't in the future. It was, after all, a small city.

The gentleman pressed on.

Do you intend to drown yourself? he asked.

Finally, the gentleman tried another tack. He wrote something on a piece of paper and told Sawyer that he would show it to her if she would disclose the cause of her grief. But a ploy that might have worked with a little boy didn't work with the despondent teenager.

In the face of Lanah Sawyer's silence, the gentleman eventually gave up and went away, leaving her alone on the riverbank.

At the same time, it was entirely possible, or even probable, that in the minutes and hours after she had left Mother Carey's house, she hadn't managed to make sense of what had happened there: that her memories were blurred and jumbled, that she was overwhelmed with fear and trauma—in short, that she wasn't at all clear about what her story was.

Yet, as the insistent gentleman's questions reminded her, at some point Sawyer was going to have to decide what to say about what had happened and whom to say it to.

For Sawyer, the waters of the bathing house may have represented a way of gaining some control over her story.

Since she had repaired her gown and the fastenings of her petticoats, the most visible evidence of what had transpired the night before was the blood on her linen shift and between her legs.

She may very well have gone to the bathing house with the idea that she could wash the evidence of what had happened off of herself and her clothing. If she had done that successfully she might have been able to give an account of what had happened the night before that did not involve sex, that did not involve the loss of her virginity, that did not involve questions of consent, coercion, and blame. She might have been able to keep what had happened the night before secret. If she could do that, her parents would still, no doubt, be upset—but they would not have good reason to disown her.

Still, that's not what Lanah Sawyer did. She did not pay the fee, go into the bath house, and clean herself up. Nor did she go to any other place where she could have waded into the water and washed herself without having to pay.

When she finally gathered the emotional wherewithal to leave the banks of the river, she walked away from the bathing house with the signs of sex and of violence still on her clothing and on her body.

If Lanah Sawyer was still not ready to face her parents, neither was she ready to take steps that might have prevented the full story from eventually coming out. Outwardly, she looked respectable enough: her gown and petticoat had been repaired more or less inconspicuously. But hidden underneath, her flesh was torn and her linens stained dark by drying blood.

At this point, her home was no more than eight or nine blocks away, a ten-minute walk. But she headed the opposite direction, walking down toward the foot of Broadway.

26 BROADWAY. THURSDAY, SEPTEMBER 5, 1793. AFTERNOON.

Lanah Sawyer's destination was "a Mrs. Bruce's near the Battery, where her aged aunt lived." The address was 26 Broadway, on the east side of the Bowling Green. As Lanah presented herself at the front door, she stood right by the spot where, in the spring of 2017, the raging bronze bulk of the eleven-foot-tall *Charging Bull* was faced down by the four-foot figure of the *Fearless Girl*—a paean to women's power and resilience that the bull's sculptor complained was too powerful; her diminutive stature and defiant posture made his oversized celebration of male muscle seem like a "threat."

Lanah Sawyer was seeking refuge in a specific kind of female space. Her aunt, Rebecca Dyckman, lived with another affluent, respectable widow from an old Dutch family, Judith (Bayard) Bruce. As young women, Judith and her siblings had married into elite families: Van Cortlandts, Livingstons, and Van Rensselaers. Her niece Eliza Schuyler was married to the treasury secretary Alexander Hamilton. Now, at fifty-three, Mrs. Bruce appeared on the most exclusive guest lists—even lists too exclusive to include the Bedlows. Her father and two late husbands had left her enough money to live independently in a comfortable house in a good neighborhood, to maintain a staff that included at least two enslaved women and several other servants, and to indulge her preference for living with a respectable female companion—Lanah's aunt.

Mrs. Bruce's house was a kind of mirror image of Mother Carey's brothel, similar in some ways but with everything reversed. Both households were managed by women, organized around women's needs and powers. But if Mrs. Carey's house represented women's sex, scandal, and shame, Mrs. Bruce's house represented women's authority, autonomy, and prestige.

The relative Lanah Sawyer was there to visit was probably her sixty-three-year-old great-aunt, Rebecca (Buys) Dyckman. Although she was not as rich as Mrs. Bruce, Mrs. Dyckman's circumstances were comfortable. She was by far the most affluent and best-connected member of Lanah Sawyer's extended family.

Mrs. Bruce's house stood on a block that had been devastated by the Great Fire of 1776. To the south was a vacant lot. To the north rose some of the city's newest, most imposing, and most expensive town houses. Through the windows of the parlor where Lanah spent the afternoon, she could look out over the Battery, across the Hudson, and down the harbor to the Narrows—and take in refreshing breezes off the water. Like the house itself, the household the two widows created represented an effort to rebuild, to construct new lives for themselves in the aftermath of loss.

Over the years, both Mrs. Dyckman and Mrs. Bruce had benefited from connections to men of property and standing, but both had been passed over in the wills of their fathers and husbands—who had favored the interests of sons and grandsons over those of their daughters and wives.

How much of their stories did Lanah Sawyer know? At least some, presumably, pieced together over time from overheard snippets and secondhand gossip.

As a young woman, Rebecca Buys married an ambitious baker, John

Dyckman—whose only sibling, Maria, had married Lanah's grandfather Peter Sawyer. Early on, the Dyckmans bought the Gold Street property that Samuel Hone now rented, living in the dwelling house and operating a bolt house (sifting flour for their own needs and likely for others) as well as the bakery. John prospered—and dreamt, like Benjamin Franklin, of retiring from business and establishing himself as a gentleman. Around 1760, both Rebecca and John inherited land from their families—in her case a portion of her family's old farm on Turtle Bay. The windfall helped finance his dreams of power and prestige. He purchased a country seat in the Bowery, about a mile north of his bakery, and his growing family moved there. A few years later, he stood for election as one of the city's seven aldermen (now called council members), with his wife's brother as his assistant. Up against members of the city's entrenched elite, the upstarts won and were repeatedly reelected.

For Lanah, it was an easy walk from her home on Gold Street to the Dyckman farm, no more than a mile—a leisurely ten minutes through winding streets to the large, stagnant pond that marked the outskirts of the city and then another ten minutes up Bowery Lane, the western side of which was dominated, for half a mile, by the sprawling Bayard estate—a two-hundred-acre property that Mrs. Bruce and her siblings had inherited. By the end of the war, when Lanah was six or seven, a grid of roads and a scattering of houses had begun to grow up the west side of Bowery Lane as the Bayards began to develop their property. Their old windmill still stood just off the lane, creaking and turning as its sails caught the breeze. Just beyond that, a jagged line of fortifications, constructed at the start of the war, cut through the landscape. Soon, both would be erased by the expanding urban grid. By 1790, residential development had overtaken the southern half of the Bayard property, up to the point at which a quarter-mile-long drive lined with shade trees cut straight through the fields and pastures—offering passersby teasing glimpses of the Bayards' grand, glamorous, mysterious country seat.

The last stretch of the road to the Dyckman property was through a landscape that, even in 1793, retained much of its rural feeling—long views across fields and pastures on both sides of the road, punctuated by country seats built by the DeLanceys and the DePeysters and an old "Negro Burial Ground." The Dyckman farm was organized in the same way as its grander neighbors: the main house fronted the street and presided over extensive formal gardens that gave way to an expanse of fields and pastures. But it had long been clear that the Dyckman family's future would depend not so much on the growth of grain and livestock as on the growth of the city. As early as 1780, when Broadway barely existed beyond the Fields, Lanah's uncle had banked on its projected route through the western end of his property, which it would open up for development as frontage along an important thoroughfare. Lanah's widowed aunt continued living there in the years after her husband's death. In 1790, Lanah would have seen Rebecca Dyckman presiding over a working farm and a household that included several of her cousins, their spouses, and children—and seven enslaved people.

When Lanah's uncle, Alderman John Dyckman, Esq., had died, she was about ten—old enough to remember him and to understand why her family continued to take pride in his memory. Aldermen served on the mayor's council and also—in an era before the city had a police force—as justices of the peace. They presided over the busy courts of General Sessions of the Peace that heard minor civil and criminal matters. They were also the men you would typically approach first if you wanted to report a more serious crime, such as a major theft, a murder, or a rape.

For her part, Mrs. Judith Bayard Van Rensselaer Bruce came from a family that, since the earliest days of Dutch settlement, had flourished—and, at times, managed to survive—because of their social prominence. Her Bayard great-grandparents both narrowly escaped execution; her grandfather was convicted of treason and then pardoned during the political tumult around the turn of the eighteenth century. And her feisty great-grandmother was convicted of witchcraft while visiting the Puritan settlement at Hartford; only her family's powerful connections allowed her to avoid hanging. When a man in New York slandered her as "a whore and strumpet," she beat him up and stoned his house.

It was likely through their family properties in the Bowery that the two widows had first gotten to know each other: the two-hundred-acre Bayard estate bordered the eighteen-acre Dyckman property. In 1793, the man who held Mrs. Dyckman's late husband's seat as the alderman for the Out Ward was Mrs. Bruce's brother.

But both women received smaller shares of their parents' property than their brothers, and both women were largely cut out of either ownership

Revolutionary New York
Circa 1776

HUDSON RIVER

EAST RIVER

MANHATTAN ISLAND

Dyckman Farm

BOWERY LANE

Wetlands

Bayard Farm

Wetlands

FRESH WATER POND

Francis Sawyer

DIVISION ST.

Rutgers Farm

Area burned in 1776 fire

New York City

Shipyards

WALL ST.

EAST RIVER

N

Fort George

Brooklyn Ferry

W E

S

Scale of miles

LONG ISLAND

In Lanah Sawyer's day, Manhattan was dominated by large farms and rural estates. During the revolution, Lanah's family lived near her father's workshops at the foot of Bowery Lane—not far from her aunt and uncle Dyckman's country seat. Mrs. Bruce's family owned the adjacent Bayard estate. Henry Bedlow's family owned Rutgers farm. Areas developed by 1776 are shaded gray.

Map by Gene Thorp

or effective control of their late husbands' estates. Rebecca Dyckman's husband had taken over the property she inherited. His will left their marital assets—including the bakery on Gold Street and the farm where they lived—in her hands only until their youngest son came of age. The same patriarchal attitude would color even the record of her burial at the Dutch Church, which listed not her name but her relationship to her eldest son: "Mother of Tunes Dickman."

Lanah Sawyer may well have heard something of the story of how Judith Bruce had been cut out of her first husband's family fortune. Back in the early 1760s, she had married a man distinguished by his "beatific" smile, his status as the next in line to inherit a vast manorial estate, and his poor health. He died when she was only twenty-six—and left her with a two-year-old son and little else. Her father-in-law, the lord of the Lower Manor of Rensselaerwyck, controlled the family fortune until his death in 1782. His will left the bulk of his vast though indebted estate to Mrs. Bruce's son, now twenty years old, under what amounted to an entail: the manor would pass, in trust, to the eldest son of the patriarch's eldest son, and so on.

The unfortunate effects such entails had on women is a topic frequently lamented in Jane Austen's novels. But, at the time, the practice was controversial not so much because of its harsh treatment of women and younger sons but rather because of its unfairness to the heir—a man who inherited an estate still under the control of the dead hand of the past. As such, entails were attacked as aristocratic and undemocratic. Indeed, to defend her son's control of the estate, Mrs. Bruce enlisted the assistance of her nephew Alexander Hamilton, who pursued the case for years and ultimately prevailed.

Still, the two widows lived together by choice, not necessity. Mrs. Bruce inherited enough property from her father and her second husband to live quite comfortably. And she certainly didn't need help with the housework, which was done by at least two enslaved Black women and, apparently, a white female servant as well. Mrs. Dyckman, too, had options—including five adult children in the city with whom she could have lived. So neither woman needed to remarry for financial reasons. Or, evidently, for any other reason. But both women, it seems, enjoyed living with a companion—which they found in each other.

Amid the trappings of wealth and ease and status at Mrs. Bruce's, did Lanah feel like an interloper? At that moment, the domain of these two prosperous matrons must have seemed a world apart. When their children were born, decades earlier, they had been respectable married women—with husbands, wealth, and social standing. Lanah was not married. She had no financial resources of her own. She had been led into danger and lost her virginity to a flirtatious liar, a fraud. Now, she might even be pregnant. Even as she sought strength from the older women's tacit embrace, Lanah was aware that they didn't know what had happened to her—and anxious about how they would regard her if they did.

Of course, there was much Lanah didn't know about them. It's quite possible that her aunt or Mrs. Bruce had engaged in sex before marriage. Many, if not most, young women did, and suffered no ill consequences. In Lanah's time, as many as a third of all women were pregnant on their wedding day—and we know that only by noting those who gave birth within seven and a half months of marriage. Presumably, plenty more single women had sex and didn't get pregnant, or at least give birth, so quickly.

For a woman to engage in premarital sex was a risk. But most young women chose their partners and their moments well. Typically, an unmarried woman would consent to sex only as part of an advanced courtship. For these women and their families, there was no real problem as long as marriage ensued and the circumstances were kept quiet.

Problems arose only when a young woman's path to marriage was blocked.

In popular lore, this was the harm of seduction: a man convinces a young woman that their love will lead to marriage, that it is safe for her to agree have sex with him; then, after getting what he wants, he reneges on his promise. This would leave the young woman in a bind and create a problem for her family if the fact that she had been despoiled became known. One solution was the proverbial "shotgun wedding"—in which the young woman's menfolk force the reluctant groom to make things right; she might end up married to a schmuck, but the family's honor is preserved.

This, indeed, may have been the point of the seduction stories—most of which were written by, and read by, women. Female writers were generally careful to avoid explicitly challenging conventional sexual morality, with its patriarchal double standards. But they could still speak to young women like Lanah Sawyer—struggling with their own fantasies and fears and rebellious impulses and facing their own decisions about young men, their parents, and sex. The proliferation of such stories of innocence and betrayal may have served not just as a warning to young women but as a kind of feminine power play, pressuring men to make good on their premarital (or simply precoital) promises.

In *Pride and Prejudice*, foolish fifteen-year-old Lydia Bennet throws her entire family into crisis by eloping with the rake George Wickham. Through charm and deception, he convinces her that they are going to get married, even though he has no intention of tying himself to a woman with such limited financial prospects. Her family races to resolve the situation before her sexual shame becomes public—because their honor and the marriageability of their other daughters is at stake. Eventually Wickham is convinced to marry the hapless Lydia by a substantial cash payment. This is done in secrecy, and the imperiled honor of all involved is redeemed.

In such narratives the betrayal of a sexually compromised woman was transformed into a battle between men. This was all too often the case in real life, too—as Lanah Sawyer would ultimately learn from her own experience.

At the same time, the fear of sexual dishonor was powerful enough that a young woman could sometimes turn it to her advantage in struggles with her parents over generational power. Sometimes the obstacle standing between a young woman and marriage was the fact that her parents did not approve of her choice. The increasing cultural power of the love match encouraged young people to follow their inclinations, not their parents' ideas of what was suitable.

Lanah Sawyer's problem, however, was not going to be solved by marriage. Even if she found some way to rationalize marrying Harry Bedlow after what he had done to her, there was little reason to imagine that he would ever agree to marry her. The social distance between their two families meant that there was little chance that he could be forced or bribed into doing so.

Flashing through Lanah Sawyer's mind that afternoon was, no doubt, the fear that what had happened the night before might leave her pregnant. For a woman who engaged in illicit sex with a man she didn't end up marrying, the most obvious solution was simply to cover it up. But pregnancy would make that more difficult. For enslaved and servant women, a sexual assault or an illicit liaison could lead to terrifying desperation—covering up her pregnancy, giving birth in secret, killing her newborn baby, and attempting to hide the body. Even a woman with greater freedom and more options could end up desperate to "destroy the fruit of her body and conceal her sin and shame." Abortion was not illegal, but it was shrouded in secrecy. There were people in the city who knew about how to prevent conception or induce abortions, but even if Lanah managed to connect with one of them there was no guarantee that the proposed treatments would be safe or effective. Some women, afraid to confide in their mothers, turned to friends for advice. And by the 1790s, better advice was becoming available. Still, the cases that have come to light ended badly. One young woman from a respectable family agreed to have sex with the young man who had been courting her. But by the time she revealed that she was pregnant, he had decided he no longer wanted to marry her. Instead, he pressured her into drinking an herbal abortifacient, and, when that didn't work, into arranging for a shady doctor to attempt a mechanical procedure. In the end, the botched abortion left her dead—and left him free to marry another woman.

Over the course of that long afternoon at Mrs. Bruce's, Lanah kept her troubles to herself.

It was obvious that she was deeply distressed. One of the women there later recalled that "she appeared very much down and dejected." But the woman didn't pry—and neither did anyone else.

For Lanah, the visit to her aunt likely offered a temporary respite, a female world of ritual and reassurance. The two older women embodied matriarchal power, authority, and autonomy. From their proximity she could draw strength, the emotional energy she needed to refuel her depleted psyche. From their acceptance she might have felt she could still be seen as who she had been before, that despite what had happened she might be able to go on being who she had been.

Mrs. Bruce's house proved to be a good refuge. Lanah's aunt was sufficiently removed from her parents' immediate circle of friends and relations that there were no alarming interruptions. No one came and spread rumors that would have called her to account; no one burst in looking for her. And even if her stepfather had shown up, he might well have been sufficiently cowed by the two matriarchs to check his temper and compose himself.

A study for George Romney's The Seamstress, *about 1787.*

Lanah passed the afternoon sitting with the other women—half listening, perhaps, as they chatted or read aloud from some magazine or novel or book of sermons and she worked a sewing project in her lap. Was she calmed by the familiar rhythms of the needle and thread, by her skill and confidence, by a task that she could control—and by the excuse to keep her head down? Or was she too distracted and distraught and exhausted to do anything right, and worried about getting a job done on time? At some point, no doubt, there was something to eat and hot tea—served, along with white sugar and silver spoons, in delicate porcelain cups that rattled, in their matching saucers, on the unforgiving surface of a tabletop polished like a dark mirror.

Perhaps, over the course of the afternoon, Lanah Sawyer's deeply distraught, sleep-deprived seventeen-year-old mind conjured up some scenario or other that seemed to offer a way out of her predicament. What if her aunt could provide her with some kind of alibi for her absence, and she could quiet her parents' upset and go on as she had before? What if she confided in her aunt and was met not with disappointment and disapproval but rather with compassion and protection? Perhaps, drinking tea, she was waiting for the right moment to broach the topic. If so, the moment never came.

Around the time the light raking through Mrs. Bruce's front windows began to dissolve into the warm glow of sunset, Lanah realized that she could not stay there forever. If she lingered too long, questions would be raised. The older women, presumably, would want to know why she wasn't going home. Word might even reach her parents.

Moreover, whether Lanah was conscious of it or not, indecision had a cost. As she delayed going home, her ability to keep control over the story of what had happened—and to keep it quiet—was slipping away. As time passed, and as morning turned to afternoon and afternoon approached evening, her parents' alarm at her absence would only intensify. Eventually, news would spread that young Lanah Sawyer was missing, that her parents were deeply agitated, that some scandal was in the air. At that point, it would be not just her parents' questions that would require answers but those of a widening circle of relations and friends and neighbors.

That evening, the sun set at 6:23 p.m., and twilight had faded by 6:52. As darkness settled over the city and people began lighting candles and lamps, Lanah finally summoned her courage and got up to leave Mrs. Bruce's.

It was "about seven o'clock" when Lanah Sawyer stepped back on the wide stone sidewalk of Broadway. But even then, about twenty-four hours since she had set out for her walk with lawyer Smith, she still wasn't quite ready, or able, to make herself head home.

SEPTEMBER 5, 1793. TWILIGHT, APPROACHING 7:00 P.M.

Leaving Mrs. Bruce's, Lanah remembered that she had an errand to run nearby—and took the excuse to put off heading home. She walked a few short blocks down toward the foot of the East River waterfront, to the home of a Mr. Jones on Dock Street, probably to drop off or pick up some work. But as she drew close to her destination, she saw that the door was shut. Out in front, there were "some Frenchmen on the stoop"—a hideous reminder of the lewd, aggressive men she'd encountered on Broadway eleven days earlier, her mounting sense of panic, and the false relief she had felt at her rescue by "lawyer Smith."

Taken aback by fear, Lanah Sawyer could not proceed to Mr. Jones's. She turned away.

Then, she noticed that one of her gloves was missing. It was a sign of her preoccupation. Had she left Mrs. Bruce's incompletely dressed? Had she dropped it and failed to notice? Lanah retraced her steps to Mrs. Bruce's and went back in. It wasn't there.

Once again, she stepped out onto Broadway's wide stone sidewalk—conscious, now, that she was showing more skin than was really proper. It was about seven o'clock. Darkness was overtaking the city. Lanah Sawyer decided that it was time to head home. But, first, she had one more thing to do. Anxious about how her parents would receive her, she headed up north to the home of her friend Miss Pine, on Spruce Street.

For the rest of the evening, Lanah benefited from the support and protection offered by a network of female friends, relations, and older women. This was a classic pattern for young women in difficulty, especially sexual difficulties they were anxious about disclosing. A young woman typically confided first in female peers, then approached her mother.

Lanah Sawyer had known Miss Pine for years. For a time, they had lived a few doors down from each other on Gold Street. Both girls experienced the sorrow and disruption of their fathers' early deaths. Miss Pine's father, a painter, had died a few years earlier, leaving a widow in her mid-thirties struggling to support herself and her daughters. They moved again and again in the years to come, as the Widow Pine sought to make ends meet as a seamstress. Perhaps it was at her hands that Lanah had learned her trade as a sewing girl.

Lanah turned down onto Spruce Street. As darkness fell, the block between Nassau and William Street was alive with energy. Mr. Robert Towt was in the street, heading to the home of a neighbor. He saw Miss Pine looking out over the bottom half of her house's Dutch front door. He saw Lanah approaching. And he went about his business.

Miss Pine, "looking over her door," called out to her friend, and they spoke.

Would you or your sister go home with me? Lanah asked, and Miss Pine agreed.

Meanwhile, Mrs. Sarah Towt had also spotted Lanah in the street and observed her conversation with Miss Pine. Unlike her husband, she intervened.

By this point, Mrs. Towt was aware that something was wrong. Perhaps she had overheard enough of the two young women's conversation to gather that there was a problem. Or, more likely, Lanah's mother, Jane Callanan, had dropped by earlier, looking for her daughter. If so, Sarah Towt was one of the first people Jane Callanan had approached and trusted with the potentially scandalous news that Lanah had gone missing.

The Towts were considerably more prosperous than the Callanans—though they lived in a modest, rented house at 26 Spruce Street, they enslaved a worker and owned several valuable houses in town, including one just around the corner from Mrs. Bruce's. Mr. Towt held an appointment from the mayor as one of the city's inspectors of leather, a position that reflected the number of tanneries, with their noxious smells and putrid vats of soaking hides, still operating within the city. Perhaps more relevant, Mrs. Towt had plenty of experience raising teenage girls. She had six daughters and stepdaughters, including one close to Lanah's age and several who were older. Whatever Jane Callanan might worry about was probably something Sarah Towt had already dealt with.

She called out to the two teenagers.

Mrs. Towt saw that Lanah was anxious about returning home. So she told the girls she would send her husband to escort them.

Lanah refused the offer.

But Mrs. Towt insisted. She called her husband out of the neighbor's house and told him that she wanted him to take the girls home, since Lanah "was afraid of her father."

He offered to go with them.

Lanah demurred, saying she did not want to "trouble him."

Lanah's impulse was to feel judged and mistrusted. She assumed that Mrs. Towt was "apprehensive they would not go home" and wanted her husband to go along to make sure they did.

But Mr. Towt had no such concern. He considered Lanah a "decent girl" and "had no apprehensions that they would head to any improper place." He agreed to escort Lanah only because she was so "afraid of going home."

Fragile emotions and misperceptions notwithstanding, Mrs. Towt prevailed.

For his part, Mr. Towt did what he could to put the teenage girls at ease. Respecting the young women's privacy, he followed them at a discreet distance, walking on the "other side" of the street.

The anxious procession had no more than three blocks to cover.

Some five minutes later, the moment Lanah Sawyer had been avoiding all day long finally arrived.

She was home.

But the dreaded confrontation with her parents would be postponed once again.

When Lanah finally arrived home—the dark stains of blood on her body and her linens hidden by her petticoats and her torn, repaired gown—she found that "her father and mother were both out."

She had just missed them.

They had gone out looking for her.

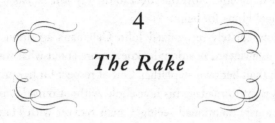

4

The Rake

In a city like New York, there were many hazards that could keep a child from coming home. At the same spot on Broadway where Bedlow forced Lanah down Ann Street, the son of George Washington's dentist was nearly trampled to death by a raging horse: he scrambled behind a public water pump and then leaped through an open Dutch door moments before the deranged animal crashed into the stoop. Others were not so lucky, their bodies crushed under the wheels of carts and carriages. Murders were rare, and fatal accidents typically befell boys and working men. These were not the kinds of misfortune that first came to mind for parents of a seventeen-year-old girl when she went out in the evening and didn't come back.

By Thursday evening, Lanah Sawyer's stepfather was, as he put it, "extremely alarmed" at the absence of his daughter. Having slipped away the previous evening, she had now been gone some twenty-four hours. Either something bad had happened. Or something worse.

All day, Lanah's mother had delayed going out to search for her. Raising the alarm, calling attention to the problem, carried its own risks. On the one hand, she wanted to find her daughter, to see if she was all right, to discover what had been going on. On the other hand, she had good reason to keep this domestic drama discreet. The honor of a woman like Jane Callanan, and the honor of her husband, depended on what their dependents did—or, at least, how they were perceived.

And so it was not until shortly before Lanah finally arrived home that her parents began their search in earnest. Lanah's mother seemingly went to confide in Mrs. (but not Mr.) Towt—and had already come and gone by the time Lanah walked up Spruce Street. Meanwhile, Lanah's stepfather headed directly across the street to the Dyckmans' bakery to ask his friend Samuel Hone for help.

Hone immediately recognized John Callanan's agitation and found himself in an awkward position: he knew more about what was going on with Lanah than her own stepfather. Out of respect for her privacy, or for his friend's right to manage his household without outside meddling, he hadn't previously mentioned seeing Lanah Sawyer with Harry Bedlow. Now, he did.

For Callanan, the revelation suddenly clarified the nature of the problem. "She was with him," he concluded. He asked Hone to go with him "in search of her," and the two men set out.

The news that Lanah had been out with Harry Bedlow was both good and bad—good because it brought the problem into focus, gave it a name; bad because Bedlow was precisely the kind of man a young woman's father would worry about. Whatever his daughter had done, whatever had been done to her, Callanan's problem had grown.

John Callanan and Harry Bedlow were from different worlds. Callanan's was a world of working men: men who ranked above the city's poor, the unskilled, and the enslaved, but who still struggled to support their families, struggled to have their voices recognized, struggled with the humiliations of a deferential social order. Harry Bedlow's was a world of wealth, family connections, power, and privilege.

When Callanan and Hone caught up with Bedlow, these two worlds would collide: two men from opposite sides of the social and political fault lines that were reshaping the face of the city and the future of the new republic. The battles then gathering in the city and across the nation would either tear down the old hierarchies or reinforce them.

Scouring a city of some forty thousand souls for one or two individuals was not easy. The search would take a father through the gathering gloom into the places he would least want to find his teenaged daughter. But Callanan and Hone did have some advantages. Bedlow's notoriety meant that when they made inquiries, people were likely to know whom they were asking about. And, amid the mass of men in the city—among enslaved and free men of color, among sailors and working men, and even among actual lawyers and other young gentlemen—Harry Bedlow cut quite a figure.

A portrait miniature is an intimate object. The one that shows Harry Bedlow around the time he met Lanah Sawyer is tiny: a fragile film of watercolor on an ivory disk not much bigger than a quarter, protected by a gold-and-glass case and mounted on a long, sharp pin. Like a jewel, it was intended to be worn—a gift to a mother, a wife, or, most likely, a woman he was courting, as a sign of love, a sign of possession. A sign that he belonged to her, or that she belonged to him.

To make out much detail—the brilliant blue eyes; the smooth, pale skin; the dark, arched eyebrows; the carefully coiffed cloud of white-powdered hair—you have to hold his face right up to your own. He sports a frill of snowy linen at his neck and a deep-blue coat with a high red collar and glittering gold buttons. The white, the dark, and the flash of color emphasize the thin rosebud of his lips—pulled back slightly into a hint of a smile or, perhaps, a smirk.

The image reflects not only how Harry Bedlow looked, but also how he wanted to be seen: young, proud, confident; a gentleman coming of age and relishing his privilege. His hair was a more fashionable version of a style still favored by men of the previous generation, like George Washington, who as president still wore his hair powdered white, pulled away from his face, tied into a queue in the back, and poufed out on the sides. Hair like that took time and money. The white powder had to be blown on while your clothes, your face, your eyes, were kept covered. Then someone had to clean up the mess. In New York, a fastidious gentleman could arrange for a hairdresser to make daily house calls.

Bedlow's look made a statement. It announced his sense of himself as a gentleman, a man of fashion, a high Federalist who supported John Adams, Alexander Hamilton, and their hierarchical vision for the new nation—a vision of a republic, to be sure, but a republic in which poor and working men would defer to gentlemen of property and standing. Increasingly, it was a statement his peers chose not to make. The white wigs and powdered hair of the previous generation had reflected that era's veneration for age. But the new republic increasingly celebrated youth, the right of the rising generation to cast off the dead hand of the past.

Even at the time Bedlow posed for his portrait, the image of the young high-Federalist gentleman divided Americans: some saw rising elites, entitled to prestige and respect, claiming their place in a natural aristoc-racy. Others saw arrogant, irresponsible young bucks—dismissive of their supposed inferiors, selfish, and even predatory. By the summer of 1793, this is how many in the city saw the twenty-six-year-old Harry Bedlow: as a rake, a "man of gallantry," a man who accumulated debts he struggled to repay and who took advantage of unsuspecting women. A man who might be appointed an officer in the local militia but who, instead of showing up and serving as required, simply posed in his uniform long enough to have his portrait painted.

❧

Harry Bedlow was born in early 1767 to parents who, for nearly twenty years, had longed for a son, an heir. From the time of their marriage in 1749, their family record had been a litany of heartbreak. Their first four children were either "Born Dead" or died young—a crushing record even at a time when almost every family suffered the death of at least one infant. Eventually, the Bedlows had a child who survived: Catharine, born in 1758 and named after her mother. But the babies that followed struggled and faltered. By the time Harry was born, on January 3, 1767, his mother was in her mid-thirties, his father in his mid-forties. Over the course of their marriage they had shifted their allegiance from the old Dutch church to the Church of England and had adopted anglicized versions of their names: Willem became William, Catharina became Catharine. They christened the new baby Henry, and nicknamed him Harry, making him the first member of their extended family to start out with an English name. In his family Bible—on a blank page after the Apocrypha—the anxious father, William Bedlow, offered up a little prayer for his son: "God Grant him to Live and Grow up in Knowledge & True Holyness."

Young Harry would, at least, live.

Both of his parents came from prosperous, old Dutch families—though, by the time he was born, the fortunes of the Bedlows were flagging. His great-great-great-grandfather had helped finance the so-called Glorious Revolution of 1688, which overthrew the British monarch James II and installed the Dutch prince William of Orange on his throne. Meanwhile, in New Amsterdam, the Bedlows accumulated large grants of land—including the island in New York harbor on which the Statue of Liberty now stands. It was long known as Bedlow's Island.

As a young man, William Bedlow had pursued a career as a ship captain. He braved the hazards of the sea, enduring long voyages to the West Indies, across the Atlantic to English ports, and, on occasion, to West Africa to buy captives he could sell into slavery in the Americas. Yet none of Captain Bedlow's efforts proved sufficient to breathe new life into his family's fortunes. His widowed mother had been forced to sell the island. Now it was used by the city as a quarantine to prevent contagious diseases from entering the city. Captain Bedlow himself was confined there at the end of a voyage shortly before Harry was born—waiting, among the sick and the dying, to see if he, too, would fall ill.

Around the time Harry Bedlow turned eight, his father took a bold risk and aligned himself with the Sons of Liberty in the escalating imperial crisis. New York had long served as the headquarters of the British military presence in North America and the city was full of staunch Loyalists. With its unparalleled harbor and access to the Hudson River Valley, it was clear that if the fighting spread beyond the Boston area, New York would be "a post of infinite importance," as the newly appointed general George Washington put it. During the summer of 1775, as the military conflict in Boston unfolded, William Bedlow was named to the Committee of Safety that effectively took charge of the city. The colony's insurgent Provincial Congress then appointed him to a secret committee charged with fortifying the Hudson River in the Highlands, an area about fifty miles north of the city. Bedlow's committee helped plan a series of forts, including West Point, and devised a massive chain, suspended across the river, to block the passage of British warships.

Late in the summer of 1776, the Continental Army, which had briefly occupied the city, retreated northward in the face of an overwhelming British invasion—and many of the city's residents, including the Rutgers clan and the Bedlows, fled. The city had numbered about twenty-five thousand residents a year earlier; soon barely five thousand were left. Most of the Rutgers clan took refuge in Albany, but William Bedlow moved his family only as far as the Highlands, which would serve as the headquarters of the Continental Army for the rest of the war. There, drawing on his social connections, he arranged to rent the childhood home of Governor George Clinton, a comfortable farmstead in New Windsor with magnificent views across the valley.

For William Bedlow, then in his early fifties, the war was an opportunity to distinguish himself. His early embrace of the Patriot cause and his social connections might have set him up for distinguished roles. Instead, he ended up in a series of unglamorous civilian support posts that he hoped might lead to some other advantageous appointment. Meanwhile, to supplement his income, Bedlow operated a kind of general store out of his rented home.

A long-anticipated British raid up the Hudson River finally came in late 1777: an amphibious force sailed northward up the river from New York, and an army under the command of General John Burgoyne marched south from Quebec, intending to meet the northbound troops in the Hudson River Valley and cripple colonial resistance by cutting New England off from the other rebellious colonies. For the Continental Army, it was a glorious turning point. General Benedict Arnold managed to force the surrender of the British army marching south—a victory that essentially ended British efforts in the region and emboldened the French to enter the war as allies of the nascent United States.

But for William Bedlow, the campaign was a disaster. The great chain across the Hudson proved useless. The British sailed right through it and set about raiding Patriot strongholds in the Highlands. The British troops never did make it to New Windsor, but locals took advantage of the chaos and plundered Bedlow's house and store. Soon thereafter, he heard that he was about to be relieved of his position.

Bedlow responded by dashing off long, plaintive letters to his powerful patrons—a pattern he would repeat in the coming years. "What a wound then it must be to a person of the least sensibility," he exclaimed, to be treated with such a lack of consideration. His wheedling secured the intervention of at least one influential figure, General Alexander McDougall, who in early 1779 sent him to George Washington with a generous introduction and a plea for help. Soon, the Continental Congress named him one of the army's five auditors. It was important work and brought him close to influential figures. While Baron Kościuszko came to the Highlands to design and build the fort at West Point, he sketched a portrait of William Bedlow, showing a slightly built man with a bald pate and a dour expression. But with his prickly personality, undistinguished performance, and tendency to provoke petty quarrels, even his patrons saw him as less promising than pitiable. At the end of the war, the best Governor Clinton could say of him was that "he has been much injured by the times."

For his part, young Harry Bedlow spent much of the war doing schoolwork. At age thirteen, in 1780, he was sent up the Hudson River to the Washington Seminary, a classical academy opened the previous year. There, Bedlow studied Latin, higher mathematics, and advanced English with the scions of some of New York's richest and most powerful families.

On November 15, 1783, just as the British were unwinding their long occupation of New York, William Bedlow paid £4 to hire a sloop to move his family back home. Ten days later, Harry Bedlow, now sixteen, witnessed the ceremony completing the British evacuation and Washington's triumphant Grand Entry.

The city the Bedlows returned to was devastated by the war, largely depopulated, and tense with political and personal antagonisms. Fires that had broken out during years of British control had destroyed a large swath of the city, including almost everything between Broadway and the Hudson from the Battery up past St. Paul's Chapel—and the burned-over areas had not been rebuilt. Trinity Church was in ruins. People who could not afford better were living in damaged, sailcloth-covered structures in an area called Canvas Town. Many of the most active Loyalists had fled with the British, but others remained.

Resentments flared—and for Harry Bedlow's family, they were personal. What rights did Patriots have when they returned to property that had been appropriated by Loyalists during the war or left damaged? Bedlow's great-aunt, who had inherited the old Rutgers town house and a nearby brewery, initiated the most high-profile legal battle, *Rutgers v. Waddington*—seeking some £8,000 in back rent from the man who had been using her property for the previous seven years. The case became an early test of American constitutional law and the principle of judicial review; it also established young Alexander Hamilton's reputation as a brilliant legal mind. In the years to come, he would continue to advocate for a strong federal government and for reconciliation with wartime Loyalists.

The future of Harry Bedlow's immediate family lay in another Rutgers property—a hundred-acre farm that stretched along the East River from the outskirts of the city to Corlears Hook. During the British occupation, the property had been appraised at the staggering sum of £80,000. Originally, the fields and orchards there had served to support the family's breweries, but in the 1750s Harry's grandfather Hendrick Rutgers had begun to see himself, his land, and the growing city in a new way. To proclaim his status, Rutgers built a fine brick mansion on the model of a country villa, with expansive views across the farm toward the developed part of the city and down along the city's bustling waterfront. And he also hired the city surveyor to draw up a plan to transform his pastures, his orchards, his fields of barley and hops, and even his brewery into a dense grid of building lots—rectilinear blocks separated by wide, straight roads, unlike anything the crooked, cramped old city had ever seen.

Harry's family also saw this property with new eyes because a substantial portion of it was now theirs. The Rutgers patriarch had died in Albany during the war and left his property to his children. Harry's uncle Colonel Henry Rutgers got the lion's share, including the mansion house, the brewery, and more than half the land; Harry's mother and two aunts divided the rest—about a hundred building lots each.

At the time, there was little indication on the landscape itself of his grandfather's vision for the future. Some of the lots along the waterfront had been sold, and a busy shipyard joined the Rutgerses' wharf, but mostly the farm was still fields, orchards, pastures, and hilly, swampy wasteland strewn with wartime fortifications. Simply the task of surveying the property and deciding which parcels of land would go to each sibling would take more than a year. Then they would have to carve out roads and level uneven ground.

Meanwhile, the war had left the city largely depopulated. After the British and Loyalists left, the city's population was only about twelve thousand, half what it had been a decade earlier. It would take years for the real-estate market to rebound. And the Rutgers family's other income-generating businesses—the nail factory, the distillery, the brewery—had fallen into disrepair during the war and required new infusions of capital and expertise to return to profitability. The mansion house itself bore signs of its use during the war as a British military hospital: a large arrow slashed into the front door by the officer who commandeered the property and Union Jacks carved into the woodwork by bored patients—scars the Rutgers family regarded as badges of honor.

Harry Bedlow's father had been rewarded for his wartime service with the office of postmaster of New York. Decades earlier, Benjamin Franklin had turned a similar position into a substantial fortune, but William Bedlow enjoyed neither Franklin's entrepreneurial savvy nor his sense of thrift. Bedlow rented a series of large houses on prestigious streets and eventually settled at 8 Wall Street, a commodious three-story brick house in the heart of the city's center of power. Despite the future potential of his wife's inheritance, money was tight. To help reestablish himself in the city, he borrowed money from an army colleague—money that he struggled to repay. "My health has not been good," he wrote; "my office as postmaster hasn't yet begun generating enough income to cover even the salaries of my clerks; and my property"—meaning his wife's portion of the Rutgers farm—"is in such a Cituation from British Conduct as to render me nothing till next Spring."

Coming of age in the war-ravaged city, Harry Bedlow focused on the Rutgers property as the key to his future. Many of his peers went on to college at Columbia or Princeton or Yale or Harvard; they apprenticed with lawyers or merchants to prepare for careers in business, or in politics, or simply managing complex estates. But Harry Bedlow does not seem to have planned for any profession other than that of a gentleman of property and standing.

Not content with the portion of his mother's inheritance that he expected to share with his sisters, Bedlow began to look toward the even larger estate of his uncle Henry Rutgers—who had never married and had no children of his own. By the patriarchal conventions of descent, young Harry came to see himself as his uncle's heir. How his family managed this windfall would be crucial. The difference between selling lots prematurely and leasing them with an eye to the future would be the difference between fleeting prosperity and the creation of one of New York's first great real-estate fortunes.

Harry Bedlow's life to this point had been one of privilege and opportunity, his father's failings cushioned by family money and social connections. His parents moved in the highest circles and were conscious of their claims to rank. In an age of republican simplicity, they continued to have their Dutch family crest engraved onto their silverware. And as the abolition movement gained traction, they continued to enslave people. Harry grew up with five enslaved servants: Flora, who was about eleven years his elder; her three daughters, Nan, Rosanah, and Flora; and a man whom the Bedlows called "Mars" (a wry reference to the Roman god of war) but who called himself "Mack." Shortly after the war, Mack "absconded"—claiming his own freedom. How did the experience of growing up as a member of a master class affect Harry's development? Thomas Jefferson, who was in a position to know, warned that a child in such circumstances is "nursed, educated, and daily exercised in tyranny"—and rarely emerged with his "manners and morals undepraved."

So much we can surmise from traces of Harry's early life in documents written by others. The only document to survive in his own handwriting from before his encounter with Lanah Sawyer is a blank page in one of his father's old logbooks on which young Harry practiced writing his name.

B, B, B, B, B, he wrote in a row across the top. Then some Hs and "Henry"s and "Bedlow"s, amid spatters and blots of ink. At one point, he turned the paper on its side and wrote a row of signatures. Dissatisfied, he crossed them out and tried again. Eventually, he arrived at the signature he would use for the rest of his life. Alongside these versions of his name, Harry Bedlow wrote only one other thing, a single word in large letters: "Dominion."

❧

At eighteen, Harry Bedlow found himself in the thrall of love. It was no idle dalliance or passing crush; instead, it seems to have been a consuming passion that rocked and, for a time, threatened to overturn his world. He was so smitten that he was willing to risk his relationship with his parents and his anticipated fortune rather than forsake his determination to marry his beloved.

Precisely how this romance developed is obscure. What we know is that the woman who captured his heart was Catherine Van Horne. And, in some ways, it seemed like a good match. During the summer of 1785, she was about sixteen; he was two years older—young, admittedly, but not egregiously so. Her parents, like Harry's, descended from the region's early Dutch colonists. She and Harry were distant cousins: her grandfather had married a member of the Rutgers family, and they shared a common great-grandfather. But while Harry's branch of the family had prospered, hers had not. In the years after the war, her father, James Van Horne, owned a modest house and enslaved a worker, but he never amounted to more than a small-scale grocer. Even then, his business was unstable; he moved almost yearly between a location near the Fly Market (close to the Battery) and the New Market (now Fulton Market), half a mile up the East River shoreline at the edge of the old Rutgers farm.

When Harry told his father he wanted to marry Miss Van Horne, William Bedlow forbade the match. But Harry was defiant. By the summer of 1785, he and Catherine had been married—though neither in the Episcopal church favored by his parents nor in the Dutch Reformed church favored by hers.

Harry's parents responded the way parents in seduction stories responded to their ruined daughters: they disowned him.

In the record of family events William Bedlow kept in his Bible, he noted the marriage of Harry's older sister a few years earlier with obvious pride. In 1781, Catharine Bedlow had married Dr. Ebenezer Crosby before a gathering of prominent witnesses at the house they rented from the governor, which the proud father could not resist calling "Clinton House." Crosby was, as the expression went, "a man of parts." A longtime friend of John and Abigail Adams, he served with distinction during the war as the physician to George Washington's elite Life Guard and would go on after the war to be well respected and well connected. Crosby's financial interests included a plantation in the West Indies. When William Bedlow wrote his account of the event, he emphasized its importance by setting it off with a scroll and signing his name with a flourish at the end.

In stark contrast, William Bedlow made no record of his son's marriage to Catherine Van Horne. It was as though the marriage had never taken place. Indeed, the angry, anguished parents were determined to act as though Harry had never been their son.

Why the disapproval? Money, most likely. Harry's marriage took place in the middle of a major cultural and social shift: the age-old pattern of propertied families arranging marriages for financial and social reasons was being challenged by the revolutionary idea of romantic love. For the rich, especially, marriage was far too important to be left to the whim of lovestruck children. The merging of two families was a crucial opportunity to promote social standing, advance business interests, and consolidate wealth.

In Harry Bedlow's world, it was one thing to engage in a sexual dalliance with a woman of no fortune; it was quite another to marry one.

For some time after Harry's impetuous marriage, his parents were anguished—torn between their determination to disown him and their inability to tolerate the breach. William Bedlow shared his troubles in a series of letters to an old friend, John Moore—a well-connected merchant and a pious Anglican. Their friendship had survived their divided political allegiances—though, at the end of the war, the Patriot Bedlow had been allowed to return to the city while the Loyalist Moore had been banished. On August 24, 1785, Bedlow wrote that he and his wife had decided to reconcile themselves with what their son had done and take him back.

Moore's response was a mixture of sympathy, reassurance, and pious reflections on the spiritual value of worldly disappointments—the disappointment in this case being that young Harry had defied the mores of social class and the wishes of his parents to marry the daughter of a storekeeper. "I received inexpressible pleasure in finding that your kind, Parental Arms, had again clasped to your bosom a much loved child," Moore wrote. "I had greatly lamented the step he had taken, so contrary to your advice & approbation and which appeared to me big with inconvenience." While the Bedlows had been justified in disowning their wayward son, they were also right to forgive him, Moore wrote.

Even after the Bedlows took Harry back into their hearts and home, their attitude toward his wife seems to have remained chilly. When it became apparent that she was pregnant, the family's attitudes began to thaw somewhat. At the end of November 1785, both Harry Bedlow's parents and his uncle Henry Rutgers gave him parcels of land on the old Rutgers farm that amounted to wedding presents—lots 193 and 295, on one of the first blocks to be developed.

Over time, these lots would grow in value, and in the meantime, they would produce rental income. For the first time, Harry Bedlow owned a portion of his anticipated inheritance. In his deed, Henry Rutgers extended a symbolic olive branch, stating that he was giving the land to both his nephew and his nephew's wife—even though that did not give her any additional legal rights. But the Bedlows evidently were not willing to go so far, and in their deed granted their lot to their son alone.

In any case, the marriage did not end well. The following summer, William Bedlow recorded in his Bible the birth of a grandson: "July 7th: 1786 Was Born: William, Son of Henry Bedlow and Catherine Van Horn." In private, William Bedlow followed the Dutch convention of using a married woman's maiden name in family and church records. Evidently, they were fearing the worst. A cousin who was an Episcopal minister was present at the Bedlow house and baptized the infant immediately. Almost as an afterthought, the grandfather added, "Catherine Van Horn, wife of Henry Bedlow Dyed in Labor of this child." At the time, childbirth was far more dangerous than it is today—and, in Catherine Van Horne's generation, cut short the lives of as many as one woman in ten. In this case, it seems, the baby died soon after his birth.

The death of the unwelcome daughter-in-law, it turned out, was an opportunity for the Bedlows to recast her as a respectable part of their family. A public notice appeared in the city's newspapers: "Mrs. CATHERINE BEDLOW, consort of Mr. Henry Bedlow, and daughter of Mr. James Van Horne, of this city" had "died suddenly" and been buried the following afternoon in the Rutgers vault in the New Dutch Church Yard.

❧

What did Harry Bedlow learn from the tragic end of his tumultuous teenage years?

He had been swept up by love, become a husband, and, briefly, a father—only to see his young wife and newborn son die. After that, he seems to have turned away from the path of romantic love and marriage. Instead, he entered his twenties in the pursuit of sex without attachment, pleasure without responsibility—earning a reputation as a rake, a man of "gallantry," the kind of young gentleman who frequented places like Mother Carey's.

He had defied his parents and suffered disownment—only to see them capitulate and take him back. Instead of accepting this reprieve with humility and gratitude, he seems instead to have remained impetuous and self-indulgent, unconcerned about the consequences of his actions for others.

In early 1788, Harry Bedlow played an unseemly role in the furor that erupted when it became clear that medical students and faculty at Columbia College were dissecting bodies they had robbed from the city's Black and paupers' graveyards. That winter, a group of free Black men petitioned the City Council to stop the practice; one published a lurid account describing the wanton desecration that outraged the city's people of color, free and enslaved. Bodies left exposed by the grave robbers were consumed by birds and beasts—including, on one occasion, free-ranging swine that were found "devouring the entrails and flesh" of recently buried Black women. Meanwhile, stolen human bones were being bought and sold for the purposes of anatomical study. Nonetheless, it was not until an ugly incident involving Harry Bedlow's friend John Hicks, one of the medical students—who reportedly waved a severed arm out a window to frighten off some curious boys—that public outrage erupted into the so-called Doctors' Riot of April 1788. A mob of hundreds of men, perhaps as many as two thousand, occupied the medical school, destroyed anatomical equipment, reburied the human remains they found, and chased after the fleeing students and faculty. The search for Hicks traced him to a house on Broadway, which he managed to escape by crawling out through a scuttle hole in the roof. After that, as one of his comrades recalled, he was spirited out of the city to Long Island by his friend Harry Bedlow, where they continued to "kick up" new "capers."

In the coming years, Harry Bedlow continued to test the limits of his parents' indulgence. When his family gave him little portions of the Rutgers farm in the fall of 1785, they had been making peace overtures and also putting him to a kind of test—a test of his prudence, his financial self-discipline, and his ability to shoulder larger responsibilities.

But he does not seem to have distinguished himself, except as vain, financially imprudent, and sexually profligate. As his family endured a series of crises and humiliations and the health of his aging father worsened, Harry Bedlow ran up debts, shirked his responsibilities, and got himself into a series of petty legal conflicts that he handled badly and lost.

At the same time, there are suggestions that he had a winning personality—that he had a way of inspiring others to trust him, even when doing so ultimately got them into trouble. As his attorneys would later attest, he was fond of the company of women and willing to go to great lengths to get them into bed. While much of that information is shadowy, we do know something of what happened when he convinced other men to trust him with their money.

By the fall of 1788, Harry Bedlow had gotten himself into a pickle. On October 14, 1788, he borrowed £15 from John J. Remsen, a member of a prominent mercantile family. The sum involved was significant but not huge—enough to hire a laborer for two weeks, or to pay a hairdresser to come to your house every day for a year. At the time, various kinds of loan instruments were used, generally reflecting the anxiety of the lender, the amount of money at stake, and the borrower's perceived trustworthiness. Remsen was evidently convinced that there was no real risk. He could have required some kind of security for the loan, but he simply asked Bedlow to sign a promissory note—acknowledging receipt of the money and promising to pay it back, with interest, "on demand." Of the various ways of securing a loan, this was the closest to a gentleman's agreement. It was also the most difficult for the lender to enforce if there turned out to be a problem.

Evidently, Bedlow hadn't told Remsen the extent of his financial troubles. A week after taking out the £15 loan, Bedlow sold one of his only tangible assets: the lot of land his uncle had given him two years earlier, for £48. And, instead of using part of his proceeds to repay Remsen, Bedlow went about raising yet more money. He turned to another man, John Harris, and borrowed £14 using another unsecured promissory note. Then, four days later, he sold his other lot, the one his parents had given him, for £32. The two lots were of the same size, around the corner from each other, and the buyer was the same man. The lower sale price Bedlow got for the second lot suggests that the buyer sensed Bedlow's desperation and was able to take advantage of it.

Smelling trouble, the two men who had just made loans to Bedlow asked for their money back. It was, after all, due "on demand." But at this point, Bedlow's powers of persuasion seem to have finally failed him.

Part of his problem was that his two creditors had begun to compare notes. The two men—presumably annoyed by Bedlow's deceptive representations and concerned about ever seeing their money again—joined forces and hired a lawyer. Meanwhile, the man who had bought the two lots quickly registered his deeds—something that often was done years or even decades after a sale.

Summoned to appear before the Mayor's Court in mid-December to respond to the claims against him, Bedlow compounded his problems again by failing to respond to the lawsuits. His best option would have been to strike a conciliatory tone, negotiate an agreement to repay the loans, and get the lawsuits dismissed.

Instead, Bedlow behaved as though the lawsuits had never been filed. He didn't hire an attorney to represent him and didn't respond to a series of summonses to appear in court. In early February 1789, the court lost patience, found against him by default, and ordered him to appear at a special inquest to determine precisely how much he owed. Again, Bedlow failed to show up. The result was that his combined debt of £29 and a few months' worth of interest was magnified by fees and court costs: he was ordered to pay a total of more than £47.

For Bedlow's family, this petty humiliation could hardly have come at a worse time.

Just as Harry Bedlow's lawsuits were coming to a head, the family of his older sister, Catharine, was struck by repeated tragedies. In the spring of 1788, her newborn baby died. A few months later, in July, her husband, Dr. Ebenezer Crosby, who had been suffering from some kind of "consumptive" illness, died, too. Soon, the grieving widow herself fell sick. In February 1789, when it became clear that she would not recover, she made a curious decision.

"On her death-bed Mrs. Crosby committed her sons to the care of their great uncle, Col. Henry Rutgers," one of her granddaughters wrote many years later, explaining that she chose "him in preference to nearer relatives on account of his ardent piety, as her chief solicitude was, that they should be brought up in the fear of God." Her granddaughter, by emphasizing religious motives, may have been trying to distract attention from mercenary motives: Uncle Henry was far richer than Catharine's parents and had no children of his own. Why shouldn't her children share in the fortune her brother Harry was looking to inherit? And it is hard to escape the suspicion that there was some darker concern, that she did not want her boys to grow up under the influence of her immediate family.

Meanwhile, William had suffered another blow—from which he seems never to have entirely recovered.

For most New Yorkers, the spring of 1789 was a time of excitement, renewal, and pride, as the city assumed its role as the first capital of the newly reconstituted American nation. After six months of furious work overseen by Pierre L'Enfant, the cramped old City Hall had been greatly enlarged and entirely refashioned into a suitable home for the new government—now known as Federal Hall. Congressmen began arriving from up and down the new nation and settling in, along with others attracted to the bustling center of national power. The city was now growing vigorously after the devastation of the war and the depression that followed it. And in April 1789, the newly elected George Washington made his dramatic entry into the city. As a crush of spectators in the streets looked on through pouring rain, Washington stood behind an elegant wrought-iron railing on the balcony of Federal Hall, bent down to kiss a Bible, and was inaugurated as the nation's first president. The Bedlows' fine house just down

Wall Street gave them a privileged position from which to observe this momentous event.

Among the new president's first official acts was to discharge William Bedlow from his position as postmaster for New York and give the office to a man he considered more deserving, more capable, or more useful politically.

Bedlow responded to the loss of his government position with a long, complaining letter directly to President Washington—a sufficiently august figure that he addressed him only hesitantly.

"Sir," Bedlow began, "If these lines should be improper by being addressed to you, Pardon the freedom, as nothing but the distressed cituation I am put in by being deprived of my Office at this season of the Year could induce me to trouble you with a detail of it." The rest of the letter was a catalog of self-pity and woe. What with the "excessive high" rent for a house "Convenient for the Office," the salary of his clerk, and the costs of firewood and candles, he was left with a profit of "not £200 a Year." At the same time, he wanted the president to know he wasn't actually poor. He derived some income from "the small productive part of my Estate," he wrote, alluding to his wife's share of the Rutgers farm. But, he went on, "to sell part of my property now would be to a great disadvantage."

President Washington was evidently unmoved by Bedlow's wheedling; he did not respond, much less intercede. Soon, William Bedlow was forced to move his family out of the expensive house they had been renting on the city's most fashionable street.

By 1790, the Bedlows had moved to another rented house at 170 Queen Street—which had a large lot and an attached "store." At that point, Harry and his younger, then-unmarried sister, Mary, were still living with their parents, a white woman who was probably a servant, and three enslaved women. The two Crosby boys were living in the Rutgers mansion with their uncle Henry and an even larger staff.

That fall, Harry had run up a tab that the Wall Street tailor Christian Baehr began to find worrisome. As a safeguard, the tailor asked Bedlow to formally acknowledge the accuracy of their accounts. Bedlow did so with such conviction that the tailor agreed to make up, fit, and trim additional "Garments Clothes and Wearing Apparel." But when Bedlow was pressed by his tailor to pay up the £30 he owed, it became clear it was easier to get him to open his mouth than his purse. Alarmed, the tailor hired an attorney and filed suit in late 1790, accusing Bedlow of "Craftily" and "Subtily" contriving to "Deceive and defraud" him.

This time, Bedlow could not entirely ignore the problem. Soon after the suit was filed, he was arrested by the sheriff. Typically, this was a mere formality: the "arrest" would consist of the sheriff accosting the defendant, informing him that the suit had been filed, and asking him to post a bail bond to ensure his appearance in court. If the defendant didn't show up, the sheriff himself would be on the hook for the sum in question. Usually this wasn't much of a worry—signatures were often just a fictional "John Doe"—but perhaps remembering Bedlow's behavior the last time he had been sued, the sheriff demanded that the bond be signed by an actual person. Forced to come up with a real person to bail him out, Bedlow turned to his aunt's husband, Dr. Stephen McCrea, a well-respected physician. (Dr. McCrea's sister was the celebrated Jane McCrea, whose death during the war at the hands of Wyandot warriors allied with the British had become a cause célèbre as Patriots sensationalized the image of a white maiden gruesomely murdered by Native men to stoke up revolutionary fervor.) Now, if Bedlow didn't show up in court, the physician would be liable for the amount they had pledged the sheriff.

And that is exactly what happened. Following his earlier pattern, Bedlow ignored court summonses, failed to hire an attorney, and was eventually ordered to pay not only the original debt but also interest, court costs, and the tailor's legal expenses. Meanwhile, both Bedlow and his uncle faced a new lawsuit from the sheriff—whom they hadn't paid for the forfeited bond.

By this point, it was not just Harry Bedlow who was having financial troubles. As William Bedlow had hinted in his letter to President Washington, his family was land rich and cash poor. Taking the best advantage of the family real estate involved a long-term strategy of holding, renting, and making capital improvements. Surviving family accounts show payments to laborers to dig out high areas and fill in low areas. In the early 1790s, both the Bedlows and the McCreas were building wharves along their East River waterfront—which involved purchasing massive timbers and paying carpenters and other laborers.

But after losing his position as postmaster, William Bedlow does not seem to have made a serious effort to reestablish himself as a merchant. In

June 1790, he was forced to sell a number of parcels his wife had inherited from the Rutgers estate, and began suffering health problems that disrupted his ability to conduct business of any kind.

Bedlow's financial anxieties also produced an increasingly ugly quarrel with his brother-in-law Stephen McCrea. For years, the two had disputed the expenses for room and board incurred at the end of the Revolution, when the McCreas were living with the Bedlows at Clinton House in New Windsor.

By 1792, the Bedlows were too short on cash—and, it seems, patience—to continue joint investments with the McCreas in grading lots and building wharves. Testily, William Bedlow wrote his brother-in-law to stop ordering supplies and labor on his account. Around that time, Dr. McCrea attempted to resolve the family quarrel by writing directly to Mrs. Bedlow—a gesture that only inflamed William Bedlow's injured pride.

Through all of this back and forth, Harry was reduced to the role of messenger—dispatched to carry letters around the corner from one house to the other.

❧

That morning in Mother Carey's back room, Harry Bedlow put on his clothes, warned Lanah Sawyer to do the same, and, at around eight o'clock, set off into the city. He seems to have gone about his business as usual—though precisely what his business was is not entirely clear. There is no indication that he felt any need to lie low or cover his tracks—or that he had any reason to suspect that he might be in danger.

Harry Bedlow had every reason to expect that he would be protected by the social armor of a gentleman in a hierarchical society. Even in the fantasy world of seduction stories, gentlemen were almost never held accountable for their behavior with women they paid for sex, seduced, or worse.

Once Bedlow left Mother Carey's on Beekman Street that morning, the most obvious place for him to go was home. His parents had recently abandoned their efforts to remain within the fashionable parts of downtown and had rented a house toward the far end of the old Rutgers farm, near his uncle Henry in the old family mansion. It was about a three-quarter-mile walk from Mother Carey's. At home, Harry could get breakfast, change into fresh clothes, and get help fixing his hair.

In any case, he was soon back out on the streets. Around ten o'clock, he was spotted by Lanah Sawyer, who had finally dragged herself out of Mother Carey's. Bedlow passed near the fateful corner where Ann Street opened out into Broadway. She saw him, but there is no indication that he acknowledged or even noticed her.

At one point, the young man was observed by Thomas McCready, a "house-carpenter" who, at times, worked for Bedlow's father. He saw Bedlow "in the streets attending a building." Presumably Bedlow was supervising some aspect of a construction project, repair, or rental on the Rutgers farm—or another family holding.

Still, when they set out that evening, it took John Callanan and Samuel Hone more than an hour to track him down. By then it was well after nightfall, about nine o'clock. Perhaps they caught sight of him in the street, passing under a streetlamp, as he sauntered away from his parents' house and toward another night on the town. Perhaps they spotted him stepping out of some tavern, or down into some oyster cellar, illuminated by the light escaping through an open doorway. Or perhaps they spotted him after passing through one of those doors themselves, across a room full of gentlemen or a mixed company of miscreants—noisy, red faced, basking in the warm glow of candlelight and alcohol. Or perhaps what caught their attention was the click of his walking stick on a dark side street. And perhaps, after spending so long searching, it took them a moment to realize that they really had caught up with their quarry.

There he was. But not Lanah.

Closing the distance between them, the anxious, agitated stepfather accosted the slightly built gentleman.

If Harry Bedlow was surprised when John Callanan confronted him, he kept his cool. He did not have long to size up the situation, but he certainly knew the kind of man John Callanan was. He had been to his house at least three times in the previous weeks and knew that it was a modest, crowded dwelling on a street populated by working people. Probably Sawyer had told him something about her father's work, and in any case, a man's social standing was easy to read from his appearance and clothing. Unlike gentlemen, who typically wore expensive knee breeches, closely tailored coats, and waistcoats, working men like Callanan and Hone wore sturdy, loose-fitting pantaloons and smocks made of durable materials and designed to allow free movement.

If Callanan had been a gentleman, Bedlow's response might have been different. He might have had to consider the dangerous possibility of a duel. But the code duello only applied if the antagonists were both men of honor—and no gentleman was obliged to recognize honor in his social inferiors.

And so, Harry Bedlow attempted a bluff.

Where is my daughter? Callanan demanded.

I know nothing about her, Bedlow lied.

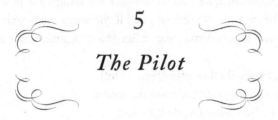

5

The Pilot

Even a smooth liar can get tripped up, especially when he misjudges his mark. Harry Bedlow could see that the man accosting him was no gentleman. He had the rough hands, ruddy skin, and creased face of a man who worked on the water. But when Bedlow faced off with John Callanan, there was plenty he didn't know.

He didn't know that claiming he had never met Lanah Sawyer would backfire. It wouldn't give Callanan pause; it would enrage him. And Bedlow didn't know that Callanan would dare to attack him.

The two men may have lived in the same small city—residing only a few blocks apart, their paths crossing and recrossing—but they inhabited different social worlds. Typically, the privileges of the elite went unchallenged, everyone showed deference to their betters, and violations of the social order were vigorously suppressed. But the entitlement that Bedlow could generally take for granted was only as powerful as the willingness of others to respect it.

Two things happened next.

Callanan got physical. What he would later describe as a "scuffle"—and Bedlow as a criminal "assault"—broke out between the two men. It was an astonishing breach of convention—in its way, a kind of revolution.

And Bedlow changed his tune. He did know Lanah Sawyer, he acknowledged. He had been with her. Then, trying out a new lie, he claimed that he had just "taken her home."

As John Callanan headed back off into the dimly lit streets toward his small, crowded house to see if his daughter really was there, Harry Bedlow may have comforted himself that this would be the end of the matter—that he would hear no more from Callanan or Sawyer.

But if John Callanan was worried about his stepdaughter, about what had happened to her, he was also concerned about what that meant for him, for his reputation, for his honor.

Around nine o'clock, Callanan got home. His wife, Jane, was there; Lanah was not. The nature of the problem was now pretty clear. But where was Lanah?

Meanwhile, Samuel Hone returned to his own home across the street and learned that Lanah had been there for hours. Once again in the uncomfortable position of knowing more about Lanah Sawyer than her own parents, he worried how Callanan might behave when reunited with her. Hone knew his neighbor to be "a very violent man." So, before he revealed what he knew, he made Callanan promise not to beat her.

Callanan agreed.

"If my daughter is [in the] wrong, I will turn her out of doors," he declared. "If she is [in the] right, I will say nothing to her about it."

As it turned out, Harry Bedlow had badly underestimated both Lanah Sawyer and her stepfather.

The story of how John Callanan got the confidence, the nerve, and the sense of power to take on a man like Harry Bedlow involves both his experience as a workingman—and the political upheavals that rocked New York in the Age of Revolution and defined the emerging American nation.

The story begins with the approach of war in 1776, the year Lanah Sawyer was born.

ON THE WATER OFF SANDY HOOK. FEBRUARY 9, 1776. MORNING.

It was a lonely journey as John Callanan sailed his pilot boat out past Sandy Hook and into the most dangerous encounter of his career. At twenty-three, he was one of about two dozen men licensed by the governor to guide ships through the long, treacherous passage into and out of port. One of the city's merchants, informed that his ship had arrived "below," had asked Callanan to go down and guide it up. In ordinary times, no such request would have been necessary. Pilots vying for work typically haunted Sandy Hook, on the lookout for incoming vessels. But the winter of 1776 was no ordinary time, and Callanan's was the only pilot boat on the water.

By the end of the day, the young pilot would demonstrate qualities that would serve him well in the years to come. He had steady nerves and did not shrink from danger. He was good at reading men and gaining their confidence. And, perhaps most surprisingly, he was politically savvy and understood the power of legal paperwork.

On a typical morning, Sandy Hook looked like a scene painted some years later by a British navy officer. Soft sunlight warms the clouds and glitters across the green-gray waves. In the distance, a pale lighthouse tower rises from a low, sandy beach. Two small pilot boats and a square-rigged merchant ship bear eastward, running lazily with the wind into port. There is no sign of the mad dash a few moments earlier to see which boat could reach the ship first and put its pilot on board. A ship captain was required to hire the first pilot to reach his vessel. The resulting need for speed led to the development of swift schooners—like the sleek, gaff-rigged boat tacking out into open water in the foreground. On deck are four men, dressed in black hats, bright-blue coats, tawny trousers, and dark shoes. Atop the foremast, a lookout perches precariously—one arm outstretched, pointing to a new prospect.

New York enjoyed a magnificent natural harbor, with waters deep enough to accommodate even the largest vessels and an abundance of safe anchorage, but the passage in and out of the harbor required the expertise of pilots. A vessel approaching New York from the Atlantic would see almost eight miles of open water between Sandy Hook, on the Jersey coast, and Coney Island, at the western tip of Long Island—but just under the surface loomed massive sandbars. Only a few hundred yards were navigable. If the man at the helm didn't know how to judge exactly the right opening, failed to maintain exactly the right course, or was surprised by the tides, the winds, or the currents, he risked running aground and breaking apart. Beyond the hook lay other hidden dangers.

The work of branch pilots required skill, physical endurance, years of training, and steady nerves. Callanan earned his living by boarding other men's vessels, assuming command, and guiding them into or out of port. Taking the helm of a ship was an individual responsibility, but piloting was social work. Pilots had to be able to inspire confidence in the ship captains who gave up control of their vessels. And pilots functioned only as part of a team. The branch pilots were also charged with assisting ships in distress, a role later assumed by the coast guard.

Callanan's job required braving dangers and taking risks. A pilot boat might labor home from the hook on a cold winter's day with every man on board injured by frostbite. A sudden "flaw" of wind could overset a pilot boat, split her sails, or send the boom across the deck—knocking a man overboard or entangling him in fast-moving ropes and yanking him to his death. In fog, a pilot boat could run aground. In winter, it could be sunk by ice. In storms, it could be blown out to sea or splintered by lightning.

The winter of 1776 was no ordinary time for the port of New York. The Sons of Liberty had taken over the colony's government, the royal governor had taken refuge on one of the British warships in the harbor, and a Royal Navy fleet was daily expected to arrive off the hook with thousands of soldiers to retake the city and return it to its long-standing role as Britain's military headquarters in North America. During this standoff, the branch pilots served as the port's eyes and ears—and as its most effective gatekeepers. The Sandy Hook pilots were given secret orders: if any vessel carrying British troops was seen offshore, they were not to board it; instead, they were to report it immediately. But, in a city of divided loyalties, suspicion grew that some of the pilots were secretly collaborating with the British. Unable to distinguish which pilots to trust, the Committee of Safety effectively closed the port. On January 15, John Callanan and the other pilots were summoned to city hall and given new secret orders: a few pilots were to serve as lookouts, but the others, unless given special permission, were to stay away from the hook altogether.

In early February 1776, panic seized the city: the British invasion seemed imminent. On Saturday, February 3, the pilot posted at the hook raced into the city. Two British warships had arrived—and other pilots, defying Patriot orders, had boarded them. The next day, a cold, stormy Sunday, the Continental Army's General Charles Lee arrived with news that the British were finally evacuating Boston. He had come to prepare New York's defense. Messengers were dispatched to summon militia companies from New Jersey, Pennsylvania, Dutchess County, and Connecticut. The Committee of Safety advised the city's remaining civilians to flee, and thousands scrambled to gather their possessions. A crush of carts and wagons jammed the roads out of town. Soon, the city felt eerily deserted.

Five anxious days later, John Callanan arrived at the hook and spotted a waiting vessel. Was it the merchant ship he had been sent down to meet? Or a British troop transport? Instead of racing up to it, he hove to about a mile away and watched. Even through a spyglass, he could only see so much. Figures clambered down the ship's side, boarded a tender, and began to cut across the cold, gray water.

By the time Callanan saw who they were, it was too late.

Captain Primrose Kennedy of His Majesty's Forty-Fourth Regiment of Foot introduced himself, presumably with a show of arms, and announced what he wanted. His vessel, the *Kitty*, was the second troop transport that had sailed from Boston under the protection of the *Mercury*, but it had been separated from its small convoy by a storm and had taken all week to make its way to the hook. He wanted Callanan to pilot it into port.

Callanan refused. Just days earlier, another recently appointed deputy pilot had helped a similar British troop transport into port—only to be berated by his brother pilots and hauled off to prison.

Captain Kennedy insisted.

There is not any person aboard my boat, Callanan reiterated, *who can pilot your ship up*.

I am under necessity to press you, Kennedy informed Callanan, pointing to his men and their weapons.

Soon, Callanan was climbing out of the British tender and up the steep sides of the hulking troop transport. With vessels of different sizes rolling and pitching with the waves, it was easy for a pilot to slip and fall, breaking bones or plunging into the water. In minutes, even a good swimmer could be swept away or frozen to death.

Safely aboard, Callanan faced another challenge. He had to take charge of the British warship.

When a pilot took command of a ship, he temporarily disrupted the extreme hierarchies that ordered maritime life. Between the hook and the harbor, the man in charge was not the captain but the pilot. Generally, pilots managed these potentially fraught relationships with ship masters smoothly—but not always. One pilot who antagonized a captain ended up beaten to death.

To do his job, John Callanan had to be comfortable taking command and be able to inspire confidence. But he was on the *Kitty* under duress. And Captain Kennedy didn't trust him.

Run this vessel aground, Kennedy warned, *on pain of death*.

Callanan had spent most of his young life working on the water, but only recently had he earned the right to pilot ships on his own. The Sandy Hook branch pilots were organized like a traditional guild—a trade regulated by the government and structured by rigid hierarchies of rank. Each pilot passed through a long, rigorous process of training and certification before receiving his government-issued license, or "branch." The system benefited pilots by limiting competition, standardizing their fees, and making it easier for them to collect payment. It was a trade often passed down through families.

Callanan does not seem to have enjoyed any such leg up. He was born around 1753, but no records survive to indicate precisely when or where—or even who his parents were. The Callanan surname indicates that the family came from Ireland, making them some of the earliest Irish immigrants to New York. Several Callanans appeared in early city records, but none of them seems to have been very prosperous: they didn't buy or sell real estate or record a will.

John Callanan likely started working on the water as a boy, bound by his parents or a guardian as an apprentice to one of the city's pilots. His contemporary David Morris was bound to a deputy pilot at age nine. At that point, he would have left his parents' house and moved in with his new master until his term ended—typically, at age twenty-one. He was to be trained in his profession, decently fed and clothed, and, generally, taught reading, writing, and arithmetic. If he were abused or restless, he could not simply leave. An apprentice who ran away could be advertised and hunted down like someone trying to escape slavery. Callanan, however, seems to have completed his apprenticeship successfully. By late 1774, around the time he turned twenty-one, one of the senior pilots had chosen Callanan as his deputy, the master and wardens of the port had affirmed his competence, and he had earned the right to pilot ships on his own.

As Callanan maneuvered the *Kitty* through the narrow channel off Sandy Hook and bore northward past Staten Island toward the Narrows, her deck milling with soldiers and army officers in brilliant red uniforms, he and the British did their best to pry intelligence from each other. Callanan counted the officers and soldiers he saw on board. He learned what he could about their plans. And he devised a plan to avoid trouble when he returned to the rebel-held port.

Working with a gun to his head, Callanan cultivated a rapport with Captain Kennedy and then asked for a favor. The British officer agreed: he wrote out a formal certificate attesting that he had "pressed" Callanan "by force" and "obliged" him to pilot the *Kitty* into the city's harbor.

When Callanan disembarked, he took the certificate with him, strode up from the waterfront to the old city hall, where the Committee of Safety met, and asked for an opportunity to report on what had happened in his encounter with the *Kitty*. They told him to come back the next day. Overnight, alarming rumors spread. The morning's papers reported the arrival of a second British troop transport.

Saturday afternoon, amid frantic preparations, the Committee of Safety heard Callanan's account—which was calculated to demonstrate his fidelity to the rebel cause. Like a good spy, he had gathered useful intelligence (an accurate account of the *Kitty*'s movements and of the number of troops and officers on board) and spread strategic disinformation (giving the British an exaggerated view of the strength of the rebel forces in the city).

The committee concluded that he was blameless and issued a new certificate clearing his name.

The imminent threat of invasion soon passed. After tense negotiations with rebel leaders, British authorities sent the two troop transports back out to sea. But the standoff continued. Thomas Paine's *Common Sense* roused revolutionary sentiment. George Washington and his army arrived to garrison the city. Massive fortifications were thrown up across the Rutgers and Bayard farms to block invaders from the north. And both sides, knowing the strategic importance of the city's maritime approach, began capturing and imprisoning pilots they suspected of disloyalty.

Through all of this, John Callanan managed to stay out of trouble.

Finally, on June 29, word reached the city that the British fleet was on its way. The next day, pilots spotted the first sails off Sandy Hook. On July 9, news arrived that the Continental Congress had declared the United States an independent nation.

That evening, the Declaration of Independence was read aloud in the city—to troops mustered at the Fields, to civilians assembled in front of City Hall—as more than a hundred British warships and troop transports, the largest fleet ever assembled in American waters, rocked at anchor, biding their time. Later, men gathered on the Bowling Green and pulled down the city's most prominent symbol of royal authority: the great, glittering gilt-lead statue of George III. They cut off its head, mounted it on a pike, and hauled the rest of the statue off to Connecticut, where patriotic women melted it like candle wax and molded some 42,088 musket balls. One rebel quipped that the king's troops would end up being shot at with "melted majesty."

When the onslaught came in mid-September 1776, the American forces were powerless to stop it. As the Continental Army fled north, the British occupied Manhattan and assumed control of the abandoned city—which would serve as their military headquarters until the end of the war. The city's residents had numbered some twenty-five thousand when the hostilities began, but the mounting military conflict had left it largely depopulated. A year earlier, when the rebels had taken control, about a third of the city's inhabitants had left. Since then, at least as many had rushed to escape the British takeover.

Among the few New Yorkers who remained in the city through all of these reversals were John Callanan and Lanah Sawyer's parents.

⌘

No more than a baby when the British invaded, Lanah would grow up in a city garrisoned and besieged. Her father, Francis Sawyer, had avoided being conscripted into the Continental Army that summer when he and the city's other firefighters had formed their own militia unit to defend the city. Most of them marched off with Washington's retreating army, but not Sawyer. Perhaps, like most Americans at the time, he didn't care that much who won the war. Perhaps, as a skilled carriage maker and wheelwright, he felt his prospects were better in the city. Perhaps he was simply loath to leave his wife and new baby alone. Throughout the long conflict, Francis Sawyer, like John Callanan, remained neutral—neither affiliating with either side nor attracting undue attention. The war would bring hardship enough.

Within a week of the British invasion, the first of two great fires ravaged the city. Lanah's father was among the only experienced firemen available to answer the frantic calls, and the conflagration burned out of control, consuming most of the area west of Broadway. As many as a quarter of the city's structures were destroyed. The houses left standing were soon crowded by thousands of British military men—and by Loyalists streaming into the city. Meanwhile, the war disrupted the supply of provisions from the countryside. Food grew expensive. Firewood grew scarce. Soon, almost all of the trees on the city's streets had been cut down.

Lanah's family lived on the northern outskirts of the city, at the foot of Bowery Lane—just north of a road cutting across the Rutgers farm called "Love Lane." Development was poised to overtake the area, but the surrounding landscape was still dominated by swamps and hills, windmills and orchards, fields and the country seats of gentlemen like Lanah's uncle John Dyckman.

Most of Francis Sawyer's work was likely building, mounting, and fixing the sturdy wooden wheels on which the business of the city rolled— the hundreds of carts that carried goods around the bustling port, the wagons and stagecoaches that transported produce and people longer distances. Only a tiny portion of the city's elite could afford carriages and the constant maintenance they required. The varied skills required by Sawyer's trade are suggested by a bill he submitted in early 1778: he had repaired the body of a carriage, furnished a new seat cushion, replaced several spokes, installed two axles, and nailed new metal tires onto three of its wheels.

Given the small number of New Yorkers who remained in the city during the war, it is not surprising that the families of John Callanan and Lanah Sawyer crossed paths. By 1778, Lanah's parents were friends with a woman named Catharine Callanan—probably a relative of the pilot. That year, the Sawyers asked her to serve as the godmother of their newborn son. Four years later, they named Lanah's baby sister Catharine.

By then, Lanah was about six. Up to about that age, young children were not sharply differentiated by sex: they were typically cared for together, and boys and girls alike were dressed in the same loose-fitting gowns. But around age five or six, children in working families were considered old enough to perform useful work and began transitioning to adult roles. When Lanah's brother Peter turned five, in 1783, he would likely have been "breeched"—taken out of his infantile gowns and dressed in small versions of men's shirts, coats, and breeches.

For girls like Lanah, there was no such ritual, no dramatic break. And, on the path to womanhood, there never would be. Her life would remain centered around domestic labor—washing, cooking, errands, helping to care for backyard animals and younger siblings, knitting when it was too dark to do other kinds of work and, when it was not, sewing and mending. As a girl, she would be a helpmeet in her father's household; as a woman, she would be a helpmeet in her husband's.

As soon as a girl could manipulate a needle, she began to learn plain

Lanah likely carried a sewing roll like this expertly crafted example.
PHOTOGRAPH © 2022 MUSEUM OF FINE ARTS, BOSTON.

sewing—the routine work of stitching together the seams of new sheets, pillowcases, towels, and shifts. Given that Lanah's parents were literate, she and her siblings likely got some schooling. The curriculum of the charity school operated by Trinity Church was typical. All children were given basic instruction in reading, writing, and arithmetic. Boys were also taught accounting and prepared for "suitable" trades. Girls were taught "Needle-work." Over time, a girl might learn more specialized skills—how to mark linens with cross-stitched initials; how to make unobtrusive repairs; how to sew shirts and other garments that required careful fitting, precise seams, and advanced stitches. Most girls learned from their mothers. But in the city there was also a regular supply of self-proclaimed experts offering formal classes in the "finer branches" of technique and style.

Lanah's girlhood was interrupted, when she was about seven, by the death of her father. The circumstances are obscure; the only record of his death is a notice published by her mother in late July 1783, calling on the "Creditors of Francis Sawyer, deceased . . . to meet at the Widow Sawyer's, near the Fresh-water Pump" to receive their due—and calling on his debtors to pay what they owed.

For Lanah and her family, the loss must have been traumatic. First, of course, there was grief. How does a seven-year-old child understand the death of a parent? Then there was the burden her mother faced. Without her husband's income, how would Jane Sawyer support herself and her young children?

For a working-class woman, the best option was to remarry quickly. Within months, Lanah's mother did just that. Viewed as a prospective husband, John Callanan's attractions included his steady, reliable employment in a skilled trade.

How did Lanah react to her new stepfather? Did she mirror her mother's sense of urgency and feel relief that there would once again be a man in the house—a protector, a provider? Did Lanah resent the notion that a new man would take her father's place? Did she worry about the pilot displacing her mother's attention and affections? Was she self-possessed enough to focus on his personality—that he was shaped by the rigid hierarchies, the strict discipline, the violence, the authoritarianism of the maritime world?

On September 26, 1783, John Callanan paid a ten-shilling fee to the royal official in charge of the city for a marriage license, stood before the Reverend Benjamin Moore of Trinity Parish, and bound his fate to the twenty-eight-year-old widow Jane Sawyer and her four young children.

By that point, the British had just begun to evacuate. Two years after the Battle of Yorktown, New York was the last British stronghold in the new independent republic—crowded with locals, with military men, with throngs of Loyalist refugees from elsewhere, and with some thousands of men, women, and children escaping slavery. Finally, in late November 1783, the last of the British forces set sail—taking some Loyalist branch pilots with them, even as the most committed rebels among their ranks prepared to return to the city. In triumph, George Washington marched the Continental Army back into the city—marking the end of the military standoff, the independence of the American nation, and the beginning of a long process of reconstruction, reconciliation, and reintegration.

John Callanan had started the war as a young, single man and one of the most junior of deputy pilots. Now, he was starting a new chapter in his life—as a married man, as a husband and father, as a senior pilot, as an embodiment of the patriarchal ideal of republican citizenship.

For seven-year-old Lanah Sawyer, it was a new beginning too. She would have to reconcile herself to her father's death and to the start of a new life with her stepfather—even as the landscape of the city shifted, once again, around her.

THE FIELDS. WEDNESDAY, JULY 23, 1788. 10:00 A.M.

The federal ship *Hamilton* fired ten cannon shots and set sail, through a cloud of acrid smoke, down Broadway. John Callanan, his brother pilots, and most of the other white men in the city had spent the morning at the Fields, preparing for a massive procession designed by the city's Federalist elite to celebrate the new republic's new constitution, to push New York to become the eleventh state to ratify it, and to project an idealized vision of the American social order.

Before the war, every man, woman, and child in the city had been the subject of a far-off king. The revolutionaries had proclaimed that "all men are created equal," but the new republic they created was far from democratic. In the city, more than a thousand people were still enslaved. And lining the streets, crowding windows, jostling for a view of the procession, were others excluded from the political order: free people of color, white women, and children—people like twelve-year-old Lanah Sawyer, her siblings, and her mother.

Even the city's white men were not equal, as the procession emphasized. Some six thousand men paraded through the streets in groups representing "the various classes of citizens." Foresters with axes were followed by farmers with their plows and an array of tradesmen, artisans, maritime men, and, finally, college students, merchants, lawyers, and clergymen. Each man had a role to play, but he was also expected to know his place.

The city's maritime men stole the show. The *Hamilton*—a thirty-foot-long, ten-foot-wide model of a frigate manned by officers and sailors, and sporting the procession's ceremonial cannon—was followed by a scaled-down pilot boat carrying a senior pilot and "four lads." Both vessels were mounted on horse-drawn wagons. But they were also fully rigged and, precariously, under sail.

As the *Hamilton* reached the Bowling Green she signaled for a pilot, raising a jack and firing a cannon. After the long, straight expanse of Broadway, the crooked, narrow streets of the old part of the city were like the treacherous approach from open water through Sandy Hook. The pilot boat drew up to the *Hamilton*, hailed it, and asked the "necessary questions."

"From whence came ye?" asked the pilot.

"From the old Constitution," answered the *Hamilton*'s captain.

"Where bound?" asked the pilot.

"To the new Constitution," came the answer.

"Will you have a pilot?"

"Ay," came the response.

On board the frigate, the pilot took charge and guided the awkward vessel around to the ruins of Fort George, where the president and members of the Continental Congress were assembled, brought her to, and fired a salute. Then, he guided the *Hamilton* up along the East River waterfront to the Rutgers farm and back to the Fields. As squalls came on, a newspaper report gushed, the "pilot displayed his skill in navigation," tacking back and forth through the hilly landscape, much to the delight of spectators.

When the parade ended smoothly, its organizers were delighted, too—and relieved. For the city's elite, any large gathering of lower-class men was a risk, especially when free beer was on offer. Memories were still fresh of the "tea parties" and popular protests that had helped provoke the recent war. In France, the popular unrest that led to the storming of the Bastille—and touched off a bloody revolution and a radical transformation of the social order—had already begun. In New York, a minister from the court of Louis XVI, looking out at the crowd and not seeing a strong military presence, wondered aloud: How were all these men going to be dispersed without "riots, intoxication, and disorder"? A local gentleman assured him that the good men of New York didn't need the threat of force to act with propriety. "They act as Freemen," he declared, puffed up with pride.

Freedom, however, meant different things to different people. And so did equality.

The end of the war had not brought an end to questions about the kind of nation America would, or should, become. Would it replicate the hierarchies of colonial society and the politics of privilege? Or would it introduce a new kind of democratic equality? Gentlemen like Harry Bedlow expected deference from their social inferiors. But workingmen like John Callanan were not always happy to oblige. They celebrated the dignity of their labor, claimed their own virtue, and asserted the equality of all republican citizens. For years to come, unresolved tensions and resentments would continue to rankle.

After the new constitution was ratified, the right to vote was still restricted by race, sex, age—and wealth. In New York, only three in five adult white men owned or rented enough property to vote at all, and only about one in five owned enough to vote for higher offices, like governor and senator. In the city, an exception was made for men designated "freemen" by the mayor—as Lanah's father had been in the 1770s and her grandfather in the 1740s. Men with skilled trades, like branch pilots, routinely became freemen upon completing their apprenticeships. The city's 1789 tax rolls show John Callanan as typical of the other senior pilots: he had little taxable property and he lived with his family in a modest, rented house. The pilots thus belonged to the middling group of white men below the small elite of gentlemen and prosperous tradesmen whose right to vote was unrestricted, but above the large swath of poor and laboring men who could not vote and whom the tax assessors didn't even bother to list.

Pilots enjoyed an exalted metaphorical role as just the kind of leaders the nation needed. "In such tempestuous times, it requires the greatest skill in the political pilots to keep men steady and within proper bounds," wrote a young Alexander Hamilton at the start of the war. Such imagery was classically republican: a man earned authority through his character and actions. But it was not democratic; exceptional leaders were needed because ordinary men required guidance.

The stark hierarchies that structured the world of the branch pilots were painfully exposed about a month after the Federal Procession, when the most severe thunderstorms anyone in New York could remember passed through in the dead of night. John Callanan was safely at home, but his boat, *Fortune*, was out by the hook. At her launch, eighteen months earlier, she had been hailed as among "the completest vessels ever intended for that service, having accommodations far superior to any hitherto produced." But the big sails and sleek lines that made such vessels fast also made them vulnerable. As the squalls came on, the crew of another pilot boat looked on in horror: the *Fortune* was caught by surprise, with some of her sails still up. The next morning, all that could be found was her skiff, floating upside down with a single oar lashed to it. Soon, the loss became one of the era's most widely reported maritime disasters.

Newspaper accounts gave pride of place to the boat's owners, identifying Messrs. Matthew Daniel, John Callanan, and Zachariah Russler by name, while relegating most of those who died to anonymity. They were described only as "Mr. Hallett, two other pilots, two boys, and a negro man." The "two boys" were no doubt apprentices; the "negro man" was probably enslaved. Several pilots, including Callanan's partner Matthew Daniel and his friend Edward Wilkie, enslaved workers—men and boys who labored as integral members of a pilot boat's crew but would never be allowed to advance into the pilots' all-white ranks.

As Callanan's joint ownership of the *Fortune* suggests, even senior pilots were bound by complex webs of coöperation and patronage. In 1790, a pilot boat cost about $800 to build and outfit—about the same as a modest house—and had to be replaced about every ten years. To cover the expense and limit risk, pilots typically banded together and borrowed the purchase price—making them dependent not just on each other but also on the merchants who financed their boats.

It was also the merchants who owned trading vessels, not the captains they employed, who paid the pilots' fees. In June 1789, a few days after taking a schooner out to sea, John Callanan presented himself at the offices of Gouverneur, Kemble & Company on Front Street, received his £1.6.3 fee, and signed a receipt. For pilots in some ports, collecting such debts and divvying up the proceeds could be difficult. But in New York, pilotage fees were handled by a clerk. The state had enacted regulations permitting the clerk of the port to bypass the regular courts and have conflicts involving pilots resolved by a single magistrate "in a summary way." Unlike most workingmen, pilots didn't need to worry about getting paid what they were owed—less, of course, the clerk's 3 percent fee.

At the same time, John Callanan and his brother pilots learned to treat the officials on whom they depended with respect and deference. Every few years, the pilots appealed to the governor and general assembly for increases in their state-regulated pilotage fees. In early 1788, the city's newspapers reported on one such petition from "David Morris, Matthew Daniel, John Callanan and 12 others, Pilots of the Port of New-York." The pilots renewed their request repeatedly, but it was years before the state finally raised their fees. The politics of patronage required patience and swallowed pride.

Open defiance, however tempting, wasn't worth the risk. In the early 1790s, Philadelphia pilots attempted to force a raise in pilotage rates by mounting a strike, but it didn't go well. New York's pilots had learned the same lesson decades earlier, when John Callanan was about ten. In 1763, the New York government attempted to spur commerce by reducing pilotage fees. The pilots howled in protest and brought shipping to a standstill. Merchants crushed the strike, officials fired the offending pilots, and the city's newspapers gloated. The only glimmer of sympathy for the pilots was a letter acknowledging that given the cost of "their Boats and Provisions" and the "Hardships and Dangers" they routinely braved, the pilots had a right to a living wage—enough to "live and maintain a Family."

A man's ability to support his family lay at the heart of the republican ideal of citizenship. And by this measure of manhood, John Callanan and his brother pilots did relatively well.

By the time John Callanan and his partners launched *Fortune*'s replacement that fall, the city was animated with new construction. To make New York into a suitable home for the new federal government, the city was busy leveling, paving, draining, and illuminating its streets—and transforming City Hall. In October 1788, the French architect Pierre L'Enfant was given five months to turn the cramped old structure into a suitable home for the new United States Congress, which would convene the following April. He tripled the building's footprint, added a monumental chamber for the House of Representatives at the rear, and redecorated the whole. Renamed Federal Hall, it was hailed as the new republic's most elegant building.

In April 1789, John Callanan and the other pilots played a visible, if humble, role in the spectacle organized to welcome President-elect Washington. To ferry him across the Hudson from New Jersey, the master of the port had commissioned an elaborate barge. Rowing it were thirteen of the city's branch pilots, outfitted in gleaming white uniforms. Lanah Sawyer, now about thirteen, and the rest of her family were no doubt among the crowd of spectators that cheered as the barge rounded the Battery and docked at an East River wharf.

That night, New Yorkers put candles and lamps in their windows, illuminating the streets in a silent collective statement of unity, pride, and hope. After the hardships of war, after the divisions between Loyalists and rebels, and after the bitter debate over the new constitution, the city came together around the figure of their president-elect.

But the moment was not to last. By the summer of 1793, when Lanah Sawyer met "lawyer Smith," the nation was in crisis, the city was in an uproar—and the branch pilots found themselves caught in the middle.

The storming of the Bastille in 1789 had briefly united Americans in their enthusiasm for another republican revolution. But France's turn toward a far more radical vision of democracy had divided Americans and exacerbated domestic conflicts. By early 1793, the body of Louis XVI lay in an obscure churchyard, his severed head at his feet. George III had declared war on the French republic. A bloody struggle to overthrow slavery was raging in colonial Haiti, driving thousands of refugees into American ports. President Washington, with no navy to defend his nation's interests, was determined to keep America out of the international war. But he couldn't keep the war out of America.

In May 1793, the thirty-two-gun French frigate *Embuscade* had sailed past Sandy Hook with a pilot at the helm, dropped anchor off the Battery, hailed the city with a fifteen-gun salute—one for each state in the expanding republic—and received a warm welcome. But, as New Yorkers began to see their long-simmering conflicts and resentments as part of an epochal struggle between Aristocracy and Democracy, the city was roiled by a series of violent scuffles, street brawls, and angry mob actions. Some, like Thomas Jefferson, welcomed the French Revolution as a revival of the "spirit of seventy-six"—and championed calls for social equality, civil rights, and the dignity of the common man. Others worried that the fragile American political order was falling apart. Federalists, like New York's haughty mayor Richard Varick, were closely aligned with Britain through both their business interests and their political values: they admired stability, tradition, and hierarchy, and they feared democratic reforms. Soon, the city's most prominent Federalist, Alexander Hamilton, would complain that the "common people" had come to see elections as battles between "the Rich & the Poor."

The trouble for the pilots arrived that summer, when a British frigate appeared off Sandy Hook, determined to take on the *Embuscade* and drive the French out of American waters. Flying false colors, the British warship captured a series of French vessels. Almost immediately, the city's branch pilots were accused of deceiving the French and luring them into the trap. Then, the British captain revealed his true identity and challenged his French counterpart to what amounted to a naval duel. But none of the city's pilots would agree to guide the *Embuscade* out of harbor. Part of the problem was that many of the pilots' boats had already been (illegally) rented out to spectators who wanted to sail down to the hook to watch the battle. Approached by French officials, one pilot explained that his boat had been promised to a group of merchants for a "fishing party." Flabbergasted by this blatant dereliction of duty, the French remonstrated with him.

I cannot help it, he replied. *Those merchants are my employers, and give me my bread.*

The *Embuscade* eventually did make it out of port on its own, faced off with the British and sent them fleeing, and was welcomed back in triumph by a crowd of thousands on the Battery. The drama had transfixed the city—and left the nation's Federalists chagrined, the emerging party of Jeffersonian Democrat-Republicans exultant, and the city's pilots exposed to a welter of public recriminations. Alongside breathless accounts of the affair in newspapers in the city—and across the nation—appeared bitter complaints excoriating the branch pilots. At a time when many artisans and tradesmen began to rebel against the Federalist vision of hierarchy and deference, the pilots, who shared their middling social status, appeared abjectly under the thumb of the city's mercantile elite.

Why, republican partisans asked, had the pilots treated the French with such treachery? "To explain this seeming mystery," came a damning answer, "it must be observed, that the pilots of New-York are generally under the influence of a British mercantile interest." Suddenly, the pilots' deference to the merchants who employed them came to be seen as craven servility, unmanly and beneath the dignity of an independent republican citizen.

The intense partisanship that August was vividly captured by Noah Webster, already famous for his spelling books, who moved to the city that fall to launch a new, reliably Federalist newspaper. Walking through the streets, he was horrified by enthusiastic chants of "Vive la France!" and ominous cries of "Down with King Washington!"

Late that summer, all this anxiety and tumult and these impassioned politics shaped Lanah Sawyer's initial encounter with "lawyer Smith" and her stepfather's attitude toward Harry Bedlow. Without the French refugees crowding the city that August, it is possible that Lanah would not have been harassed on Broadway on that stormy Sunday. Without the fear generated by the recurring street fights that summer, a Federalist gentleman like Harry Bedlow might not have felt the need to put the French in their place. And without the class resentments inflamed by republican partisans—and the attacks on the city's branch pilots for unmanly subservience to mercantile elites—John Callanan's response to Harry Bedlow might have been more deferential.

Suddenly, the attack of an arrogant, younger gentleman on the honor of a workingman seemed like a challenge that required an answer.

62 GOLD STREET. THURSDAY, SEPTEMBER 5, 1793. ABOUT 9:00 P.M.

Lanah Sawyer had been right to worry about the reception she would find at home that evening. By the time John Callanan returned to 62 Gold Street around nine o'clock, she was across the street at the Hones'. And everyone seems to have agreed that he was too agitated for a reunion with her.

John Callanan's most immediate concern was for himself. The qualities that prepared him to stand up to Harry Bedlow—his paternal pride, his violent temper, his willingness to take command and hazard risks, his self-respect as a workingman and as a republican citizen—also made Lanah's overnight absence a problem for him.

Callanan didn't need to know what had happened the night before to know that it would leave his stepdaughter damaged, and that damage to her sexual honor represented a threat to his own patriarchal honor.

If Lanah had acted of her own accord, she would bear responsibility not only for her own disgrace but also for bringing dishonor upon him. If that were the case, he was prepared to cut her off ruthlessly. So, at least, he had said to his friend Samuel Hone.

Yet for a workingman like Callanan, the possibility that a gentleman had wronged his daughter raised a different kind of problem—one without a good or obvious solution. Back in 1786, a gentleman tracked down his sister's seducer, challenged him to a duel near the Fields, and killed him with a shot that struck near the groin. But the elite code of honor that governed dueling did not include workingmen like Callanan. Nor could he simply take revenge with his fists—at least without risking a criminal prosecution.

So John Callanan remained at home. And sometime past nine o'clock, Jane Callanan went across the street to the Hones' house to see her daughter.

By then, Lanah had been sitting for some two hours with a group of women, including her cousin Lucretia Harper and Mrs. Hone. Conscious that they were in "company," the women pointedly avoided asking her any questions. But they were full of apprehension and curiosity.

When Jane Callanan burst in, things did not go well. Whatever relief she felt at the knowledge that Lanah had returned and was safe was over-powered by her rage. Like her husband, Jane Callanan was thinking not just about her daughter and her daughter's welfare but of herself, her family, and their reputation. Whatever Lanah's story turned out to be, there was no good outcome at this point, only bad and worse.

As Lanah recalled, her mother "came and was in a great passion."

"[I] was extremely angry at her," Jane Callanan later put it.

Lanah's mother was so angry and abusive that Lucretia Harper intervened. Harper was in a position to serve as a kind of surrogate mother to Lanah—she was almost the same age as Jane Callanan (who actually was her aunt), she had five daughters, including one a few years younger than Lanah, and she lived just a few doors down Gold Street.

Lanah, you should go home with me and stay the night there, Lucretia Harper said.

Gratefully, Lanah accepted the offer. At the Harpers' house, she found a candle and "went immediately to bed." Exhausted, and finally in a place where she could rest, the seventeen-year-old fell fast asleep.

Up to that point, no questions had been put to her, but everyone was curious.

After Lanah had been asleep for some time, Lucretia came up to her bedside, "drew the clothes off her and examined her linen." What she saw was exactly what she had feared. Lanah's linens were "much discolored and very bloody," Harper later recalled, and there were "evident marks of her no longer being a virgin."

The discovery confirmed that whatever had happened to Lanah, the story would have to come out, and blame would have to be assigned.

Lanah's cousin went back out into the dark to tell Lanah's mother Jane what she had seen.

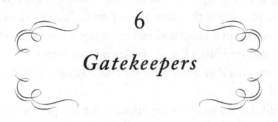

6

Gatekeepers

It was the beginning of another muggy day, the late-summer air heavy with rain not quite ready to fall. Once again, Lanah had spent the night in an unfamiliar room. Once again, she was close to home—but not home.

Her cousin Lucretia's house was a modest, narrow structure, wedged into a lot about sixteen feet wide, fronting on Gold Street and stretching back to Ryder's Alley. Lucretia was about the age of Lanah's mother; both women had married young, stayed in the city during the war, and lost their husbands just as it ended. Lucretia's husband had left behind the house, but not enough money to live on. She, too, had quickly found herself a new husband—a skilled cooper named Gideon Harper. He fashioned lumber into precisely shaped staves, pieced them together, and bound them with hot iron rings—producing the watertight barrels, firkins, and hogsheads that were the era's basic shipping containers.

Lucretia Harper's eldest daughter, Hester, was a few years younger than Lanah, but the two had much in common. They were both eldest children, they had both lost their fathers, they both now lived with their mother and stepfather and a growing brood of stepchildren.

Lanah had finally gotten some sleep—nothing had been settled, but for the moment she was safe.

Through a front window, Lanah could look out on the scene of the previous evening's abortive homecoming—and take in the sour smell of the brewery to the left, the scent of baking bread from across the street, and, since Friday was the day householders were required to put out their refuse, the stench of animal carcasses and night soil. Across the street, to the right, was the Hone property, where she had waited for her parents to return, only to be swept away from her mother's wrath. Her own home, opposite the bakery, was harder to see. If she craned her neck far enough out over the street, she could catch a glimpse of the front stoop.

Lanah had known that her homecoming would not be easy. She had expected that her stepfather would be angry, dismissive, even violent. Her mother's rage the night before had resolved nothing—but had made brutally clear that whatever was to come would be as hard as Lanah feared.

Lanah had barely made it out of bed before her mother burst in through the door, shocking Lucretia Harper with her violence. Jane Callanan needed to know, to see with her own eyes, if what she had been told the night before was really true.

"Before the girl had spoke a word," Harper recalled, Jane Callanan approached Lanah, "threw her down and examined her linen." In an echo of the violation Lanah had suffered the day before, her gown, petticoats, and shift were wrenched up. Callanan saw that her daughter's underclothes were "very bloody, that she could no longer be a virgin."

For Lanah—her skirts up, her legs spread, her mother taking in the dried blood, the blackening stains, the blossoming bruises—the moment of truth had arrived, the moment she had been dreading. And, perhaps, yearning for. All of her decisions and indecisions the previous day had made an accounting inevitable. However exhausted and confused she had been, Lanah's instinct had been to turn to female relatives, friends, and neighbors who had helped ensure that the confrontation, when it came, would be with her mother.

And so, for the first time, the young woman related "the whole affair."

For Lanah, the process of putting what had happened into words, pulling flashes of memory out of a flood of emotions, would require taking what was interior, what was private, what was urgent and inchoate and unfathomable, and producing instead a discrete set of events organized into a narrative.

The power of a narrative is that it endows events with meaning, with specific meanings. That is why narrative therapy can be healing; it helps one take control of thoughts, memories, feelings—to put them outside of oneself, to name them, to make sense of them. But the power of a narrative is also its danger. Lanah wasn't relating what had happened for herself. Her mother was not there to offer an empathetic ear, comfort, or support. Her mother was there to take in what she heard, piece together

her own narrative, endow it with her own meanings. She was there to make judgments, and to decide what would come next.

Seventeen, unmarried, a girl with an unblemished character and a reputation for modesty, Lanah Sawyer had left home one evening and not come back until the next. It was clear to Jane that her daughter was no longer a virgin, but who was to blame?

This was the question Lanah's story would have to answer. In this fraught moment, Lanah had to tell her story in a way that was coherent and sympathetic, in a way that would bring her angry mother onto her side. Lanah would need her mother's support if she was to have any hope of reconciling with her stepfather.

Lanah did tell her story. And her mother did listen. But their encounter in the Harpers' narrow house that morning was just a first step.

Having heard her daughter's story, Jane Callanan told Lanah that she was going to summon her husband. Typically, this is how families handled such things: young women like Lanah Sawyer would turn first to female friends and relatives for support, then appeal to their mothers. Sometimes, as in Lanah Sawyer's case, it was the mother who forced the confrontation—sensing that something was wrong and demanding an explanation from a daughter traumatized by what had happened and afraid of further violence. One seventeen-year-old was struck speechless for days after being raped and thought she was going to die. Almost immediately, her mother recruited the assistance of the perpetrator's mother. Together, they confronted him with the young woman's condition—only for him to deny responsibility, while she remained too traumatized to respond.

However a woman heard her daughter's story, it was generally her husband who made the crucial decisions going forward—decisions about how to handle the matter within his household and how to manage his family's public face.

When Lanah's stepfather arrived, she would have to tell her story again. Much would depend on what he heard in it. If he wasn't convinced of her blamelessness, he might disown her. Or, he might decide that they would take her back but bury what had happened in shame and silence; she would live in the shadow of violation at the hands of one man and humiliation in the eyes of her family. On the other hand, if he found her account compelling, if he took what had happened to her seriously, another path might open up before them all. But it would not be an easy one, and the risks would be grave.

Before John Callanan arrived, Lanah's mother warned her that he would be angry. It wasn't anything Lanah didn't already know. But perhaps that was the closest Jane Callanan could come to telling her daughter that she believed her, cared for her, wanted to be on her side.

In the hours, days, and weeks to come, Lanah would have to tell her story again, and again, to men and women—mostly men—who would stand in judgment of her. At each juncture, their responses would determine her range of options. At each stage, she would face the possibility of denial and disempowerment—and the possibility of gaining another, even more powerful ally. Her challenge would be to convince them to believe her story, to convince them to care.

But for the time being, Lanah—waiting for her stepfather in her cousin's house—was still in limbo.

&

In the dark of the previous night, John Callanan had blustered that if Lanah were in the wrong, he would disown her—and that if she weren't, he wouldn't say a word. Now, in the light of day, as he headed to the Harper house, things were not so clear—even for a man whose options were limited by the harsh logic of patriarchal honor.

This was the moment Lanah had been dreading: the fateful confrontation with her stepfather. Yet all that was recorded of this climactic scene from her later account was that "the story was told to him." And all we know from his account is that he heard the story from her at the Harpers' house.

It is possible that Jane Callanan was the one who went to fetch her husband. If so, she may very well have told him the outlines of Lanah's story—perhaps in a way intended to protect and defend her daughter and to deflect her husband's anger. The fact that she didn't simply take Lanah home for the face-off suggests that she was worried about his volatility—and Lanah's fragility. In another man's house, he might be more restrained, less volatile. If Jane did break the news, he may have walked into the confines of the Harpers' cramped, narrow house already having had a few moments to adjust to the broad outlines of her account, more settled, better prepared to let Lanah get through her story in her own way. On the other hand, perhaps he had been summoned by someone else—such as one of the Harper children—who hadn't told him much of anything. In that case, he may have arrived more anxious and less in control of himself, compounding the ordeal by making Lanah more nervous and her account messier and more disjointed as he interrupted with flashes of anger and exasperation and blame.

The one thing that's certain is that John Callanan would have to respond to Lanah's story by making a decision.

He could determine that Lanah was in the wrong and disown her. But that would be a drastic act: it would expose the shame his household had suffered and probably provoke a wrenching conflict with his wife. He could determine that she was not in the wrong and "say nothing" more to her about it. He could swallow his pride and try to keep what had happened secret. That might limit the damage to his family's reputation—if it worked. Was that even still possible? Each new person who had seen or heard something—that Lanah had gone missing, that she had not returned until the next day, that her stepfather had been involved in a scuffle with a notorious rake—expanded the reach of gossip.

Alternatively, if John Callanan determined that his daughter had been wronged, he could identify the man responsible and seek public vindication. Callanan was not one to back away from a challenge. And as a self-respecting workingman, he had good reason to resist the notion that an arrogant young gentleman like Harry Bedlow might dishonor his family, dishonor him, with impunity.

In any case, John Callanan listened—and, presumably, interrupted and asked questions. And then he hesitated.

For Lanah, her stepfather's uncertainty was a harsh reminder that he wasn't simply going to take her word for what had happened and who was to blame. He wasn't going to offer her the warm embrace of comfort and support. But neither was he going to dismiss what she had said out of hand.

Indeed, it appears he was inclined to believe Lanah that Harry Bedlow's treatment of her had constituted a crime. But that left him weighing whether or not to seek legal recourse. There was no guarantee that, if he took the matter to the authorities, they would take on the case, or that the prosecution would ultimately succeed. Would the costs of trying to keep the matter private be outweighed by the risks of trying to take the case to court? As far back as the *Kitty* affair at the start of the revolution, John

Callanan had understood the power of the law, of documentation, and of attorneys.

Before committing to a path forward, Callanan decided that he needed more information. In this sense, his reaction was like that of many fathers in similar circumstances. Mothers, like Jane Callanan, typically responded to concerns about sexual violation by examining the most private, intimate traces on the survivor's body. Men, like John Callanan, usually looked to more public evidence. Sometimes, they confronted the suspected perpetrator, as Callanan had already done, or they returned to the scene of the crime—to see it for themselves and to evaluate the physical space in a forensic light. One man went to the field where a woman had reported being raped to measure how far it was to the nearest house: if she had really cried out, he wanted to determine, whose ears might her pleas for help have reached?

It seems that fathers most often conducted this kind of investigation when the accused was a man, like Bedlow, with standing in the local community. If the accused was not local, or not of respectable status, making a legal complaint would carry far fewer risks. As it was, Callanan felt a need to verify aspects of Lanah's account. And, to evaluate whether her complaint should be made public, he needed to get a better sense of how strong her case might appear to others.

Callanan announced that they would visit Mrs. Carey's. As he had the day before, Callanan recruited Samuel Hone to go along. And he told Lanah to join them.

She did not want to go. But Callanan, dismissing the emotional consequences of her ordeal the day before, made it clear that he wasn't asking for her consent. Later both he and Lanah would describe this moment in the same terms: he "made her go with him."

The confrontation at 3 Beekman Street was tense. Mother Carey answered the door, and Lanah shrank back, but her father forced her to go in first. She and the two men went into a side room. There, in that confined space—in a house so charged with emotion for Lanah—John Callanan confronted Mrs. Carey.

Pointing at his stepdaughter, he demanded: Do you know "that young woman"?

No, Mrs. Carey lied. To repeated questions, Mrs. Carey insisted that she "had never seen her before in her life."

But the older woman's efforts to rattle Lanah only roused her courage.

Callanan turned to his daughter and demanded "if that was not the house."

Yes, Lanah replied, with composure that she would later reflect upon with pride: "she told him before Mrs. Carey, it was the house she had been dragged into the night-before-last."

Next, Callanan demanded to see the "back room"—where Lanah had described being raped and imprisoned overnight.

Mrs. Carey refused.

The old bawd's flat denial and her stonewalling were suspicious. Why would Lanah make up a story involving Mother Carey's house if she had never actually been there? And if Carey weren't hiding something, why wouldn't she let him see her back room?

Mother Carey's reaction bolstered Callanan's confidence in Lanah's story—and gave him new cause for concern about what it would mean for him and his family.

If Mrs. Carey were shameless enough to lie in front of three knowledgeable witnesses, she could prove a dangerous adversary. It was daunting enough to be up against a well-connected gentleman like Bedlow in a court of law. It would be harder if they were up against a witness whose interests aligned with Bedlow's and who wasn't troubled by the prospect of perjuring herself.

By the end of the confrontation with Mrs. Carey, Lanah had succeeded in winning over her stepfather. Exhausted, frightened, and traumatized, she had summoned reserves of inner grit and stood up to the complicit, indifferent, lying old woman. She had prevented a catastrophic rupture with her family.

For the first time in days, she returned to her family's home on Gold Street. And she did so having gained another crucial ally.

At the same time, another question still loomed: What would they do about Harry Bedlow? Would they try to keep it quiet—and face down any damaging rumors with a show of familial solidarity? Would they expose the crime Lanah had suffered and seek some kind of public vindication? No option would be easy. The stakes were high, the risks were grave, and so much was unknowable.

Again, Callanan hesitated. Despite his anger and agitation, he did not march Lanah off to a city magistrate to lodge a criminal complaint.

Instead, he and his daughter took several days to weigh their options. Then they took a step that was unusual—and savvy.

Like a ship captain turning to an experienced pilot when facing a risky passage, Callanan turned to someone who could offer him, and his stepdaughter, expert guidance—and who could, potentially, become another important ally.

LAW OFFICES OF EVERTSON & RIGGS, 144 BROADWAY. MONDAY, SEPTEMBER 9, 1793. DAYTIME.

Later, John Callanan would insist that the decision to publicly accuse Harry Bedlow was Lanah's, that he "never threatened his daughter, nor compelled her to bring [a] prosecution, but left her to her own will." Perhaps so. But he certainly did take forceful actions to shape their options.

Typically, a New Yorker who wanted to pursue a rape charge would go directly to one of the aldermen or to the mayor. But that was a risky step: they might not be believed or taken seriously; the defendant might never be charged, and even if he were charged and then indicted, the trial could expose the survivor to harsh scrutiny and abuse. In this case, Lanah Sawyer faced the prospect of a high-stakes battle with Harry Bedlow and his rich, well-connected family. Even if they endured all that, she and her family faced the possibility of a humiliating public loss. And even if they won, what would they win?

But John Callanan was not a man to give up. Surprisingly, he also had the money for expert legal counsel—and was willing to spend it.

And so Lanah Sawyer found herself in the modest offices of two young lawyers on the east side of Broadway, about halfway between the Battery and Mother Carey's house, at the corner of a cross street whose name would soon be changed from the royalist "Crown" to the republican "Liberty." Caleb S. Riggs and Nicholas Evertson were young men, recently admitted to the bar, just emerging from years of apprenticeship and work under established attorneys. Only a few months earlier had their names first appeared in the city directory as "attorneys at law" with their own practice. Though less experienced than many of the city's lawyers, they were smart, skilled, and hungry for work.

Caleb Riggs and John Callanan would develop a strong working relationship that fall. Nicholas Evertson had been raised in affluence; his family owned a large farm near Poughkeepsie, enslaved more than a dozen people, and sent him to Yale. Riggs's parents, although pious and well connected, struggled financially. As a speaker, he was more plodding and punctilious than eloquent. But his legal judgment was sharp and his persistence legendary.

Again, Lanah Sawyer recited her story, answered questions, and waited for judgment. Now, though, her interlocutor was a man whose job was to listen dispassionately and evaluate her story in terms of its legal merits. Could Lanah mount a viable legal case against Harry Bedlow? How strong did the case against Bedlow appear? How would lodging a criminal complaint serve their interests? What risks would they face?

No lawyer could offer such clients much encouragement. Riggs had an inexpensive edition of the standard authority on English common law, William Blackstone's *Commentaries on the Laws of England* (originally published in the 1760s), which defined rape as "the carnal knowledge of a woman forcibly and against her will." In law, rape ranked among the gravest felonies; the penalty was death. In practice, few survivors—or their families—found the law of much use. The process of reporting and prosecuting a sexual assault could be traumatic, and the odds of prevailing in court were low. Today, rape is the most underreported crime; only about a quarter of all sexual assaults against young women are reported to police, much less referred to prosecutors or taken to trial. In Lanah Sawyer's city, no one had been indicted for a sexual assault in more than five years.

As a result, trials for rape and other forms of sexual assault were rare. And even more rare were prosecutions that ended well for survivors.

The first hurdle was getting a magistrate to take a complaint seriously. When her nine-year-old daughter was raped on Christmas Day in 1765, one New York mother had to take her complaint to four different aldermen before she could find one who would pursue the matter. A few years later, another magistrate dismissed a young woman's complaint with the observation that her father was "poor," while her assailant's father was "rich." Even before a case gets to trial, he warned, such men sometimes get the better of people like you.

It wasn't just that rape accusations fell on deaf ears. Complaints against local men of standing—indeed, against almost any white men at all—were often interpreted as threats against the social order. Rarely was this more nakedly asserted than in a letter an Anglican cleric in Albany sent, along with an indicted rapist, to the attorney general in New York City, asking him to drop the charges. As the clergyman wrote, the man facing trial was a local tavern keeper, a taxpayer who rented a large property. His good character was attested by the mayor of Albany, and the accusation against him came from a "Mulatto wench." Whatever had prompted a local grand jury to send her complaint on to trial, the English-born, Oxford-educated Reverend Thomas Brown wanted it stopped. "If you can any ways befriend this Person you will oblige some Principle People in this Place," he promised. "If Negros are protected in their insolence . . . but an old Country man indicted for every little Crime, twill be time for us to leave this Country." Calling a white man to account for a crime against a woman of color was an attack on the entire colonial social order.

Lanah Sawyer was white, but she nonetheless faced a version of this same challenge as she considered a sexual assault charge against a gentleman. Often, the same social dynamics that made a woman vulnerable to sexual abuse in the first place also made a claim for redress threatening to men who enjoyed the privileges of whiteness, patriarchy, and property. Generally, rape charges were easiest to bring when the victim was either a married woman or a young girl, making the alleged assault into an attack on the honor of her husband or father—or when the alleged perpetrator was outside the body of male citizenship, most obviously if he was a man of color.

Even if a magistrate took the case seriously and persuaded a grand jury to return a bill of indictment, there was no guarantee that a survivor would ever have her day in court. In the years before the revolution, grand juries in the city repeatedly returned indictments against accused sexual assailants whose cases then disappeared from the legal record. Prosecutors always faced the possibility that a key witness—in these cases, the survivor—would decide that testifying at trial was not in her best interest. One woman testified before a grand jury, which returned an indictment for rape—but by the time the case came up for trial three days later, she had changed her mind and moved to Philadelphia.

And even if a case went to trial, survivors were seldom able to convince juries to convict white men—at least local white men—of rape. In the decades before the war, juries generally found white sexual assailants guilty only of lesser charges: attempted rape, or even just assault and battery. And even when they were convicted, no white New Yorker in the mid-eighteenth century received any sentence harsher than a modest fine. Only when Black men were accused of assaults against white women was the pattern different. They were more likely than white men to face prosecution, more likely to be charged with rape, more likely to be convicted, and more likely to receive harsh sentences. In 1734, an enslaved man convicted of the attempted rape of the fourteen-year-old daughter of a merchant was burned at the stake. In 1763, another enslaved man, convicted of attempted rape, was hanged—but a crowd of angry spectators overpowered the soldiers guarding the gallows, cut the man's body down, and dragged it through the streets.

Since the end of the British occupation ten years earlier, there had been only two sexual assault prosecutions in the city. Neither case could offer someone in Lanah Sawyer's position much encouragement.

The first started out with a remarkable jury verdict. In May 1785, Elizabeth Nesbitt secured a conviction against the impoverished white man who had raped her. It was the first time in more than half a century that a white New Yorker had been found guilty of rape. But the judge's response was even more astonishing: he declined to enter a sentence. Newspapers reported that the sentencing had been delayed—but it never came at all. The judge didn't want to see the man hanged, and he was too poor to pay a fine. The convicted rapist soon got married. He baptized a child in the church Lanah Sawyer attended and lived to a ripe old age.

The following year, the *New-York Journal* reported that Lewis D. Flynn, "a man of infamous character," was accused of raping, and communicating a venereal disease to, a mentally retarded "child" under the age of nine. While in the almshouse awaiting the disposition of his case, he was treated for venereal disease—at city expense. Still, the grand jury indicted him only for attempted rape, and the trial jury convicted him only for assault and battery. His sentence? A £2 fine. Despite repeated brushes with the law, Flynn went on to prosper and eventually marry.

In both of these cases, the presiding judge was Richard Varick.

Now, he was the city's mayor—the man Lanah Sawyer would have to face if she chose to go forward with a criminal complaint against Harry Bedlow.

The challenge facing women was illustrated again at the start of 1793, in the diary of a young New York gentleman whose friend was charged with rape: his response began with horror, shifted to fraternal sympathy, and settled on misogynistic rage. Jotham Post and Edmund Ludlow, both medical students from affluent families, were walking from a lecture on a mild January afternoon when Ludlow was arrested and hauled off to jail, charged with having "committed a rape, upon the daughter of a Parson Keteltas at Long Island." As was customary when elite men were accused of crimes, the city's newspapers made no mention of it. Post was shocked. "Most horrid idea," he wrote in his diary. "I cannot conceive the truth of it. It made me feel cold." But his concern was not for Elizabeth Keteltas and her ordeal. Rather, he worried about the reputation of his friend (who, he acknowledged, "has been a dissipated character"). Soon, the accused man was released on £4,000 bail (about half a million dollars today) and Post was relieved to hear his denials from his own lips. "Poor fellow," Post noted, "he seems when sitting still to be much agitated by contending emotions." Soon, Post was feeling sorry for himself. "Is it just that a woman should be allowed such liberty as to swear away the life of a man?" he ranted. "No man is absolutely safe, if Women are disposed to injure them."

In fact, by October 1793, Elizabeth Keteltas had good reason to worry that she might never get her day in court. Her family was too prominent and powerful to be intimidated into dropping the charges, but the accused rapist's father was a rich, resourceful attorney, and there were other ways to thwart a prosecution. Ludlow's family managed to get his case postponed again and again. Then, two weeks before Lanah Sawyer consulted with Evertson and Riggs, Ludlow jumped bail. With the help of his family, he managed to escape the reach of American justice entirely—by sailing to Jamaica, where the Ludlows had commercial interests and a sugar plantation.

Given all the legal challenges facing a woman in Lanah Sawyer's position, Caleb Riggs's job was not easy. Blackstone's authoritative *Commentaries* on English criminal law outlined a very narrow view of what made a rape accusation plausible. Citing the seventeenth-century jurist Sir Matthew Hale, Blackstone argued that the question was not simply whether a woman had been forced to have sex against her will but also whether her reputation was good enough, whether she had resisted vigorously enough, whether she had cried out loudly enough, whether she had sustained sufficiently conspicuous physical injuries, and whether she had reported the crime soon enough.

Finally, however, Sawyer and her stepfather were told what they had come to Evertson & Riggs to learn: they did have a case against Bedlow.

Before sending Sawyer and her stepfather off to the mayor's office—which was only about two blocks down Broadway—Riggs helped her draft a written deposition to ground her complaint. This precaution meant that when she approached the mayor, she was armed with a precise account crafted with an eye to the requirements of legal convention.

The fact that Lanah Sawyer managed to get this far is a testament to her courage, to her emotional endurance, and to her ability to inspire trust and sympathy. Once again, she had told her story and recruited an important ally. Once again, newly won support gave her more control, and more power, as she braced for the next challenge.

OFFICE OF MAYOR RICHARD VARICK, I CONGRESS STREET. TUESDAY, SEPTEMBER IO, 1793. DAYTIME.

For Lanah and her stepfather, fortified by their consultation with Evertson & Riggs and armed with a written statement ready to be sworn, the next step was to visit the city's chief magistrate, Mayor Richard Varick. At forty, he was "tall and dignified" (as John Adams put it), with a bald pate and an aquiline beak of a nose. Another gentleman described him as "a severe magistrate, somewhat austere and lofty in manner but humane and charitable in his disposition and conduct."

The mayor conducted much of his public business in an office that formed part of a walled compound stretching along Congress Street behind his Broadway-facing town house. Although dwarfed by the imposing residence, the office was a spacious structure, set among other amenities only the richest New Yorkers could afford: a formal portal, a well, a cistern, a large shed, a small privy, a patch of grass, and a coach house with stables for four horses. Through a side door, visitors could step directly from the sidewalk into the mayor's office, by design an intimidating mixture of private rank and public authority.

Varick was already known to Callanan, at least by reputation. Like the branch pilots, the mayor owed his position to the governor and his committee of appointments, and both the mayor and the pilots were closely allied with the city's mercantile elite—Varick as an equal, Callanan as a dependent. After years of loyalty and deference, Callanan was coming to the mayor as a citizen, to champion his stepdaughter's right to justice.

Varick had long experience in legal matters. Before being appointed mayor, in 1789, he had served as the state attorney general, and before that for five years as the city's recorder, its top legal official. As mayor, he remained one of the city's most important judicial officials. For Lanah Sawyer, he was a crucial gatekeeper to the criminal justice system. He was the highest authority to whom criminal complaints could be presented, and it was up to him whether such complaints should be referred to the attorney general for prosecution—or dropped. It was a role he took seriously.

When Lanah Sawyer came before him, Varick later recalled, "the deposition to ground the charge, came from Evertson and Rigg's office, ready to be sworn."

He did not simply accept it as presented. Like everyone to whom Lanah had told her story, Mayor Varick would take action only after carefully evaluating her story and her credibility.

The mayor began by examining Sawyer. He listened to her story and compared what she said with the text of the prepared statement. He noticed something that struck him as "a little inaccurate" and took it upon himself to make the necessary corrections. Only then would he permit Lanah to swear to its validity with an oath—and take up a quill pen and seal the document with her signature.

Still, he was not satisfied. Pressing the charge of rape against someone as well connected as Harry Bedlow was not a step to be taken lightly, even by the mayor. He and William Bedlow had served together in the New York Highlands during the war; the letters they exchanged during the war included conventional pleasantries affirming their shared membership in a small elite. As the mayor was no doubt aware, there had not been a sexual assault prosecution in the city against a man of Bedlow's status in almost four decades. The path of least resistance for him might well have been to set the complaint aside and let the charge against Bedlow lie.

Instead, he launched a brief investigation of his own to evaluate Sawyer's claim. That he took this step was a testament to Lanah Sawyer's powers of persuasion—and to the snowballing support she had already gained, turning one gatekeeper after another into allies who helped advance her cause.

The mayor summoned Mrs. Carey.

She told him the same things she had told Callanan and met with the same response.

Carey claimed that she had never seen Lanah Sawyer before in her life, and Sawyer had certainly not been at her house on the night in question. As Varick later recalled, Carey insisted that "there was nobody in her house at the time, but a young woman and a negro wench."

The mayor was not convinced. He would hardly have called Carey in if he hadn't considered Lanah's account plausible. And Carey's flat denials left no room for ambiguity: either the notorious old bawd or the respectable young woman was lying. Whether or not everything on the night in question had happened just the way Lanah claimed, Mother Carey clearly had something to hide. And she had little reason to cover up what had happened unless she knew it was something bad.

For Varick, this was hardly a welcome conclusion. The old woman's lies were a mark of disrespect for his authority—and left him with no easy excuse to let the matter drop.

The mayor decided to go forward with the charge against Bedlow.

Lanah Sawyer was now headed directly for a high-stakes legal confrontation. But with the support of the mayor and his office, she also had a new kind of power.

On September 10, a rainy Tuesday less than a week after the alleged rape, Mayor Varick issued a warrant for Henry Bedlow's arrest.

THE MAYOR'S OFFICE. TUESDAY, SEPTEMBER 10, 1793. DAYTIME.

Not long after Lanah Sawyer, John Callanan, and the arrest warrant left the mayor's office, the accused man himself walked in. As the rain continued and the air turned "Raw & Chilly" that Tuesday, Harry Bedlow had caught wind of the warrant circulating through the city. The twenty-six-year-old gentleman was not yet under arrest. Accompanied by his seventy-three-year-old father, he had come to the mayor looking to head off the rape prosecution—and exact a measure of revenge.

Their response to the news that Lanah Sawyer was pressing charges was impetuous, bold, aggressive—the response of a gentleman filled with righteous indignation yet comforted by the thought that he would be protected by his social standing and political connections. Harry Bedlow would not show remorse or apologize. Another man might try to intimidate his antagonists with the menace of physical violence, but the Bedlows would not stoop to the vulgar tactics of men with no other options. Harry's father had known Richard Varick for decades. They would go to him and demand justice.

We are here, the Bedlows told the mayor—as if the rape charge and the arrest warrant didn't exist—to make a complaint against John Callanan. Bedlow was still sore about the "scuffle" that had broken out the previous Thursday, when John Callanan had confronted him about the whereabouts of Lanah Sawyer. The Bedlows told the mayor that Callanan should be arrested for assault and battery. Such a legal counterpunch against Callanan might intimidate Lanah's family into backing away from their rape charge and serve to exact revenge for the insults they had already offered to Bedlow's honor. If the claim itself was a stretch, no matter—that would only reinforce the Bedlow family's status, manifest their ability to pull the strings of power.

Mayor Varick was back in his role as gatekeeper of criminal complaints. It was a delicate moment, but not because he took the assault complaint seriously. It didn't take long for the mayor to decide that he wasn't going to pursue the matter. The man who would be spending the night in jail was Harry Bedlow.

But Varick didn't want to be rude. He and the young man's father were hardly close, but they had spent all of their lives as members of the small city's social elite. As Varick later recalled, "not liking" to arrest Harry Bedlow himself, he discreetly sent word for an officer to come do so. While he waited, the mayor "amused" Harry by going through the motions of making out a deposition. Even when an officer arrived, Varick did not break the news to Harry himself, who, in his late twenties, was still living in his father's household. Instead, the mayor took up a pen and "wrote on a paper to the elder Mr. Bedlow that he must commit his son."

Taken into custody, Harry Bedlow was escorted from City Hall up Broadway to the city jail—retracing the route of his walk just six nights earlier with Lanah Sawyer. Then, he had been charming and disarming, maneuvering Lanah Sawyer into positions of progressively greater vulnerability. Now, the tables were turned, and he was the vulnerable one, being taken on an ignominious journey under duress and compulsion. The jail, built during the war and named after London's loathsome Bridewell prison, stood at the far end of the rough triangular park known as the Fields—along with the other municipal institutions that housed the city's most feared and despised residents, the almshouse, the hospital, and the debtors' prison—and within eyeshot of Mrs. Carey's brothel.

Amid the squalor and indignity of the city's criminal jail, Harry Bedlow had time to reflect on his predicament and the real trouble he was in. His father was probably already arranging to get him released on bail. But even in the luxury of his father's house, where his parents and several enslaved women could attend to his needs, he would still be bound to face his legal fate. Soon, a grand jury would consider whether to indict him. If they did, he would face trial. If convicted, he could be sentenced to hang.

Whether or not Harry Bedlow was ready to acknowledge his vulnerability, he was now in a fight not just for his honor but for his life.

The next public battle would come when a grand jury was called to review the charges against him and decide whether they should go to trial—or be dropped. That would happen at the end of the month, when the state's top criminal court would sit in Manhattan.

He had two, maybe three, weeks to stop it.

It was no secret that there was more than one way to defeat a criminal charge like rape. One, of course, was to arm oneself with the best available lawyers—which Bedlow's father soon did. The other was to derail the prosecution before it could come to trial—as had happened in the cases of as many as five of the last eight men to be indicted for sexual assault in the city. All of these men were white, but of low rank—a cartman, a maker of leather breeches, a common laborer, and others of obscure origins. For workingmen, the typical means of intimidation and retribution was physical violence. But a man like Harry Bedlow, with the advantages of wealth and connections, had other ways to get the better of an accuser.

The last time a gentleman had been charged with rape in a Manhattan court had been almost a half century earlier. The event provided a piercing example of the ways in which elite men could use their connections and status to fight back against a rape allegation and revenge themselves against their accuser, her family, and even the Crown-appointed prosecutor.

In June 1754, a group of four gentlemen were amusing themselves one evening at a coffeehouse and sent out for some oranges from a nearby shop. For some time, they had been eyeing the fourteen-year-old daughter of the woman who ran the shop, but the protective mother had warned them off. Now, the unsuspecting teenager arrived with oranges—and found herself alone, in a private room, with the gentlemen, who took turns pulling off her clothes and attempting to rape her as she struggled and ultimately succeeded in breaking free. When the girl's mother reported the assault to the colony's attorney general, the gentlemen were enraged and set in motion a campaign of intimidation and retribution. The girl's mother was from a respectable family in Ireland, but her husband's death had left her destitute. On the advice of a brother who promised to help set her up in business, she had recently moved to New York and opened a small grocery.

Taking advantage of the mother's precarious finances and lack of friends in the city, the gentlemen attempted to entrap her into receiving stolen goods by sending Black men and women into her shop to sell or pawn used clothing. She rebuffed several such advances. But eventually the gentlemen arranged for a red cloak of disputed provenance to be found in her shop and had her arrested. She was summarily convicted of receiving stolen goods and sentenced to be whipped. Two of the gentlemen slipped some money to the executioner, who flogged her with such violence that she fell into convulsions. But the gentlemen were still not done. Some of the city's most prominent merchants, calling her a person of "notorious ill fame," accused her of operating a bawdy house. Only after months of court appearances and attorney's fees did she get that trumped-up charge quashed.

Meanwhile, the gentlemen set their sights on the prosecutor who had brought charges against them. They accused him of abusing his office and arranged to initiate impeachment proceedings. As that matter dragged on, they got their own case delayed until the following spring. Nine months after the original incident, the prosecutor was cleared, but chastened. He had seen his prosecution of the men who had assaulted the fatherless fourteen-year-old as part of his duty to administer justice impartially to "the poor" and "the Rich" alike. After a series of attempts to hold gentlemen accountable for sexual assaults, this would be his last.

The next day, the four gentlemen came to trial.

Though they failed to block their indictment or prevent the trial, they won over the jury, which quickly rendered a verdict of not guilty. Newspapers frequently reported rape prosecutions involving enslaved, poor, or workingmen. But, as was usual, no mention of this drama ever appeared in the city's papers except for a report that the mother, Elizabeth Anderson, had been convicted of receiving stolen goods and whipped.

The gentlemen had kicked back an attempted rape charge and made their victim and her supporters pay for standing up to them—exactly what Harry Bedlow wanted to do.

About a week after Bedlow's arrest, John Callanan was given formal notice that the young gentleman had not given up trying to make hay out of their rough encounter. Having failed to convince the mayor to press criminal charges as a result of the alleged "assault and battery," Bedlow had arranged for an attorney to file suit against Callanan in civil court, seeking monetary damages. The lawyer representing Harry Bedlow was a man even more junior and less distinguished than the attorneys Callanan had turned to. Perhaps he was the only one willing to dirty his hands with Bedlow's vengeful scheme.

For Bedlow, there were several advantages to a civil lawsuit—the most obvious being that anyone could file suit against anyone else on almost any pretext. In civil court, the plaintiff had much greater control over the proceedings. There was no one in a position to refuse him the right to file a claim, the suit itself would unfold under his own direction, and it might be easier to secure a favorable judgment. Moreover, a civil case turned on money—and access to money gave Bedlow crucial advantages at every step. Often, civil litigation ended in negotiated settlements out of court, particularly when an affluent plaintiff was suing someone poorer. At midcentury, the average fees and court costs incurred in a civil lawsuit amounted to several months of a laborer's income. Indeed, simply by announcing his intention to file suit—or in this case, instructing an attorney to do so—Bedlow forced Callanan to go to the expense and trouble of hiring an attorney to defend himself.

Bedlow's lawsuit surely gave John Callanan cause for concern and added to Lanah Sawyer's anxieties in advance of the grand jury proceeding. But if the young gentleman expected his antagonist simply to fold, he was mistaken. Callanan may have sensed Bedlow's advantages in the civil arena, and for legal counsel he went back to Evertson and Riggs.

As they could tell him, Bedlow might have filed suit for several reasons—none of which boded well for Callanan. Bedlow no doubt felt his honor had been impugned by the confrontation with Callanan; he was no doubt angry about the rape charge and seeking revenge. He may also have been trying to intimidate Callanan and Sawyer—grasping for leverage as his criminal trial approached.

In the days before the grand jury would convene, Bedlow and Callanan engaged in a proxy contest in the Mayor's Court. Their legal maneuverings suggest something of Bedlow's personality—and of John Callanan's. Having filed notice of his intention to sue Lanah's stepfather for money damages, Bedlow didn't follow through by submitting his complaint. Perhaps he thought the mere menace of a potential lawsuit would be enough to intimidate Callanan and Sawyer, or his lawyer said the case was too flimsy to put in writing. In any case, on Thursday, September 26—four days before the grand jury was scheduled to convene—Bedlow's attorney asked the court for permission to withdraw the civil suit.

But Callanan refused to let the matter drop. Through his attorney, he filed a counterclaim—seeking to revive the matter and force Bedlow to spell out the nature of his claim in a formal declaration. The Mayor's Court refused to let Bedlow drop the matter but gave him until the next sitting of the court, in mid-October, to specify what Callanan had done wrong and why Bedlow thought he deserved financial compensation for it.

Increasingly, the sexual assault charge brought by Lanah Sawyer was turning into a conflict between two men, embroiled in a contest of wills, pitting their honor and masculine pride against each other. In the end, the gambits Bedlow employed to kick back the rape charge didn't work. Callanan refused to be intimidated. If Bedlow's style alternated between sniping and avoidance, John Callanan's response was characterized by fearlessness and tenacity.

Like the four gentlemen who had proven themselves so resourceful and ruthless half a century earlier, Harry Bedlow was well positioned to defend himself from the rape charge and to revenge himself against his accuser and her supporters. As a result, Lanah Sawyer and her father approached the grand jury hearing at the end of September with the threat of Harry Bedlow's lawsuit hanging over them, and the possibility that he might have something else up his sleeve.

FEDERAL HALL. MONDAY, SEPTEMBER 30, 1793. DAYTIME.

Three weeks after Lanah Sawyer and "lawyer Smith" stepped off her father's stoop for an evening stroll, a flurry of official paperwork swirled through the city. As commanded by the state's Supreme Court, the county sheriff and his deputies canvassed the city, knocking on doors and delivering summonses. Dozens of men were ordered to present themselves at the courthouse—sixteen would be needed for the grand jury, dozens of others for the various trial juries. The coroner, justices of the peace, and other officers were given notice that they would be needed. Criminal defendants out on bail were given notice to appear for the hearing on their indictments; the jail keeper was ordered to release those in custody; and prospective witnesses were summoned. Among the first to receive summonses were

Harry Bedlow and two witnesses against him, Samuel Hone and Lanah Sawyer. For the first time since Harry had walked out of Mother Carey's back room, Lanah would be in the same room with him.

Around ten o'clock, the Court of Oyer and Terminer, the Supreme Court's criminal arm, convened in the cavernous room at the rear of Federal Hall. It was a mild early-autumn day; sun streamed through the room's massive windows. On the bench were three men: one of the state's six Supreme Court justices and two local magistrates, Mayor Varick and the city recorder, Samuel Jones. Varick had witnessed Lanah Sawyer setting the prosecution in motion and Harry Bedlow's efforts to turn the tables on her. Now he would see the next act.

Once again, the matter rested largely in Lanah Sawyer's hands. If her powers of persuasion and her ability to recruit allies succeeded, Harry Bedlow would go on trial.

The court's first order of business was to impanel the grand jury. As much as the good citizens of the republic valued the protections of the English legal tradition, there were always some who ignored their summonses. Soon enough, though, sixteen jurors were selected and sworn in. They would be the last gatekeepers between a person accused of a grave crime and prosecution. The grand jury's role was not to weigh the defendant's guilt or innocence. Rather, they were there to prevent the attorney general from abusing his vast prosecutorial powers—to verify that each indictment he presented was supported by at least a minimal showing of evidence. In each case, the attorney general would present the charges he proposed to bring and some of the evidence he had gathered. There was no defense. On each charge, the grand jury had a simple question to answer: if they were convinced that there was a reasonable basis for prosecution, they would declare the indictment a "true bill." If not, the matter would end there.

Attorney General Nathaniel Lawrence had been appointed ten months earlier. For this session, he had prepared a stack of charges that reflected the continuing unrest provoked by the French Revolution—and the priority state law placed on money, property, and stable financial markets. Three Frenchmen faced charges of rioting, assault and battery, and attempted murder. Four locals faced even more serious charges related to forging deeds, thereby threatening the stability of the city's real estate market and the personal interests of some of its most prominent individuals. The punishment for forgery was death by hanging.

For the indictment against Harry Bedlow, the attorney general framed a single charge: rape. This was a risk. Increasingly, in the years after the American Revolution, prosecutors faced juries reluctant to convict men for rape—which was, after all, a capital crime. In response, prosecutors sometimes presented only lesser charges, such as attempted rape, assault and battery, or even sexual misdemeanors. Or prosecutors framed indictments with multiple counts: a charge of rape might be accompanied by a charge of simple assault and battery, essentially offering the grand jurors (and, later, the trial jurors) a fallback position.

In this case, the attorney general may have felt he didn't have much choice. His introduction to the case had been the detailed written complaint crafted by Lanah and her private attorneys to frame the narrative she wanted to convey. And it had already been investigated, amended, and endorsed by the mayor. Perhaps, if Lanah had approached the attorney general first, he might have encouraged her to consider other options. As it was, he decided not to second-guess the mayor or the account Lanah had committed to paper. He confronted the grand jurors with a single question: Was there sufficient evidence to try Bedlow on the most serious possible charge?

The burden of making this case would fall to Lanah. Her neighbor Samuel Hone had been called as well, but he could establish little more than the true identity of the man who had called himself "lawyer Smith." Lanah alone could say what he had done.

This was the largest, most public, and most intimidating audience she had yet faced. Previously, she had told her story to her mother and to her father in the privacy of Mrs. Harper's house; she had explained what had happened to the attorneys engaged on her behalf by her father; and she had faced examination before the mayor. Now, instead of finding herself in the relative privacy of the mayor's office, she stood before the grand jurymen and the officers of the court—and in front of Harry Bedlow.

The sixteen grand jurymen were an imposing group. They were all white men far above Sawyer's social station. By law, all jurymen had to be freeholders, which in the city meant that they had to own at least £60 of either real or personal property—a standard John Callanan would not have met. In a sign of deference to wealth and prominence, the foreman was Daniel McCormick, a prosperous and politically well-connected merchant and a founding director (with Richard Varick) of Alexander Hamilton's Bank of the United States. He was in his early fifties, wore his hair powdered, and lived just down Wall Street with his family and four enslaved people. Back in the 1780s, when William Bedlow had been postmaster, they had been neighbors. At the same time, McCormick was also, like John Callanan, a member of the city's small, sometimes disparaged Irish minority—a proud member, who belonged to the genteel Society of Saint Patrick. Of the other fifteen grand jurors, at least ten were also merchants. As such, they were more a jury of Harry Bedlow's peers than of John Callanan's or Lanah Sawyer's.

As Lanah walked to the witness box, the burden of proof she faced was, technically, not all that high. The grand jurors were not there to evaluate the truth of the matter, only whether the evidence was strong enough to take to trial. The hearing would not be adversarial in the sense that a trial would be. The attorney general could guide her. The grand jurymen, all sixteen of them, could pepper the proceedings with whatever questions they liked—but there would be no cross-examination by hostile defense lawyers, or any other concerted effort to impeach her testimony. The defense would present no case; the accused had no right to speak.

For Harry Bedlow and Lanah Sawyer, it was a reversal of roles. Previously, he had been well served by his charm and silver tongue; now he was silenced. Lanah, whose screams had been stifled and whose protests had been ignored, now once again had to give voice to her story—a story that was ugly, humiliating, and deeply intimate, a story about experiences that were, in any other context, too obscene to be spoken about in public.

Then it was over.

Stepping back out of the witness box, there was nothing for Lanah to do but wait. Although Attorney General Lawrence had a good track record—grand juries almost always validated his indictments—there was always the possibility that they would balk. Either way, there was cause for anxiety. If Lanah's account of having been raped did not convince the grand jurymen, Bedlow would go free. If it did, he would face trial—and she would have to face an even larger, more public, and more hostile audience.

For several days, the grand jury worked through a stack of indictments, hearing the prosecutor's presentations, calling in witnesses as needed, excusing them afterward, and deliberating in secret.

Finally, at eleven o'clock on Thursday morning, the court reconvened to hear the grand jurors deliver judgment on their first stack of indictments. First up were the four forgers—all of whom were sent on to trial, their lives at stake. Then the grand jurors turned to Harry Bedlow and announced their verdict:

"The Jurors for the People of the State of New York for the body of the City and County of New York upon their oath present, That Henry Bedlow, late of the fifth ward of the City of New York in the County of New York Gentleman not having the fear of God before his Eyes but being moved and seduced by the instigation of the devil on the fifth day of September in the year of our Lord one thousand seven hundred and ninety three with force and arms at the fourth Ward of the City of New York in the County of New York in and upon one Lanah Sawyer Spinster in the peace of God and of the People of the State of New York then and there . . . violently and feloniously did make an assault, and her the said Lanah Sawyer against the will of her the said Lanah Sawyer then and there feloniously did ravish and carnally know against the form of the Statute in such case made and provided and against the peace of the People of the State of New York and their dignity."

If the language of the indictment took Harry Bedlow aback, it was also a disturbing reminder for Lanah Sawyer: in the eyes of the law, the crime had happened "upon" her, but it was a crime "against" the people of New York. She had propelled her complaint against Harry Bedlow this far, but now control of the case was moving out of her hands and into those of public officials.

After the grand jury delivered their verdict—that it was a true bill— the attorney general moved, and the court ordered, that Harry Bedlow be "set" at the bar and arraigned.

What say you, he was asked. Guilty? Or not guilty?

Not guilty, he responded.

There would be a trial—probably within the next few days. And Harry Bedlow was not the only one with reason to worry.

For Lanah Sawyer, the grand jury's verdict represented a powerful victory. But along with relief and the savor of triumph, there was also good reason for dread.

During the trial ahead, attention would remain focused on her: on her behavior, on her judgment, on her credibility. At trial, the audience would be larger and the forum would be public; those present would include fierce antagonists. Bedlow had already showed that he would fight back against her stepfather. Now, his attorneys would do their best to discredit her. Once again, she would have to recount her sexual violation. Her decisions would be second-guessed, her integrity and morality would be attacked, and every effort would be made to bury her with scorn and shame and suspicion.

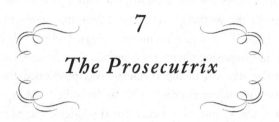

7

The Prosecutrix

Spectators streamed into Federal Hall, the city's largest, most elegant building. The city's newspapers had made no mention of Harry Bedlow's arrest and indictment for rape, shielding him with the discretion they generally afforded gentlemen, but the upcoming trial had nonetheless become the talk of the town. Some had waited in vain the previous day, like young medical student Alexander Anderson: "In the fore-noon—I went to Court to hear Bedlow's Trial, but it was postpon'd." He couldn't make it back on Tuesday, but the gaunt fifty-eight-year-old physician he worked for did. And so did a crush of others who had never before shown any interest in watching a criminal trial.

Entering the building from Wall Street, Lanah—along with court officials, lawyers, men reporting for jury duty, witnesses responding to summonses, and Bedlow himself—passed under the balcony on which George Washington had been inaugurated, along a stone-paved hallway, and into a soaring three-story lobby illuminated by a massive skylight. Stairs rose on either side to the gallery on the second floor, where the diffuse light glinted off gold-framed portraits of famous men in their Revolutionary War uniforms: General Washington, Colonel Hamilton, Governor Clinton. Ahead, doors opened into an even larger space: a vast room, some fifty feet wide and sixty feet deep, designed five years earlier as the first chamber of the House of Representatives. Sun streamed from the bank of windows on the right, flanked by pale-blue silk curtains and stretching up toward the barrel-vaulted ceiling more than thirty feet overhead. Everyone entered at the rear of the room, which was reserved for spectators. Those who could not find seats turned around and headed upstairs to elbow their way into one of the galleries that projected from the rear wall. Others pressed forward, through a gate in the railing, or bar, that set off the working courtroom. Gleaming mahogany furniture originally designed for house members—elegant, curved desks on thin turned legs and imposing chairs, their seats and backs upholstered in the same expensive damask as the curtains—was positioned for the court clerk and the contending attorneys. On the far wall, the old speaker's dais would have made an imposing bench for the judges. Tiered benches for the jurors had likely been added—as had a "bar," or dock, for defendants like Harry Bedlow and a "box" for witnesses like Lanah Sawyer.

At ten o'clock, the Court of Oyer and Terminer was called to order, and three judges took their places on the bench: the aging Supreme Court justice John Sloss Hobart; the city's recorder (or top legal official), Samuel Jones; and alderman John Campbell (sitting in for the mayor, who had been called as a witness). For those anticipating the Bedlow trial, there was another delay as the court took up the trial of an accused forger. His defense attorney, Robert Troup, tried to get the trial delayed, but he was outargued by the attorney general, and it went forward. The mayor testified for the prosecution, as did attorney Brockholst Livingston, whose name had been written on the deed in question. That trial didn't take long; the jury deliberated briefly and then returned a verdict of guilty. The forger would hang. As he contemplated his fate, attention turned to Harry Bedlow, who also faced a capital charge—and to his accuser, Lanah Sawyer.

Bedlow was accompanied by a phalanx of distinguished attorneys, including two men who quickly regrouped from the forgery trial: the defense attorney, Robert Troup, and the victim, Brockholst Livingston. In an extraordinary show of force, Bedlow's father had also hired James Miles Hughes, William A. Thompson, Richard Harison, whose nephew Edmund Ludlow was under indictment for rape in Queens County, and John Cozine, who lived two doors down from Lanah's family, at the corner of Gold and Beekman. Together, these six men comprised the region's most formidable trial lawyers.

The composition of the prosecution team was also remarkable: throughout the trial, and in the published *Report*, Lanah Sawyer was consistently identified as "the prosecutrix." This designation was evidently an informal echo of an earlier tradition in English law, when criminal offenses could be prosecuted not just by the state but also by private individuals. In the

American criminal justice system today, there is no such role. Even then, it was unusual—a strange amalgam of modern and medieval conventions. In modern American law, a crime like rape is defined as an offense against the state, not against an individual. Prosecutions are brought by the state not on behalf of the victim but on behalf of the people as a whole. And in official records, this is how the Bedlow case appeared. The lead prosecutor was New York's attorney general, Nathaniel Lawrence, who had only recently taken over an office previously held by Aaron Burr. Sensing what he was up against, he had hired an attorney in private practice, Josiah Ogden Hoffman, to assist him—as is sometimes done today. But Lanah herself was technically just a witness, with no control over her own case. For survivors of sexual assault who enter the modern criminal justice system, this loss of power can be agonizing.

So what did it mean that Lanah was described as the "prosecutrix"? While the title emphasized her stake in the trial, it didn't come with any formal authority, and it may even have worked against her. The attorney general did allow Lanah's stepfather to negotiate an unusual arrangement: at the start of the trial, John Callanan, evidently anxious about leaving the case entirely in the hands of the state—given the high stakes for Lanah and himself—made arrangements to pay another private lawyer to join the prosecutor's team. The man he hired was James Kent, a brilliant lawyer who would go on to become the state's highest legal official and the nation's most influential interpreter of the legacy of English common law. This public-private arrangement—unusual at the time, unthinkable a century later—bolstered the defense team and highlighted Lanah Sawyer's stake in the trial. At the same time, there was a danger that emphasizing her role as an individual with a private grievance could distract from the crime itself and the authority of the state. Then, as now, defendants often sought to deflect rape accusations by invoking patriarchal fears of vengeful women trying to bring down powerful men.

The trial began with the usual formalities. Bedlow took his place, and the clerk addressed him.

Henry Bedlow, prisoner at the bar, hold up your right hand, and hearken to what is said to you. These good men, the clerk went on, referring to the prospective jurors, *are those who are to pass between the People of the State of New-York, and you, upon your Trial of Life and Death.*

As each man was called and prepared to be sworn in, Bedlow had a right to object. This was the only time during the trial when Bedlow would be permitted to speak publicly. By the end of the eighteenth century, defense attorneys had become more common in American criminal trials, and the rules of evidence and procedure had become more formal. The result, by Harry Bedlow's day, was that defendants in felony trials were effectively silenced. Until late in the nineteenth century, it was held that a defendant had so much at stake in the outcome of his trial that he could not be trusted to provide truthful testimony.

As each man rose, the clerk ordered: *Juror, look upon the Prisoner; Prisoner, look upon the Juror.* If no objection was sustained, the juror was sworn in, and the clerk turned to the next man.

As on the grand jury the previous week, only men who owned enough property to qualify as "freemen" under state law were eligible to serve. In the city, this meant that juries were drawn from a minority of adult white men. For the Bedlow trial, it seems that the least affluent juror was the keeper of the city militia's gunpowder magazine. There was a prosperous grocer who lived on Beekman Street, a couple of blocks from Lanah's home, and a member of a family that owned a large stoneware factory on the outskirts of town. But the panel was dominated by rich merchants, including Benjamin Seixas, who owned a country estate in Greenwich Village and had recently built a large "double" house at 76 Broad Street that would later be the home of Delmonico's legendary hotel. Once again, it was a jury more of Harry Bedlow's peers than of Lanah Sawyer's.

Once twelve men had been impaneled, the clerk addressed them as a body:

Gentlemen of the Jury, the prisoner at the bar, stands indicted in the following words, to wit.

He then read the indictment the grand jurors had returned the week before, charging Henry Bedlow with having committed "a rape upon the body of Lanah Sawyer, a young girl about 17 years of age."

Having been indicted, the clerk continued, the prisoner had been arraigned and pleaded not guilty. Now, he was to be tried by his country. And you, Lawrence told the jurors, are that country: *Your charge is, gentlemen, to enquire whether the prisoner at the bar is guilty of the felony whereof he stands Indicted, or is not guilty; so sit together and hear your evidence.*

Then, Attorney General Nathaniel Lawrence rose to open the prosecution.

He began "with a few general observations on the nature of the evidence in an affair of this kind."

Then, as now, the issue of evidence in rape trials was fraught—in ways that have no parallel in other criminal matters. In Lanah's case, as in most other sexual assault cases involving acquaintances, two of the key facts would be effectively beyond dispute: whether she had been involved in sexual relations, and whether the prisoner was the man in question. No one was likely to bother challenging her testimony on either score. Instead, the trial would revolve around a third question: Had the sexual relations between Lanah and the prisoner been consensual—or against her will? There was only one person who could answer that question: Lanah herself. And she was there to give it. In a bitter irony, it was because of this that the defense would be left with only one obvious strategy: attacking her credibility and her character.

And so, when the attorney general began to introduce the prosecution's case, he started out defensive. In rape cases, he observed, evidence of the crime "must always be drawn from the party herself, whose testimony, if clear and positive, and not impeached, was deemed in law, sufficient to ground a conviction."

This, of course, was true of almost any criminal trial. Jurors are routinely forced to weigh evidence and evaluate questions of consent and credibility. Only moments before, Brockholst Livingston had been called as witness in a capital case against a man who had forged his name on a deed. Was Livingston's account plausible? Was he an innocent victim? Maybe he had signed the deed in question, only to change his mind and try to reverse the deal by crying fraud. Or consider the case involving a woman who worked in a brothel around the block from Mother Carey's: she had been accused by a sailor of stealing his pocket watch. The question was not whether it had been found in her possession; it had. The question involved the sailor's consent. Had he given it to her as a gift or payment for services? Or had it been taken by force or without his knowledge? In most cases, including those against the forger and the woman with the pocket watch, the legal system took the supposed victim at their word—at least on the issue of consent.

But in the case of rape—particularly in the case of rapes involving acquaintances, cases involving women of lower social standing and men of higher social standing, cases like the one Lanah Sawyer was bringing against Harry Bedlow—an elaborate body of legal commentary had been developing to call the victim's credibility into question.

Lanah's story—the story of every woman charging a man with rape—had been written out more than a century earlier by Sir Matthew Hale, who worried about malicious women bringing false rape charges against men of property and standing like himself. Hale's influential commentaries, written in the 1670s and published posthumously in 1736, advised juries to use circumstantial evidence to test a woman's credibility. Was she "of good fame" (that is, did she have a good reputation) before the incident? Did she resist physically and bear signs of injury on her body? Did she cry out for help during the attack? Did she promptly report the crime to authorities? In one scenario, she was virtuous, had been grievously harmed, and deserved to be heard. In the other, she was untrustworthy, potentially malicious, and had to be recognized as a threat.

The opinions of Hale and more recent legal scholars were not the law itself—rape was, at root, simply the "the carnal knowledge of any woman . . . against her will." Still, even before she was called as a witness, Lanah had been cast as a character in a story—a character that was not her and a story not of her making, but which everyone in the room thought they already knew.

☙

Lanah Sawyer walked across the room and stepped into the witness box. She didn't have long to take in the vast room from this vantage—the judges, the jury, the defendant, the lawyers, the eager spectators filling the back of the room and crowding the galleries. The court clerk prompted her to place her hand on a Bible and take the customary oath.

Her task was to make two things clear to the jurymen: that Bedlow's actions had met the legal standard of rape and that her own behavior satisfied Hale's concerns about a rape victim's credibility. The latter was a challenge because of the way she had been drawn in by the man who turned out to be Harry Bedlow. At every turn, the tactics he had used to isolate her and make her vulnerable had also created a kind of social camouflage that blurred the distinction between rape and seduction.

On a Sunday evening, at the latter end of August, Lanah began, *I was going through Broadway, and received several insults from some Frenchmen, whose language I could not understand. The Prisoner came up—rescued me, and then attended me to my father's house in Gold Street. He told me his name was lawyer Smith.*

As Lanah spoke in the crowded courtroom, her speech was likely filled with hesitations, pauses, and asides, and colored by powerful feelings of anger, disgust, and shame. Little of that comes through in the surviving account of her testimony. William Wyche's written report of the trial summarizes, paraphrases, and omits, making her testimony seem more fluid, efficient, and controlled than it perhaps was in the moment. But there are passages that seem to evoke not just the substance of Lanah's testimony but also the flow of her speech.

On the Sunday following, she went on, *I met with him again*. Here, catching herself, Lanah clarified: *he accosted me*. She didn't want to leave the impression that she had been so indecorous as to approach him.

They fell into conversation, Lanah testified, in the course of which he asked if she would take a walk with him the following evening.

I am engaged, she had replied.

Tuesday evening? he persisted.

I am also engaged, she had replied.

His rejoinder, as she described it, was good-humored and flirtatious.

Surely you are not engaged on every evening—you can certainly go on Wednesday.

I am not then engaged, she reported responding—not quite saying yes, not quite saying no.

Then, she testified, he escorted her home and departed.

Now, as Lanah told her story in court, the very glamour and deception "lawyer Smith" had initially used to draw her in worked against her in a new way. The act of describing his lies, his false front, put her on the defensive. Hale had emphasized the importance of a woman's public reputation, whether she was of "good fame." The prosecution could easily call other witnesses to answer that question. But Lanah's story raised other questions—about her actions, her judgment, her motives—that could not be answered so definitively. How had she been taken in by "lawyer Smith"? Why had she agreed to go out for that fateful walk to the Battery with him? What had she imagined a gentleman, so obviously of a higher social station, had seen in her?

Standing in the witness box before a throng of spectators, Lanah addressed these questions head on, relating her conversation with her

Lanah likely dressed for her walk on the Battery
like the seated woman in this 1795 view of New York.

across-the-street neighbor Samuel Hone: he had remarked on her "smart Beau" and told her that he was Harry Bedlow. In court, Lanah made it clear that she recognized that this was a warning, that Bedlow had a reputation as "a very great rake." But she also made it clear that she thought that her well-meaning neighbor was mistaken.

It could not be, she reported telling Hone, *as he had said his name was lawyer Smith.*

She had taken "lawyer Smith" at his word. That, it was now clear, had been a mistake. But how to explain her hopefulness, her inexperience, her reaction to her neighbor's paternalism, her sense that her family wasn't necessarily all that far below the status of a young lawyer, her eagerness to believe that a man like that might find her special?

In the courtroom, the problem Lanah faced was in part due to the nature of narrative: she had experienced events as they developed through a haze of misinformation and fantasy and confidence in her own judgment. But what everyone in the courtroom knew from the outset, she learned only after it was too late.

She went on to recount a whole series of deceptions as her new beau led her out for a walk. He had convinced her to leave her father's stoop with him by indicating that they would be joined by another couple, including her friend Miss Steddiford, and when she turned out not to be at home, he used that fact to get Lanah to agree to go to the Battery, whence he indicated Miss Steddiford must already have departed. The stop for ice cream—a luxurious treat that could only have increased Lanah's sense of obligation to him—and their long walk around the Battery as darkness closed in around them ended with a jolt when she heard the bells of Trinity Church strike and realized how late it was—that she was out long past the time her parents would have considered acceptable. Her anxiety was compounded by confusion about the actual time—she had heard the bells strike twelve; he said it was only ten; the night watchmen said it was one. He offered to escort her home. It was not until he pulled her past John Street and tried to steer her down Ann Street that she realized something was wrong.

I knew there were vacant lots there—and had heard the street was filled with bad people, and thought it improper for a young girl to go down there, Lanah explained. She refused, but he kept a tight hold of her.

I screamed—and he stopt my mouth, Lanah went on. *I then, for the first time, began to suspect his intentions.*

Lanah described how Bedlow "dragged her" around the block to a house on Beekman Street opposite the Brick Presbyterian Church— "with one arm round her, the other having both her hands."

As Bedlow knocked with his stick at Mrs. Carey's door, and she opened a window to speak with him, Lanah testified, she "escaped from the Prisoner" and ran. She headed toward home, only two blocks away, but before she made it to the end of Carey's block, he caught up with her.

Bedlow dragged me back again, she reported. *I again escaped, and fled quite to the corner; he forcibly made me return. I again ran away, almost exhausted, and not knowing what I did.*

Once again, Bedlow caught up with her. Keeping a "tight hold" of her struggling body, he dragged her not back to Carey's front door but into Ann Street.

He carried me down there, took me through a vacant lot, keeping fast hold of my arms, and going backwards himself, drew me through a passage, pushed open a gate, led me thro' a garden, where we were obstructed by bushes—then came to a back door, at which he knocked and demanded admittance.

The door was opened by Mrs. Carey.

"There is a room," she said.

Bedlow dragged her into it, Lanah testified. *I screamed.*

This was exactly the kind of physical resistance and crying out that Matthew Hale held up as signs of a rape survivor's credibility. Lanah's account of struggling with Bedlow in the street also helps explain Mother Carey's decision not to let him drag her in through the front door.

Inside the small, dark chamber, Bedlow asked for a candle. Mrs. Carey called for one and soon put it in at the door, which was then shut.

By the light of the candle, Lanah could see Bedlow beginning to undress—pulling off his coat, then his waistcoat.

I screamed and endeavoured to escape, she testified. *He seized me, stopped my mouth, and laughed aloud to prevent my screams from being heard.*

Then he roughly pulled off her clothing.

He then threw off my hat, tore the pins out of my gown, and placing me before him, drew it off my shoulders.

Then, she continued, *he asked my consent three or four times.*

Shockingly, Bedlow had gone through the motions of a conventional seduction narrative—as though he had not insinuated himself into her confidence with false pretenses, dragged her into Mother Carey's back room, and ignored her screams and attempts to escape. Then, as now, acquaintance rapists often tried to use only as much force as necessary, ignored or discounted resistance, and staged their assaults as consensual.

If Bedlow's attempt to manipulate reality disoriented Lanah, it also infuriated her.

I refused, she testified, *calling him a brute, a dog, a villain.*

Next, Bedlow asked her consent to put out the candle—another effort to make her complicit in the scenario he was staging. Again, she refused.

At this point, as Lanah recounted, Bedlow abandoned all pretense that she was a willing participant in his fantasy.

He snuffed out the candle and turned more violent.

He tore the strings off my petticoats, and kicked them off with his feet.

Then, she went on, *he threw me down on the bed.*

As Bedlow pulled off his remaining clothes, Lanah testified, she again tried to escape. But he forced her onto the bed.

He then threw himself upon me, laid his left arm across my throat, so that I was almost choked; and did not suppose I could live many minutes, and had his ends of me.

Here, the published *Report* interrupts the flow of her testimony to observe: "These words were explained by leading questions." Legally, the attorney general guiding Lanah's testimony needed her to affirm that Bedlow's penis had entered her vagina. He also needed her to indicate whether or not Bedlow ejaculated.

By all accounts, this had been Lanah's first sexual experience. Now, before a crush of onlookers, the powerful emotions evoked by these memories were compounded by the indelicacy of giving voice to such intimate, sexual acts.

Even the sexually experienced men who had written the most important legal commentaries discussed such matters only obliquely or through a veil of Latin circumlocutions. As Hale put it in the 1670s, a sexual assault was a rape only if there had been "actual penetration or *res in re*." In addition, an emission of semen (in Hale's words, an "*emissio seminis*") was legally significant in rape trials since, although neither strictly necessary nor sufficient, it was considered "an evidence of penetration." By the mid-eighteenth century, a broad cultural shift had only made standards of propriety more prudish. In the 1760s, William Blackstone omitted even Hale's Latin circumlocutions from his *Commentaries on the Laws of England*—regarded by Americans, even after the revolution, as the authoritative compendium of the common law. Indeed, Blackstone only exacerbated the double bind facing women in Lanah Sawyer's position: "the material facts requisite to be given in evidence and proved upon an indictment of rape . . . are highly improper to be publicly discussed, except only in a court of justice."

To make a plausible claim of sexual assault, according to male legal authorities, she had to talk in a knowing way about sexual matters they themselves considered too obscene to address clearly in print. But at the same time, according to these same writers, in order for her claim to be credible, she had to project an air of sexual innocence.

This was why the attorney general approached the sexual aspect of her ordeal through "leading" questions—questions that required Lanah to answer only "yes" or "no." Even so, Wyche considered the whole episode too obscene to reproduce in print. As he assured readers of his *Report*: "the answers to which thro' delicacy we omit; but they amounted to proof of the fact."

I did not feel his right arm, nor knew what he did with it, Lanah testified, in the only portion of this exchange that Wyche did reproduce.

Afterwards, she went on, *he turned his back and went to sleep*.

Lanah, meanwhile, frantically searched for a way out of the small dark room. Late at night, with no fire, no candle burning, no moon outside, and solid wooden shutters covering the window, it was pitch dark.

I arose to look for the door, she testified. Feeling her way around the rough plank walls she first came to the window. *I tried to open it, but could not.*

Then she reached the door.

I felt a latch but could not open it, she testified. Feeling all over the door for a bolt keeping the door locked, she found none.

She was locked in.

Bedlow hearing me, she continued, *got up and forced me to bed again, but did not offer any new violence.*

Bedlow clearly wanted her in bed next to him. Presumably, in part, he wanted to be able to better monitor and control her movements, since he didn't want her leaving Mrs. Carey's house in the dead of night. Perhaps, too, he wanted to preserve the illusion that she was comfortable with what had happened earlier by making her act the part of someone engaged in a consensual tryst.

Lanah wanted to be as far away from him as possible.

She waited for him to fall asleep again.

I again got up and tried at the window, but not being able to get out, set down in a chair, the room being very dark and impossible to distinguish any day-light, she testified. *Bedlow again got up and made me lie down.*

Eventually, she gave up. With the room so dark, it was impossible to gauge the passage of time. She lay on the bed in Mrs. Carey's back room, with Bedlow dozing next to her, and waited.

Eventually, Bedlow woke up, opened the window, swung open the shutters, and flooded the room with daylight. As he pulled on his clothing, he told Lanah that Mother Carey would want her gone.

Having told the court what had happened on the night in question, including some of its most intimate and painful details, Lanah Sawyer was still not yet permitted to end her testimony.

Now, she had to relate to the court what had happened afterward. By this point, she no doubt knew that questions would be asked about the amount of time that had passed between the assault itself and her formal complaint to the mayor.

Lanah described leaving Mother Carey's house, seeing Bedlow at the corner of Ann Street and Broadway, and her fear of her father's violent temper. She described her retreat to the bathing house where the kindly gentleman had asked what was troubling her. She described spending the afternoon with her aunt on Broadway, looking for her lost glove, and, finally, heading to Spruce Street at around seven o'clock to see if her friend Miss Pine would walk her home. She described Mr. Towt accompanying them, the wait for her parents at the Hones', and her mother's rage that forced her to spend the night at her cousin Lucretia's house. She described her mother confronting her Friday morning and her father forcing her to return to Mother Carey's. Finally, she described how Mother Carey had lied about knowing her and refused to let them into her back room.

The end of Sawyer's testimony was punctuated by a dramatic moment.

The attorney general produced the gown she had worn on the night of the rape—made of cotton calico with "a drawn frill round the neck." She had probably sewn it herself. Only a few weeks earlier, it had been a happy example of her skill and fashion sense, of the story she imagined for herself when she put it on. Now, it was an artifact of that harrowing night.

As the attorney general held it up, the thin cotton hung limp and shapeless—its tears and repairs inanimate evidence of the violence Bedlow wrought as he had ripped it off her struggling body. Sawyer had made some repairs before leaving Mrs. Carey's—so that she could go out in public "decently"—but the damage could still be seen.

A gown like Lanah's, made of an unforgiving flat-woven cloth like calico, could not simply be pulled on and off. It was likely constructed as a one-piece "round gown"—with full skirts attached to the closely tailored bodice, high armholes, and tight-fitting sleeves. Such gowns had to be partially disassembled in order to be pulled on and off. But the fabric had little give, so care was required. On Lanah's gown, the bodice was designed to open up in front—the two halves held in place with straight pins. In the event, they pulled out smoothly enough. But other fastenings were less forgiving: fixed ties and drawstrings that gathered the frilly neckline, held up the skirt's drop-front panel, cinched the waist, and secured the petticoats. If the strings were not untied, they would pull and bind as the gown was forced off. And then, either the strings or the fabric itself would rip. Or both.

As Lanah testified, two or three "strings" had been torn off, and the gown had been torn in a "few places" when Bedlow had "pulled" it off over her shoulders.

Was the significance of this evidence fully appreciated by the all-male, mostly affluent jurors? From Wyche's account, it is not clear what the attorney general felt was necessary to explain. For a young woman of modest means like Lanah Sawyer, a gown was an expensive object, and this one was probably her best. The cost was almost entirely comprised of the material: in this case, yards of cotton calico. Her own labor, even when others were paying for it, was worth precious little. This is why surviving gowns from this period often show evidence not just of alterations to fit changing bodies, but wholesale refashioning as styles changed. Lanah was not likely—even supposing she had been driven by the heat of passion—to be so heedless as to tear her best gown. She knew where the fasteners were; she had long practice undoing them; and preserving her investment in the garment was important to her. But Harry Bedlow was quite another matter.

With the production of this single piece of forensic evidence, the prosecution rested, and Lanah Sawyer's direct testimony, guided by the attorney general, came to an end.

Now she had to brace for cross-examination.

It was only to be expected that Bedlow's lawyers would focus on attacking her, on poking holes in her narrative, on undermining her credibility, on impugning her motives.

Still, the cross-examination gave Lanah her first indication of how exactly they would go about doing so—though the point of some of their questions was not immediately clear.

After leaving the Battery, who did you see in the street? one of the defense lawyers asked.

I saw nobody in the street, she answered, *after passing the three watchmen.*

When did you first suspect the true identity of the man you were with?

I did not know that the lawyer Smith was Bedlow, Lanah replied, *till we got to the Corner of Ann-Street, when, from his behavior, suspecting his intentions, I thought I had been deceived and that he really was Harry Bedlow.*

One line of questioning raised the suggestion that Sawyer had been pressured by others into fabricating the charge of rape. Were you influenced by your father, or any other friends, to bring on this prosecution? she was asked.

No, she insisted.

Another set of questions sought to cast doubt on whether she had really done all she could to cry out for help or escape from Mother Carey's back room. It was established that there had been a child sleeping in a corner of the room, boarded off from where she and Bedlow were. And Lanah acknowledged "that no noise had awakened him." For jurymen unaware of how soundly toddlers can sleep, this may have seemed significant.

The defense did not progress logically through the sequence of events Lanah had laid out but rather jumped around from one moment to another, trying to deprive her of the confidence and stability provided by narrative control.

Her answer to one question was: *The first light I saw in the room was from the Prisoner's opening the window.*

Her answer to the next: *I did not stamp in the room with my feet.*

Then, there were two disconcerting questions about her whereabouts on the night after the alleged rape.

Had she returned to Mrs. Carey's house the next night? Or gone to Mr. Bedlow's?

No, she replied. *I did not even know where the latter was.*

Ominously, these questions implied that the account she had just given was incomplete, that she had left out important information, that the defense was preparing to offer a very different narrative of her whereabouts that evening. This was one of the great advantages the defense team possessed. They did not necessarily need to follow up on such insinuations with evidence of their own. Sometimes, just posing questions was enough to sow the seeds of doubt.

With that, the defense team announced that they were done with her.

Lanah stepped down from the witness box. And the attorney general rested the prosecution, satisfied that she had made their case.

~

The defense case was opened by William Thompson, who, in a self-deprecating nod to his distinguished colleagues on Bedlow's legal team, introduced himself as its "youngest member."

Thirty-one years old, Thompson had graduated from Yale toward the end of the war, trained with his father in Connecticut, and established a lucrative practice there. Like Bedlow, he had married a woman in her teens, who had died young. He then set his sights on her sister. They could not marry in Connecticut (which hewed to an Old Testament definition of incest), so in 1791 they relocated to New York City and, for a time, lived on Cherry Street, near the Bedlows. Thompson's services were in high demand, but he struggled with stress. Within a few years of the Bedlow trial, he would retire to a rural property upstate—worried that overwork and lack of exercise would drive him to nervous exhaustion.

Thompson's opening statement was his chance to reframe the jurymen's attention: to outline the "nature" of the defense case and to preview "the most material evidence" he planned to present.

He began by reminding the jurors that the stakes could not be higher: Bedlow was on trial for his life. Thompson repeated Matthew Hale's famous comment that rape "is an accusation easy to be made, hard to be proved, but harder, much harder to be defended, by the party accused though perfectly innocent." It was an apt summary of the defense strategy: Thompson would not attempt to prove his client's innocence. He would not dispute that Harry Bedlow had insinuated himself into Lanah Sawyer's confidence through false pretenses, that he had carefully planned her ruin, that he was a man of low moral character, that his actions on the night in question were despicable, or even that he had left her grievously harmed. Thompson didn't want to call any more attention than necessary to Bedlow's behavior. He wanted the jurors to focus instead on the jeopardy Bedlow now faced—as a result of Lanah Sawyer's accusation.

Thompson made it clear that Bedlow's defense would revolve around his purported victim—attacking her character, challenging her story and her motives. To justify this approach, he relied heavily on the authority of Hale's commentaries.

"As it is an offense of so dark a nature, so easily charged by the woman, and the negative so difficult to be proved, putting the life of a citizen in the hands of a woman, to be disposed of almost at her will and pleasure," he told the jurymen, "you will therefore find it necessary in the first place to examine with strictest scrutiny into the character of conduct of her upon whose evidence he must stand or fall."

The standard Thompson proposed for evaluating the credibility of a purported rape victim went far beyond anything Hale himself had suggested: "Her character, her conduct, to entitle her to be that evidence who shall take away the life of a citizen, ought not only to be perfectly chaste, but through the whole scene should not leave the slightest suspicion of impropriety; she ought indeed to be a person who would have avoided the house in which she pretends the fact was committed, as she would have avoided her own ruin." The simple fact that she had been inside Mother Carey's house, according to Thompson, proved that she was not the kind of woman who was "intitled to belief by a jury of the country." There could be no more stark example of how Bedlow's tactics could be used after the fact to impugn Sawyer's character and motives.

Having outlined how he wanted the jurors to evaluate Sawyer's testimony, he turned to what he planned to establish by calling his own witnesses. His narrative would begin with the moment Harry Bedlow and Lanah Sawyer first approached Mother Carey's house. He would call witnesses who would prove that far from trying to escape Bedlow and screaming for help, Lanah Sawyer had approached Mother Carey's house in a "very agreeable conversable mood" and had entered willingly; that no cries or other indications of resistance had been heard by the other occupants of the house that night; that, to the contrary, both Bedlow and Sawyer had been heard laughing and talking "in a soft agreeable manner." Testimony, he promised, would prove that the house was so cramped and its walls so flimsy that anything that had transpired in the back room would have been overhead by everyone else there that night; that the window hardware and door latch were both broken and thus Sawyer could not have been locked in. Witnesses, instead, would establish that Sawyer voluntarily remained in the room the next morning for hours after Bedlow departed—and that she "left it with a degree of apparent complacency and satisfaction in her looks and conduct." Finally, witnesses would establish that far from reporting the alleged crime at her earliest opportunity, Lanah Sawyer had been hoping to rekindle her romance with her alleged assailant.

For Thompson, the basic questions he proposed to answer through the testimony were all drawn from Hale's concerns. Did Lanah Sawyer physically resist Bedlow either before or after entering Mother Carey's? Did she cry out in distress? Did she attempt to escape—or voluntarily remain in that back room until late the next morning? The answer, as witnesses would prove, he told the jurors, was no. The only real question, he suggested, was: Why had she claimed to have been raped in the first place?

"If we can prove these facts," Thompson told the jurors, "you will without hesitation, discover that the whole is a scene of iniquity, contrived to extort money from an aged infirm father, or to deprive an innocent man of his life."

What Thompson promised the jury was nothing less than a counternarrative that evoked Hale's worst fears of female malice, greed, and vengefulness. There would be no ambiguity about the defense. The jurors would be confronted with a binary decision: to believe either Lanah Sawyer's testimony or the testimony of the defense witnesses. If they believed one narrative was true, they would have no choice but to conclude that the other was false. For the defense, this meant arguing that behind Lanah Sawyer's accusation lay some dark motive. As Thompson promised, the defense witnesses would reveal Sawyer to be "full" of "iniquity," prove that "she yielded herself a willing sacrifice on the altar of prostitution," and expose the prosecution of their client as "a scene of fraud and falsehood."

After making so much of the moral purity required of a woman to be entitled to belief in a rape case, William Thompson called his first witness: Mother Carey. She could plausibly testify only about what she had witnessed within her house—but that was all the defense strategy required. Carey would lay out the basic defense narrative and, unsurprisingly given her profession, there were at least two other women in the house that night that the defense would be able to call for confirmation and elaboration.

Mrs. Carey's testimony began with her account of the moment when Harry Bedlow knocked on her front door on the night of Wednesday, September 4. At the time, she was in bed in her front room; it was shortly after ten o'clock when the knocking roused her. This timeline was a subtle challenge to Lanah Sawyer's account, supporting what Bedlow had claimed on the Battery rather than what Sawyer heard from the clock striking and the night watchmen. More important, what Lanah Sawyer had described as a scene of resistance, repeated attempts to escape, and cries for help, Mother Carey described as a scene in which Sawyer accompanied Bedlow contentedly and would have had various opportunities to seek help or escape if she had been under duress. A number of people, Mrs. Carey testified, were "passing and repassing the street" as Bedlow and Sawyer stood outside her door; he did not seem to be holding "the Prosecutrix, who made no noise, nor struggles." Carey recounted how Bedlow demanded entrance and how she turned him away. She then returned to bed, only to be awoken by noise at the back door, where she was surprised to find Bedlow, once again demanding entrance. Carey testified that she asked Bedlow how he had gotten into her yard.

By jumping over the fence, he had replied.

This was a pointed challenge to Sawyer's account of Bedlow pushing open Mother Carey's back gate. Carey testified that this was not possible because the gate was "fastened at night so that nobody could open it from without." And if Bedlow had to jump over the fence, it would have given Sawyer a chance to escape if she had been so inclined.

Mother Carey went on to testify that she didn't even see Sawyer at the back door when she let Bedlow in, or later on—and that Sawyer "made no noise in the night." Carey went further, testifying that if Sawyer had made noises she would have heard them. She did not go back to sleep that night, she claimed—and "words spoken in one room of her house could almost be heard in any other."

Having challenged Sawyer's claims that Bedlow had forced her into the house and that she cried out in protest, Mother Carey went on to challenge Sawyer's account of having been trapped in the dark room.

Carey testified that there were "no fastenings to the windows of the room" and "no fastening to its door." Moreover, Carey insisted, there was no means of making the room where they slept "totally dark, for part of the shutter was broke, and the least light might be seen through the cracks." Here, Carey's testimony was misleading—though the prosecution seems to have let it pass. Whatever the state of the window shutters, with no moon that night, the room would have been completely dark once Bedlow snuffed out the candle. The sun hadn't begun to rise the next morning until about five thirty.

In the morning, Mrs. Carey continued, the family arose, had breakfast at eight o'clock, and "passed and repassed thro' the entry several times." Sawyer did not come out of the room until ten o'clock. Carey confirmed Sawyer's account of their exchange in the hallway—"except as to wishing to meet her father"—and added that "she appeared perfectly composed and satisfied."

Up to this point, Carey's account generally conformed to the broad outlines of Sawyer's testimony—the basic sequence of events closely overlapped. The main difference was in what Carey described as Sawyer's demeanor. By depicting her as complaisant, Mother Carey indicated that the young woman had failed three of Hale's tests. She had not resisted. She had not cried out. And she had not reported the assault at her earliest opportunity.

The defense had carefully planned their argument so that the answer to all of these questions was no. After Carey's testimony, Thompson would call other witnesses to support her version of events. But first, he had another job for the aging brothel keeper. He wanted not just to undermine Sawyer's credibility but also to give the jurors an explanation for her behavior. Why would she have made a false accusation against Bedlow? That was the question Mother Carey was about to answer.

If Sawyer and the prosecution had been wondering why she had been asked on cross-examination about having revisited Mrs. Carey's house the next evening and whether she had gone to Bedlow's house, the answer came as a stunning surprise.

Mother Carey told the court that on Thursday evening "at the hour of lighting candles"—about seven o'clock, when twilight faded—Miss Sawyer reappeared on her doorstep.

"The Prosecutrix called," Mrs. Carey said, "and enquired for Mr. Bedlow."

He is not here, Mrs. Carey replied.

Mother Carey invited Lanah in and offered her some pumpkin pie. She had some herself, and gave some to another woman who was also there in her front room.

Sawyer refused the pie, according to Carey, but lingered even after the two women finished eating.

When the other woman went into the kitchen to see her son—the toddler who had slept in the back room—Mother Carey asked Lanah to move into another, more private, room. It was evening in a brothel, after all, and she thought "some gentlemen might come in."

No, Lanah replied, according to Mrs. Carey, *I cannot stay.*

If you leave a message for Mr. Bedlow, Mother Carey reported offering, *it will be conveyed to him.*

"Give my love to him," Sawyer allegedly said, "and tell him if I can get out tomorrow-evening, I will meet him."

Then, Mrs. Carey testified, Sawyer departed.

And with that image of an awkward, anxious Lanah Sawyer desperate to rekindle a romance in which Harry Bedlow had already lost all interest, Mother Carey's testimony concluded.

This testimony was a bombshell. In her own testimony, Lanah had described going to Mrs. Carey's only twice—the first time on Wednesday night when she was raped, and the second time on Friday with her father and Mr. Hone. Under cross-examination, Lanah had specifically denied stopping at Mrs. Carey's that Thursday evening.

By testifying that this extra visit had taken place, Mrs. Carey opened up an irreconcilable challenge to Sawyer's account. The jurors might have been able to convince themselves that there was some reasonable explanation for the other differences in Lanah's and Mrs. Carey's accounts—all of which involved Lanah's comportment on the night of the alleged rape. Perhaps Lanah really had been there unwillingly, had struggled, and even cried out for help—and Mother Carey had simply not perceived, or correctly interpreted, what was happening. Perhaps Sawyer had attempted to get out of the room that night and failed—even if the shutter was broken and the door without a latch. Sawyer might simply have been too upset and confused, fumbling around in the dark, to find her way out.

But this alleged visit on the evening after the rape forced a decision one way or the other. Either Mrs. Carey was lying about that Thursday evening visit or Miss Sawyer was.

To bolster their case, Thompson lined up a series of witnesses to confirm the essential points of Carey's account—and, in some cases, to elaborate on it.

After Mother Carey's explosive testimony, the rest of the defense witnesses were anticlimactic—most of them called by Thompson simply to confirm key aspects of Carey's story.

The first of these witnesses was Ann McFall, the "lady" Mrs. Carey had described as present that Thursday evening when Lanah Sawyer had supposedly come by in search of Bedlow. McFall lived in a humble rental around the corner on Spruce Street, was currently married to a house carpenter, and worked as a laundress—menial work that involved cauldrons of steaming water and heavy physical labor. The two women were related by previous marriages to members of the Glover family—and young Thomas Glover, who slept in the back room, was both Ann Glover McFall's son and Ann Glover Carey's godson.

Thompson's purpose in calling McFall was simple: to confirm Mrs. Carey's claim that Lanah Sawyer had returned Thursday evening in an effort to reconnect with Bedlow. As the *Report* put it, McFall "repeated exactly the story of the pumpkin pie." According to McFall, she knew Lanah by sight, having frequently passed by her home and noticed her looking out over the bottom half of the front door.

The next two witnesses were women who evidently worked in Carey's brothel and had been there on the night in question: Mary Franklin, who testified that she was in bed with Mrs. Carey when Bedlow arrived at the front door, and Elizabeth Smith, who testified, pointedly, that she spent the night "alone" in bed in another room at the back of the house. Like Mother Carey, they attested that at no point did they see or hear any sign of resistance from Sawyer—no "struggling," no "noises," no "screams." Franklin confirmed Carey's account of the structure of the house and the window shutters and door in the back room. Indeed, her only departure from Carey's account was that she reported that Bedlow and Sawyer did make some sounds during the night: "she heard them converse, and a woman's laugh." Smith's testimony mirrored Franklin's on almost every point. Finally, Smith added that she "Saw the Prosecutrix go out next morning, perfectly composed and easy."

Next, the defense called Thomas McCready, a house carpenter. If it were unclear at first what a carpenter who neither knew Sawyer nor had witnessed any of the events in question could offer by way of evidence, soon all was revealed. He opened his testimony by reporting that "by the desire of the Prisoner's father" he had inspected Mrs. Carey's property and made detailed observations. Given the Bedlows' deep involvement in real estate development and McCready's trade as a carpenter, he may well have worked for them before. Certainly, he knew Harry Bedlow by sight: McCready reported that "after the affair" he had seen him both "in the streets" and "attending a building." Now, he appeared in court on Bedlow's behalf as a kind of expert witness.

Weeks earlier, when Mrs. Carey had refused to allow John Callanan and Samuel Hone into the back room she had, in effect, maintained control over information about the state of her property at the time Lanah Sawyer had been there. Hiring McCready had been part of the defense team's efforts to capitalize on this advantage. The defense had made the physical structure of Mrs. Carey's house central to their case. They had asserted that Bedlow could not have dragged Sawyer by pushing open the back gate and that she could not have been trapped in the back room. Moreover, the defense had not contented itself with the claim that none of the other women in the house that night had heard any indication of struggle from Lanah Sawyer. They had used the flimsy construction of the house to make the argument that if no sounds of struggle or distress had been *heard* it could only have been because they had not been *made*.

In the witness box, McCready noted that "the height of the garden gate was 7 foot"—supporting Thompson's characterization of the back fence as "high." Evidently, though, he did not go on to describe its fastenings—or explain how Bedlow could have "jumped" over such a barrier. His testimony about the house itself was more detailed. Unsurprisingly for a structure that could not have been more than twenty-five feet wide, he reported that quarters inside were close. The back passageway was only three feet wide. The distance between the bed in the back room where "the fact" had taken place was no more than thirteen feet from the bed in the room opposite where Elizabeth Smith had been sleeping—and no more than fourteen feet from Mother Carey's bed in the front room. Sound would not have had to travel far from Lanah Sawyer's lips to reach the other women's ears. Moreover, while plaster and lath walls might have dampened sound, McCready testified that "all the rooms in the house are divided from each other by a thin boarded partition." These aspects of his testimony were consistent with the claims of Carey and the other women in the house that night. But in the surviving record of his testimony, there is no mention of the state of the window shutter in the back room, nor of the nature of the fastenings, if any, on its window and door.

The last witness called by the defense was the mayor, Richard Varick.

For the defense, this was something of a gamble. There were several key facts that the mayor was well positioned to confirm. One was that he had not issued the warrant for Bedlow's arrest until September 10, almost a week after the fact. This went to the question of whether Lanah Sawyer had waited longer than necessary to file an official complaint. Second, the defense wanted to emphasize Bedlow's response to the news that he was facing arrest. Instead of attempting to flee—a sign, according to Hale, of guilt—he and his father had voluntarily presented themselves at the mayor's office. In the witness box, Varick left it unclear whether Bedlow had come to him knowing that an arrest warrant for him had already been issued. The mayor told the story of Harry Bedlow's complaint against John Callanan for assault and how he had "amused" the young man with making out his complaint while he summoned an officer to take him into custody. Presumably, the defense—conscious of the weight Hale lent to the danger that a woman might charge a man with rape as part of some other, nefarious scheme—also wanted it known that the complaint itself had been prepared by the law partnership of Evertson & Riggs. This the mayor confirmed, adding vaguely that the statement "was a little inaccurate, & amended by the Witness." All of this, presumably, they were using to build the case that Sawyer had not reported the alleged crime promptly enough, that her enraged stepfather may have encouraged her to fabricate the rape charge, that the attorneys may have encouraged her to press charges as part of a plan to extract money from the Bedlows, and that Harry, far from having avoided legal authorities in the aftermath of his interactions with Sawyer and her father, had gone to the mayor himself.

At the same time, the defense was well aware that there were risks in calling the mayor to testify—and exposing him to cross-examination by the prosecution. The mayor's condescending attitude toward young Bedlow was hardly helpful. Nor was the fact that he had been clearly confident enough in Sawyer's complaint to issue the warrant in the first place. But it was the last portion of the mayor's testimony that was most damaging to the defense—for it went to the credibility of their key witness, Mother Carey.

The defense team was helpless to stop the mayor as he testified what happened when he had summoned Mrs. Carey and examined her about the events involving Miss Sawyer and Mr. Bedlow. As the mayor told the court, when he had questioned her—in his capacity as a magistrate in an official investigation into an alleged rape in her house—she had lied.

The court had just heard Mother Carey describing in great detail Sawyer's arrival and departure from her house. And then the court had heard from two other women who had been present in the house at the time.

As the mayor told the court, he had asked her about the night in question.

Carey had responded by insisting that neither Lanah Sawyer nor Harry Bedlow had been at her house. Indeed, the mayor reported, "she said that there was nobody in her house at the time, but a young woman and a negro wench."

Clearly, Mrs. Carey had been lying to the mayor—in the same way that Sawyer had described the old bawd lying to her father and Mr. Hone.

The defense was now forced to close its presentation of evidence, leaving the jury with the question: If Mother Carey had lied to the mayor about that, what else might she be lying about?

In the end, the defense strategy left little room for confusion or ambiguity. They wanted to confront the jury with a stark decision. Either Mrs. Carey or Lanah Sawyer had been lying. Which woman did they believe?

☙

For her part, nothing could have prepared Lanah Sawyer for the ordeal of the defense case. Even if she had been warned about what to expect, the concerted attack on her character, her motives, and her credibility had been shocking. She had summoned her courage. She had stood before a packed courtroom, not far from Bedlow himself. She had laid bare her truth. But now the outcome of the trial—Bedlow's fate, and her own—was out of her hands. What if all that she had endured, all that she had done, had not been enough?

For the attorney general, it was a practical question; his job was to manage the prosecution's trial strategy. Whatever doubts had been raised about Mrs. Carey's testimony, the prosecution team decided they needed to address several issues the defense had raised. Attorney General Lawrence asserted his right to call a series of rebuttal witnesses to prove three things—each of them tied to specific issues Hale had emphasized as important in evaluating the credibility of a woman in Lanah Sawyer's position: first, that Sawyer's "character was blameless"; second, that there had indeed been "marks of violence" on her body; third, that there was no basis for the defense lawyer's insinuations that her accusation against Bedlow was part of some dark scheme for revenge or financial gain.

The first witness for the people called by the attorney general was Lanah's stepfather, John Callanan. His testimony was primarily a chance to emphasize that both Harry Bedlow and Mrs. Carey had lied to him in the same way Carey later lied to the mayor. When he learned that his daughter had been "absent" that fateful Wednesday night, Callanan began, he was "extremely alarmed." Callanan recounted how he had learned from Samuel Hone that she had been with Bedlow, how they went out to "search the city," and what happened when they caught up with Bedlow. When Callanan "accosted" Bedlow and "demanded where his daughter was," Bedlow had responded with one lie after another: "the Prisoner, at first, said he knew nothing about her—but afterwards pretended he had taken her home." Callanan then launched into an account of the "scuffle" that broke out. At this point, as the *Report* of the trial indicates, Callanan "was stopped by the Court." This altercation, however colorful and important to Callanan's sense of masculine honor, was irrelevant to the rape charge—and the defense may well have objected in an effort to stop Callanan before he recounted how Bedlow had attempted to use this incident to intimidate Callanan in the run-up to the trial.

Callanan's testimony resumed with his return home that evening, only to find that Sawyer was not there, and his subsequent conversation with Samuel Hone, in which the younger man offered to tell him where his daughter was if he "promised not to beat her, which he did." For the prosecution, the decision to call attention to this incident was a risk. On the one hand, it supported a key element of Sawyer's account, showing that she was not alone in worrying that her stepfather might react to her return with impetuous violence. This, in turn, addressed the defense claim that she had taken too long to report her rape; it offered the jurors a simple rationale for why, after leaving Mother Carey's, Sawyer hadn't just gone home immediately. On the other hand, the image of a violent, domineering stepfather could also be turned to support the insinuation of Bedlow's lawyer William Thompson that Callanan had coerced Sawyer into lodging the rape complaint. To navigate these pitfalls, Callanan explained that "he told Mr. Hone if his daughter was wrong, he would turn her out of doors, if right he would say nothing to her." Then, Callanan testified that he had not repeated this declaration to his daughter and that he didn't have any reason to believe that it ever "came to her ears."

Finally, Callanan testified that after he saw his stepdaughter the next morning and heard her story, he "made her go with him and Mr. Hone to Mrs. Carey's." His detailed testimony about what happened next was another opportunity to corroborate Sawyer's earlier account. And it was another opportunity to reiterate that Mrs. Carey's response, when confronted about her involvement in what had happened to Sawyer, had— like Bedlow's—been to lie and stonewall. He told the court how he "demanded of Mrs. Carey whether she knew the Prosecutrix," and how "Mrs. Carey repeatedly said, in answer to different interrogatories, that she had never seen her before." Callanan then "demanded a sight of Mrs. Carey's back room." But she refused.

At the end of his testimony, presumably prompted by a pointed question, Callanan returned to the defense insinuation that he had pressured his daughter into making the accusation against Bedlow. In the witness box, Callanan had acknowledged his violent temper and harsh treatment of his daughter. He had described his anger at her absence, his confrontation with Bedlow, his neighbor's fear that he might beat Sawyer impulsively before hearing her out, and the fact that he had "made" her return to Mrs. Carey's against her will. But Callanan told the court that he "never threatened his daughter, nor compelled her to bring this prosecution, but left her to her own will."

The next witness for the people was Samuel Hone. He had been at Callanan's side during most of the events just described, but he had also witnessed crucial events before that. Hone's testimony began some five weeks earlier, on the late-August Monday morning after he had seen Bedlow accompany Sawyer home. His account of their exchange—his comment about her "smart Beau," whom he identified as "Harry Bedlow," and her response that the man was actually "lawyer Smith"—matched hers almost verbatim, with one exception. Hone testified that "he did not mention the character of the Prisoner to her, or that he was a great rake." That correction aside, Hone's testimony emphasized the lengths Bedlow had gone to in order to deceive and manipulate Sawyer. It was a scheme that could only have succeeded because of her innocence, guilelessness, and naïveté.

He described Callanan as "much alarmed at what had become of his daughter" and recounted their search for her and the confrontation with Bedlow, who at first denied knowing Sawyer and then claimed to have escorted her home. And he described his concern, after returning home, about how Callanan would react when reunited with Sawyer: "knowing Mr. Callahan to be a very violent man, and apprehensive he might beat her, he exacted a promise from him, not to do it, before he discovered where she was." Hone went on to say that he didn't tell Sawyer about her stepfather's threat "nor knows that she heard it" from anyone else. The upshot was that her fear of her stepfather's violence and anger were realistic, but that there had been no threat influencing her decision to point the finger of blame at Bedlow. Finally, Mr. Hone described their visit to Mrs. Carey's the next day: "Mr. Callahan asked her if she knew that young woman; Mrs. Carey replied she had never seen her before; Mrs. Carey also refused to shew her back room."

Hone was, thus, the second witness (along with Callanan) to testify that Bedlow had lied about having been with Sawyer. And he was the fourth witness (along with Callanan, Sawyer herself, and the mayor) to testify that Carey had lied about Sawyer's ever having been at her house. His testimony also reiterated that Carey had denied them a chance to view the back room, the physical features of which would become so important to the defense case.

Next, the prosecution turned to a series of witnesses—Lanah's mother; her neighbor Mrs. Hone; and her cousin Mrs. Harper—to corroborate Sawyer's account of how she returned home and disclosed her story and to establish that they had seen, in the attorney general's words, "marks of violence on her."

Sawyer's mother, Jane Callanan, began with the scene at the Hone house that Thursday evening when she saw Lanah for the first time after her return. She acknowledged that she was "extremely angry" at her daughter and that her "relation" Mrs. Harper had taken Lanah home for the night—only to return shortly thereafter to report that "her daughter's linen was discoloured, and that she must have had connection with a man." In the morning, Callanan went to Mrs. Harper's and "examined her daughter's linen, and found it very bloody; and that she could no longer be a virgin; her daughter then told her the whole story." Callanan testified that she mentioned to Sawyer "her father's anger." For Jane Callanan, speaking about such things in so public a setting could not have been easy; for Lanah, hearing her mother describe these intimate details must have been a new humiliation.

Mrs. Hannah Hone was then called, and testified about the events that she had witnessed the evening after Sawyer had gone missing—the timing of which had become more crucial now that Mrs. Carey had claimed that Sawyer had been at her house looking for a way to rekindle her relationship with Bedlow that evening around dusk. Hannah Hone testified that Sawyer had come to her home on Thursday evening at "a little after seven." Because company was there, Hone didn't ask her any questions. Sawyer stayed until after nine o'clock, when her mother arrived and Mrs. Harper took Sawyer away.

This sequence of events was confirmed by Mrs. Lucretia Harper, who testified next. She described her visit at the Hones' that evening, Sawyer's arrival "a little after 7," the tumultuous reunion with her mother around nine, and her intervention and decision to bring Sawyer back to her house to spend the night. She described her clandestine examination of Sawyer's "linen, and evident marks of her no longer being a virgin," her report to Jane Callanan, and the scene the next morning, when Jane Callanan arrived, threw Lanah down, examined her linens, and demanded her story.

In addition to confirming the signs of violence on Sawyer's person, there were two other key aspects of Harper's testimony. First, she confirmed that the time Lanah arrived at her house was "a little after 7." This was about half an hour after sunset, the time when twilight faded and night fell. That, in turn, was precisely the time when Sawyer had, according to Mother Carey, called at her house, lingered while she and Mrs. McFall ate pumpkin pie, and then spoken privately about reconnecting with Bedlow: "at the hour of lighting candles," in Carey's words; "at dark" in McFall's. There simply wasn't time for that interlude to have taken place—if Sawyer's own account of her movements that evening were accurate. Sawyer had said that she had finally left Mrs. Bruce's shortly before seven, gone up to Spruce Street (about a twelve-minute walk)—where her friend Miss Pine and a neighbor, Mr. Towt, had agreed to escort her home (about a five-minute walk)—and then, finding that her parents were not there, she had gone across the street to the Hones' and arrived there shortly after seven. That endpoint had now been confirmed by two other witnesses.

The second crucial part of Harper's testimony was that on Friday morning, when Sawyer finally got a chance to tell her mother what had happened, the story she told was "extremely similar to that given in evidence." Despite the vagaries of human memory, it was typically assumed then—as now—that if a witness's story remains consistent from one telling to the next it is more likely to be true. Moreover, Harper's account challenged the defense claim that Lanah had invented the rape accusation under pressure from her father.

Finally, at the end of Harper's testimony, the focus shifted to another line of argument: that Sawyer was a young woman of good character. This was significant because the English legal authorities Hale and Blackstone had made establishing whether a woman pressing an accusation of rape was of "good fame" a crucial barometer of her credibility—as Bedlow's lawyer William Thompson had emphasized in his opening argument. Harper attested, perhaps in response to a question from the attorney general, that "the character of the Prosecutrix is generally good and she reputed to be a discreet, prudent girl, never kept much company."

To support this characterization of Sawyer, the attorney general turned to a series of other witnesses, beginning with two men of property and standing—men of approximately the same social status as the jurors.

Robert Dowle was an English-born clock- and watchmaker who lived a few blocks south of Sawyer in a substantial house he rented at the corner of Gold Street and Maiden Lane. He testified that he had known Sawyer for some time, that he had always "esteemed her a modest girl," and that she was "generally reputed to be so."

George Warner was a prosperous sailmaker, with a reputation as a staunch Patriot and as a deeply religious member of Trinity Parish, who hosted "meetings of exhortation, singing, and prayer." Warner testified that the "general character of the Prosecutrix was good" and that she was "esteemed to be modest and prudent."

The district attorney also presented two women who knew Sawyer personally, and as peers thus had a more intimate knowledge of her character and behavior. Isabella McDonald lived up near the Bowery on Harman Street (which was named after Harry Bedlow's maternal grandfather). Somewhat older than Sawyer, she had been married for just over a decade to a schoolteacher. She testified that she had been acquainted with Sawyer for two years and "thought her a very discreet, prudent, modest girl" and confirmed that "she was generally esteemed so."

Elizabeth Aubrick—a relative of the tanner Earnest Aubrick, who lived a few blocks up Gold Street from Lanah's home—came next. She testified that she had known Sawyer about fourteen months and had actually lived for two months in the same house with her—presumably the Callanans'—"without ever seeing any lightness in her conduct." Invoking a familiar litany of maidenly virtues, Aubrick attested that Lanah "was generally thought a modest, prudent, and discreet girl."

Finally, the attorney general presented two witnesses as part of an effort to show that Mother Carey's pumpkin pie story could not be true. He wanted to prove that Lanah Sawyer's own testimony about her movements on that Thursday evening had been accurate. And he did so by focusing on the timeline, which other witnesses corroborated: there simply hadn't been enough time for that interlude given the time Lanah left Mrs. Bruce's and the time she arrived on Spruce Street.

He began with the question of when Sawyer's visit with her aunt that afternoon had ended. A witness named Mary Caswell—likely a servant of Mrs. Bruce's—had been there that evening and confirmed the crucial details of Sawyer's account. Caswell attested that "the Prosecutrix, on Thursday afternoon, came to Mrs. Bruce's to see an aged lady, that she appeared very much down and dejected; stayed to tea, and went away between 6 and 7—nearer 7."

The final witness in the trial was Robert Towt, a prosperous shoemaker who had been named one of the city's two inspectors of sole leather shortly after the revolution. Although he owned two valuable houses in the city's most fashionable neighborhood near the Battery (as it happened, on the same block as Mrs. Bruce's house), he rented them out and lived in a much more modest dwelling he rented on Spruce Street, with his wife, Sarah, several daughters around Lanah's age, and an enslaved worker.

Towt testified that "on Thursday evening, about seven, or a little after" he saw the Prosecutrix walking down Spruce Street. Sawyer was "called to by Miss Pine, then looking over her door." Towt went into another neighbor's house but was, sometime later, called out by his wife to accompany Sawyer home. Towt and his wife were not apprehensive that Lanah might deviate from the route home and go into "an improper place." "She was a decent girl," Towt emphasized. Rather, she needed an escort because "she was afraid of her father." Towt arranged for Sawyer to walk with Miss Pine while he would follow discreetly on the other side of the street for the short walk to her home. He witnessed Sawyer arrive at her stepfather's house, discover that her parents were not home, and go over to the Hones' dwelling. She was, he attested, "generally known to be of good character, modest and virtuous."

❧

With that, the first phase of the trial was over. Over the course of the day, sunlight had shifted around the courtroom: from almost overhead when the trial began around noon, evenly illuminating the large room, and then farther to the west as the afternoon progressed, until the low, raking light of late afternoon was blocked by the front of the building, suffusing the room with the indirect glow of twilight. At around seven, the huge windows went dark, and the huge candelabras hanging from the ceiling were lowered, lit, and raised back into position. Flames on the desks of the judges, court officials, and lawyers cast smaller pools of light. The trial had been going on for about seven hours—and was far from over.

Lanah Sawyer, her family, her friends, and the prosecution team all had good reason to feel optimistic. From the outset, they had known that successfully prosecuting a rape charge would require overcoming substantial challenges. The peculiar ways in which the crime of rape had come to be understood in English law after the publication of Matthew Hale's *History of the Pleas of the Crown* (1736) meant that the prosecution case would be judged by the tests he had proposed for evaluating a woman's credibility.

Lanah had explained why the timing of her reporting the crime to her parents and then to the mayor was reasonable. Her parents, several neighbors, and other relatives had shown their support of her through their testimony. They, and other witnesses—including a number of prosperous, respectable men with families of their own—testified that she had a good reputation for morality, discretion, and chastity. She had explained how she had struggled and been overpowered, how she had cried out, screamed, and spent the night trapped in the dark room at the back of Mrs. Carey's brothel. She had borne marks of violence on her clothes and on her body, and these had been inspected and seen for what they were by her cousin Lucretia Harper and by her mother. And, in telling her story, Lanah Sawyer had shown the court something about her character.

The nasty tone of Thompson's opening remarks had made it clear that Bedlow's lawyers would fight back ruthlessly. The testimony of Mrs. Carey and the women associated with her had been a challenge. They denied being aware of any unwillingness on Sawyer's part that evening; denied having heard her scream, cry out, or struggle; denied that the window or door fastenings could have prevented her from leaving at will; denied that she seemed upset in the morning. And they had also testified that she had come back looking for Bedlow later that day. The implication was that she had come willingly, been jilted, and then cried rape for revenge. On the other hand, this testimony came primarily from Mrs. Carey, a notorious brothel keeper and admitted liar, and from women who worked for her—all of whom could have been accused as accessories to Sawyer's rape. How credible would the jurors find them?

Taking no chances, the prosecution had rebutted Mrs. Carey's counternarrative on three fronts. As for whether Lanah had been trapped in the room, they had brought forward witnesses who testified that Mrs. Carey had refused them access to it immediately after the crime—suggesting that the window fastening and door latch might have been altered after the fact. As to whether Lanah had come back to Mrs. Carey's looking for Harry Bedlow, the prosecution had brought forward witnesses to show that no such visit could have taken place because there had not been time for it. Most damningly, perhaps, at least three witnesses had testified that Mrs. Carey was a liar. The mayor himself had testified that she lied to him about Sawyer and Bedlow during his official inquiry. Lanah's stepfather and Mr. Hone also had testified that she had lied to them the week before, when they had first confronted her.

Ultimately, it would be up to the jurors to decide who was telling the truth.

But before then, a phalanx of attorneys stood ready to argue for their own positions—about what to believe and about who mattered.

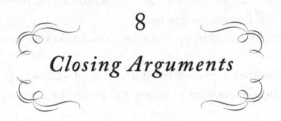

8

Closing Arguments

A s the attorneys shuffled their notes and prepared for their closing arguments, Lanah had no reason to suspect that among the spectators shifting in their seats was a thirty-year-old English gentleman struggling to make a permanent record of the proceedings. He was not a reporter; the city's newspaper rarely published anything about criminal trials other than the names of those found guilty. The clerk, as well as the judges and the lawyers for the prosecution and defense, typically took notes for their own purposes, but shorthand was not yet in common use, and they could capture only so much of what was said. There was nothing like a modern stenographer preparing a word-for-word transcript. In the official minutes of the Bedlow trial, all that was recorded of Lanah Sawyer's testimony was her name, at the head of a list of witnesses. No record was made of the names of the contending attorneys, who were set to play such a crucial role piecing together the evidence, crafting narratives, and telling the jurors how to interpret them in light of the law.

The young Englishman William Wyche had arrived with the tools he needed to take careful running notes—folded sheets of paper and a pencil, perhaps, or a lap desk complete with quills and ink. But the cramped seats and jostling elbows he encountered in the "crowded auditory" disrupted his plans. He observed the trial intently, wrote down what he could, and relied for the rest on a memory trained by long years of schooling that emphasized learning by rote. Ultimately, the detailed record he produced became the first published report of an American rape trial.

Wyche's interest in the trial was both professional and personal. An ambitious young lawyer, he sought to distinguish himself in his adopted homeland by capitalizing on his training in London, a metropolis with a population twenty times that of New York and a far more sophisticated and elaborate legal culture. Since his arrival in New York two years earlier, Wyche had been clerking for the prosperous attorney Cary Ludlow—whose son Edmund was, at the time of the Bedlow trial, under indictment for rape in Queens County. For Wyche, the Bedlow trial was a rare chance to observe prominent attorneys at work in a high-stakes trial involving another gentleman accused of raping an acquaintance. But if Wyche felt an obligation to defend the interests of his patron's son, he also had good reason to resent the deception and especially the false show of chivalry Harry Bedlow had used to gain Lanah Sawyer's confidence and make her vulnerable.

The way "lawyer Smith" had "rescued" Lanah from street harassment was a dark inversion of the incident that had forced Wyche to leave his homeland two years earlier. According to a somewhat cryptic account in a London newspaper in the spring of 1791, Wyche had "interfered between" another gentleman and "a Lady in the Street." Enraged, the other gentleman challenged Wyche to a duel. He accepted. Neither man was much of a shot; they both missed on the first round. But neither would back down. Finally, on the third round, Wyche blew a hole in his opponent's shoulder. Soon, the illegal affair bled into the press, and Wyche had to flee the country.

Now the proceedings were coming to the stage that Wyche, as a lawyer, found most interesting: the closing arguments, in which the various attorneys attempted to control the narrative of the case and what it meant. Although often described as "summations," closing arguments could be quite long. Every lawyer on both sides of the case typically got to present his own. Taken together these summations often consumed nearly as much time as the evidence phase of the trial. In Wyche's published report of the Bedlow trial, the closing arguments went on for twice as long as the presentation of evidence. Then, as now, the sheer length of closing arguments could be strategic, an effort by the defense to drown out the voice of a sympathetic victim like Lanah Sawyer with a torrent of talk.

At the same time, the closing arguments had special legal importance. In any trial, the evidence presented is specific and unique. But the arguments made by lawyers and the opinions of the judges could have much broader application and shape future cases. Lawyers could learn from each other's trial strategies and successful arguments. Trial by trial, the law itself was constantly evolving.

In New York, as in England, the crime of rape was still defined by a brief, vague, medieval statute—a single convoluted sentence written more than five hundred years earlier. It provided that none shall "ravish," or kidnap by force, any maiden under age (either with or without her consent) or "any other Woman against her will." Private prosecutions had to be initiated within forty days; there was no such limit on Crown prosecutions. Ten years later, the statute was amended to make rape a felony. Under Elizabeth I, the age of consent was specified as ten. But no statute answered some of the basic questions in a case like Lanah's. What precisely did a woman like Lanah Sawyer have to prove in order to make her case? What questions could the defense legitimately raise in order to cast doubt on her story? What standards of proof and persuasion should be applied to her testimony? Because the statutes left so many crucial questions open, lawyers and judges and commentators had wide latitude for interpretation.

In preparing for the trial, both the prosecutors working with Lanah Sawyer and the defense lawyers working for Harry Bedlow had two opportunities to shape the proceedings: they could plan the narrative of the case they wanted to advance by selecting potential witnesses and considering what their testimony might add, and they could tailor the legal implications of the narrative they presented by searching through published legal treatises for favorable arguments. Researching local case law was cumbersome; nothing like a modern compilation of case reports for New York's courts would be available until early in the next century. So American lawyers relied heavily on English legal reports and especially on English legal commentaries. Consequently, legal interpretations, expectations, and assumptions shifted over time, as lawyers, judges, and codifiers pushed and pulled—sometimes subtly, sometimes boldly—in one direction or another.

The rights of rape survivors like Lanah Sawyer were generally favored by the first major eighteenth-century work on English criminal law, William Hawkins's 1716 *Treatise of the Pleas of the Crown*. He dismissed as "very questionable" the old canard that only a consensual sexual encounter could leave a woman pregnant. He insisted that every woman was protected by the law of rape, whatever her prior behavior—even if she were a "common strumpet." He argued that anyone present and assisting a rapist could be charged as a principal offender—a position that, in the Bedlow case, would have put Ann Carey in jeopardy. He remarked on a claimant's credibility only once, noting that it would reflect badly on her if she didn't make her complaint "in a reasonable Time after the Fact." Most prominently, he offered a realistic discussion of coercion, emphasizing that the mechanisms of compulsion used against a woman could be emotional as well as physical. A sexual assault is still rape, he opined, even if "the Woman at last yielded to Violence, if such her Consent was forced by Fear of Death, or of Duress."

The problem for Lanah Sawyer and the prosecutors working the case was that subsequent publications had pushed the law forcefully in the other direction, effectively narrowing the definition of rape. Sir Matthew Hale's commentaries (1736) focused on the threat false rape accusations posed to men of property and standing like himself—or Harry Bedlow.

Hale's circumstantial tests of a woman's credibility tended to undermine charges that challenged prevailing social hierarchies and validate those that reinforced them: charges against men who were marked as outsiders, men of low status who targeted women with powerful champions, men whose only means of compulsion was physical violence. Was the woman of "good fame"? Was the place where the rape allegedly took place "remote from people, inhabitants or passengers"? Had she cried out for help? Were there signs of violence on her body? Did she report the crime "presently"—or did she "conceal the injury for any considerable time after she had opportunity to complain"? Did the accused stand to face trial—or flee? These were questions that might be satisfactorily answered by a married woman overpowered in a blitz attack by a stranger—or by a white twelve-year-old who reported being threatened by an enslaved Black man. But these conditions would not favor a delivery girl targeted by a group of gentlemen in a tavern, or a servant pressured by her master—or a young woman like Lanah Sawyer, who reported being enticed, deceived, isolated, and caught off guard, as well as physically coerced and terrorized, by an acquaintance.

Eager to limit the ability of women like Lanah Sawyer to mount effective cases, defense lawyers embraced Hale's views. And so did other authorities, like Oxford law professor Sir William Blackstone, whose

Commentaries on the Laws of England (1766–1769) quickly became the most important legal authority both in Britain and in the new American nation. Blackstone adopted Hale's discussion of the credibility of women bringing rape charges, quoted a long passage about "false and malicious" rape accusations, and emphasized the centrality of violence to the crime. Raising the bar for women like Lanah Sawyer, he and other commentators specified physical force as the form of coercion that constituted rape. Hale, following the ancient statute, had defined rape as "the carnal knowledge of a woman *against her will*." But in Blackstone's rendition, rape was "the carnal knowledge of a woman *forcibly and* against her will."

For Lanah, this narrowing of the effective legal definition of rape made prosecuting her case against Harry Bedlow more difficult. The closing arguments from both sides would be grueling. The defense's cross-examination of Lanah, and the testimony procured from Mother Carey and others, showed that they intended to challenge the key aspects of Lanah's story. Against her own account of being deceived and shocked, of crying out and struggling to escape, of being manhandled and fearing for her life, they would offer an account of a jilted lover lashing out in anger—a story not of rape but of seduction. They would challenge Lanah's account of what had happened that night and contest the legal standards by which it should be judged. Would the defense team content themselves with the standards Hale and Blackstone had set forth? Or would they seek to shift the law of rape even further, exaggerating distrust of women like Lanah Sawyer and sympathy for men like Harry Bedlow?

❧

Brockholst Livingston rose to begin a stream of defense arguments questioning Lanah's testimony that would go on for hours. Nearly forty, Livingston had short, dark, Roman-style hair that suggested his republican politics and a prominent, aquiline nose that marked him as a member of one of the region's preeminent families. He lived in one of the most expensive, extravagantly furnished homes in the city with his second wife, several children, and four enslaved people. Livingston's father, recently retired from a long stint as the governor of New Jersey, had started out as an attorney; back in 1754, he had represented the four gentlemen accused of raping twelve-year-old Mary Anderson in a tavern, securing their acquittal and savaging her mother. Since then, no woman in the city had dared to bring another sexual assault charge against a gentleman—until Lanah. Now, Livingston faced the same challenge his father had: presenting a simple, compelling theory of the case that would convince the jurors that the real victim in this case was not the naïve young sewing girl who had testified earlier but rather the self-indulgent gentleman confined to the prisoner's box.

Lanah sat silenced—reduced to the role of an observer in this phase of the trial. The defense would not bother trying to shift the jurors' impressions of Harry Bedlow's character. They didn't need him to be anything other than what he already seemed: a rake. They would focus instead on creating a new version of Lanah—on transforming the young woman who had testified earlier in the day into someone entirely different.

"Gentlemen of the Jury," Livingston began, "the magnitude of the offence, the wild character of Mr. Bedlow, the stories which have been circulated, have excited the attention of the publick and have no doubt created strong prejudices against the prisoner." But, he promised, a "fair and impartial view of the evidence" would "prove that the present prosecution is founded on fraud and malice."

"The talk, gentlemen, may be long, and the hour is late; but you will not require an apology for that length, when the life of a fellow-citizen is at stake."

The jurors were not all as rich as Henry Bedlow, but they could take pride in their status as men of property and standing. This gave Livingston powerful advantages; he could play upon gender- and class-specific cultural scripts of respectability, allying the affluent Bedlow with the jurors. Lanah Sawyer, in contrast, was not only a woman but also of a much more modest background. A woman who had to work to support her family faced a double bind: her life, social world, and options were far removed from those of her elite contemporaries—but their model of gentility and decorum set the standards by which she would be judged.

Livingston began with a characteristic sleight of hand: lionizing "Lord Hale" as the principal authority on the law of rape (and referring to him by a title that reflected his brief tenure in the 1670s as England's Lord Chief Justice) while misrepresenting what Hale had actually written. Livingston told the jurors that Hale defined rape as "the carnal knowledge of a woman, forcibly and against her will." In fact, that was Blackstone's language. Hale, following the ancient statute, had not attempted to narrow the definition of the crime with a reference to force.

"Gentlemen," Livingston continued, "I by no means pretend to justify the conduct of Mr. Bedlow."

"*Prisoner at the Bar*," cried a spectator, objecting to the politesse with which Livingston had referred to the accused rapist.

"I will call him Mr. Bedlow, or the Prisoner at the Bar, as I think proper for his defense," Livingston huffed.

"Gentlemen, as I was going to observe," he continued, "Mr. Bedlow may have been highly culpable, and yet not guilty of a Rape."

This was Livingston's essential argument: Bedlow might have seduced Lanah Sawyer by devious means, but he was too genteel to resort to the gross violence of rape. Sawyer "may have fallen victim to a seduction," Livingston admitted, "but she has not experienced the monstrous brutality of a rape."

One advantage of this argument was that it allowed Livingston to address Bedlow's bad reputation. "The prisoner is known," he admitted, to be "fond of women." But "he is not known to be a wretch, so lost to every sense of honor and decency, as to be capable of satisfying his lustful appetite by a recourse to the brutality of force."

Livingston turned to a detailed examination of Sawyer's testimony—which, he argued, did not meet the standards Hale set forth. Livingston organized his summation around the questions Hale had suggested as ways of evaluating a complainant's credibility, but repeatedly misrepresented what Hale had actually written.

"What is her reputation?" Livingston asked, before conceding, "A cloud of witnesses have sworn that she is a modest, discreet, prudent girl." It would seem then that Lanah Sawyer satisfied the first of Hale's concerns: that she was indeed "of good fame" (and she was "supported by others").

If Lanah felt satisfied that the defense had been forced to concede this point, the sensation was fleeting.

Livingston next launched into an argument that the true issue was not Sawyer's public reputation but rather her inner character. "She may have had the art to carry a fair outside, while all was foul within," he suggested.

Now Lanah was becoming not just an object of observation and evaluation but of unbounded speculation. Earlier in the day, she had been a young woman full of life—someone with friends and neighbors who looked out for her, with a family that cared for her, with work to do, with dreams and fears strong enough to cloud her judgment. Now she was being reinvented as an abstraction, unmoored from specificity and humanity—a stereotype of womanhood at its worst.

From her first acquaintance with Bedlow, Livingston claimed, Sawyer's behavior revealed a lack of prudence and discretion. "She walks alone through the city, at a late hour of the night—picks up the Prisoner (then an utter stranger) in the street, suffers him to convey her home, and appears to be pleased with his conversation," he began. The next Sunday, she allowed him to walk her home again and actually made an appointment to walk with him on the Battery.

Livingston acknowledged that the prisoner, in "concealing his name and assuming that of lawyer Smith," harbored guilty intentions. "This concealment is consistent with an intention to seduce," Livingston observed, but "we cannot suppose, without doing violence to our reason, that Mr. Bedlow at that instant meditated a rape."

Livingston returned to the narrative of the fateful evening, ridiculing Sawyer's behavior: "Knowing this to be Mr. Bedlow, yet willing to be deceived, she accompanies the Prisoner at a late hour on a walk; goes with him to Corre's hotel, and instead of taking a single glass of ice-cream, and returning, as would a girl, jealous of her reputation, she stays with him here a full hour and a half." Then, instead of heading home, Sawyer went with Bedlow to the Battery and stayed out very late.

The lawyer attacked Sawyer's testimony about why she was confused about the lateness of the hour, and continued, "From here, we have a lamentable tale of her being dragged by him to the door of Mrs. Carey; of her screaming aloud; the inefficacy of her resistance; and of her finally being exhausted." None of this, he claimed, was remotely credible.

But it brought Livingston to two of Hale's considerations: whether she had physically resisted and whether she had cried out. Livingston claimed that Sawyer could not have physically resisted because Bedlow wasn't strong enough to overpower her, and that the two were of equal strength.

Consider the scene at Mrs. Carey's house, he went on. How could the prisoner, exhausted by his previous exertions, hold her down and stop her mouth, while also managing to knock at the door? She was "willing to go in," he declared, and once in the room with the prisoner could have had no doubt about his intentions.

"Let me ask all of you, gentlemen, whether the description she gave amounted to a rape? Was she forced? Did the Prisoner accomplish his wishes against her will?"

After "the affair," as Livingston euphemistically termed it, Bedlow fell asleep. Why, then, did Sawyer not escape, he asked. She could not open a window without a fastening or a door without a latch? In the morning, she heard no noise as others walked through the passage. For hours after the sun rose, she saw no light coming through the broken window shutter.

Dismissing Sawyer's account as a "string of falsehoods," Livingston shifted to Mother Carey's testimony. Admitting that Carey's occupation as a brothel keeper might harm her credibility, Livingston did his best to discount previous testimony that showed the old woman had lied repeatedly and suggested that even though she kept a whorehouse, "still it is one of a decent kind."

Carey's credibility was important for Livingston, because her testimony was critical to the defense arguments on two issues raised by Hale.

First: Had Sawyer actually cried out during the alleged assault? To answer this question, Livingston told the jurors, he had directed Mr. McCready to examine Carey's house and "measure the distance from room to room, from bed to bed." The results proved that "if a noise had been made, it must have been heard" by Mrs. Carey and the other women there that night. "Yet," Livingston continued, "none were heard by three people who lay in the same house; they all tell you they heard a talking and the laugh of a woman, who appeared perfectly satisfied and pleased." By emphasizing McCready's testimony about the construction of the house, Livingston skillfully drew attention away from the fact that the real question was whether Mrs. Carey and her "girls" were more credible than Lanah Sawyer. His own account was clearly exaggerated: two of the women had indeed said they heard talking and a woman's laugh, but Mrs. Carey had insisted that Lanah made "no noise" at all.

Second: Had Sawyer reported what had happened soon enough? Far from it, Livingston argued. Actually, she had missed a series of opportunities. "When Miss Sawyer went out in the morning, did she make any complaint to Mrs. Carey?" Livingston asked. "Did she say I have been injured in your house, I demand redress?"

Once Sawyer was out in the street, Livingston pressed on: "Did she immediately pursue the offender? When Mr. Bedlow passed her, did she call to the people passing, stop that ravisher?"

Lanah Sawyer wore a dress like this, made of printed cotton and held together with a combination of straight pins and drawstrings.

1

Henry Bedlow (1767–1838) around the time he introduced himself to Lanah Sawyer as "lawyer Smith." His hair is styled fashionably and powdered white.

2a

2b

Susanna Rowson (1762–1824), around the time she published Charlotte Temple: A Tale of Truth *(1791), a novel about a young woman who faces ruin on the streets of New York after being misled and seduced by a rake.*

3a

Street life in Lanah Sawyer's New York. This 1810 painting shows a couple looking over a Dutch door, a sawyer cutting firewood, a boy waiting on a stoop, windows covered by solid wood shutters, and a water pump at the corner.

3b

Lanah joined "lawyer Smith" for an evening stroll in the new park at the Battery. In this view, drawn earlier that summer, couples promenade, climb up the tower, and admire the French frigate Embuscade *in the harbor.*

4 *View of New York in 1794, looking south across the Rutgers farm, with Staten Island in the distance. The fence runs along Division Street; the red roof of the Rutgers mansion is visible at the left. Henry Bedlow lived with his parents in the cluster of houses along the riverfront at center. Lanah Sawyer and her family lived downtown, near St. George's Chapel—the first steeple from the left. At the far right, Trinity Church stands at the corner of Broadway and Wall Street. This view was drawn by a refugee from the French Revolution.*

Lanah Sawyer's father was a carriage maker who built and repaired expensive vehicles like this coach, made around 1770 by the Beekman family, who emblazoned it with their family crest and had it repainted about every five years. Lanah's father died at the end of the Revolutionary War, when she was about seven. Her mother soon remarried.

Lanah Sawyer's stepfather and younger brother worked as branch pilots.
This 1795 painting shows a sleek pilot boat at sunrise racing to meet an
inbound ship and guide it into port.

Lanah Sawyer faced off against Henry Bedlow in the courtroom at the rear
of Federal Hall, which dominates Wall Street in this circa 1798 view.
In the distance, across Broadway, is Trinity Church.

Among those troubled by the outcome of the rape trial—and the defense team's disparaging treatment of Lanah Sawyer—was Frances Harison, who was married to one of Bedlow's lawyers. She is shown here, about 1795, in a fashionable white chemise dress with a drawn frill about the neck.

7a

7b

The keys to the city's debtors' prison in the 1790s, where Henry Bedlow was confined for almost two years—as attorney Alexander Hamilton worked to get him out. The larger of the two keys measures about 8½ inches.

As a girl, some of Lanah's first lessons in sewing would have been in how to repair torn and worn-out patches in clothing and linens. This ambitious darning sampler, worked in cotton thread on woven linen, was made between 1790 and 1830. It illustrates the extraordinary skill needed to match the pattern and texture of damaged fabrics.

In fact, Livingston declared, Sawyer's emotional response was consistent not with a rape but with seduction. If she had been raped, Livingston asserted, she would have been consumed with outrage: all she had to do was mention the "atrocious injury" she had received to "a single citizen," and he would have seized Bedlow and delivered him into the hands of justice. And if "delicacy" had made her reluctant to complain in the streets, she could have returned home immediately. Instead, she loitered—sitting by the river, visiting her aunt—all day.

A woman's "natural" responses to rape and seduction were almost polar opposites, Livingston insisted: on the one hand, outrage; on the other, shame. "Had she been seduced; had she been overcome through the entreaties of the Prisoner at the Bar to consent to her ruin, this would have been very natural; we might reasonably suppose that a sense of guilt had filled her with contrition and remorse; that afraid to look her parents in the face, she had retired to ruminate on her crime in solitude."

This guilt, fear, and longing drove Sawyer back to Mrs. Carey's that night, where "she enquired in a friendly manner after Mr. Bedlow" and left a solicitous message seeking to reconnect with him.

The issue, of course, was whether this visit had happened at all. "The girl denies it," Livingston acknowledged dismissively. But "who, Gentlemen of the Jury, are you to believe?" He went on, "A single interested witness, or two who derive no benefit from the event of this trial?" (Here he was referring to Mrs. Carey and Mrs. McFall, whom he described as "a poor decent woman.")

As for Sawyer, "An idea of a rape never entered her head," he insisted, until after this second visit to Mrs. Carey's, when her romantic hopes regarding Bedlow began to unravel. Even then, Livingston claimed, she failed to volunteer what had happened. "Had it not been for the impertinent curiosity of Mrs. Harper, it would have rested to this day in silence," he claimed. Instead, her secret was exposed and she was "thrown down" by her mother, who demanded an explanation: "The girl obliged to account for these appearances, to justify herself from these marks of guilt, to allay the wrath of her parents, invents this rape."

Livingston emphasized that five days passed before there was any official complaint—and no reason was given to explain this "delay."

"Another strong mark of Mr. Bedlow's innocence," Livingston declared, "was his continuance in this city, walking about the streets as usual, perfectly unconcerned." Indeed, Bedlow had even gone to the mayor to file an assault complaint against "the father of the girl." Livingston repeatedly emphasized that this visit had taken place after Bedlow had heard that a warrant for his arrest had been issued—though, in fact, no evidence had been presented to support this claim.

Ultimately, Livingston argued, the trial came down to whether one believed Mrs. Carey and her associates or Lanah Sawyer. The former had no reason to lie, he insisted, however implausibly—but the latter did.

"Keep in mind *the strong interest Miss Sawyer has* in the event," Livingston told the jurors. If a woman prosecuting a rapist does not succeed, he said, "her reputation and character are irretrievably lost, she is shunned by her former dearest connections, and life itself must become a burthen."

Miss Sawyer, he suggested, was also motivated by malice and seeking revenge. "You all know how strong the passion of revenge exists in a female breast; a deserted woman sets no bounds to her anger," he continued.

This, in short, was the defense theory of the case: "How probable is it that Miss Sawyer, finding Mr. Bedlow had no farther occasion for her, and neglected to meet her on the second night, filled with malice, meditated his destruction?"

Livingston concluded his remarks by addressing the jurymen directly: "By this time you well understand the complexion of this charge; you see the prosecutrix in her true colours; you discover her secret springs and motives, and can have no hesitation to acquit the Prisoner." Sometimes when a case was very clear, Livingston added, the jurors might declare their verdict from their seats, without even leaving the courtroom to deliberate. This, he said, was such a case. And Harry Bedlow, whose "public character" had been impugned, deserved no less. *"Renew to him the reputation destroyed through malice,"* Livingston urged the jurors, *"by acquitting him without leaving the bar."*

❦

Lanah was powerless to object as the second member of the defense team rose to continue the disorienting assault on her account, her character, her reality. Robert Troup was a man in his mid-thirties with a big belly; a round, pink face; small, dark eyes; and a calm, confident, inquiring gaze. A longtime friend of John Jay and Alexander Hamilton, he was a leading Federalist partisan and one of the region's best, and best-paid, attorneys.

*Robert Troup in the formal
robes of a counselor,
painted by Ralph Earl, 1786.*

Friends valued his "sound Sense & ardent & generous feelings." But on this occasion, his job was to be an attack dog.

Troup began with an aggressive claim. "This cause no doubt will be discussed with considerable eloquence by the Gentlemen on the opposite side," he predicted. "They will attempt to awaken your passions and feelings in behalf of the youthful Prosecutrix." But he would not stoop so low. "Reason," he assured the jurors, "is sufficient to acquit the prisoner of this scandalous yet inconsistent charge." It was a delicate maneuver. Then, as now, a juror's duty was to evaluate the evidence rationally and apply the law fairly. It was improper for lawyers to try to sway jurors with emotional appeals and the arts of eloquence.

Like Livingston, Troup cast Henry Bedlow as a man imperiled by an emotional rush to judgment—and the jurors as the guardians not only of his welfare but also of the new republic's hard-won liberties. Bedlow might not be free from "all degree of blame," but he was not the kind of "abandoned wretch" who could be guilty of a violent sexual assault. Also like his colleague, Troup cited Hale's authority while distorting what Hale had actually written. Beginning with the questions Hale had proposed as examples of circumstances that might help a jury evaluate a witness's credibility, Troup claimed instead that they constituted a rigid checklist of legally required elements. According to Hale, he told the jurors, for a woman's charge of rape to be valid, her character "must be pure and unblemished," she "must have made all the outcries in her power," and she "must have made immediate complaint of the outrage."

Troup didn't simply dismiss the testimony of Lanah Sawyer's supporting witnesses (as Livingston had done), he attacked them with open scorn. During the trial, he acknowledged, a "multitude of Witnesses" had attested that Miss Sawyer was characterized by prudence, discretion, and modesty. But who, he demanded, were these witnesses? "An obscure set of people," he declared, "perhaps of no character themselves."

Troup described Sawyer herself even more scornfully than Livingston. "Was it prudent to pick up a man in the streets, and become instantly acquainted with him?" he asked, blaming Sawyer for Bedlow's actions. "Was it discreet to go on the Battery with this stranger, and amuse herself with him beyond midnight?" The rest of her story—her account of having been dragged through the streets without raising an alarm, of being pushed through Mrs. Carey's locked back gate, of screaming for help without being heard—was, Troup declared, not just "improbable" but actually "impossible."

The defense team's basic theory—that Sawyer had been seduced but not raped—had two advantages: it offered an alternate narrative that exculpated their client from the charge of rape, and it allowed them to argue that even if he deserved blame so did she.

The defense faced two challenges: the jurymen's natural sympathy for Lanah Sawyer, who had clearly suffered grievously, and their natural skepticism of Mrs. Carey and her associates, who were beyond the pale of respectability. So the defense ignored Carey's previous lies, the danger the prosecution posed to her illegal business, and the jeopardy she faced as an accessory to a capital felony.

As for Lanah Sawyer, the defense strategy involved emphasizing the emotional distress that lay at the heart of her complaint: having stayed out all night and lost her "chastity," Troup argued, Sawyer faced the "horror" of "impending ruin." Desperate, she returned to Mrs. Carey's and tried to reconnect with Bedlow, but that effort failed, and her "only alternative" was "to acquit herself of blame by inventing a rape."

The third defense lawyer who rose to speak was, for Lanah, a familiar figure. A stout man in his mid-fifties, John Cozine lived and worked just two doors down from her, at the corner of Gold and Beekman streets—along with his wife, four children, and four enslaved people. He was later remembered as "good-humored and amiable, inclined to indolence, corpulence, and high living." But if Cozine's appearance was genial, his arguments were ugly. And for Lanah Sawyer, who had known him as a neighbor for years, they were personal.

Cozine insisted that when Sawyer accepted the invitation to walk on the Battery with "lawyer Smith," she all but agreed to have sex with him. Consider their stations in life. "Was it probable that lawyer Smith had any honorable designs in his connection with a sewing girl?" Why would he buy her ice cream if not with a view toward "illicit commerce"?

Having already employed sexualized language, Cozine seized on what he claimed was an inconsistency in Sawyer's testimony about the rape itself. "She tells us that in the act of which she complains that Mr. Bedlow did not use his right hand." But without his right hand, Cozine protested, Bedlow could not possibly have committed a rape.

Did Cozine expect the jurors to overlook how he was misrepresenting Sawyer's testimony? She hadn't said that Bedlow didn't use his right hand, only that she couldn't say what he had done with it while his left arm was across her throat, pinning her down, and choking her. But Cozine was focusing the jurors' attention on Sawyer's body during the physical act of sexual intercourse, taking advantage of attitudes deeply rooted in Western culture associating sex acts with shame and sin—and female virtue with virginity and innocence—to further degrade Sawyer in the eyes of the jurymen.

For Lanah Sawyer, this line of attack was no doubt shocking and humiliating, which may have been Cozine's purpose: to push the jurors to see her not as an innocent maiden but as a sexual creature engaged in the act of intercourse, a ruined woman who deserved neither their respect nor their concern.

In the end, Cozine insisted, the rape charge was unfounded.

"How far she may have been seduced by the Prisoner at the Bar, or won over by intreaty to consent to his desires, is a question not for me to determine," Cozine observed. Then came a final reminder that Bedlow was facing a possible death sentence. "Whatever other punishment he may deserve, the laws of this country do not for that, incur a forfeiture of his life."

⚲

As Cozine returned to his seat, yet another defense attorney rose. At forty-seven years old, Richard Harison was one of the city's richest and most distinguished attorneys. A staunch Federalist, he had been appointed the first US attorney for New York by President Washington in 1789. By 1793, he was also a trustee of King's College, the secretary of the US District Court for New York, and one of the directors of Hamilton's Bank of the United States. Through his second, much younger wife, he was related to William Wyche's patron, Cary Ludlow, whose son was the medical student under indictment for rape. Walking up and down Broadway, Lanah had repeatedly passed the Harisons' imposing town house—with its own stables, lavish furnishings, and a staff that included two free, and two enslaved, people of color.

In his long "summation," Harison repeated his colleagues' arguments that there was insufficient evidence to prove rape and that the crime, if anything, had been seduction. But he went further than Troup in disparaging the witnesses who had testified in support of Lanah's good character. Playing on common stereotypes about poor and working folk, the patrician attorney argued that the prosecution witnesses were not only socially "obscure" but also morally loose and sexually profligate. "Some young people have testified that they esteem Miss Sawyer to be a modest, discreet and prudent girl," he sniffed. But the standards of people "belonging to the same condition of life with the Prosecutrix" were far removed from those of respectable people. Young women like them, he asserted, were "accustomed" to allowing "male friends" to take "liberties."

Then he took a new tack. "Throughout the whole of her intimacy with the Prisoner," Harison argued, "the infatuation which led her on to ruin is too apparent to leave room to believe that the force used by the Prisoner to accomplish his ends, was of the kind which is necessary to constitute a rape." Having already told the jurors that the element of force was essential to the crime of rape, Harison now claimed that only a particular kind of force counted.

Essentially, Harison presented the jurors with an early version of the modern rape-culture formula of "No means yes." For a man to play along with that pretense by applying a little force was not just expected, Harison argued, it was courteous. While a man might openly embrace sexual desire, no respectable woman would acknowledge such feelings. "Any woman who is not an abandoned Prostitute, will appear to be averse to what she inwardly desires; a virtuous girl upon the point of yielding, will not appear to give a willing consent, though her manner sufficiently evidences her wishes." But this, Harison reiterated, is not the "kind of force which can be said to constitute a rape."

Rape was made a capital crime, he claimed, to punish not the "seducer" who accomplishes his aim by "entreaty, persuasion, apparent force," but rather the "ravisher" who immediately overpowers an "unwilling woman" with sheer physical "strength." Harison's implication was that whatever might happen between acquaintances like Lanah Sawyer and Harry Bedlow wasn't really rape. There was no brute, no blitz attack. All but admitting that Bedlow was guilty of seduction, though not of rape, Harison argued that criminal court was not the proper venue for holding him to account; it would have been better for Sawyer to have brought a civil action and recovered a compensation in damages for seduction. It was Bedlow's purse that should be at stake, not his life.

Finally, Harison turned to the image of Sawyer's bloodied body. "Some witnesses of the prosecution, have deposed that marks of violence appeared on the linen of Miss Sawyer, after the affair," Harison observed. But all this proved, he claimed, was that she had lost her virginity, not that she had been raped. In fact, that wasn't true—at least according to Hale. One of the circumstances he had identified for evaluating a woman's rape charge was whether she bore physical signs of blood and injury. This was the one issue raised by Hale that the defense studiously ignored.

In treating Sawyer's feelings with such callous disregard, in sexualizing her and repeatedly focusing on her body, the defense attorneys were modeling the attitude they hoped the jurors would adopt: that she was unworthy of their sympathy and concern.

❧

With the defense team's withering attack on Lanah Sawyer's character finally over, it was time for the prosecution to respond. James Kent, the private lawyer hired at the last minute by John Callanan to assist the prosecution, rose first. He was thirty, with brown, slightly hooded eyes and a penetrating, even flinty, gaze. A staunch conservative, he was long-time friends with the defense attorney Robert Troup and had served a couple of terms in the state general assembly with his fellow prosecutor Josiah Ogden Hoffman, who may have been the one who had recommended him to Callanan. Although he was a brilliant attorney, at the time of the Bedlow trial, he was struggling financially and emotionally. After moving to the city that spring, he later wrote, "I was poor and had but little business and lived in a narrow, dirty street." Then, a smallpox inoculation sparked a fever that "swept off" his young daughter. Wracked by grief, he was still struggling with depression at the time of the Bedlow trial.

Kent launched into a vigorous effort to rebut the defense case, arguing that the very aspects of Miss Sawyer's testimony that Bedlow's lawyers had sought to use against her were, in fact, evidence of her good character and credibility. He began by drawing the minds of the jurors back hours earlier, when Sawyer had stood before them to deliver her emotional testimony. "The appearance of the girl; the modest manner in which she delivered her evidence; the effect it had upon her feelings; all forcibly struck me, Gentlemen, and I trust it did you, with the opinion that truth, and nothing else, flowed from her lips."

The defense attorneys had tried to represent Sawyer as a malicious, calculating liar, motivated by vengeance and greed. In fact, Kent insisted, she was innocent and "artless," a girl who had been terribly wronged and needed the jurors' protection. Her testimony made this clear in three ways. The first was her candor: "Her very indiscretions, which the council for the Prisoner tell you impeach her credibility"—by which he meant the way in which she had allowed Bedlow to insinuate himself into her acquaintance and her decision to go out for a walk with him—Kent reminded the jurors, "she openly and unasked revealed to you." He went on: "Examine every part of her testimony, and I trust you will see a well connected tale, highly artless and probable; you will see the chequer of indiscretion and imprudence which is a forcible mark of its truth."

The second sign of Sawyer's credibility was her remarkable consistency. "She relates [her story] to her mother, then to her father, and when she comes in court and relates it again upon oath, her friends and relations tell you it is the same she told to them." Through each relation, Kent emphasized, "she does not vary from her tale a single iota."

Finally, her account was corroborated by reliable witnesses. "Every part of her testimony which could receive confirmation, has been confirmed," Kent observed, and by people "of reputation."

This confirmation left unaddressed only those aspects of Miss Sawyer's account that had—or had not—taken place inside Mother Carey's house. This, Kent emphasized, was a place where only "the most abandoned of their sex could be witnesses." Who, Kent asked the jurors, were they to believe? "An artless simple girl who never varies from her tale ... or a woman whose constant life is a scene of iniquity and guilt?"

Emphasizing his outrage and exasperation, Kent reminded the jurors of Mrs. Carey's repeated lies. "Can you believe, gentlemen, that a woman who dares to tell a lie before a public Magistrate, will scruple at perjury?" Aside from the claims of these "scandalous witnesses," Kent insisted, there was no reason to doubt the truth of Miss Sawyer's resistance, her outcries, or even the "brutal force which she experienced from Mr. Bedlow."

His final point was that Sawyer's behavior after the assault was entirely consistent with her emotional response to the assault.

The "dictates of nature" in such a circumstance, Kent concluded, are illustrated by a famous story from Roman history—the story of Lucretia. It was a story well known to many in the courtroom through countless retellings in classical works as well as renditions in contemporary poems, paintings, and excerpts in the popular press.

Lucretia was the virtuous wife of a Roman officer; while he was away, she spent her time industriously spinning alongside enslaved workers rather than relaxing in luxury like the wives of the other officers. A nobleman, jealous because she was more virtuous than his own wife, came to her villa under false pretenses, was received as an honored guest, and then crept into her bedroom at night, held her down with his left hand, and attempted to persuade her to have sex with him. When she rebuffed his entreaties and threats, he raped her. Then, according to Livy, Lucretia "sunk under the pressure of her misfortune." She sent a messenger to Rome to summon her father and her husband, who arrived to find her "sitting quite disconsolate in her bed-chamber." She burst into tears and told them what had happened: "But though my body is polluted, my soul is without stain." She implored the men to avenge her lost honor by killing her rapist—and then took up a dagger and committed suicide. Galvanized by Lucretia's rape, and moved by a host of other outrages committed by the dissipated monarchy, her family's quest for vengeance developed into a broader revolution that overthrew the ruling family, abolished the monarchy, and created the Roman republic.

For those in the courtroom—just a decade after their own revolution and the start of their own national experiment in republican rule—the story had deep resonance. For the American revolutionaries, the Roman republic had served as a powerful model and inspiration. By associating the notorious rake Bedlow with the dissipated nobleman who raped Lucretia, and the seamstress Lanah Sawyer with his virtuous spinning victim, Kent sought to do more than validate Sawyer's account of having been emotionally devastated by the assault she had survived. He was also trying to turn the defense team's snobbery and elitism back on them, as part of a republican critique of aristocratic vice. In this light, Henry Bedlow could be seen as a symbol of the debauchery and luxury of an aristocratic order overthrown by the revolution, and Lanah Sawyer and her peers—hardworking, modest, and unpretentious—as the true representatives of republican virtue.

It was the duty of the republican citizens on the jury, Kent concluded, to heed Lucretia's legendary injunction and hold the rapist to account.

❧

The trial dragged on. The court generally pushed hard to complete trials in a single sitting, even if that meant working late into the night. Eventually, the jurors would start showing such obvious signs of exhaustion that the judges would agree to recess until morning. But that point had not yet been reached on this night. The second member of the prosecution team took the floor next. After the long, audacious defense arguments, things had not looked good for Sawyer. Now, the prosecution had another chance to change the tone.

Josiah Ogden Hoffman was a young gentleman with a stylish look. At twenty-seven, he was only a year older than Bedlow and wore his hair the same way—pulled back from his forehead, powdered and frizzed, hanging down over his ears, and tied into a queue at the back. He had big gray eyes under dark brows, and a mild, inquiring, slightly plaintive air. Another prominent Federalist, he lived in an expensive house with stables on Broad Street—just a block south of Federal Hall—with his young wife and their two young daughters. His longtime friend James Kent described him as "very sociable, lively, & acutely intelligent." He was particularly renowned for his skill in the "examination of witnesses and the management of juries."

Hoffman vowed that he would refute the defense case using only evidence and reason. And he proceeded to do just that—offering a long, detailed rebuttal of the opposing lawyers' arguments about the issues raised by Hale. Curiously, though, he followed Kent's example and refrained from addressing the defense team's significant misrepresentations of Hale's actual arguments. The result was that the prosecutors allowed the defense to dictate the basic terms of the legal battle.

"It has been laid down," he began, "that a witness entitled to belief in a charge of this nature, ought to be of spotless fame." And, he argued, Sawyer met this standard. Various witnesses—including one who had lived in the same house with Sawyer for two months—had testified that she had, and deserved, a reputation for being "modest, discreet, and prudent." It was absurd to claim, as Bedlow's lawyers had, that she might have simply appeared virtuous to others.

Indeed, Hoffman emphasized, it was Sawyer's youth and good nature that had made her vulnerable to Bedlow's villainy. Was it her fault that he had struck up an acquaintance with her under false pretenses? That she had been taken in by his gallant behavior and solicitous manner? That she had believed him when he said that they would be escorted on their walk to the Battery by a friend of hers and another gentleman? "We have been told," Hoffman scoffed, that Bedlow might have set this plan in motion without the intention of going any "further than seduction"—and that a man contemplating seduction could not possibly commit a rape. But this notion was absurd. "The man who will seduce, will ravish if opportunity serves," Hoffman declared, for there are no limits "to the lawless irregularities of sensual desire."

Sadly for Lanah Sawyer, it was only when Bedlow tried to force her down Ann Street that she "suspected his baseness."

The counsel for the prisoner had claimed that Bedlow could not have dragged Miss Sawyer around to the back of Carey's house because he was too slightly built and she was too strong. Hoffman instead emphasized her feminine delicacy: "Her age, her sex, her fears, her alarms, all account for her want of strength; she tells you, besides, that with the force of the Prisoner she was quite exhausted." And what happened next? "She was brought into the room where the fact was perpetrated, by a combination of art and force, against her will."

Dramatizing this moment, Hoffman shifted to the present tense: "The Prisoner finding his prey in his power, exulting in the success of his schemes, now seizes the unhappy victim; forcibly tears off her clothes, and accomplishes his diabolical scheme."

He urged the jurors to bring the scene to mind: "Recollect the situation of the Prisoner; the whole weight of his body on the Prosecutrix, his left arm across her throat" so that she could not move. As for his right hand, Hoffman concluded: "There is no doubt, gentlemen, of its being used, you can conceive in what manner, though from her innocence she could not."

It was hardly surprising that Miss Sawyer had screamed for help and not been heard, Hoffman observed. Bedlow had, by turns, stopped her mouth, laughed aloud to drown out her voice, and forced her into a place where her outcries would fall on deaf ears. The prisoner's counsel had claimed that the "*respectable* Mrs. Carey and the *Ladies* of her house" had no reason to lie. Railing against the defense lawyers' hypocrisy, Hoffman threw Hale's vaunted queries back in their faces. "Are these witnesses of good fame?" he demanded. "We are told that the Prosecutrix is not—therefore, you ought to pay no attention to her evidence." But what about "Mrs. Carey and her *creatures*?" They lead lives of utter depravity, he declared. "Abandoned to every species of vice, how can you expect their adherence to truth?"

For Lanah Sawyer and her supporters, it was a moment to savor—a resounding vindication after hours of humiliating insinuations.

We have been told, Hoffman continued, that upon leaving Mrs. Carey's house and passing Mr. Bedlow in the street, Miss Sawyer should have called out and demanded his arrest. But this expectation, Hoffman insisted, was not reasonable. She was not, as the defense lawyers had insinuated, the kind of robust, lusty, low-class woman whose concerns the jurors might simply dismiss. Instead, Hoffman insisted, Miss Sawyer was the kind of innocent maiden celebrated in genteel culture, the kind of young woman who deserved their protection. "Overcome with horror at the transactions of the night, with shame at the involuntary loss of what was dearer to her than life, her fears and alarms reduced this miserable girl to a desponding situation." And, in fact, she had reported what had happened to her parents at her first realistic opportunity. Aware of her stepfather's violent temper, she was anxious about returning home. "This accounts for her behavior—for her retirement to solitude, to ruminate on her sad situation, and to devise the fittest means of obtaining redress for her injured innocence."

Sawyer had good reason to be cautious about advancing her official complaint, and to proceed with deliberation. Consider, Hoffman urged the jurors, the difference between her family's modest circumstances and Bedlow's great wealth: "She was going to disclose an unfortunate occurrence to the world; poor and unknown, she was going to oppose a man of rich family and connections, who might through influence and art, or the quibbles of law, obtain an acquittal."

And finally, Hoffman observed, Bedlow's decision to stay in the city to "defy" the charge against him was proof not of his innocence but rather of his "matchless assurance"—his confidence that he would be secure under the "shelter of riches, influence and the perjury of his witnesses." Bedlow's lawyers, Hoffman told the jurors, had attempted to "influence your passions in his favor" by stressing the fact that the prisoner was facing the penalty of death. But that matter, he emphasized, was not within their purview as jurors. "You are solemnly sworn to give a verdict according to evidence," he concluded. "If indeed you believe Mrs. Carey and her creatures, you must acquit him. But if you do your duty, and believe respectable testimony, you can do no otherwise than find him guilty."

ℂ

As Hoffman delivered his powerful summation, confidence in the prosecution case rose. By the time he returned to his seat, it was close to midnight. Attorney General Nathaniel Lawrence weighed his options.

At thirty-two years old, Lawrence had a long face, quizzical eyebrows, and blue, somewhat world-weary eyes—an expression of restraint, caution, control. He had left college to fight in Washington's army and gone on to hold several distinguished public offices. Despite his youth, he was not a vigorous man; it was later said that his constitution had been weakened by his experience as a British prisoner during the war, confined in one of the notorious prison hulks that haunted New York's harbor. In any case, by this point, the trial had been going on without a significant break for about twelve hours.

The defense strategy of dragging out the trial with long, elliptical closing arguments had worked to their advantage. Because the prosecution customarily spoke last, they would bear the brunt of the jurors' fatigue, the court's impatience, and their own fading spirits.

Finally, Attorney General Lawrence made his decision.

If he had read the jurors' faces and thought them to be unsympathetic to Lanah Sawyer, he presumably would have exercised his right to make one last effort to persuade them. However, he was confident about the case, reassured by the effective arguments his colleagues had just delivered, and optimistic about the mindset of the jurors.

He rose only long enough to say that because the hour was so late and his colleagues had advanced the cause of the prosecution so effectively, "he would not trouble the Court and Jury with any further observations, convinced that the Prosecutrix would obtain justice for her wrongs."

By the time the closing arguments were finally over, it was well past midnight. For Lanah, the trial had become not just a search for the truth, and a struggle to define reality, but also a test of the power of sympathy. All day she had been an object of observation and speculation—first, as she had testified, and then as witness after witness and lawyer after lawyer had talked about her. Not about what had been done to her, not about the man who had done it, but about *her*: what she had done, what she might have done, what she should have done; what she had believed or imagined or feared or desired. Ultimately, the defense team's dizzying effort to dispute and distort reality had been part of a relentless effort to transform a young woman who mattered into one who didn't. The question now facing the jury wasn't so much whether they believed Lanah Sawyer's account of what Bedlow had done but whether they cared.

In a nod to the late hour, justice Samuel Jones turned to the jury and signaled that his instructions would be brief.

"Gentlemen of the Jury," he began. "The evidence has been so fully stated by the different counsels on each side, that it is unnecessary for me to recapitulate."

Indeed, the role of a judge was not to repeat or evaluate evidence but rather to clarify for the jury key points of law and the basic questions they would have to answer, a role for which Jones was eminently qualified. He served both as a state senator and as the city's highest legal official—a role that had given him long experience presiding over trials and giving juries their instructions. Five years earlier, the governor had chosen him and Richard Varick as the best legal minds to edit a new compilation of the state's laws—and the result was widely acclaimed as masterful.

"The principles of law, quoted by Lord Hale, are extremely just," Jones told the jurors, "and ought to govern you, gentlemen, in determining the weight of the evidence." Then he reviewed four of the "circumstances" Hale had pointed to as indicators of a rape victim's credibility. In doing so, he echoed the claims advanced by Bedlow's lawyers and discounted the case mounted by the prosecutors. In effect, Jones completed the transformation of Hale's commentaries from suggestions written by a retired jurist into rigid rules that defined the nature of settled law and that were binding on the jurors.

As for Lanah's character, Jones told the jurors, she had been proven to be "pure and unblemished." But they still needed to consider the possibility that she was lying—because of her "strong interest" in seeing Bedlow convicted of rape, a possible desire for "revenge," or pressure from her family. As to whether she had made outcries, Jones told the jurors that they would have to decide who was more credible: the prosecutrix, who testified that she had screamed, or the three women (albeit women whose own character was "clearly impeachable") who testified that she had not. Like the defense attorneys, Jones skipped entirely over the next issue Hale identified: whether the prosecutrix's body or clothing had showed signs of injury. And on the last two questions identified by Hale, Jones told the jurors there was no room for debate: the answers reflected badly on the prosecution.

There had been no immediate pursuit of the prisoner, no warrant for his arrest was obtained until six days after the fact, and the private disclosure "the girl" had made to her parents in the meantime was simply "not sufficient in law," Jones told the jurors. Here, Jones had evidently been convinced by the defense team's efforts to rewrite the law of rape; neither Hale, whom he cited, nor any other published authority claimed that a rape complaint had to be formal and immediate to be valid. As to whether Bedlow had fled prosecution, Jones told the jurors, the answer was clear: he had not fled—and had actually presented himself at the mayor's office after the warrant for his arrest had been issued. This, of course, was literally true—but implied that Bedlow had gone to the mayor with the intention of turning himself in, which the evidence had shown was not at all the case.

Having made his sympathy with the defense clear, Jones concluded.

"From revolving all these circumstances in mind, you, Gentlemen of the Jury, are to determine whether the Prisoner is guilty, or not. If you are of opinion that the Prisoner's witnesses have sworn the truth; that no outcries were made; that no complaint was made to a magistrate in a reasonable time, and no legal reason assigned for the delay, and that the Prisoner's not flying is a mark of his innocence, you will undoubtedly acquit him. But if you should be of opinion that the testimony of the Prosecutrix is true, you will find him guilty."

By the time Jones finished, it was about half past midnight. The trial had arrived at the moment of decision. The jurors were informed that it was time for them to render their verdict.

The first clue to their leanings came when the jurors conferred briefly and the foreman told the court that they wished to retire to the jury room to deliberate: they would not, as Brockholst Livingston had urged, render an immediate acquittal from the bar. Clearly, they had issues to discuss. But there was no way of knowing, as they filed out, how long it would be until their return. Surrounded by attorneys, supporters, and spectators, Lanah Sawyer and Harry Bedlow waited.

After a trial of almost fifteen hours, William Wyche noted, the jurors deliberated for only fifteen minutes.

Court was called back into session, and the names of the jurors were called out, each in turn. Then the prisoner was ordered to hold up his right hand.

At one o'clock in the morning, the jury announced its decision: "NOT GUILTY."

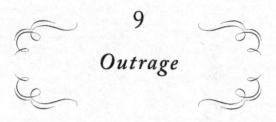

9
Outrage

As nightfall settled over the city on the sixth day after the trial, the crack of a gunshot rang out—deep and unmistakable. Lanah, no doubt, heard it with a jolt. After days of angry talk about the Bedlow trial, calls for action had roused hundreds of men to venture out into the mild evening air to enact their own kind of justice. Among them, very likely, were Lanah's hot-tempered stepfather and her fifteen-year-old brother. Others, too, heard the gunshot and immediately "suspected the cause." The earnest medical student Alexander Anderson was in a French class near the college at the time—and responded to the sound with a thrill of excitement. Having complained all fall about his fellow pupils' lax discipline, he jumped up and raced down the street, across the Fields, and to the foot of Beekman Street. In the soft glow of moonlight, he saw hundreds of men crowding the street in front of Mother Carey's house, prying up cobblestones and hurling them at the flimsy wooden structure. "Cary," he was told, had "fir'd from the house and wounded some of them which serv'd to exasperate them more."

The city's newspapers had passed over the Bedlow trial in almost complete silence. As usual, the only explicit reference in the city's papers to the entire session of the criminal court was a brief notice that Monday morning naming those convicted of capital crimes and the dates of their impending executions. Yet Saturday's *Weekly Museum* had included a letter to the editor that posed two cutting, if oblique, questions about the trial. The first referred to Mother Carey's role as a key witness for Henry Bedlow's defense, even though she could have been charged as his accessory: Was it justifiable "for any Court of Justice to admit as evidence, persons

The buttonwood tree in the churchyard to the left overlooks Mother Carey's house, which is blocked by the church itself, in this circa 1798 view south down Nassau Street and Park Row. To the right are St. Paul's Chapel and the Fields.

who are *parties concerned* in committing *atrocious crimes*, whose chief study and business it is, and who get their livelihood by it"? The second question referred to the sense that justice was effectively up for sale to anyone, like Bedlow, who could afford enough high-powered attorneys: Was it "conducive to the public good, to have so many Lawyers among us, especially in a Republican Government"? Under the letter's posture of sardonic gentility was a sense of outrage—that the legal system had failed to dispense justice, that the new nation deserved better.

The anger that erupted in the riots had been building for days. The spectators at the trial, including those who had hissed and stomped their feet at the defense team's tactics, reported what they had witnessed and shared their opinions about what it meant. According to one snobbish gentleman, citizens of "a particular class" were angered by the trial and wanted to see Bedlow hanged. "They spoke warmly against him in different companies, and upon different occasions, until, by such means encreasing the fermentation of their passions, they broke out into the extravagancies of a licentious mob." A more sympathetic observer, Alexander Anderson, noted that the rioters' sense of grievance and their choice of targets were, in fact, tightly focused: "Mrs. Cary was the Bawd whose evidence was admitted in favour of Bedlow and in whose house he was said to have forc'd Miss Sawyer," Anderson explained to his diary that night, and "this had enrag'd her acquaintances and the Public in general and it seems they were determin'd to rout this Mother Damnable."

As the men smashed their way into the house that night, Mrs. Carey and her associates fled out the back and down the alley. The men set about destroying everything left behind: first the contents of the house, and then the house itself. Anderson took up a safe vantage along with other spectators—like the baker Samuel Hone's thirteen-year-old brother Philip, who perched in a large buttonwood tree in the churchyard across the street and watched the action with boyish glee. Members of the crowd "show'd their dexterity in tumbling" the brothel's furnishings out into the street: feather beds, mahogany furniture, mirrors, and women's clothing. Meanwhile, other men hoisted themselves onto the roof and began to pull off the shingles. Working their way downward with "great industry," they tore apart the house's interior walls and dismantled its structural timbers. Soon, the ground was littered with debris, and the air was "fill'd with Feathers."

The street uprising at Mother Carey's house continued into the night and began to spread. For Mayor Richard Varick, news of the unrest was particularly unwelcome, coming as it did at the end of a day of pomp and circumstance marking his reappointment by the governor. Arriving at the scene outside Mother Carey's, he confronted a crowd in no mood to respect his authority. In emergencies, he could call upon the city's watchmen and constables, but they were no match for the hundreds of rioters. When Varick himself tried to disperse the protesters, he suffered much abuse and was forced to retreat, nursing kicks and bruises.

At ten that night, Alexander Anderson went home to bed, his coat "bedeck'd with feathers." The men were still hard at work. Some focused on razing Mother Carey's house; others broke off and attacked other bawdy houses. The protesters were joined by spectators like the young gentleman John Barent Johnson, who had attended the trial the previous week. Having spent the evening on a whirl of social calls, he stopped on the way to his lodging house to view "the operations of a Mob, who tore down the houses of Mrs. Carey—and of others of like fame."

The next morning, Alexander Anderson returned to "view the ruins" of Carey's house and found that some of the rioters had never left: "they were busy pulling down the last Timbers, which were . . . carry'd off by the poor people."

Over the course of the day, wild rumors spread through the city, terrifying the Bedlow family and their allies. Already on edge because of the partisan violence and tensions over the French Revolution, the young attorney Charles Adams, the vice president's son, feared the worst. The attorneys who had represented Bedlow in the rape trial were besieged with ugly threats and, as darkness came on, were forced to quit their houses for safety. "We will tear your houses down around your ears," the protesters blustered. And, worse: "we will show you how things are done in France." Harry Bedlow's family was forced to hire armed guards to protect their home. And Harry himself, fearing for his life, fled the city.

That evening, the rioters regrouped in larger numbers, perhaps some six hundred strong—but they also faced much more substantial opposition. As the rioters fanned out to half a dozen or more brothels, a group of citizens dedicated to "good government" rallied at Federal Hall. The mayor called up extra watchmen, more than doubling their numbers. The city's rank-and-file militiamen could not always be relied upon to turn out to quell riots, especially riots that enjoyed broad public support, but that night, a troop of elite "Light Dragoons" that reported to Bedlow's uncle Colonel Henry Rutgers did mobilize to police the city. Mounted on horses and accompanied by fanfare from a cornet player, they were mobile and intimidating. The protesters were forced to disperse.

The dragoons were back on patrol the following evening, and the Bedlows kept guards at their house for several days. The protesters did not regroup.

The battle in the streets was over. But it had changed things.

Suddenly, Lanah Sawyer and her family were not alone in their sorrow, their grief, their anger. What had been a private ordeal for her, a triumphant relief for Harry Bedlow, and a passing spectacle for others had exploded into the streets. The hundreds of men who gathered in the dark that week transformed Lanah Sawyer's failed prosecution of Harry Bedlow into a cause célèbre.

Never before in New York history had the outcome of a criminal trial provoked such mass unrest. How did so many men come to see Lanah Sawyer's ordeal as a personal affront, a political outrage? And what did it mean that her cause was, once again, in the hands of men? Indeed, by focusing their ire on female bawdy-house keepers, the protesters echoed the example of Bedlow's defense lawyers, blaming the bad behavior of men on the wrongdoing of women.

The street battle, in turn, gave rise to something equally extraordinary: a war of words in the city's newspapers that, in the days and weeks to come, reverberated across the American republic. The newspaper war made it clear why the Bedlow trial provoked such strong feelings, and it revealed bitter disputes underlying the public response.

Back during the revolution, Abigail Adams had privately voiced concerns to her husband about the exclusion of women from public affairs in the new American nation—alluding specifically to the link between women's lack of political representation and their vulnerability to sexual exploitation. And since its publication the previous year, Mary Wollstonecraft's *A Vindication of the Rights of Woman* had caused a stir on both sides of the Atlantic. Wollstonecraft forcefully claimed her own right to participate in public political debates and analyzed the sexual double standards that hobbled and degraded women. But she also faced fierce resistance—and devastating ridicule.

For weeks, Lanah Sawyer's challenge had been to tell her story and to have other people take it up. Now, hundreds of people with competing agendas were taking it up—and threatening to take it over.

❧

Even as scavengers were carting away the remains of Mother Carey's house on Tuesday morning, the street battle had begun to spread into the city's newspapers. So far, news about Lanah Sawyer's ordeal and Harry Bedlow's arrest, about the trial, about the proposed riots, had spread by word of mouth—in coffee shops and markets, in the lines for water at public pumps, in alcohol-fueled rants in taverns, and in more or less discreet tones as Lanah passed by in the street. Now the war of words, the struggle to shape the story and define its meaning, was moving into the realm of print—transferred from fixed blocks of type to sheets of paper that could be disseminated faster and farther, creating common texts that could be read, repeated, interpreted, debated, and preserved. Print had the power to transform the meaning of the riots and of Lanah's story: on the one hand, to amplify the rioters' own accounts—to explain who they were, what they had done, and why; on the other hand, to present counternarratives—to dispute, dismiss, and distort. The tendency of the popular press to exaggerate and sensationalize was on the mind of one gentleman reporting on the riots in a letter to friends in Connecticut. By the time this letter gets to you, he joked, the papers will be reporting not that six or eight brothels had been destroyed and a few people injured but rather that "one quarter" of the city has been pulled down and "half the inhabitants murdered."

To Lanah, it may have been hard to tell whether the world was coming down around her—or turning upside down. After the glare of scrutiny during the trial, she was now exposed again, the focus of a new kind of attention and controversy. What had happened to her had inspired the riots; it was rumored that her stepfather, John Callanan, had set them in motion. In reports of her ordeal, hundreds of men who had never laid eyes on her had come to see themselves. In attacks on her body and character, they had come to see attacks on their own standing, their own dignity, their own honor. For Lanah, in the aftermath of a trial in which she had effectively been erased, redrawn, and ultimately dismissed, this may have felt like an extraordinary affirmation. Yet whenever one individual's experience is used to mobilize the power of sympathy, there is always a tendency to distort and appropriate. In making Lanah's story their own, the rioters, the newspaper writers, and others also—inevitably—made it about themselves.

The newspaper war opened on Tuesday with a letter to the editor of the *Diary* that championed the previous night's attacks on bawdy houses as part of a venerable tradition of popular protest calling attention to grievances the government either would not or could not address. "You have no doubt heard that the noted Brothel, kept by Mother Carey, was demolished by a number of citizens, who met for the purpose, last evening," the letter began. The account emphasized that the protesters had destroyed property—leveling the house to its lower floor and demolishing its furnishings—but were not to blame for the night's only serious violence. "We were sorry to hear, if the report be true, that one man lost his life, by the firing of a gun, out of the house, and that two others were wounded." (In fact, the report was not quite true; several men were wounded, but none seriously.) Such protests were unfortunate, the letter continued, but they had been made necessary by the failure of the city fathers to protect the public good. "'Tis said that this noxious house has been too liberally supported for a number of years," the writer observed. "Have we not magistrates? Have we not law to punish licentious houses?"

In this telling, the attack on Carey's house bore all the hallmarks of the theatrical protests the Sons of Liberty had so effectively mobilized during the prewar imperial crisis. Such protests were highly disciplined crowd actions that avoided violence and looting and focused instead on destroying symbolic property to express a sense of political outrage. A case in point was New York's Tea Party of 1774, which John Callanan had special reason to remember. In order to protest imperial tax policies, the Sons of Liberty had charged the branch pilots with keeping English tea ships out of port. When one lying captain with fake books tricked a pilot into taking him into port, a crowd gathered on the East River waterfront, forced their way on board, discovered the proscribed cargo, and dumped it into the water. While that captain made his escape, another tea ship captain— shaken, but not harmed—was ceremoniously drummed out of port on a pilot boat. This protest tradition lived on in the years to come. On another occasion, a group of men, convinced that one of their comrades had been murdered in a bawdy house in the Holy Ground, organized an operation to demolish it. In 1788, the Doctors' Riot had been sparked not just by the revelation that students and faculty at the medical school had been stealing freshly buried bodies and illegally dissecting them but also by the failure of the city fathers to stop them. In 1792, the city again exploded in fury and frustration when the collapse of a massive financial scheme wiped out the savings of New Yorkers from all walks of life and plunged the region's economy into recession.

The day after the letter about the Bedlow riots appeared, the city's leaders struck back with a heavy-handed effort to take control of the emerging public narrative. The piece was headlined "NOTICE BY THE MAGISTRATES"—a group that included Mayor Varick and two of the men who had presided over the Bedlow trial, the recorder Samuel Jones and the alderman John Campbell—and was pointedly addressed only to the city's adult, white, male citizens. Like the defense lawyers in the previous week's trial, the magistrates focused on disparaging the rioters as low-class rabble unworthy of regard. "It is with regret the Magistrates observe to their Fellow-Citizens," the notice began, that a large portion of those involved in the "shameful riots" of the previous two nights were "Apprentices, and Negroes, as well as Sailors." Ignoring the rioters' targets and grievances, the magistrates decried the destruction of private property without due process of law. The problem, as they saw it, was a breakdown of patriarchal household governance. "We seriously recommend it to all parents, masters and mistresses," they concluded, "to keep their children, apprentices and servants, at home in the evenings."

This was not the first time the haughty mayor had overplayed his hand—and it would not be the last. In the aftermath of the riots, it was obvious that the magistrates' notice had completely ignored or fundamentally misrepresented the protesters' tactics, their social identities, their targets, and their underlying grievances. In fact, the so-called rioters had restricted themselves to tried and true tactics: they had avoided violence and focused instead on destroying, rather than looting, property—and their targets had been a series of brothels. Their motives were clearly not greed or self-interest but rather a broader sense of political grievance sparked by the previous week's trial. And they had obviously enjoyed considerable public support: in a city of only about forty thousand inhabitants, it was reported that the protesters on Tuesday night numbered some six hundred men.

So who were these men? Because the riots were illegal, no one ever publicly acknowledged participating in them. But arrest records from other incidents suggest two basic patterns. First, rioters typically hailed from across the city—indicating that actions like the attack on Mother Carey's brothel were not personal squabbles or neighborhood conflicts but broader expressions of widely shared moral or political values. Second, rioters came from a broad range of the city's middling and lower ranks. Gentlemen had little need to participate in such actions; they had other ways of making their concerns known. But the rioters were not just men on the margins, as the magistrates had implied. Among those most likely to riot were workingmen like John Callanan and his brother pilots—acting on their conviction that street protests were a legitimate, necessary way to maintain a free government.

Lanah Sawyer's stepfather was, to all appearances, just the kind of man to organize a successful protest, which required strong social networks and effective leadership. In the fall of 1793, John Callanan was one of the city's senior pilots and a member of the largest pilot company. This brotherhood of pilots, deputies, and apprentices was bound together by a dense web of social connections. Like Lanah and her family, many of the pilots worshiped at Trinity Church and, along with their wives, regularly stood as witnesses at each other's marriages and as godparents for each other's children. Moreover, most of the pilots chose to live in a small area of the city, clustering together within a block or two of John Callanan's house.

Lanah herself was connected to the city's volunteer firefighters—another tight-knit corps of men whose camaraderie, organization, and skills made them especially valuable to anyone looking to mobilize a protest. Back in the 1730s, her grandfather had been one of the founding members of the city's first official fire company; in the 1770s, her father had joined their swelling ranks. Most firemen, like the men in Lanah's family, were skilled artisans; they took pride in the strength, skill, and courage it took to safeguard their community. Even after her father's death, some of his fellow firefighters remained connected to Lanah's family. One of them was George Warner, the prosperous sailmaker who had testified on her behalf during the trial—only to be disparaged by the defense attorneys, including his neighbor Robert Troup, as part of a group of obscure and disreputable witnesses. In fact, during the Constitutional Procession of 1788, Warner had marched as the leader of his trade; by 1793 he was an influential spiritual leader within Trinity Church, the foreman of his fire company, and the president of the fire department's board of trustees. In addition to their broad social networks, firemen had the training and leadership needed to work together effectively in chaotic situations. And they were skilled in the use of fire hooks and axes to dismantle structures in order to keep fires from spreading—precisely the skills needed to destroy a brothel in the dark.

If riots are the "voice of the voiceless," as Martin Luther King Jr. later observed, what did these workingmen have to say? What about the Bedlow trial had struck them as a personal affront?

Only one of the rioters can be identified with any certainty—a supposed ringleader, who was arrested for an attack on the house of Polly Frazier, around the corner from Mother Carey's on what is now Park Row, during the second night of rioting. Anthony Clawson was only one man among hundreds, but what we can discern about him is suggestive.

Anthony Clawson was a cartman who lived with his wife, sons, and a lodger or two in a small, crowded house on Whitehall Dock, at the southern tip of the East River waterfront. His immediate neighbors included another cartman, a common laborer, a boatman, a shoemaker, two oystermen, a grocer, and a tavern keeper. The fact that Clawson didn't live close to either Mother Carey or Lanah Sawyer suggests that his motivation to join the riots was not a personal grudge or neighborhood grievance but rather some broader sense of common cause.

For a workingman like Anthony Clawson, what happened to Lanah Sawyer may well have seemed like a matter of honor. Presumably Clawson wasn't the kind of man who had the leisure to spend all day in court as a spectator at the Bedlow trial. But he had evidently heard enough to take offense: perhaps just that a gentleman had been allowed to grievously harm the daughter of a pilot with impunity; perhaps that the gentleman's attorneys had spent hours disparaging and dismissing the victim and those who had stood by her during the trial as too obscure to merit consideration even as they exalted the credibility of a notorious bawd who, by her own admission, had colluded in the young woman's ruin. In this sense honor became not a matter of truth or virtue but a question of power. And what the trial had said about power was that a profligate gentleman mattered and a workingman's daughter didn't.

By the time of the Bedlow trial, the city's cartmen, who numbered in the hundreds, had been primed to see their political resentments crystalized in the image of an aristocratic sexual predator protected by the courts. Against the backdrop of the French Revolution, the Federalists' paternalism and demands for deference had begun to rankle. Carrying merchandise and household goods throughout the bustling seaport, cartmen like Clawson earned a decent living and kept the wheels of commerce turning. Their trade was open only to men licensed by the mayor, and he, in exchange for his patronage, demanded political loyalty. In a bruising incident two years earlier, Mayor Varick had overplayed his hand, threatening to revoke the licenses of cartmen who failed to vote as he directed. Varick's political opponents had seized on the incident to inflame workingmen's resentment of Federalist elitism and to promote a more democratic vision of republican citizenship.

For workingmen like Anthony Clawson, struggling to assert their political equality and social respectability, the presence of houses of ill fame in their neighborhoods had begun to seem troublesome—a threat to their patriarchal right to regulate sexual morality and women's behavior. Since at least the end of the war, the area where Clawson lived—particularly Moore Street, an alley cutting up from the waterfront between Whitehall and Broad—had been known for its concentration of brothels. They had long been tolerated both by the city and by their neighbors. But, eventually, a group of local workingmen—grocers, barbers, house carpenters, and tavern keepers—organized a concerted effort to spur the law into action. On a single day in February 1791, the same group of eleven neighbors testified in court against four local disorderly-house keepers. Their goal was not to drive out an egregious nuisance or two but to clean up the neighborhood as a whole. It was a process that would be repeated again and again over the next century, in the city and across the country—until prostitution had been effectively pushed out of emerging working-class neighborhoods and confined to distinct red-light districts.

In the meantime, what the citizens of Moore Street got for their efforts was a lesson in frustration. All four of the disorderly-house keepers they targeted that winter were indicted, but the attorney general, Aaron Burr, allowed charges against the two men to be dropped, almost allowed one of the women to get off on a technicality, and secured only a trivial conviction against the other woman, Eleanor Ogden. Undaunted, the men determined to clean up Moore Street kept at it doggedly. When Mother Ogden emerged from her brief spell in prison only to reopen her business a few doors down Moore Street, they pursued her for almost two years. Only after her third conviction did she finally give up her trade—or, at least, move her business elsewhere. Still, the problem persisted. Long after the city prosecuted Anthony Clawson for rioting against Polly Frazier's house in the fall of 1793, a shifting coalition of local men were still working to clear Moore Street of bawdy houses.

And so, when men like John Callanan or Anthony Clawson wanted to express their outrage at what had happened to Lanah Sawyer, they did not directly challenge the powerful men immediately responsible for Lanah Sawyer's ordeal: Harry Bedlow, his lawyers, the judges responsible for the conduct of the trial, or the jurors who determined its outcome. Rather, the rioters targeted Mother Carey and other women whose guilt was only by association: Mother Giles, Mother Gibbons, and Polly Frazier are the names we know. Symbolically, these bawds were soft targets. Indeed, like the defense lawyers, the rioters focused attention not on the bad behavior of men but on the sexual disorder of women. And like city fathers who sought to shame working-class rioters by calling for more rigorous household discipline, the rioters sought to vindicate their own honor by asserting their patriarchal authority to blame, and shame, and discipline women whose only business was to serve the illicit desires of men. Instead of confronting the misogyny that had so powerfully shaped the trial's outcome, they blamed women they deemed "disorderly."

At the same time, the protesters' careful adherence to a legitimate tradition of popular protest shielded them from the efforts of the city fathers to demean and dismiss them. The magistrates' "Notice" circulated quickly within the city and beyond—but as a work of propaganda it failed. It didn't take much for newspaper readers, even those far from the city, to see its obvious distortions and omissions. And it did not appear alone. Almost a dozen competing accounts of the riots were soon circulating in the city's newspapers and in periodicals up and down the East Coast, from Charleston, South Carolina, to Windsor, Vermont.

On the day the magistrates' notice appeared, so did two other pieces about the riots. One was a studiously neutral report, in the *Daily Advertiser*, that "a number of people" had gathered and attacked several houses of "ill fame," including Mother Carey's; that gunshots from within Carey's house had wounded some of the protesters; and that the mayor himself had received minor injuries. Reprinted alongside the magistrates' notice, as it often was, this and other reports had the power to make the notice seem less an indictment of the riots than an illustration of the authoritarian elitism that sparked them.

The other piece that appeared alongside the magistrates' notice in Tuesday's papers was a sardonic send-up under the headline "AN AIRING!" Ultimately, this was the rhetorical strategy that seemed destined to defang the rioters and their potential for political subversion: not heavy-handed paternalism but lighthearted satire. "The night before last," it began, "Mother Cary's nest of CHICKENS, in the fields, was sadly interrupted by about 600 enraged citizens." It went on to mock the magistrates' remonstrations about the rioters' destruction of private property by listing some of the items thrown out of Mother Carey's windows: "all the wardrobe, consisting of petty-coats, smocks, and silks, together with the downy couches, or feather beds of the innocents." Now, the report concluded, Mayor Varick was scrambling to arrest the likes of *"Nickey Rapevenger, Ickabod Whorehater, Ebenezer Justicemonger, &c."* The piece struck a chord. It was likewise widely reprinted up and down the East Coast—and followed by a welter of other pieces treating the riots primarily as an opportunity for wordplay, innuendo, and wry humor.

In all of this, Lanah Sawyer herself was increasingly sidelined. Reading between the lines, a newspaper editor in rural Vermont observed that the magistrates' account, which described respectable men standing idly by as spectators, implied that whatever had sparked the riots must have been some "atrocious crime." None of the early reports about the riots made any mention of the Bedlow trial, the charge of rape, or Lanah Sawyer. The only individual named was Mother Carey, and few details about her were given—as though having a name like that was sufficient explanation for having one's house pulled down. What had happened to Lanah Sawyer, and the reasons Harry Bedlow's trial had been so upsetting to so many, was irrelevant. With no role in the public response to the trial, with no voice, Lanah was in danger of being erased and overwritten as men, locked in struggles with other men, spun new stories around her.

❧

68 BROADWAY, NEW YORK. WEDNESDAY,
OCTOBER 16, 1793. BEFORE 9 P.M.

Women, too, were shocked and disturbed by the Bedlow trial—and they, too, struggled to make their voices heard. A few days after the trial, the forty-six-year-old defense attorney Richard Harison decamped for Albany, leaving his twenty-seven-year-old wife, Frances, in charge of their imposing town house on Broadway, her teenaged stepchildren, her own young daughter, her aged mother-in-law, and a staff of servants that included at least two free people of color and two enslaved people. In his absence, she was besieged by ugly gossip about the trial—and then came the riots. By Wednesday, she was upset enough to write her much older husband an uncharacteristically forceful letter.

A fashionable dresser with an abundance of curly auburn hair, a long face, and penetrating blue eyes, Frances Harison typically filled her letters to her husband with affection, deference, and self-deprecating humor. She would ask for advice about minor business matters and report on her endless rounds of social visits, including sewing circles at which she and her friends sat "at our work" while "chattering about Furniture, Politics,

[Dances], and Deaths." But, in the aftermath of the Bedlow trial, their "chatter" was neither idle nor amusing. With her cousin Edmund Ludlow also facing rape charges that fall, it was hard not to take reaction to the Bedlow trial personally. And members of her social circle were shocked by what they had seen and heard about the trial—particularly, it seems, about the defense team's tactics. Shamed by the gossip about her husband and shaken by the two nights of street protests, she sat down to compose a letter to him about the riots and what their friends had been saying. Frances Harison was clearly anxious about the letter's implied criticism of her husband's professional conduct—and for good reason.

Richard Harison didn't keep his wife's letter, but she kept his response—which began by acknowledging that she had been "truly frightened" by the riots, which he went on to ridicule before dismissing everything else she had written. "I could hardly refrain from laughing," he wrote, at your "tragicomical Description of the Mob," the dragoons, and "the vast Effusion of Feathers." For Harison, the rioters were nothing more than members of "an uninformed & unsteady Populace." Even so, he was aware that the trial had been ugly—and that Bedlow wasn't exactly innocent. It was his professional duty to defend his client to the best of his ability, Harison explained, "whatever might be the Indecency of the Trial, or the Criminality of the Prisoner." Nonetheless, he went on, "I have not disgraced myself by uttering a Sentiment favorable to Vice, or occasioning a Blush in the Cheek of Modesty, which could possibly be avoided." This rebuke, it seems, had the desired effect; a week later, he wrote back to accept his wife's apology.

This was pretty much the response Abigail Adams had gotten to her 1776 letter asking her husband to remember the ladies. John Adams treated his "saucy" wife's letter as a joke. "I cannot but laugh," his response began. But he recognized her comment's radical implications. The Continental Congress was already being accused of encouraging Natives to resist settlers, Blacks to rebel against their enslavers, and apprentices to desert their masters. But we men, he concluded, know better than to give up the privileges that keep us from being completely subjected to the "Despotism of the Petticoat."

Public events thus remained the domain of men. Elite women learned to keep their political opinions to themselves—even when they were outraged by the seduction of a member of their household by a neighbor's son, or felt that the failure of city governments to curb vice justified vigilante attacks on brothels. And women writers—among the most prolific and popular writers of the day—typically restricted themselves to religious essays, sentimental poetry, and moralistic fiction. One of the features that allowed seduction novels to enjoy such widespread popularity was the moral ambiguity the genre afforded. Where one reader might see righteous anger against men's callous behavior and unfair double standards, another reader might see a pious warning that a young woman could not be too careful.

A year earlier, Mary Wollstonecraft had provoked a sensation with her trenchant critique of sexual double standards. *A Vindication of the Rights of Woman*, published in London in 1792, enjoyed brisk sales and positive reviews in journals like *New-York Magazine*. By early 1793, the book was being heavily promoted by New York booksellers. Almost immediately, Wollstonecraft's work launched "the rights of women" into common parlance. But most of the time, at least in the city's newspapers, it appeared as a joke. As one piece observed, didn't women already have the "right of scolding, crying, falling into fits, . . . and running up bills?" Another piece asserted that while women had the right "to expostulate with temper" in family arguments, their happiness ultimately depended on their submission to patriarchal household governance. In the coming years, Wollstonecraft turned to fiction as a way to explore the sexual double standards and legal disabilities that made women "slaves" to their husbands, forced poor women into prostitution, and made the consequences of seduction so dire. Her novel, left incomplete at her death, was called *Maria: or, The Wrongs of Woman*.

So it was all the more remarkable that, as Frances Harison was anxiously awaiting her husband's response to her letter about the Bedlow trial, another woman in the city was writing a letter of her own—a forceful critique of the sexual double standard at the heart of the Bedlow trial and a stinging rebuke of the magistrates' paternalistic calls for "law and order."

Then, she sent it to the editor of the *Diary* for publication—using the pen name "Justitia," after the ancient Roman goddess of justice. The letter, and its author's sex, gave him pause. On Friday, October 18, he did publish it—along with a patronizing disclaimer. "As the following Address came from the hand of a Female author," he wrote, "we could not refuse indulging her, though she is rather severe."

It was indeed a forceful letter. Justitia called attention to the sexual double standard at the heart of the controversy over the brothel riots. And, for the first time in print, she linked the civil unrest to its cause, the Bedlow trial.

The demolition of "Mrs. Cary & Co.'s houses," Justitia began with an air of wry detachment, seems to be a "matter of great grief to many of our male citizens." This was "no wonder," she went on, "considering what comfortable hours they have passed in these peaceful abodes, far from the complaints of a neglected wife, or the vexatious cries of hungry children." Earlier in the week, other writers had cast bawdy houses run by women like Mother Carey as sinks of immorality. But Justitia focused on the men who kept them in business. The magistrates have neither shut down such establishments nor shown their disapproval of them, she wrote. Instead, she concluded, it was rumored that the patrons of these establishments included some of the magistrates themselves.

The real "outrage," as Justitia saw it, was not the brothel riots but rather their provocation: "the unexpected issue of a late very important trial." The jury's astonishing verdict reflected the sexual double standard at the heart of the trial, which had revolved around "the protection of a wretch" and "the blasting of a spotless reputation."

Justitia's critique touched off howls of protest.

Monday's *Diary* included two vigorous attacks on Justitia that echoed the attacks Bedlow's lawyers had directed at Lanah Sawyer. Writers calling themselves "Candidus" and "Civis" excoriated her for daring to cast aspersions on the city fathers. It was simply wrong, Candidus claimed, to imply that the magistrates either patronized brothels or went easy on them. Justitia's letter, Civis argued, was a "gross libel" upon the city's magistrates, "fabricated" for "wicked purposes." Those wicked purposes, both men agreed, were to lessen the authority of the city fathers, to threaten the privileges of respectable citizens, and to excite "tumult among the lower classes."

Justitia was undaunted. Her response in the pages of the *Diary* two days later was a remarkable rhetorical performance, countering the anger and exaggerations of her attackers with a masterly display of coolheaded reason and wry humor. Certainly, she was well informed—even about the sentences typically meted out to convicted bawdy-house keepers.

"To the gentlemen whose sagacity pronounces my piece a libel, I have only to observe, that among our decent and thinking citizens, there are some," she wrote, "who do not consider ten pounds, or a few weeks confinement, as a sufficient correction for these disorderly places."

The power of Justitia's letters stemmed in part from her style: her aloof tone and steady composure gave the lie to the claim that only men were suited to citizenship because of their supposedly greater command of rational thought and self-control. Her letters certainly struck a nerve. A few days later, a man calling himself "Justitius" responded with a letter that was both openly misogynistic and shockingly personal.

Since the riots, Lanah Sawyer had been largely sidelined in the evolving public debate. Even the reference Justitia had made to the Bedlow trial had been vague and oblique. But Justitius's letter opened with an unmistakable reference to her—cast in the same dismissive, demeaning narrative that Bedlow's lawyers had spun out during their unending closing arguments.

"THE most penetrating mind, on observing a professed rake strolling the streets of our metropolis in the dead of night, with an unalarmed female, would scarcely have supposed that he discovered the embryo of a r—e," Justitius began, as though it were more indelicate to write out the word "rape" than to accuse Lanah Sawyer of perjury and malice. Addressing the problem of prostitution, Justitius argued that the fault lay with women—both unmarried women who refused men their sexual favors and married women who failed to sustain their husbands' sexual interest. Suggesting that Justitia herself was one of these frigid, neglected women, he concluded by chastising her "indelicacy" in writing, and writing publicly, about sex and politics.

The controversy about women authors—and appropriate topics for them—was part of a broader cultural and political conflict about the rights and capacities of men and women. The furor over Justitia's letters provoked a long critique of Civis's and Candidus's claims, and a scornful note, evidently from Justitia herself, challenging Justitius to a duel—as well as an essay vigorously defending Mary Wollstonecraft's *Vindication of the Rights of Woman*. This essay included a long reflection on the tendency of the nation's newspapers and magazines to dismiss Wollstonecraft's work, citing attacks on women's right to do anything other than "to dress, to dance, and to talk nonsense," and attacks on the book's champions as "antiquated virgins, who, having lost all hopes of making conquests by their withered persons, have commenced a new and furious" front in the war of the sexes with what "they call mental accomplishments." Before leaping to such conclusions, the essay suggested, such critics might want to first try actually reading the book. In doing so, the piece promised, they would find strong support for the conclusion that "THERE IS NO NATURAL DIFFERENCE IN THE INTELLECTUAL FACULTIES OF THE TWO SEXES."

Just as the controversy over Justitia's letters seemed to be playing itself out—her final public comment, challenging Justitius to a duel, appeared on October 25—another female voice was heard. On Saturday, October 26, the *Weekly Museum* featured a long assessment of the Bedlow trial and the ensuing controversy, written under the name "Maria."

"MUCH has been said upon the decision of a late trial," Maria began, quickly making it clear that her sympathies lay with Lanah Sawyer. The verdict's "apparent vindication and support of vice" as opposed to "unprotected innocence and virtue," she observed, has "greatly electerized" the "feelings of many." There had been much talk about the propriety of a woman walking in public with a man who turned out to be a rake. But why should innocent women be faulted for the behavior of devious men? No woman should be blamed for trusting in the good nature of a man "where there was no foundation for a suspicion of premeditated injury." The kind of confidence Lanah Sawyer had placed in "lawyer Smith" revealed nothing more than a woman's feminine virtue.

By assuming the role of arbiter of feminine propriety, Maria was using her obviously genteel social standing to vouch for Lanah Sawyer. The ugly insinuations made by the defense lawyers during the trial and by others afterward, she argued, were grossly unfair. "Credulity is the result of inexperience," she insisted, and "unsuspicion the offspring of innocence." Were women really supposed to regard every man as "an enemy"?

Most men, Maria insisted, are good. Indeed, it was this male regard for virtue that explained the outrage expressed in the aftermath of the Bedlow trial: "The riots which lately have taken place is an evidence of its existence, and warmly glowing in the breasts of the male citizens of New-York." She even held out hope that Harry Bedlow himself would ultimately come to feel regret over what he had done.

By the time Maria's letter appeared, more than three weeks after the trial, the newspaper war was already dying down. Her moral reflections roused no public response. Indeed, the last word on Mother Carey and the riots was a joke that appeared about a month after the trial.

In early November, the *American Mercury*, published in Hartford, Connecticut, produced a fake report about the forthcoming publication of a tell-all by Mother Carey. This work had supposedly been saved from destruction during the recent riots and now promised to become the greatest literary curiosity of the age. It would, the advertisement promised, include detailed accounts of the men of "all descriptions," both "respectable" and "other," who had patronized her establishment—from men of state to "truckmen and coalheavers." And it would name names. The result, it was promised, would have a salutary effect on both public and private morals—as men would be frightened into better behavior. The joke was hardly original: a generation earlier, the fictional Moll Placket-Hole had responded to the riot that destroyed her own brothel with a similar ploy—threatening to "expose" her customers if they didn't build her a new, better house, which they promptly did.

What did all this mean for Lanah Sawyer? The riots and the ensuing newspaper debate had focused attention on conflicts among men and the tendency to blame and shame disorderly women. Now, Justitia and Maria had shifted the public debate—insisting that the problem was men's behavior and the sexual double standards that confronted young women with so many dangerous decisions and dire consequences. Did Lanah take courage from these sisterly expressions of understanding and support? Did she take comfort in the knowledge that these bold, elite women saw themselves in her ordeal, that she was not entirely alone? Or was all of that overwhelmed by the patriarchal backlash that engulfed them all? By the condescension and misogyny, the personal insults, the cruelty of dragging her case into print? And by the tendency of men to laugh the whole thing off?

❧

On the same day that the fake report about Mother Carey's purported exposé was published, another advertisement appeared in the city's newspapers. *"Just Published,"* began the brief notice in the *Columbian Gazetteer* for November 4, 1793, "A REPORT OF THE LATE TRIAL OF HENRY BEDLOW, Containing an accurate statement of the process, with the arguments of both counsel: Taken by a Gentleman of the profession." For Lanah, it must have seemed that the relentless attention would never end. Now she would be exposed in a new way, with the record of those legal proceedings made public and permanent, available for all to examine. And she was not the only one worried about the report. News of its publication filled Bedlow's lawyers with dread.

Never before had a report of an American rape trial been published. Trial reports of any kind had always been rare in North America; in the ten years since the end of the war, only a few accounts of criminal trials had appeared. The anonymous "Gentleman" behind the report of the Bedlow trial was the young lawyer William Wyche, recently arrived in the city from London, where such publications were common. Indeed, the high criminal court, the Old Bailey, routinely produced them itself. For Wyche, the intense public interest aroused by the Bedlow case offered a chance to bring this practice to America. As he wrote in an editorial note, "a fair and unbiased statement, reported by a Spectator unconnected with either party, cannot but afford data whereon to exercise the general judgment, and serve as a means of developing the true principles of the Verdict."

Such works capitalized on the dramatic potential of criminal trials, which were becoming increasingly adversarial in the late eighteenth century, as attorneys took on a more prominent role—playing on their skills and savvy as each side presented a coherent case, staging witness testimony, debating points of law, and mounting moving closing arguments. Wyche's *Report* offered those who hadn't been present at the trial a way to see for themselves why it had aroused such attention. It offered readers a chance to sit in the same position as the jurors: to follow the presentation of the contending cases, to evaluate the evidence and arguments, and to come to their own conclusions.

Those who snapped up copies of the Bedlow trial report included, no doubt, some attorneys and law students looking to learn by example, as well as many others attracted by the promise of a dramatic narrative that turned on volatile social issues and titillating sexual themes. That seems to have been the lesson the local printers took from the reception of Wyche's *Report*. Before the end of the century, New York printers had produced five other reports of trials involving young women and sexual themes: three rape trials, a seduction lawsuit, and a murder case in which a man was accused of killing the young, working-class woman he had been courting. Meanwhile, London's high court had stopped publishing reports of trials for rape and other sex crimes—deeming them too "indecent" for public view. While these jurists may well have been concerned about such reports attracting prurient interest, they may also have been concerned about how they themselves and the defense lawyers in such cases might appear in the eyes of readers.

Certainly, that was the case for Bedlow's lawyers—who, at this point, hadn't even been paid. Even before the trial report was available, Bedlow's lawyers worried about how it would make them look. One of them was overheard blustering—even before he had seen a copy—that he knew Wyche's *Report* would be "trash," that "it could not be accurate," and, in a particularly eloquent turn, that "it would be all fudge."

He had good reason to worry. The oblique queries published a few days after the trial had expressed unmistakable disapproval of the defense attorneys for relying on witnesses like Mother Carey—and the darker implication that the Bedlows, in hiring them, had managed to buy justice. Then came the riots and the extended newspaper debate. Meanwhile, Richard Harison, for one, had also heard an earful about his performance in the trial from his wife and friends.

When Bedlow's attorneys actually read Wyche's *Report*, they were horrified. Their attacks on Lanah Sawyer looked harsh. Their reliance on Mother Carey was troubling. And then there were their snobbish attacks on the workingmen and -women who had testified for the prosecution. It was one thing to make disparaging comments and sly insinuations in passing during a trial—or, in Harison's case, in a private letter to his wife. It was quite another to have them fixed and circulated in print.

Their first impulse was to have the report suppressed.

Bedlow's lawyers quickly discovered the anonymous author's identity and asked him to withdraw it from circulation. This put Wyche in an uncomfortable position. His purpose in publishing the report had been to advance his standing within the New York bar. Now he had antagonized some of its most powerful members. But if he was ambitious, he was also not one to back away from a fight. Wyche refused to pull his report.

Infuriated at this rebuff, the four most distinguished members of Bedlow's defense team—Richard Harison, John Cozine, Robert Troup, and Brockholst Livingston—agreed to try another tactic. They produced a long, angry attack on the report and its author, which they published, under their own names, in the city's newspapers. Although the report announced itself as having been "impartially taken by a Gentleman of the Profession," it was, they scoffed, neither impartial nor the work of any kind of gentleman. Its author had recklessly "trusted to his memory alone" in reporting on a "subject which employed fifteen hours in the discussion."

The letter, which may have been drafted by Richard Harison, echoed the themes of his letter to his wife. "Our duty as professional men obliged us to employ every talent we possessed in the defense of our client," the lawyers wrote, especially since we were trying to save a "human being" from an "unmerited death." They also claimed the report garbled the substance of their arguments and distorted the language they had actually employed.

Indeed, Wyche's account of the trial was not a verbatim transcript. He frequently summarized proceedings and paraphrased testimony. And, as noted in the text, he skipped over some graphic parts of Lanah Sawyer's testimony and some repetitive parts of the closing arguments. In another note, Wyche acknowledged that his work might contain minor errors, expressed the hope that his readers would excuse them, and insisted that he had accurately represented all "material parts" of the evidence and of the attorneys' arguments. In fact, given that Wyche didn't have access to copies of the file papers (now destroyed) or official minutes, his account was remarkably detailed. And what can be verified against the surviving court records reflects well on its accuracy.

For Bedlow's attorneys, the worst aspect of Wyche's *Report* was the way it exposed their snobbish attacks on Lanah Sawyer's supposedly low-class character witnesses. "We do positively deny," they blustered, "that in any stage of the trial, a single expression fell from any of the counsel for the prisoner—reflecting upon the witnesses who testified to the character of the prosecutrix, as being 'an obscure set of people,' or of 'no character themselves,' or, 'as requiring testimony in behalf of their own reputation.'" Only an "idiot" would have made such observations, they claimed, given "the well known respectability of those witnesses in general, and the mature age of several." This, at least, was one point on which their readers could agree.

Just as the magistrates' pompous "Notice" ended up backfiring, so too did the lawyers' attack on Wyche's *Report*. Their full-throated denial of having disparaged the prosecution's working-class witnesses was met with incredulity and mockery. A flurry of letters appeared in the city's newspapers ridiculing the defense lawyers and defending the accuracy of Wyche's work. One correspondent, pointedly calling himself "One of the Higher Class," demanded, with mock horror: What would happen to the reputation of these attorneys—and of the city as a whole—if the report were accepted as accurate? "The inhabitants of the neighboring states will exclaim with amazement and indignation, Is this a specimen of New-York eloquence?" Pressing on in this sarcastic vein, he warned his fellow citizens that their honor depended upon dismissing the report. After all, what were the assertions of a host of observers who had been in the courtroom, he demanded, compared to the denials of men like Robert Troup, Richard Harison, and John Cozine—whom he quoted as disparaging the prosecution witnesses as "*a set of obscure people, of no character themselves*"?

Another writer was more direct. "I . . . read the publication in question, and it forcibly struck me as a very accurate statement both of the evidence and argument." What was astonishing about the report, in this writer's view, was the "extreme anger" with which the defense attorneys had attacked it.

A third writer, who also claimed to have attended the trial, was more precise but no less damning. Brockholst Livingston, he noted, could be "cleared from the charge of slander and indelicacy." But the same could not be said for all of his colleagues, particularly Harison and Troup. "Both with respect to sentiment and mode of expression, the speeches of these *gentlemen* have been deemed unbecoming in a high degree." And for good reason—if anything, their arguments had been even more "indecent" in court than they appeared in Wyche's account.

Did William Wyche pause while compiling his report to consider what its publication would mean for Lanah Sawyer? For him, the report was largely about advancing his own professional ambitions. For many readers, it offered an opportunity to see the dramas of their own lives played out in someone else's experience. In any case, its publication made Lanah, once again, into an object of examination, evaluation, and entertainment. Was she comforted that the debate over the report wasn't about her but rather about the shameful behavior of the attorneys who had done her wrong? Or did she feel newly exposed—and then newly dismissed and disregarded?

❧

The extraordinary explosion of outrage after the Bedlow trial transformed Lanah Sawyer's ordeal. Never before had a crime against a woman provoked men in the city to riot. But as different groups seized on the trial and Sawyer's experience with Harry Bedlow, they did so through the lens of their own agendas. What began as a court trial emphasizing the wrongs of women, and turned into a public vindication of the rights of women, ended up as a conflict over the rights of men—specifically, the right of the city's white workingmen to respect and dignity.

"What has been the result of all this clamor and writing?" asked one writer, after two days of rioting, two months of controversy, and more than two dozen separate pieces published, and republished, in newspapers across the nation. "Do these disputes tend to ease the minds of those who were agitated against the conduct of Bedlow?"

Some of the last echoes of the public conversation appeared in newspapers far removed from New York, items that included sensational rumors and new details—and were often strikingly sympathetic to Lanah Sawyer. About ten days after the riots, the editor of the *Vermont Gazette* published a lurid account, which he admitted could not be verified: "A young woman of character was by some means decoyed into one of the sinks of infamy, in the fields, a house of ill fame kept by a mother Cary: on her refusing to submit to personal violation, it is said the old woman, with three or four of her prostitutes held the unhappy victim of lust and forced her to endure the cruel violence of her hell enflamed ravisher." Another letter, two weeks later, added that Carey's "false evidence" was blamed for the "young lady" losing her case in court. Full of righteous indignation, "the people" swore that "if justice did not come by fair means, it should by foul."

As the story circulated through Vermont and western Massachusetts, as late as mid-December, even the sober Federalist John Adams came to see the outrage over the failed prosecution of Harry Bedlow in the same basic terms as Justitia. In late November, as the danger of yellow fever subsided and Adams made his way back to Philadelphia, he stopped in New York to visit with his daughter Nabby (whom he felt he had saved from marriage to a rake ten years earlier) and his son Charles (who he feared might turn into one). He evidently heard about the Bedlow trial and the subsequent riots while there, as well as from other sources. When Charles sent him a letter expressing sympathy with Harry Bedlow and outrage at the riots, Adams sent a stinging rebuke. Defensively, Charles wrote back insisting that he had not wished it to be "inferred that I wished to advocate the cause of infamy or that I had partially related circumstances." If Adams fretted that one of his sons remained, two months later, so exercised about Bedlow's prosecution and the brothel riots, he could take some comfort in the fact that another of his sons had just argued his first case in court—launching himself into the "great Work of Reformation" with the "Prosecution of a disorderly house."

Lanah Sawyer and Harry Bedlow were still on the vice president's mind a few days later, when he wrote to his wife, Abigail ("My dearest Friend"). Like so many others who generally deplored mob actions, Adams was inclined to sympathize with the protesters in this case, who he believed really had been "excited by gross offences against Morals." Echoing Justitia's analysis, Adams blamed the city's lack of a "virtuous magistracy" for the continuing problem of prostitution. As for the Bedlow trial, he wrote, the defense lawyers had "treated the Subject with too much Levity." They had, he wrote, treated "virtuous creditable Women with too much indifference and Mother Cary the old Beldam with to[o] much respect."

Even far from New York, people who had never met Lanah Sawyer were unsettled by the conclusion that she had been deeply, repeatedly wronged—first by Harry Bedlow, then by his defense lawyers and Mother Carey, then by the trial jury, and finally by hostile commentators.

But even those who shared a sense of outrage found it difficult to focus on Lanah Sawyer herself—her experience, her ordeal. John Adams, like the hundreds of men who rioted against the brothels, remembered Mother Carey's name but not Lanah's. All of these men saw her ordeal through the lens of other preoccupations: disgust at the city's corrupt legal system, or the moral rot of prostitution. Even when Justitia, Maria, and others shifted attention to men's hypocrisy, sexual double standards, and the unfairness of judging women for the faults of men, they were building on the interest aroused by Sawyer's case to press their own priorities.

What did all of this mean for Lanah Sawyer—to be the subject of such intense and often harsh scrutiny, of such violent outrage, lurid speculation, and fierce debate? It might seem that she and her family had reason to take heart in the public outcry against the jury's verdict, the massive demonstrations targeting Mother Carey, the public support of feminist writers, and even the private sympathy of men like John Adams. But over and over, Lanah Sawyer found herself not so much the center of attention as a weapon taken up by others waging their own battles, less a person than a symbol.

In New York, there was no public mention of the emotional toll the trial and its aftermath had on Lanah Sawyer. The only glimpse into her ongoing ordeal was an excerpt from a letter written in the city in late October and published in the *Vermont Gazette*.

"The grief of the young lady is inconsolable," the New Yorker reported. Far from feeling vindicated by the riots and the public discussion in the newspapers, Lanah Sawyer was overcome with despair.

Sunday, October 20, had been a beautiful fall day, brisk and clear; but that evening there were light showers and rumbles of thunder.

Ten days after the trial, almost a week since the riots, as the newspaper war raged on, Lanah Sawyer climbed up into the garret of her father's house, wrapped a shawl around her neck, and hanged herself.

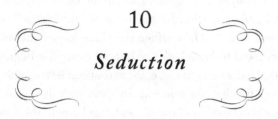

10

Seduction

If Lanah Sawyer's story had been invented by a writer at the time, this is how it would have ended: with her alone in the garret of her stepfather's house, succumbing to despair, wrapping a shawl around her neck, and hanging until the weight of her body exhausted her ability to resist, until she could no longer breathe.

An early death was, in the popular stories of the day, the inevitable fate of a "ruined woman." Even a maiden who lost her innocence through no fault of her own, who had been forced, not seduced, was said to face a life that was hardly worth living. In an essay puzzling over the verdict of the Bedlow trial, William Wyche wrote that in the act of rape, "a virtuous woman is robbed of her innocence, of all that can form her happiness." The crushing effects of such hopelessness were recognized a few years later by a coroner's inquisition over the body of Polly Traner—who, it was determined, "came by her death by excessive grief and vexation."

But that is not how Lanah Sawyer's story ended. She was discovered in time. She was taken down. She survived.

None of this was ever discussed in the city—at least publicly. Such events were rarely mentioned in local newspapers. Indeed, we would know nothing about this crucial moment of crisis if not for a few lines published in a Bennington, Vermont, newspaper under the heading "Extract of a letter from Newyork to the editor, dated October 27."

This letter may very well have come from the pen of the celebrated writer Susanna Rowson, author of *Charlotte Temple: A Tale of Truth* (1791), the era's most popular seduction story. She and the editor of the *Vermont Gazette* were cousins. They had known each other as children in Boston but had been separated by the war; when she was about fifteen, her Loyalist family had returned to England. Then, in the fall of 1793, she came back to America. Landing in Philadelphia in the midst of the yellow fever epidemic, she was forced to take refuge elsewhere for several months—and may have ventured to New York just in time to see the Bedlow trial and its aftermath. In the years to come, she exchanged letters with her cousin that combined familial affection and city news with their shared business interests: "my good coz" was how she addressed him in the only complete example of their correspondence that has survived, asking whether he could sell any copies of her latest novel. In late 1793, he published excerpts of three letters from an unidentified correspondent (rather than, as was typical, "from a gentleman") in New York; the first, dated about two weeks after Rowson's arrival in Philadelphia, reported on the effect of the fever on the printers there. The second, written a week later, offered a vivid account of the brothel riots—and included a telling detail (that "several" rioters had been arrested) that was not reported elsewhere. The third followed up, a week later, with an explanation of the event that had provoked the riots—and news of the inconsolable young lady's suicide attempt.

Did Lanah really want to die? Today, it can be tempting to dismiss a suicide attempt, especially by a young woman, as a gesture—a plea for help, an expression of anger. Women are far more likely than men to attempt suicide, yet men are far more likely to die by suicide. In part, experts explain, that's because men typically use more lethal methods, like guns. But no one makes a serious suicide attempt unless they feel an overwhelming need to die. The method Lanah chose, hanging, remains one of the most lethal. And she chose a place where it was relatively unlikely that she would be discovered in the few minutes it would take her to suffocate.

How did Lanah come to feel that death was her only option? Today, the experience of rape often leaves survivors deeply traumatized—especially if the assault, like Lanah's, involved both sexual intercourse and physical force. A sexual assault is always an intense emotional, physical, and moral violation. Survivors are far more likely than others to attempt suicide. For someone Lanah Sawyer's age, the damage can be especially severe. She encountered "lawyer Smith" when she was seventeen—a time when she was, no doubt, struggling to form her own identity, beginning to break free from her parents, and exploring the wider social world. Then suddenly, in the dark at the mouth of Ann Street, reality shifted: the man she was with was not the man she had thought he was. For many, this experience alone can be a dizzying, disorienting blow to their sense of safety and self-confidence, their sense of their own ability to accurately assess other people. And then came a terrorizing assault. (*"He . . . laid his left arm across my throat, so that I was almost choaked, and did not suppose I could live many minutes."*)

If, in the weeks that followed, Lanah's prosecution of Harry Bedlow gave her some sense of purpose and direction, the trial itself and its outcome were crushing blows. Then came the riots and the relentless newspaper war. As another young woman, two centuries later, who suffered the consequences of becoming a human flashpoint put it: "when everyone in the world thinks they know who you are, *you* don't want to be yourself."

Today, the utter hopelessness that drives people to suicide often involves a combination of two powerful emotions: a feeling that one is a failure, a disappointment, a burden, that others would be better off without you—and a feeling that one is alone, without support. Lanah may very well have felt that she had brought shame to her family, that she had failed to live up to her parents' expectations, and that, in the rape trial, she had been demeaned and dismissed as an outsider, as someone who did not matter.

If Lanah's family had been unaware just how distraught she had become, her attempted suicide made it painfully clear. In response, they may very well have tried to offer some of the comfort and support she needed.

She may have found a new sense of purpose and connection in her stepfather's ongoing legal battle with Harry Bedlow. All fall, the two men had been facing off through their attorneys in a series of skirmishes in civil court. Back in September, after Lanah had launched her rape complaint against Bedlow, he had attempted to use his "scuffle" with John Callanan to strike back. When the mayor refused to take his assault complaint against Callanan seriously, Bedlow hired a lawyer to sue him for money damages. That didn't work either. The branch pilot didn't have the young gentleman's long experience with civil litigation, but he refused to be intimidated. And the attorneys he hired, Caleb Riggs and Nicholas Evertson, were savvy and tenacious. When Bedlow attempted to withdraw his lawsuit, Callanan fought to get it reinstated. He also slapped Bedlow with a countersuit, presumably over damages he had suffered during the scuffle. All fall, Bedlow sought to dodge a reckoning—and Callanan pursued him doggedly.

Even if John Callanan prevailed, all he was likely to get was a court order requiring Bedlow to reimburse his legal fees. But just as Harry Bedlow had fatefully underestimated Lanah Sawyer's gumption when he first targeted her, so, too, he had underestimated her stepfather. The branch pilot was determined to vindicate his honor.

The legal battle between the two men finally came to a head in mid-December. Bedlow, having fled the city during the riots, still had not returned. In his absence, the Mayor's Court granted Callanan's request to reinstate Bedlow's withdrawn lawsuit. When Bedlow failed to appear for a crucial court date on December 19, he lost the case and was ordered to pay Callanan's legal fees, which, at £3.15.3, represented a day or two's work for a pilot. At the same time, Bedlow forfeited the £50 bail bond he had posted with the sheriff. And the sheriff lost no time hiring Callanan's attorney to file a new suit against Bedlow and his father (who had secured the bail bond), to recover what he was now owed. For John Callanan and Lanah Sawyer, these developments were, no doubt, gratifying. But they also meant that Callanan's countersuit against Bedlow had been further delayed.

During the break between the court's December and January terms, the sheriff caught up with Harry Bedlow, and they settled the matter. But the Bedlows defied the court order requiring them to reimburse John Callanan's costs and fees—prompting the relentless pilot to pay his attorney to file more paperwork, in January 1794, to initiate a new legal process to force Bedlow to pay.

By then, John Callanan and Lanah Sawyer had given Harry Bedlow something far more serious to worry about.

During the rape trial, Bedlow's own attorneys had emphasized that his behavior had been deplorable and that the damage he had done to Lanah Sawyer was likely to be ruinous. But they had insisted that he was being pursued via the wrong legal avenue—that rather than being prosecuted for the crime of rape he should have been sued in a civil action for seduction. As Richard Harison put it: "Had the Prosecutrix and her friends been well advised, they would have had recourse to the proper mode pointed out by the law for her relief. They would have commenced a civil action, and have recovered a compensation in damages for the seduction of the Prosecutrix; it is the purse and not the life of the Prisoner which they can affect."

In the end, that's exactly what John Callanan did.

By this point, Callanan had good reason to doubt that he would ever get justice from the Mayor's Court—which, month after month, had allowed the matter to languish in legal limbo. The magistrates who presided over the court, Mayor Varick and Recorder Jones, had both been involved in the rape trial. And the aftermath of the trial—the riots and public controversy—can hardly have endeared Callanan to either man. So, in January 1794, Callanan's attorney used a complex legal maneuver to ask the state's supreme court to assume jurisdiction over the case. Such requests generally involved some claim of bias against the lower court. When granted, they started the case anew, wiping away everything that had previously happened—including a murky complaint by one of Bedlow's attorneys back in November about some unspecified "irregularity" on Callanan's part. The supreme court granted the request. *John Callanan v. Henry Bedlow* was scheduled for trial in the now-familiar courtroom in Federal Hall in mid-April.

John Callanan had until mid-March to file his formal declaration, specifying his cause of action against Bedlow, detailing his complaint, and naming the financial damages he was seeking to recover. When he did, the result was astonishing. Callanan was not suing for petty damages stemming from his "scuffle" with the young gentleman—at least not anymore. He was suing for a staggering sum, representing the damages he had sustained as a result of Harry Bedlow's seduction of Lanah Sawyer.

A seduction suit was potentially a much more powerful form of legal action than a simple assault claim. Plaintiffs filing seduction suits almost always won—and the damages juries awarded them were typically far higher than was customary in simple assault cases. On the other hand, a seduction suit had to be grounded upon a very specific set of formal requirements and legal fictions.

Although seduction suits emerged in this period as a powerful way of holding men to account for sexual harms against women, they were steeped in arcane legal conventions and an extreme form of patriarchal thinking. Lanah Sawyer had no standing to sue Harry Bedlow for her own seduction, but her stepfather did. The suit would be in his name, and any damages awarded would be his to claim. Legal conventions and pretenses aside, a seduction suit amounted to an absolute claim of a man's sexual ownership of "his" women—his daughters, his servants, his wife.

But a seduction suit was the most promising strategy, and the most powerful, for a woman in Lanah Sawyer's position: it offered a way to pursue in civil court the accountability the criminal process had failed to provide. Indeed, it promised not only to punish the perpetrator but also to provide her family with meaningful restitution.

This strategy depended on an alliance between Lanah Sawyer and her stepfather, John Callanan. Just as she could not have mounted a rape prosecution without his support, he could not sue for seduction without hers. In a seduction trial, she would be the principal witness in her father's suit. Once again, this would involve someone else appropriating what she had endured for their own purposes. But it was the best chance either of them had to hold her rapist accountable. It was also an opportunity for Lanah and her stepfather to share a sense of purpose, standing together against a common foe. The seduction suit required John Callanan not just to take on, but to literally take ownership of, Lanah's ordeal.

◈

The formal declaration John Callanan's attorney filed in March 1794—six months after Lanah Sawyer's first, fateful encounter with Harry Bedlow, five months after his trial for raping her and his acquittal—is brief and formulaic. But the claim it sets forth is bold, even audacious. It represented the first time in New York's history that a seduction suit was used to seek redress from a man who was also prosecuted for rape.

And then there was the fact that almost nothing in the written claim was actually true.

According to the complaint, "on the first day of August in the year of our Lord one thousand seven hundred and ninety three" in the city of New York, Henry Bedlow "with force and arms &c. to wit, with swords, staves, and knives made an Assault upon one Lanah Sawyer then and there servant of the said John Callanan and in his actual service and employ." Then, Henry did "beat wound and imprison and have Carnal Knowledge of" Lanah—and keep her imprisoned "for a long space of time, to wit, for the space of three days without any lawful cause." As a result, during those three days, John Callanan "was deprived of the reasonable service of the said Lanah to the Damage of the said John Callanan of five thousand Pounds."

None of this, of course, was literally true.

Six months earlier, Lanah Sawyer had pursued a well-grounded rape prosecution and failed to secure a conviction. Why, now, did her step-father or anyone else imagine they could succeed with a civil suit so easy to expose as a patchwork of fictions? Everyone knew that Lanah Sawyer was Callanan's stepdaughter, not his servant; that she had not been beaten with swords or staves or knives; that she had not been kidnapped for three days; and that even if she had been, £5,000 represented nothing like the value of three days' worth of a maidservant's labor—more like a hundred years'.

But as Lanah Sawyer and her stepfather learned from the attorney who wrote the claim, none of that mattered in a seduction suit. The law was full of archaic formulas and necessary fictions. Assault claims always included stock language about staves and swords and knives in addition to whatever weapons had actually been used. In seduction suits, legal con-vention required the woman in question to be described as a servant and the alleged damages as the value of the labor her master had lost. In court, everyone would recognize that a seduction suit was a pretense—a vehicle for holding men who had committed sexual harms responsible.

As a form of action for sexual harm, the seduction suit was the prod-uct of inventive lawyers seizing on an old provision in the law of servi-tude that allowed a master to recover damages if someone else improperly "seduced" away one of his servants. The right of a servant to choose a more attractive opportunity with another master or mistress was, in the context of a seduction suit, irrelevant. It was a conflict between two employers. Moreover, by the patriarchal logic of Anglo-American law, a household head had the right to the labor not only of his actual servants but also of any minor children living under his roof; if the household head was a mar-ried man, he could also claim the labor of his wife. All of these dependent members of a household could be technically construed as his "servants." Typically, seduction suits were brought by a man—the father of a seduced daughter or the husband of a seduced wife—but in some cases they could be brought by a widowed mother, an adult brother, or a guardian. Defense attorneys objected when mothers or brothers brought seduction suits, but the courts consistently recognized their right to do so.

Thus, according to the logic of a seduction suit, Lanah Sawyer was regarded as her stepfather's servant, and the harm he supposedly suffered was the loss of her domestic labor. A form of legal action that originated in disputes between masters over their right to the labor value of servants became a form of action between men over the sexual ownership of women.

The patriarchal logic of seduction suits meant that they reframed the question of consent. In a rape case, a crucial issue was whether a woman had consented to sexual relations or not. But in a seduction suit, her consent was irrelevant. The issue was her father's consent—or her husband's.

This point was explained by William Wyche in his *Treatise on the Practice of the Supreme Court of Judicature of the State of New-York in Civil Actions*, published in the spring of 1794, while Callanan's suit against Bedlow was in progress. Wyche, it seems, had succeeded in using his report of the rape trial to build support for this more ambitious effort to bring English forms of legal publication to America. His *Treatise* was the first comprehensive guide to civil practice in New York—and perhaps in the nation.

To illustrate the issue of consent, Wyche gave the example of a suit brought by a husband whose wife had been involved in an adulterous liaison. In such a case, any sexual relations a woman might have had with someone other than her husband could be construed as an assault at the hands of her lover. Why? Because when she married, she transferred to her husband her legal capacity to exercise consent in sexual relations. By the same token, a married woman could not charge her husband with rape: "in respect to him, her consent is as nothing."

Although seduction suits could be a powerful legal tool against men who had sexually harmed women, they were not common because they required making public a woman's involvement in an illicit liaison. Indeed, a seduction suit was generally brought only when the woman in question became pregnant and gave birth to a bastard. In this sense, lawsuits for seduction and breach of promise were like prosecutions for sexual assaults—which most often went unreported, especially if the perpetrator was an acquaintance. If a young woman was seduced by a man or lured into losing her virginity by a false promise of marriage, the first priority of most families was to hush things up. Their silence enabled their victimizers but preserved their family's honor. Pregnancy, however, made it much harder to keep an illicit liaison secret.

Lanah Sawyer's case was one of a handful of seduction suits that didn't involve a pregnancy. She and her family had long since given up any possibility of keeping what had happened to her quiet. Two other cases also involved women who had been sexually assaulted—but who had chosen not to pursue rape charges. One, brought in 1808, involved a married Black woman, Sylvia Patterson, who was working as a domestic servant when she was sexually assaulted by her white employer. She did not file criminal charges, but her husband pursued and won a seduction suit.

Another case was making its way through the New Jersey courts at the time John Callanan filed his suit—and it was a case eerily like Lanah Sawyer's own. It involved a young seamstress, Ann VanHorn, who over a period of weeks in the summer of 1792 was courted, then propositioned, then raped by a young lawyer, Alpheus Freeman. She had been boarding with an older woman in order to learn the skilled trade of dressmaking, but was so devastated that she had to move home so her family could care for her. Her father, a clergyman, attested that she had been so distraught by the assault—and by the fear that she might become pregnant—that she was unable to work for months. The young man was not prosecuted for rape, but VanHorn's father sued him for seduction and won, though the young man dragged out the matter for years on appeal. He argued, logically enough, that the Rev. VanHorn didn't have standing to sue because at the time of his daughter's "seduction" she had been living on her own and supporting herself as an apprentice dressmaker. How then could her father claim her as a dependent and make a claim based on his supposed loss of her labor value?

The young lawyer's most astonishing claim was that, based on the young woman's own testimony, he was being pursued for the wrong offense. Inverting an argument made by Bedlow's lawyers during his first trial, Freeman argued that the proper form of action against him was not a lawsuit for seduction but rather a criminal prosecution of rape. Ann VanHorn had testified that she had not consented to his sexual overtures—she had been physically overpowered and forced. A seduction suit, he argued, had to be based on a fictive sexual assault—not a real one. Audacious as the move was, he was not the last man who gambled that he would fare better in a criminal prosecution for rape than in a civil suit for seduction—risking a far more draconian outcome against the likelihood that he would thus elude responsibility altogether.

In any case, Freeman found that none of his fussing about facts and logic mattered in the realm of seduction law. As the appeals court ultimately ruled, seduction suits were not about such literal parsing of the facts, they were about a more abstract sense of justice. After all, the judge opined, a seduction suit was the only way in which the family of a victim could recover damages: "It is in general a mere fiction of the law, in order to give some kind of compensation for an injury of the most atrocious kind, which would otherwise be remediless."

The other fiction underlying the seduction suit John Callanan brought against Harry Bedlow involved the amount of the alleged damages: £5,000 New York currency. Even by the standards of seduction suits at the time, this was an extraordinary sum. Because Sawyer was not pregnant, her stepfather could not claim direct expenses relating to the seduction—only the value of her lost labor for three days. Certainly, the amount sought in his suit was entirely out of proportion to any material harm he could conceivably have suffered.

Until the late 1780s, seduction suits in the region had involved relatively modest sums. In cases that ended up in the New Jersey Supreme Court before 1789, claims were typically about £200. And the amounts plaintiffs received were even lower. Most cases were evidently settled out of court—which a defendant would typically not agree to do unless it was for less than the amount claimed in the suit. The one jury award on record was for only £60 plus costs. Especially for people of modest means, this was a substantial sum, roughly equivalent to two months of a workingman's wages. It reflected the practical costs associated with a woman being pregnant, giving birth, and caring for a newborn infant—which the women at the center of all of these suits had done. Thus, seduction suits did not offer seduced women much in the way of compensatory or punitive awards to recognize the damage done to reputation and family honor, or to deter other men from engaging in such behavior.

By the early 1790s, this pattern began to change. Plaintiffs began to make larger claims—though still not nearly as large as Callanan's. And jurors gradually began to respond with larger awards. After Eleanor Coryell's suitor initiated a sexual relationship by promising that they would soon be married, only to abandon her when she became pregnant, she and her father both filed suit against him. She sued him for breach of promise to marry, claiming damages of £1,000. Meanwhile, her father sued him for seduction, claiming damages of £300. The Coryells won both cases, but the jury awards were modest: £77 in the marriage case, £75 in the seduction suit. Other seduction suits over the next several years followed the same pattern. It was not until the VanHorn case, initiated in 1792 and still dragging through the courts in 1794, that a jury responded to these new, higher claims (in this case, £1,000) by awarding a significantly higher judgment: £250 plus costs.

As claims and judgments in seduction suits grew, they became increasingly detached from practical considerations and reflected a new sense of the damage done to the victims. And the shift in the size of jury awards shows that jurors agreed. Increasingly, jury judgments reflected new ideals of feminine delicacy and a new horror of injured innocence. This cultural shift was reflected in the popularity of seduction literature in the 1790s and was clearly part of the challenge Lanah Sawyer faced in mounting her rape prosecution: the cult of female innocence raised a new standard of female respectability. For a young woman who had to work for her living and go out in the streets unchaperoned, it was a standard that was almost impossible to uphold.

In his claim, John Callanan was embracing this developing trend and boldly trying to push it further. And yet, as powerful as seduction suits could potentially be, there was good reason for John Callanan and Lanah Sawyer to wonder whether this strategy would work in their case. Nobody in the city's history had ever attempted to use the law of seduction in quite the way they did.

No man in New York, or New Jersey for that matter, had been both prosecuted for rape and sued for seduction. This may help explain the most astonishing aspect of the claim John Callanan brought against Harry Bedlow—and the only obvious peculiarity not explained by the requirements of legal convention or by shifting cultural norms—the allegation that he had kidnapped Lanah on August 1, 1793, and imprisoned her for three days. This was clearly false, as the rape trial had established. It's possible that Callanan's attorney, Caleb Riggs, simply made a mistake. But it seems more likely that he deliberately organized the seduction lawsuit around an invented narrative in order to avoid another legal problem.

At the time, it was not clear whether it was legally permissible to prosecute a man under criminal law and sue him under civil law for the same offense. In the English common law, the merger doctrine provided that when a private harm was also a public wrong, it should be merged with the public wrong. Until the nineteenth century, the practical implications of this doctrine remained unsettled. Did it mean that the criminal case had priority and had to be resolved before any civil suit could be pursued? Or did it constitute a form of double-jeopardy protection, blocking a civil suit entirely if there had already been a related criminal prosecution?

Riggs seems to have shared this uncertainty, though he addressed it in an audacious way—by simply doubling down on the legal fictions at the heart of any seduction suit. After all, a seduction suit was little more than an elaborate pretense, a fictional excuse to hold a man liable for real harms. And there was good reason to think that jurors in this case would agree that Harry Bedlow deserved to pay for what he had done.

ℂ

FEDERAL HALL. WEDNESDAY, APRIL 23, 1794. AROUND NOON.

On Wednesday, April 23, 1794, the parties to John Callanan's seduction suit against Harry Bedlow—all of whom had previously been involved in the rape trial—assembled once again in the monumental courtroom at the rear of Federal Hall. Caleb Riggs had submitted his declaration in mid-March, ensuring that Bedlow would be required to respond with a formal plea by mid-April, in advance of a trial during the Supreme Court's next session in the city later that month. But even though the seduction suit was little more than a pastiche of contrivances, Bedlow's response suggests that he took it seriously. Unlike most previous lawsuits he had faced, he could not ignore this one.

Under a court order to respond to Callanan's declaration within twenty days, Bedlow waited until almost the last minute and filed his plea the day before the court's April term began. Represented once again by James Hughes, Bedlow insisted that he was "not Guilty" of the allegations against him and would take the matter to trial. Callanan's attorney indicated that he, too, wished to proceed to trial, and the court scheduled the trial for Wednesday, April 23. The two sides had about ten days to prepare.

Even as Lanah Sawyer and her stepfather were bracing for another high-stakes showdown, Bedlow and his attorney set about securing a delay. After months of evasion, and no longer facing an indulgent Mayor's Court, they could not simply ignore the matter. So they came up with a legitimate excuse: they could not go to trial without a key witness who was unavoidably detained elsewhere. In an affidavit prepared by Hughes, Bedlow said he was told that he could not "safely" proceed to trial without the testimony of a man named William Allsee—who, Bedlow attested, was then "on a Voyage to the Coast of Africa" but was expected back in time to appear for the circuit court's next sitting in the city. On April 21, 1794, Bedlow signed the affidavit, and later that day, Hughes prepared a formal notice informing Callanan's attorney that he would be seeking to have the trial delayed.

Callanan and his attorney had less than forty-eight hours to determine who William Allsee might be and how he figured in the defense strategy. An English-born mariner, Allsee had married and had two children in the 1770s before abandoning his wife and moving to New York, where he took up with another woman. By the fall of 1793, he had been living in the city for two years and had become friendly with Bedlow's family. On Tuesday, September 3, 1793, he had appeared before the Mayor's Court with a petition to be naturalized as a citizen of the United States—and the witness who supported his petition was Bedlow's rich brother-in-law John Beekman. As Callanan could have learned without much difficulty, Allsee was currently engaged in an effort to break into the transatlantic slave trade. Around the time of Bedlow's rape trial in early October 1793, the *Daily Advertiser* reported that Allsee had set sail at the helm of a schooner bound for Africa. By January, they had arrived at Bunce Island, a major slave trading center in the Sierra Leone River. This was unusual: despite sporadic ventures, New York merchants had never managed to horn in on the transatlantic slave trade, a potentially profitable but unusually risky business. William Bedlow had made at least one attempt before the revolution, and since the war only a handful of attempts had been made. Moreover, by the 1790s, the slave trade was increasingly controversial—and had been outlawed in many of the northern states. In New York, many leading figures joined the antislavery movement, which focused above all on the moral opprobrium of slave trading.

Allsee had not been mentioned during the rape trial. So it seems most likely that his role in the seduction suit, unless it was simply to provide an excuse for a delay, had to do with providing Bedlow with an alibi during the first three days of August—in an attempt to prove that the fictional prosecution narrative was, in fact, fictional.

In any case, Bedlow got his delay. On April 23, the court put the trial off to the next circuit court sitting in the city. At the time, the full Supreme Court held four several-weeks-long sessions each year, two in New York and two in Albany. In addition, individual judges were empowered to hold sessions in various counties around the state as needed—which, given the crush of business in Manhattan, meant several additional times a year in the city. As it happened, Captain Allsee did not arrive home in time for the next circuit session in the city. And even after he did, Bedlow kept asking the court to put the trial off. In July, the full Supreme Court, sitting in Albany, set a final trial date. The case would go forward at the next circuit court session in New York, which was scheduled to begin on Monday, September 29, 1794.

During these long months of delay, there was little Lanah Sawyer could do to prepare for the lawsuit. Most likely she spent the year living at home with her family, taking in sewing jobs, helping to take care of her eighteen-month-old stepbrother—and battling dark thoughts. Perhaps Lanah heard news of Mother Carey—who, after the demolition of her house during the riots, had attempted to regroup in a more remote part of the city, opening what was called a "tavern" out past the Rutgers farm at Corlears Hook, an area that later became a notorious haven for prostitution and may have been responsible for the term "hooker." Lanah may also have heard that this new venture failed. By midsummer, the old bawd had been driven out of the city.

Lanah likely heard echoes of her own case in the trials of her fifteen-year-old brother Peter. He was apprenticed to one of their stepfather's fellow branch pilots, who lived around the corner and who, in early May, beat him savagely. Once again, John Callanan turned to the attorneys he had been using in his battle with Harry Bedlow and filed suit to protect his stepson's interests, claiming damages of £200—a tiny fraction of the amount named in the seduction suit. This was typical: cases over reputation and honor were generally worth far more than cases over even the most severe physical injuries. This lawsuit came to trial in the Mayor's Court on Saturday, September 20—just over a week before Lanah's seduction trial was scheduled to begin. Callanan, acting as Peter's guardian, prevailed. But the jury award was paltry—a mere £2.10, less than half what it had cost to pursue the matter.

That evening, one of their neighbors, returning home, noted "a violent storm threatening."

❧

FEDERAL HALL. MONDAY, SEPTEMBER 29, 1794.

Almost exactly a year after Henry Bedlow's rape trial, Lanah Sawyer returned to the massive courtroom at the rear of Federal Hall. It was a very warm day, overcast in the morning, clearing by afternoon. There was the usual buzz of activity as case after case came before the circuit court, and plaintiffs and defendants and attorneys and witnesses and prospective jurors waited to be called. This time there was no great crush of spectators. Some of those who had made a point of attending the rape trial seemed unaware of the seduction suit. But Harry Bedlow, despite his tendency to ignore minor civil cases, clearly felt there was too much at stake to lose by default. His attorney, one of the six who had represented him in the rape trial, was there—as was Callanan's, Caleb Riggs. The two presiding justices called the seduction suit to trial. Prospective jurors were brought forward, questioned, and sworn in until twelve had been impaneled. Once again, the trial would revolve around the testimony of a single principal witness. And that witness, Lanah Sawyer knew, was her.

From her experience a year earlier, Lanah would have been familiar with the basic format of the trial. Civil and criminal trials followed the same pattern: her stepfather's attorney would open the case, explain their allegations against Harry Bedlow, and emphasize the damage he had done by destroying a virtuous young woman's sexual innocence.

Then all eyes would turn to Lanah, as she once again made her way to the witness box and prepared to tell her story.

What Lanah actually said is impossible to know. The court's archive reveals only the barest outlines of Callanan's claim and its legal journey. Did Bedlow himself show up for the trial? In one document he is described, ambiguously, as appearing "~~with~~ by his attorney." Did the defense produce their supposedly essential witness, the slave-ship captain William Allsee? We don't know. Nor do surviving records tell us how Lanah navigated the pitfalls of the case—a case based on a narrative, crafted by her stepfather's attorneys, about a three-day kidnapping that never happened.

As in the rape trial, Lanah's basic challenge was to explain how a chaste young woman from a modest family could have been swept away by the attentions of a gentleman.

Another victim of seduction who faced this same challenge some years later was Catharine Saffen. Like Lanah, she was a young woman who worked as a seamstress and enjoyed a spotless reputation—until, while out walking on the Battery, she met a man who insinuated himself into her confidence under false pretenses and lured her into a brothel run by an old woman. Following the death of her father some years earlier, Saffen's family had slipped into grinding poverty. Her widowed mother had to take in boarders to support her five children and was so poor she had to borrow the $50 her attorney required in order to take on the case. Still, Saffen played into the cultural ideal of genteel femininity with dramatic effect.

In the courtroom, she struck an observer as a "young lady of slender and delicate figure." Stepping into the witness box, she visibly faltered—seemingly "in tears" and "too much affected to stand." A chair was brought, and she was granted a few minutes to prepare for the emotional ordeal ahead.

In some ways, Lanah Sawyer's story was like Saffen's. But Saffen's efforts to represent herself as an innocent victim were complicated by her acknowledgment that her first sexual encounter with the defendant had not been forced. She was persuaded, she testified, by his repeated assurance that his "intentions were honourable" and that he "would do well by me." Then, she had been strung along by his false promises for the better part of two years—and had two babies—before he finally abandoned her, unmarried and ruined.

When it was time for the defense to present their case, a host of witnesses were called in an effort to smear the young woman with lurid accounts of improper behavior. As in the Bedlow trial, it was clear in the Saffen lawsuit that either one side or the other was lying. The judge in the Saffen case seemed to sympathize with the unfortunate young woman, and he told the jurors that anything that happened after the young woman's initial loss of virginity was irrelevant. The question for the jurors was whether the defendant was her "seducer." If so, he told them, no punishment they could lay upon him "would be too severe."

In this sense, the challenge Lanah Sawyer now faced was simpler than it had been during the rape trial.

In sexual assault trials, the issue of a woman's consent was endlessly fraught. Defense lawyers and legal commentators dwelled on the fact that in most sexual assaults the only person who really knew whether an encounter had been consensual or not was the alleged victim herself. Given all the reasons to doubt her, they asked, how could the truth of the matter be established? Only indirectly, they answered, by assessing circumstantial evidence. This was the reason Bedlow's lawyers had given in the rape trial for their endless questioning of Lanah's behavior and motives. Had she been imprudent? Had she offered sufficient resistance to Bedlow's advances? Had she really said no? In raising these questions and supplying their own answers, Bedlow's lawyers had demonstrated how a perpetrator's tactics could provide a kind of social camouflage and obscure the question of consent.

Theoretically, this same problem of proof and persuasion lay at the heart of the seduction suit. Seduction was also a form of sexual assault. It, too, turned on the question of consent. But in the seduction suit, the consent in question was not Lanah's but rather her stepfather's. As Wyche had explained in his *Treatise of Practice*, in a seduction suit it was presumed that the woman in question had no legal capacity to either give or deny sexual consent. If Lanah had been seduced, it was her stepfather's right of consent that had been violated.

Logically, the same factors that had supposedly made the question of Lanah Sawyer's consent so difficult to discern in the rape trial should also have clouded the question of John Callanan's consent in the seduction suit. In practice, seduction suits often brought to light clear evidence that the plaintiff (typically the father) had been aware of the relationship between his daughter (or wife) and the defendant—and had tolerated it. Nonetheless, in seduction suits the question of consent was hardly mentioned, much less disputed. Jurors—and everyone else involved—generally took the woman's father at his word.

As a result, in the seduction suit Lanah didn't necessarily need to convince the jury of anything that Bedlow's own attorneys had not freely admitted during the rape trial: that he was guilty of seducing Sawyer and that, as a result, she had suffered great, and irreparable, harm. Even the literal facts of the case, it could be argued, were now less important than the moral questions at its heart.

There was a dramatic difference in the outcomes of seduction suits and rape trials. In a seduction suit, the defendant almost always lost—and was very often ordered to pay significant monetary damages.

It is hard to escape the conclusion that this regard for men's sexual rights and suspicion of women are what made acquaintance-rape prosecutions so difficult to win—and seduction suits so easy. Looking back, it is easy to imagine that this disparity was due to the different standards of proof that apply in criminal as opposed to civil trials—"beyond a reasonable doubt" versus "the preponderance of evidence." But it is not clear that this distinction was even made in American courtrooms until the nineteenth century. In England, it was not until the 1780s that a "reasonable doubt" standard first appeared in a judge's instructions to a jury. It is also possible that the reluctance of jurors to convict men accused of rape was caused by their hesitation to apply the death penalty. In 1795, New York changed the punishment for rape from hanging to a prison term. But even after that change, juries remained prone to acquit defendants in rape cases—particularly in cases in which the defendant and the victim were acquainted.

By the time Callanan sued Bedlow, the basic question in a seduction suit was not whether a young woman had been seduced, but how much the loss of her sexual innocence mattered. Theoretically, an action for seduction could claim damages only for the *material* consequences of nonmarital sex rather than for their *moral* consequences—such as damages to the woman's reputation or innocence. Nonetheless, in eighteenth-century New Jersey seduction suits, plaintiffs often claimed compensation for three separate things: the value of the victim's lost labor, the direct costs associated with the pregnancy and childbirth, and, finally, the abstract damage to the woman's reputation and her family's honor. As one man complained in 1792, the seducer responsible for "Deflowering" his granddaughter had plunged their entire family "into great Infamy and disgrace." Over time, increasing emphasis was placed on the woman's lost innocence. A large judgment in an 1825 New York case resulted in reports in more than twenty newspapers from Maine to Florida, in which the jury award was explained as compensation for "the destruction of family peace and joy" by the "seducer of a lovely young woman, who, till his arts had succeeded, was as pure as the summer's rose, and as unsullied as the lily of the valley."

In this sense, the Saffen suit was a case in point. The plaintiff's lawyer sought to frame the case around intangible moral and emotional qualities, casting the young woman in terms of a cultural script of middle-class femininity that belied her family's poverty.

The defense, in turn, sought to diminish the damage done to the victim by tarnishing her claims to innocence and virtue. An attorney representing the plaintiff in the Saffen case made this point directly. He assured the jury that, when it came time to assess the amount of damages they should award his client, they did not have to restrict themselves to the literal value of the seduced woman's labor. He told the jurymen that they had a "boundless field" in considering these injuries—not just lost services but also "feelings wounded—family disgraced—a daughter ruined." Indeed, he exhorted the jurors to "give an exemplary verdict." The community, he declared, was looking to them to punish "this apostate seducer," to serve as the "avengers of violated chastity."

Callanan's lawsuit presented the jurors with little more than the most thinly veiled pretext. It was based on the premise that he was the one harmed by what Bedlow had done to Lanah Sawyer. The damages he demanded were barely connected to the facts alleged. By convention, the facts in seduction suits were always framed as technical abstractions. But Callanan grounded his claim on an entirely unconventional sort of fiction: a sequence of events that clearly never happened. He was asking the jury to set aside the superficial facts and see only an underlying moral truth.

It was a remarkable gamble. But it paid off.

We do not know precisely how Lanah handled the peculiar demands of a case organized around legal fictions and a narrative that was morally, but not literally, true. What we do know is that she succeeded in swaying the jurors' sympathies. She had the advantage, of course, of the widespread outrage in the city over the outcome of her previous showdown with Harry Bedlow. Even after the riots, the newspaper war, and the debate over his defense team's tactics had died down, there was a lingering sense that he had gotten away with something he shouldn't have and that she deserved better. How pitiful, one writer in the city's newspapers urged the previous winter, that a man with so many advantages had sunk so low as Henry Bedlow—"his name a common bye word"—and been forced to flee the city. "Repent Oh Henry!" he was urged. Return and acknowledge your past conduct, the writer went on—after giving public notice of your arrival so that parents could lock up their daughters to prevent them from being taken on "nocturnal Battery walks."

After Lanah's testimony, the jurors didn't need anything more than the thinly veiled pretext of the seduction suit to come to a stunning verdict. They accepted Callanan's claim and found Bedlow guilty of seducing Lanah Sawyer. Then, they ordered him to pay an enormous sum in damages: £1,800 New York currency, or about $4,500.

The jurors were not simply compensating Callanan for whatever harms he and Lanah Sawyer had suffered. They wanted to punish Harry Bedlow.

⁓

The lawsuit over the seduction of Lanah Sawyer was a harbinger of change. Increasingly, in the decades to come, jurors responded to claims of seduction and breach of promise with large, punitive judgments. Increasingly, the families of women who had suffered sexual harms turned to the law of seduction for restitution and accountability. Yet the same shift in values that made seduction suits a powerful form of redress for some women began to put them beyond the reach of others—including women of color, poor women, and even white women from working families, like Lanah Sawyer.

Seduction suits had always rested on a scaffolding of arcane technicalities and legal fictions, but over time they became increasingly detached from practical considerations. More and more, women were judged by a middle-class standard of sexual innocence far removed from the everyday realities of women who had to earn money to help support their families, who lived much of their lives in the streets, who were exposed to rough language and harassment, who often had no choice but to manage as best they could on their own. The emerging ideal of women as essentially nurturing, maternal creatures, all but devoid of base, masculine sexual passion, may have really existed only in the world of print: in fictional stories, sentimental poems, and religious strictures—and, of course, in the law of seduction. In court, the value of a woman's sexual honor was rendered brutally literal, a numeric figure representing more or less cash.

In the coming decades, both the amounts plaintiffs demanded in seduction suits and the amounts juries awarded continued to grow, though it was a long time before they equaled the astonishing figures in Lanah Sawyer's case. In early-nineteenth-century currency, John Callanan's claim was about $12,500, the jury award about $4,500. In one suit in 1825, the plaintiffs explicitly stated that their $10,000 claim was almost entirely punitive; the family was affluent and the woman in question did not have to work to help support the family, so the practical damages the family had suffered were limited to about $500 in costs related to pregnancy and childbirth. The jury responded with a damages award of $9,000—double the amount in Lanah's case. Increasingly, the less practical loss a family suffered, the higher the value juries tended to place on a young woman's sexual honor. This issue was openly contested in an 1829 case, in which the young woman's family made no effort to show that they had suffered *any* financial damage as a result of the seduction. The defense argued that the suit was supposedly about the value of the young woman's lost service— and that if there was no loss, there should be no suit. The court swept that logic aside as a literal-minded quibble. In seduction suits, the court observed, the largest judgments were often awarded in cases in which the young woman in question didn't provide the family with any "real" service at all—which was to say, in cases in which the young woman's family had actual servants to keep their house clean, tend their fires, wash their laundry, care for their children, and make and mend their clothes.

Meanwhile, juries found it difficult to see much value in the sexual honor of women who did not enjoy such pampered, cocooned existences. The result, effectively, was to narrow the range of women who could successfully hold men to account for sexual harms. In 1808, the husband of the Black domestic servant Sylvia Patterson prevailed in his seduction suit against her employer—but the jury awarded only the insulting sum of "ONE dollar." Her honor may have been compromised, but in the eyes of the jury it had no value. A subsequent suit over the seduction of a Black woman by a white gentleman in the city ended with a verdict in his favor, her prosecution for criminal conspiracy, and openly racist newspaper reports about the "*dingy* lass." Poor white women, whose lives did not dovetail with middle-class ideals of feminine innocence and fragility, were also effectively denied recourse. In 1818, Catharine Saffen, whose family had been impoverished by the death of her father, became one of the few victims of seduction whose case ended with a not-guilty verdict.

This narrowing of the range of women whose seduction mattered in court reflected a tendency to reduce the most abstract qualities—a woman's virtue and sexual honor—to the most literal, financial values. Race, class, education, family ties, reputation, demeanor, and beauty all entered into calculations of a woman's worth as a potential wife and mother. Whether seduction damaged her value, and, if so, by how much, depended upon how well she embodied the feminine virtues prized by the men who sat on juries.

The same cultural shifts also restricted the kinds of women who could mount prosecutions for sexual assault. For much of the eighteenth century, rape claims emphasized physical harms and lost work, which were meaningful losses for a woman whose physical labor and earning power were important to her livelihood. It seems to have helped rape prosecutions if they could show that the woman in question fought back vigorously and physically. But starting in the 1790s, the emphasis in rape trials was increasingly on injured innocence—and a rape survivor's conformity to middle-class standards of respectability and ideals of delicacy was crucial to prosecuting cases successfully. Even fighting back physically against an assault came to be seen as indelicate; the idealized response for an assaulted woman was to faint. For working women, this standard was unrealistic.

John Callanan's seduction suit against Harry Bedlow did not quite end with the trial before the circuit court at the end of September 1794. The verdict in the circuit court still had to be ratified by the full Supreme Court, which wouldn't begin its next term for several weeks. Sitting in Albany, in late October, the court did ratify the jury's verdict and added up the costs and fees for which Bedlow was also liable, bringing the total amount due John Callanan to £1,826.3.9 in New York currency, or about $4,565 in federal currency. That was on October 23, 1794—almost a year to the day since Lanah Sawyer had been driven to attempt suicide.

If, in the aftermath of the rape trial, Lanah had felt hopeless—that she was a burden to her family, that she was all alone—she may well have continued to struggle with dark thoughts. But now she also had reason to feel effective and valued. Together with her stepfather, she had mounted an audacious battle to hold her rich, resourceful assailant to account. Her family had stood by her, offering her a sense of purpose, a way to make a contribution, a path forward. If the jury in the rape trial, with their surprising, crushing verdict, had made the world seem off kilter, the jury in the seduction suit had declared resoundingly that they wanted to set things to right. This time, the men on the jury had seen that what Harry Bedlow had done to her was wrong, and that it mattered—that *she* mattered, that she belonged, that she had enormous value. It was a powerful vindication not just of Lanah personally but also of her sense of justice and of reality. In this sense, the jury's verdict was a tremendous moral victory. And then there was the money—a staggering sum with the potential to change the lives of everyone in her family.

Of course, as Lanah Sawyer no doubt knew all too well, there are wounds that no kind of familial embrace, no measure of public vindication, no amount of money can heal.

Nor was the lawsuit itself quite over. By law, the official record of a Supreme Court case was a judgment roll—a running account of the key events in the case, written by the lawyer representing the victorious party on a roll of parchment. Properly prepared sheepskin was expensive, so attorneys used only as much as they needed for each case, cutting off pieces they didn't need or stitching multiple sheets together. For this case, Callanan's attorney chose a large, pristine rectangle—about the width of a sheet of letter-sized paper and twice as long—that, two hundred years later, remains white and supple, albeit somewhat greasy and faintly smelly. When the result of the final hearing in October was added, the ungainly record was rolled up, tied with a piece of the proverbial red tape, and handed over to the court clerk for the chief justice's signature. Only with his seal would the outcome be official.

For almost three months, John Callanan waited.

Finally, on January 11, 1795, the judgment roll was signed by Justice Morgan Lewis, who had ratified the judgment in October. Two days later, the court clerk officially marked it "filed."

The lawsuit was now legally over.

For a time, John Callanan may have imagined that, court order in hand, it would now be easy to get Harry Bedlow to pay up. If so, he was wrong.

And Lanah Sawyer would have been wrong, too, if she imagined that, with the end of their second legal battle, she could put Harry Bedlow behind her. As she would learn in the years to come, Bedlow didn't have to attack her body again to attack her dignity, her reputation, or her confidence in the power of truth.

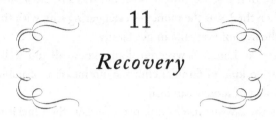

11

Recovery

T hree years after Harry Bedlow first met Lanah Sawyer, he contemplated an extraordinary letter. It was a letter full of sorrow and regret, an abject apology, a plea for understanding and forgiveness—addressed to the "sweet and affable" victim of an "unfeeling wretch." But this was not an apology from Harry, pleading with the woman he had wronged. It was the opposite.

> *July 13th, 1796*
>
> *MY DEAR BEDLOW,*
>
> *WHEN I sit and reflect on things past, it rends my heart to think how I have deceived you, what an unfeeling wretch I have proved to you and your family, but all I can do is to ask forgiveness, which I am positive your sweet and affable disposition can and will do. You know full well the cause of my going, the question was, Will you go to Mrs. Carey's? and I consented, I was therefore as willing to go as you was; but you see what it is to want a friend; at the time not one there was to intercede for me, but all threatening with taking my life, or turning me out of doors, to whom should I go, if that had been the case? how did I know whether you would ever countenance me after what happened? gone perhaps on the wide world for every one's cull, but not being that way inclined I was compelled to appear in court, and there swear to things that I knew was false, to bring scandal to your family, and more to my own; but he did not know what injury he was doing himself and me, but if he had the least spark of regard of parental affection for me, he would never did as he has done; but he has dug a pit for you and me to fall in, but let him take care of himself. What will such a father have to answer for—for the sake of*

*indulging himself in an idle, a careless, a thoughtless habit, that cannot
afford the least satisfaction beyond the present moment if in that, and
which must be attended with deep remorse when he comes to reflect, think
seriously on these things, and in time resolve on such a course as may
bring credit to yourself, justice to all you deal with, peace and pleasure
to your mind, comfort to your family, and which will afford at the same
time the highest satisfaction to your affectionate friend H.S.*

   I am dear sir,

   Your affectionate friend,

                      HELENAH SAWYER.

For Harry Bedlow, the letter could be his deliverance: the key to his
release from the long train of troubles and humiliations he had endured
over the past three years, the key to restoring his family's good opinion of
him and to restoring the honor of the Bedlow name.

The key Bedlow needed most that summer was made of black iron and
about the size of a pair of modern kitchen shears. It operated the locks of
the city's old prison—where, by mid-1796, he had been confined for the
better part of eighteen months.

When the hulking stone prison at the head of the Fields had been new,
before the war, it had housed all manner of miscreants; during the war,
the British had used it to secure suspected Patriots. But for years now it
had been used as a debtors' prison. Those who owed small sums could be
held only for thirty days, but those whose debts were large enough could
be held indefinitely. So the city's poor—tailors and sailors and cartmen
whom nobody would trust with more than a small sum in the first place—
were constantly shuffling in and out. But the city's fallen elite—those who
had been rich enough to incur debts of more than £1,000—tended to
accumulate. They were there until they came up with the money they
owed or until they struck a deal with their creditors. Or until they died—
and the jailer turned his massive keys in the locks so that another corpse
could be taken out to an ignominious pauper's grave.

It was a nasty place, uncomfortable, depressing, and stinking. The
city budgeted only about £1 a month for each prisoner's subsistence—
including food, clothing, bedding, and firewood. If that left the inmates
hungry, sleeping in rags on the dank stone floors, and freezing, that
was not the city's problem. Prisoners could appeal to their families and

friends for help. Ghost stories about the prison circulated through the city. When several dozen debtors broke out in the spring of 1798, their skeletal, emaciated bodies elicited shock and horror.

Back in October 1794, when the jury announced its verdict in the seduction suit, John Callanan's triumph over Harry Bedlow had seemed complete. After the devastating loss in the rape trial, the verdict was, for Lanah Sawyer, a resounding moral victory. A jury of Bedlow's peers had declared that he had wronged Sawyer—and that, when his wrongs were translated into pounds and shillings, the only adequate figure was hyperbolic. John Callanan was vindicated. Henry Bedlow was humiliated. And in practical terms, the financial award was big enough to change both men's lives.

Still, it could take more than a jury verdict or even a court order for money to actually change hands. If Bedlow proved unwilling or unable to pay what he owed, John Callanan had two legal options. He could get a court order to seize Bedlow's assets. But it wasn't clear that Bedlow had enough property in his own name to seize: he was still living with his parents and had long since sold the only two parcels of land he had ever owned. So instead, Callanan went after Bedlow's body. Maybe seeing their son in debtors' prison would convince his parents to pay up.

For a workingman like John Callanan, the damages he had been awarded in the seduction suit—£1,800 plus costs—was a staggering sum. If the city's tax assessments are a reliable guide, it was enough money for him to buy the house he rented on Gold Street and half a dozen like it. Even for a gentleman like Harry Bedlow, it was a large amount. His parents probably earned about £1,000 a year from their real estate on the old Rutgers farm—a figure suggested by his aunt Mary McCrea's surviving rent books. But the Bedlows were loath to sell their holdings, which were rapidly increasing in value.

In sending Bedlow to debtors' prison, Callanan would be able to exercise his power, exact revenge, see his nemesis punished. But as a way of extracting money, incarceration worked best as a threat. Time behind bars might increase a debtor's motivation to pay up, but it would not increase their ability to do so. As Callanan likely knew, sending Bedlow to debtors' prison was tantamount to giving up on ever seeing the full amount he was owed.

But the two men were in no mood to compromise. Early in 1795 John

Callanan and attorney Caleb Riggs initiated the process of having Bedlow hauled off to prison.

When a constable attempted to arrest him, Bedlow lashed out violently. On January 30, he was brought before a grand jury in Federal Hall and indicted for assault and battery on a constable in the execution of his office. The next day, the court approved Callanan's request and packed Bedlow off to debtors' prison. Flailing for leverage and revenge, Bedlow hired an attorney to file a new lawsuit against John Callanan over an alleged assault the previous fall, claiming damages of £5,000—the same figure originally named in the seduction suit. Bedlow didn't bother following through with his lawsuit, but he did force Callanan to deal with the hassle of getting the suit quashed.

By this point, John Callanan was feeling good about his future. Two days after sending Bedlow off to prison, Callanan improved his own family's living situation. On Monday, February 2, 1795, he became a homeowner for the first time. The house he bought was just around the corner from the property he had been renting on Gold Street. The new property, at 88 Fair (now Fulton) Street, was long and narrow. Saddle maker John Young and his wife Margaret attested that they had been "well and truly paid" the purchase price of £1,000.

John Callanan could not have imagined, at this point, how long and ugly his battle to extract money from Harry Bedlow would be. Or the toll it would take on everyone involved—on Bedlow, of course, but also on himself, and especially on his stepdaughter, Lanah Sawyer.

As winter turned into spring and then summer, it became clear how determined Harry Bedlow's family was to secure his release from prison without having to pay John Callanan. To that end, they hired the nation's most famous lawyer, Alexander Hamilton, who had recently resigned his position as treasury secretary and moved back to New York to make money. But as summer turned into fall and then into winter and spring and then another summer, it became obvious that they were not going to be able to circumvent John Callanan.

That's when the letter from "Helenah Sawyer" appeared.

Several years earlier, in an effort to clear himself in an investigation into financial improprieties, Alexander Hamilton had produced letters from a woman he claimed to have seduced. Political opponents had gotten wind of large payments Hamilton had made to a shady political operative, and they suspected him of abusing his high office at the treasury by funneling money into speculative ventures and profiting from his insider knowledge and ability to direct federal policy. When a congressional committee confronted him, Hamilton claimed that he had been guilty not of financial improprieties but of marital infidelity: he had engaged in an affair with a married woman named Maria Reynolds, only to be found out by her husband. The husband could have sued him for seduction but instead agreed to keep the matter quiet in exchange for a series of payments totaling about £1,000. To convince the congressional investigators to accept this story, Hamilton promised them evidence, which he soon produced—in the form of a series of plaintive, tearful letters from Maria Reynolds, documenting their turbulent affair. The tactic worked; the congressmen agreed to close their investigation and to keep Hamilton's secrets. While the matter remained under wraps in the coming years, the possibility of public disclosure by his political enemies hung perpetually over Hamilton's head.

Soon, Hamilton would use the Helenah Sawyer letter in much the same way—in an attempt to break the stalemate between his client and John Callanan. Like Maria Reynolds, Lanah Sawyer would once again become a pawn in a battle between men.

Reading that letter within the stone and iron confines of New York's old jail, Harry Bedlow could hardly have asked for a more abject apology or better proof that in the matter of Lanah Sawyer, he was the real victim—that the charge of rape had been false, that the seduction suit was an extortionate scheme devised by John Callanan. The letter was exactly what he needed to turn the tables on his enemies, to secure his release from prison, and to redeem his reputation.

Why else would he have written it?

※

For some men, being hauled by a constable past the gallows and whipping post in front of New York's debtors' prison was enough to inspire a sudden change of heart. "Terrified" by the thought of "being committed to such a place," one man agreed to pay a disputed debt upon reaching the prison's door. Passing through that door, Harry Bedlow entered a shadowy world of desperation and denial. Even if they eventually found a way out, long-term inmates were often scarred by the experience, haunted and embittered.

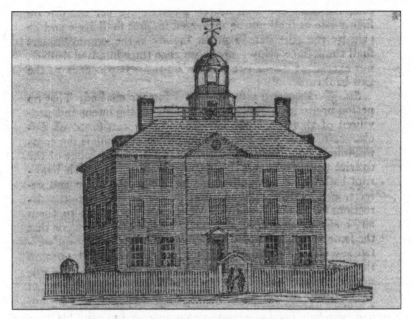

The debtors' prison as depicted in Forlorn Hope *in 1800.*

After his initial shock, Bedlow found that his fellow debtors had created a complex social system inside the prison—a hierarchical world, in which their status largely correlated to the size of their debts. The prison was a three-story structure, about seventy by sixty feet, built of rough local stone, with iron bars on its windows and a walkway, surmounted by a cupola, on its roof. The front door opened into the first floor, with a staircase dividing the prison-keepers' quarters from a large hall that housed the prisoners with relatively small debts—a rotating population of ragged, malnourished men and women from the city's lower ranks. Without friends on the outside to bring them much in the way of money, food, liquor, or anything else, their deprivation was the most extreme—but also the most likely to end. Those who owed less than £10 could be held for only a month.

Those who owed large sums were accorded more dignified accommodations on the building's second and third floors, where they often spent months or even years. Bedlow landed on the second floor, which had the same basic layout as the third but with higher ceilings and larger windows.

Six rooms opened onto a central hallway, each room housing about five men. Some of them were gentlemen like Bedlow; others were skilled artisans. Typically, they had been prosperous enough that they had been trusted with substantial sums of money. Even now, those who were deepest in debt on the outside seemed to have the best access to conveniences and luxuries on the inside—including liquor and prostitutes.

But none of that entirely masked their helplessness. On Bedlow's floor, the most prominent inmate was William Duer, the former deputy secretary of the treasury under Alexander Hamilton—whose shady dealings while in office had called Hamilton's own integrity into question, and whose subsequent financial collapse in 1792 had provoked riots and an enduring recession. With nowhere else to go, his impoverished wife and children had moved into the prison, where the other prisoners allocated them a room of their own. Year after year, Duer spent his days poring over paperwork, trying to figure out a way to reverse his fortunes, so busy that his visitors required appointments. Some years earlier, the improvident artist Ralph Earl had, with help from powerful patrons, managed to paint his way out of the prison with portraits of social luminaries, including Eliza Hamilton, Robert Troup, and John Cozine, all posed against the same improvised, or imagined, background (see p. 179). In 1800, a reform-minded lawyer produced a short-lived newspaper from the prison; it did nothing to get him out but did capture the horror of the place. He called it *Forlorn Hope.*

Men who enjoyed dignity and honor on the outside, who were accustomed to exercising authority over others and envisioning grand schemes, were now subjected to endless humiliations. Bedlow might have a friend willing to smuggle in a little rum, only to have it confiscated by the turnkey and offered to the other prisoners for sale. His visitors were searched to prevent them from slipping him some tool he might use to escape, such as a crowbar he could work against window grates, or a rope he could throw off the roof and climb down.

Escape was difficult, so the debtors on the prison's second floor turned to escapism. By early 1795, the adult men on the second floor had organized themselves into a kind of shadow republic. To defend what they saw as their customary rights against their jailers and to resolve the conflicts that inevitably arose among themselves, they created their own form of republican government. They wrote up a formal constitution for what they liked to call the "Middle Hall" and then invited all the adult men on the hall to literally sign on. The chief institution of the debtors' republic was its "Supreme Court." During regular elections, the citizens chose the court's three judges, a district attorney, a sheriff, and a clerk. In the desperate confines of the debtors' prison, Harry Bedlow and his fellow inmates created a new world of their own invention. It was a world in which incarcerated bankrupts reimagined themselves as republican citizens defending their rights and claims to respectability. It was a world in which the old stone prison could be remade, at least in the court's official minutes, into "York Castle."

Soon after his arrival, Harry Bedlow was elected one of the court's three judges—an honor the debtors of Middle Hall reserved for the most elite among them. The earliest surviving minutes of the court date to July 17, 1795. A few blocks away, Mayor Varick, presiding over the city's Mayor's Court, handed Bedlow another defeat by dismissing his most recent lawsuit against John Callanan. But in the Middle Hall of York Castle, the Honorable Henry Bedlow was the one standing in judgment of others. The case before him was typical of the petty squabbles that constituted much of the court's business: a debtor was accused of sexual slander against another man's wife—calling her, according to one witness, "a damn'd Whore." The jury found him guilty. The presiding judge signed the official record with an aristocratic affectation, writing only his last name in large letters, underscored with a flourish, as though he were a high-ranking British nobleman: "Bedlow."

Over the course of the summer, Margaret Frean, the Hall's only female debtor, filed several more complaints. One inmate had slandered her by saying that in her former life she "had Kept a bad house" and that her room in the prison was no better; another interrupted her sleep with all the noise he made at night. Surely, she told the debtors' court, she was entitled to that "Peace Harmony & Good Order which ought [to] Subsist in every civilized Society." Her most serious charge that summer was against the turnkey assigned to the second floor: he had threatened to expose her plan to get out of the prison with her assets intact by filing for bankruptcy with fraudulent accounts.

The prisoners hated that turnkey, but even the debtors' supreme court understood that it did not have the power to hire and fire prison employees. So, in November 1795, Bedlow and his fellow judges ordered their sheriff to call a meeting of the members of the Hall "to consult which will be the most proper means of regaining our lost Priviledges which we

Conceive to be decreasing rapidly." In a petition to the prison keeper, they listed a series of demands—including the removal of the offending turn-key. In the world of the Middle Hall, some crimes, like slander, looked pretty much the way they did on the outside. But smugglers were to be encouraged, and informers were anathema. In this desperate atmosphere, nothing was more sacred than the right of a debtor to try to find a way out—by fair means or foul.

By late 1795, as the prisoners' constitutional crisis dragged on, Harry Bedlow devised a plan to get out of the prison by declaring bankruptcy.

Under New York law, a debtor whose obligations totaled more than his assets could go through an elaborate procedure to document his insol-vency, turn almost all his remaining property over to his creditors, and obtain his release from prison—and possibly a full discharge from his debts as well. Fraud, of course, was a constant problem. There were two basic ways to cheat: concealing one's assets or inflating one's debts. The more fake debt held by friendly parties, the less one needed to pay one's real creditors. This, it seems, is the strategy Harry Bedlow and his attorney Alexander Hamilton pursued.

John Callanan had no reason to allow Harry Bedlow to proceed with insolvency, no reason to trust him, and no reason to believe that he had significant assets. By law, there was only one way to get around Callanan's objection. Bedlow would have to show two things: that the sum he owed Callanan (slightly over £1,800) was no more than a quarter of his total debt and that the creditor or creditors to whom he owed the other three quarters (at least £5,400) were willing to go along with his bankruptcy and accept a portion of his remaining assets in lieu of full payment. The man who stepped in to play the role of Bedlow's principal debtor was his father.

On December 26, 1795, William Bedlow formally petitioned the judge who oversaw insolvency proceedings to allow his son to declare bank-ruptcy. Harry was briefly released from prison for the occasion. He had to swear that the accounts he presented were accurate, that the inventory of his assets was complete—and that all of the debts he listed were legit-imate.

As was customary, the judge scheduled a public hearing so that any of Bedlow's creditors could review the accounts he submitted and raise any objections they might have. Then, as required by law, for six weeks in advance of the hearing, a notice signed by Henry Bedlow, as the debtor, and by William Bedlow, as the "petitioning creditor," was published in the city's newspapers.

The hearing did not go smoothly. Someone showed up and urged the judge to reject the Bedlows' proposal. Most likely it was John Callanan or his attorney—arguing that their accounts were fraudulent. The judge agreed. Ruling that there was "sufficient Cause" for concern, he denied the petition. That didn't stop Hamilton from submitting his bill, or William Bedlow from paying it. On February 4, 1796, Hamilton noted in his "Cash Book" the receipt of $25 from "Mr Bedlow on application for his son upon insolvency Act."

By then, Harry was back in prison, his prospects gloomier than ever.

A month later, the citizens of the Middle Hall greeted their new jailer, Thomas Hazard, with a petition outlining their basic rights and demanding that he stop their turnkey from ratting out their (fraudulent) insolvency petitions. Hazard was open to negotiation. He granted many of their demands and promised to reassign the turnkey to another floor if he were "detected in doing any thing tending to prevent a Prisoner get[ting] his Liberty."

After his insolvency petition was denied, Bedlow knew that to "get his Liberty," he needed John Callanan's consent. By summer, he had set in motion another scheme to obtain it.

The first reference to the "Helenah Sawyer" letter was in a note Bedlow's mother sent to Alexander Hamilton in early August 1796. When her husband's health was poor—as it had been for years—Catharine Bedlow took responsibility not only for managing their household but also for transacting the family's public business. The letter, dated July 13, had been in her hands for some time, perhaps a couple of weeks. She had hoped to hand it to Hamilton directly, but he didn't stop by as expected. Finally, she grew impatient and composed a brief note, an efficient mix of social niceties and urgent business.

New York Augst. 2, 1796

Sir

    Inclosed is the Letter of Helena Sayer which I Should have been Sent you before, but being daily in Expectation of Seeing you, it was defered to be given you till then. I could wish a Leasure Houre will

> *permit you to call & see us as Mr Bedlow Continues Ill unable to trans-*
> *act any Business.*
>
> *I am with Esteem yours*
>
> Catharine Bedlow

Satisfied, she folded the Helenah Sawyer letter into a small square, wrapped her note around it, sealed the packet with red wax, and dispatched it to "Honl. Alexr. Hamilton Esq. / Broad Way."

For Hamilton, the question was how to put the extraordinary letter to use. The letter clearly spoke to Harry's emotional needs. It absolved him of the charge that he had forced Lanah Sawyer into Mother Carey's brothel—and, without quite saying so, it implied that he hadn't committed rape. It validated the claim his lawyers had made repeatedly during the rape trial: that Sawyer's account was false. It supported their insinuations that she had perjured herself at the behest of her volatile, moneygrubbing stepfather. And it even supported Mother Carey's claim that, after the alleged rape, Sawyer had pursued a romantic connection with Bedlow. Now, it offered Bedlow the cold comfort that Sawyer was suffering, too, for what her stepfather had made her do.

The letter offered Bedlow moral vindication, the hope he could regain some of his lost honor. And it promised to expose John Callanan as a man who could force his stepdaughter to lie in the most public and intimate ways for his own gain, prostituting her for his own purposes. In the aftermath of the rape trial, John Callanan had been built up as local hero, attracting fierce support and enormous outrage. This letter called all of that into question.

And in this, Alexander Hamilton saw an opening.

According to a later account, when the letter was put into the hands of Bedlow's counsel Alexander Hamilton and Peter Jay Munro, they sent for John Callanan and confronted him with the letter. They read it aloud. They let him examine it.

He did not recoil in horror.

He dismissed the letter as a fraud.

For one thing, he told the two lawyers, the handwriting did not match his stepdaughter's. Moreover, her first name was misspelled: she was "Lanah," not "Helenah." And the style of the letter, its gushing, overwrought tone, its gentility and precision, its profession of enduring love did not seem like what a young seamstress would write to a man she had prosecuted for rape and sued for seduction. Even Bedlow's own lawyers had not tried to convince anyone that he had a "sweet and affable disposition."

The letter seemed like a fantastical ploy. Perhaps it only made sense in the shadow world of "York Castle"—that new republic of denial and reinvention.

Faced with John Callanan's rebuff, Bedlow obtained two more documents in the coming weeks: another letter, signed with Lanah's actual name, and an affidavit from a Philadelphia alderman attesting to its authenticity.

How did Bedlow manage to procure these documents from the confines of New York's debtors' prison?

One person Harry Bedlow did know in Philadelphia was Mother Carey. About nine months after the riots that destroyed her house and possessions, she and her husband had moved to Philadelphia and bought a house in a side street in Southwark, a working-class district on the outskirts of the city. Their new home was tiny: a two-story wood-frame structure about twelve feet wide and seventeen feet deep on a narrow ribbon of land. By the summer of 1796, Carey's husband had died, and her own health was failing. But Mrs. Carey was surprisingly well off. She had almost £1,000 in bonds held by merchants in New York and Albany—which likely produced enough income for her to get by.

Even after her move to Philadelphia, Mother Carey maintained an expansive social network that included Ann McFall in New York and a brother-in-law in Ireland. Like many other women, it seems that even though she never learned to write, she had learned to read. To stay in contact with the merchants who held her money and her far-flung friends and relations, she no doubt had experience turning to others to write letters on her behalf. In New York, one of her friends was a schoolmaster; in Philadelphia, she became "good friends" with a literate tradesman who lived around the corner and, a few years later, would serve as a justice of the peace.

So it is possible that Harry Bedlow was in correspondence with Mrs. Carey that summer—and that she was in a position to help him. Who better than Mother Carey to find a young woman to present herself to an alderman and swear out an affidavit serving Harry Bedlow's needs?

Bedlow remained in prison. Through the end of the summer and into the fall, he served on the York Castle supreme court and attended meetings of the citizens of the Middle Hall.

As he approached the end of his second year in confinement—and after the failure of two fraudulent ploys concocted with the help of Alexander Hamilton—Harry Bedlow and his father came to a humiliating realization: the only way they were going to get Callanan to agree to Bedlow's release was by paying at least part of the money they owed.

By this point, John Callanan, too, was ready to make a deal. Every month that passed made it clearer that his chance of recovering the full amount of the jury award was slim. If Bedlow himself didn't have the wherewithal and if his family were willing to tolerate his extended confinement, Callanan might not get any money at all for years—or, perhaps, ever.

So both men had reason to negotiate.

Although court costs and two years of interest had swollen the sum at stake, both sides remained focused on the original jury award: £1,800.

In late November 1796, Bedlow and his father agreed to pay half of that amount: £900. In exchange, Callanan agreed to give up any claim to the rest of the debt and to give Bedlow an unconditional discharge from prison. In a later account, Bedlow claimed that the deal was struck at a meeting that involved his attorneys Alexander Hamilton and Peter Jay Munro and Callanan's attorney Nicholas Evertson. The agreed-upon sum was to be paid in two installments: the first half down and the second half in the form of a note that Harry Bedlow's widely respected uncle Henry Rutgers agreed to secure. On November 24, 1796, in New York City, William Bedlow signed a promissory note pledging to pay John Callanan £450, with lawful interest, in twelve months' time.

For Harry Bedlow, at least, the deal worked. After almost two years, the big iron key turned for him, the prison door swung open, and he stepped out.

❧

Even after his release from prison in late 1796, Harry Bedlow wasn't really free. More than three years after he first encountered Lanah Sawyer, he was still haunted by her—or, perhaps more precisely, by the image of himself reflected in the disputed letter from "Helenah Sawyer": a man wronged, humiliated, and brought low; a victim of a lying woman and her grasping father—a man who deserved to recoup his lost honor, to restore his reputation, to resume his rightful place in the world. He wanted to regain the upper hand against John Callanan and to find a way out of the deal his family had been forced to strike to get him out of prison. Once again, the instrument he wanted to use for that purpose was Lanah Sawyer.

Soon after his release from prison, Bedlow headed to Philadelphia in an effort to track her down. He had heard that she had moved there—probably at the end of the previous summer, when Alexander Hamilton had confronted her stepfather with the "Helenah Sawyer" letter. Now, with encouragement from his attorney, Bedlow seems to have hoped that if he could find Lanah Sawyer he might be able to convince her to produce some more persuasive documentation. Perhaps he had in mind some new affidavit, validating the substance of the letters Callanan had dismissed as fraudulent and vindicating him as the victim of an illegitimate persecution motivated by malice and greed.

It is not clear why he imagined that Lanah Sawyer would have ever agreed to such a request. To give Bedlow anything like what he wanted would have required branding herself a liar, acknowledging that she deserved to be regarded as sexually ruined, betraying her stepfather, and dishonoring her family—and all for the benefit of the rapist who had nearly driven her to suicide.

Unsurprisingly, Bedlow's trip to Philadelphia proved an expensive failure.

A few months before he arrived, Mother Carey had died. In 1796, sensing that her health was failing, she had made out a will leaving her house, clothing, furnishings, and money to more than a dozen individuals—with the largest portion going to Thomas Glover, the young boy who had been sleeping in the back room of her New York house on the night of the rape. She left her house and some money to his mother, Ann McFall, stipulating that it was "to be paid into her own hands and for her own Use without the Control of her ... Husband." To the end, Mother Carey was wary of men's tendency to exploit their power over women.

Her death deprived Harry Bedlow of his most obvious contact in Philadelphia. By mid-January 1797, Bedlow had run out of money and was appealing to his uncle Henry Rutgers in New York for more. He needed money to pay off his debts and to return home—some $125 at first and then, two weeks later, another £50. Rutgers was better positioned than the Bedlows to arrange for credit in Philadelphia. He turned to his friend and political ally Edward Livingston, a prominent attorney who had just been reelected to his seat in the House of Representatives.

Rutgers made it clear to Livingston that he was not giving his notorious namesake any warm embrace. He introduced Bedlow not as his nephew but rather as his brother-in-law "Mr Bedlow's" son. As for the young man's business in Philadelphia, Rutgers noted only that he had been sent there on the advice of an attorney "to avail himself of certain advantages which might arise from his being there." But the trip had proven fruitless. Rutgers asked Livingston to extend sufficient credit "to enable him to return home again"—which he clearly wanted Bedlow to do before racking up any more expenses.

Did Harry Bedlow simply fail to track down Lanah? Or did she refuse to give him what he wanted?

All we really know is that if Lanah Sawyer hadn't wanted to be found, it would not have been difficult for her to disappear. In an era before identity cards or even much in the way of public vital records, there were many ways to disguise or reinvent oneself.

Back in New York, Harry Bedlow found himself effectively imprisoned again, this time in his parents' grand new house on the East River shore of the old Rutgers farm. While he had been in Philadelphia, a rich brewer and real-estate speculator who lived a block from John Callanan had sued Bedlow for debts of at least $4,000. Bedlow could avoid arrest by simply holing up at home; by law, the sheriff could not force his way into a private dwelling—a fact that sometimes resulted in tense negotiations through open windows. But, the Bedlows wondered, was that really the best strategy? At a social event one evening, William Bedlow ran into Edward Livingston, who had just returned to the city, and importuned him for free legal advice. The next day, he followed up with a plaintive note: "The disagreable situation of my Son in being confined to the House, on account of that Villianos affair I mentioned to you, makes me solicitous to have your Advise." Livingston tried to put him off, but the elder Bedlow persisted.

The only surviving indication of how the Bedlows understood the Lanah Sawyer affair was an offhand remark in a second self-pitying note. The "Villiny" of the current lawsuit, the senior Bedlow wrote, was "only equalled by the prosecution of Callanan," which, he hoped, would "impress on your mind the persecution my Son has laboured under for four Years."

A few months later, the threat of scandal that had dogged Alexander Hamilton for years suddenly exploded into public view. If Bedlow had hoped that by going to Philadelphia he could double down on the "Helenah Sawyer" documents and force Callanan to back down from claiming the money he was still owed, Hamilton's response to the so-called Reynolds Affair may have been a cautionary tale.

In a series of pamphlets and letters published in newspapers over the summer of 1797, the republican scandalmonger James Callender presented a sensational account of the affair. Back in 1792, he wrote, Hamilton had been accused of abusing his office as secretary of the treasury by engaging in improper, likely illegal, financial speculations with a shady operative named James Reynolds (who had previously been brought to court in New York for trying to bilk a Revolutionary War veteran of his benefits). A small group of congressmen opened a discreet investigation. Hamilton had claimed that he was guilty only of seducing Reynolds's wife, Maria—and paying them hush money. As a cover story, Callender insisted, this was "absurd." Why would Hamilton, a well-known adulterer, pay blackmail over yet another "illicit amour"? The world already knew, he quipped, that in "the secretary's bucket of chastity" there was not a drop to been seen.

To back up his claims, Callender reproduced a series of documents compiled five years earlier by James Monroe and the other congressional investigators. There were several unsigned letters to James Reynolds that Hamilton admitted writing in a "disguised" hand to obscure his identity. There were also reports of two sensational meetings. After putting the investigators off for several days, Hamilton met with them on December 15, 1792, told them his story, and showed them a cache of passionate letters he claimed to have received from Maria Reynolds. (The investigators didn't copy these letters and returned them to Hamilton, leading Callender to believe that he had subsequently destroyed them.) The investigators' assessment of Hamilton's story was damning: "We left him under an impression [that] our suspicions were removed."

Another memorandum, which Hamilton had not previously seen, described another meeting two weeks later in which James Monroe was briefed on a conversation between Maria Reynolds and one of her husband's associates. Reportedly, Mrs. Reynolds confirmed that her husband

and Hamilton had been involved in shady financial dealings that they tried to cover up by concocting false evidence. When told that Hamilton claimed to have been involved with her in an illicit affair, Maria Reynolds burst into tears, denied the assertion, and denounced it as a "fabrication of colonel Hamilton."

In the end, the congressional investigators decided to drop the matter and promised Hamilton they would keep his secrets—though the investigators had the House clerk copy the documents they had gathered. And rumors spread. In mid-1796, just as Hamilton was trying to use the "Helenah Sawyer" letters against John Callanan, his political enemies published a thinly veiled threat to expose the Reynolds Affair—and he himself threatened to expose Thomas Jefferson's sexual relationship with Sally Hemings, a woman he enslaved.

The following summer, when the public scandal broke, Hamilton responded with righteous indignation. He railed against the original investigators, demanded to know which of them was Callender's source, and importuned them to state publicly that they believed his version of events. Monroe acknowledged that he had given a copy of the documents to Thomas Jefferson but insisted that neither of them was the source of the leak. This was true: the source of the leaked documents, it is now clear, was a copy made by the clerk of the House. But Hamilton didn't know that. In a heated meeting in mid-July, Hamilton all but called Monroe a liar, Monroe did call Hamilton a "scoundrel," and the two men ended up on the brink of a duel—which was averted only by the intervention of Aaron Burr (who had recently helped Maria Reynolds get a divorce). Even then, Monroe would not produce the kind of public statement Hamilton demanded. I would if I could, he told Burr, "but in truth I have doubts upon the main point."

Then, about two months after the scandal first broke, Hamilton defied the advice of his friends—who argued that the best response to Callender's allegations would be silence—and published a long, indignant pamphlet of his own. He described his relationship with the Reynoldses as an illicit "amour" that had ensnared him in a plot to extract more than $1,300 in blackmail. "This confession," he noted, "is not made without a blush." But he insisted that it was necessary to "effectually wipe away a more serious stain."

At the heart of Hamilton's account were the disputed letters he claimed to have received from Maria Reynolds. Instead of tracking her down, as Callender had suggested, so that the world could hear what she had to say, Hamilton had spent weeks trying to recruit third parties to attest that the letters in his possession were in her handwriting. A Philadelphia printer forwarded a letter from Maria Reynolds as a sample of her writing, but Hamilton didn't make use of it. Instead, the proof he included in his pamphlet was an affidavit from a woman in Philadelphia who ran a boarding-house that Maria Reynolds had never stayed in. In addition, Hamilton wrote that he had deposited the original letters with an attorney in Philadelphia, where they could be examined by any "gentleman" he referred.

Hamilton's claim that he had left the letters available for inspection may have been nothing more than a bluff. The only individual with the effrontery to ask to see them was Callender himself—and Hamilton was too angry to give him any response at all. Later, the attorney Hamilton supposedly left the letters with wrote that they "never were deposited with me."

Unable to resist kicking Hamilton while he was down, Callender followed up with a new work mocking Hamilton's melodramatic indignation and fraudulent defense.

"This martyr of virtue, this exulting object of persecution," Callender wrote—in terms that could just as accurately have described the Bedlows' self-pitying attitude—"has published ninety-three pages to prove" a claim that didn't make sense in the first place: "I am a rake, and for that reason I cannot be a swindler."

As for the "love-sick epistles" supposedly written by Maria Reynolds, Callender argued that they were clearly forged. This was apparent from the published texts alone: they were written in a highly literate prose but strewn with gross errors in spelling and punctuation—a discrepancy that pointed to a clumsy effort by an elegant writer to impersonate someone less well educated. "Send for the lady, or pay her a visit," Callender insisted. "Take her before a magistrate, and let us hear what she has to say."

Hamilton's response to the Reynolds Affair was widely regarded as a disaster. His wife was devastated. Her family was so humiliated that they attempted to withdraw the pamphlet from circulation by buying up all available copies. But the damage was done. Hamilton's political career was effectively over. As his old friend Robert Troup put it: "His ill judged pamphlet has done him incomparable injury."

Hamilton never did attempt to track down Maria Reynolds. Back in

1792, Hamilton had offered the Reynoldses incentives to leave town and make themselves unavailable to the congressional investigators. After the public scandal broke, he evidently saw no advantage in encouraging her to come forward. Nor, for that matter, did James Callender. For both men, she had become not so much a real person as an image, a tool, an instrument in their ongoing battle.

Through all of this, Maria Reynolds never raised her voice publicly. She could have sent a statement to a newspaper editor, or sworn out an affidavit, or offered up samples of her handwriting. Yet, all through the summer and fall, she kept silent. Then, she and her family set sail for England—putting the scandal behind them and beginning a new life.

For Harry Bedlow, the unfolding public spectacle hit close to home. Like Hamilton, he had been accused of a serious public crime, rape, and his defense had been that he was guilty only of a lesser, private wrong: seduction. Then, with Hamilton working as his attorney, he had attempted to prove his version of events with written documentation from the woman herself. But Bedlow's "Helenah Sawyer" letter had already been dismissed by John Callanan as a fraud.

All of that hung over Bedlow's head as his father's legal battle with Callanan dragged on.

The Reynolds Affair was winding down, in late 1797, when the note William Bedlow had given John Callanan to secure Harry's freedom came due. Now the question was: Would he honor it? The answer, as soon became clear, was no.

With Harry Bedlow out of jail, Callanan's only recourse was to go back to court. And with no valid reason for refusing payment, all William Bedlow could do was try to drag the proceedings out.

At first the elder Bedlow attempted to evade the sheriff by holing up in his house. John Callanan flushed him out by going to the newly appointed city recorder—his former attorney James Kent—who declared that the law against "absconding and absent" debtors was applicable and ordered a series of newspaper notices branding the elder Bedlow a "concealed debtor." William Bedlow was able to stomach only so much public humiliation. In July 1798, at a circuit court in Federal Hall, the matter came to an ignominious end. Three times, William Bedlow was called to answer Callanan's claim. Three times, he failed to appear. Bedlow was ordered to pay what he owed Callanan—the second half of the £900 agreement they had come to in late 1796, plus interests and costs. This verdict was quickly certified by the full court, and the judgment roll was filed on August 7.

In the weeks to come, John Callanan would once again begin the process of collecting a legal judgment against the Bedlows.

Harry Bedlow, even long after his release from prison, was still tormented by the specter of the seventeen-year-old sewing girl he blamed for his troubles.

❧

POUGHKEEPSIE. THURSDAY, SEPTEMBER 27, 1798.

A year after Alexander Hamilton issued his pamphlet regarding the Reynolds Affair, responding to accusations that he had tried to cover up grave crimes by publishing copies of letters purportedly written by a woman he claimed to have seduced, Harry Bedlow contemplated following his example.

For five years, Lanah Sawyer, the flesh-and-blood woman he had accosted on a stormy August day, had been the public face of his downfall. During his dark days in prison, he had dreamed that the agent of his redemption would be another version of her, a disembodied figure of shame and regret conjured up in black and white, in ink on paper. But "Helenah Sawyer" had not served her purpose; instead, she had been dismissed as a fraud. Nonetheless, following Hamilton's example in the Reynolds affair, Bedlow had retrieved that letter and the other documents he procured from Philadelphia that summer and, ever since, had kept them close to his person.

Like a talisman with the power to ward off suspicious glances and the glare of ignominy, Bedlow took the cache of documents with him when he traveled up the Hudson, late in the summer, to take refuge in Poughkeepsie.

At the end of that hot summer, Bedlow had good reason to get out of New York.

As if John Callanan's most recent legal victory at the supreme court hadn't been humiliating enough for the Bedlows, it was followed, two weeks later, by another sensational trial that invited invidious comparisons. A Methodist preacher had insinuated himself into the family of a pious young woman, seduced her with a promise of marriage, and, when she became pregnant, abandoned her. The trial at Federal Hall attracted crowds of spectators and was followed by detailed newspaper accounts of the courtroom drama and a published trial report, *The hypocrite unmask'd*. At the same time, the case of the other New York gentleman charged with rape back in 1793—Edmund Ludlow, who had avoided trial by skipping bail and fleeing the country—was back in the news. The survivor in that case had petitioned the state legislature to turn Ludlow's forfeited bail bond, reportedly £4,000, over to her. And the general assembly, feeling that she deserved some kind of compensation, had agreed.

Meanwhile, a deadly outbreak of yellow fever was advancing up the East Coast. News that it had reached Philadelphia gripped New Yorkers with dread; soon, many of those who could were fleeing to the safety of the countryside. Harry Bedlow's aged parents decided to stay home, even after the disease broke out in the city. But having been trapped in prison during the deadly outbreak in 1795, their son took advantage of his freedom.

In Poughkeepsie, Bedlow was safe from the epidemic—but not from gossip, suspicion, and shame. Even swelled by refugees from the city, it was hardly more than a village of several thousand inhabitants. People were curious. They talked. And some even had the indelicacy to raise uncomfortable questions.

Bedlow had come prepared. He kept the "Helenah Sawyer" letter and the other documents he had procured two years earlier close at hand—so that when people seemed inclined to doubt his word, he could show them proof. But now, like his erstwhile attorney Alexander Hamilton, he found that the very documents he had obtained to prove his innocence were exposing him to a new charge: fraud. And like Hamilton, Bedlow's instinct was to double down by publishing a long, bitter account—along with copies of the disputed documents.

Of course, Hamilton's determination to defend his reputation at all costs—the same instinct that had already led him into half a dozen affairs of honor—was widely seen as self-destructive. Still, he and Bedlow seem to have fed each other's darkest impulses—basing their fantasies of vindication on new, public attacks on women.

Bedlow also failed to heed another implicit warning. Earlier that year, his friend William Allsee had used a similar tactic against a woman who had emerged from his past and crossed the Atlantic, claiming to be his wife and making financial demands. In response, he published a big lie:

a newspaper notice claiming that she wasn't who she said she was, that they had never been married. What reader would be in a position to say otherwise? Faced with notices like that, women almost never responded. But Elizabeth Allsee did—publishing a stinging "Counter-Notice," which pointed out, among other things, that their marriage certificate had been validated by a New York court just the previous week.

On September 27, 1798, Harry Bedlow wrote a self-pitying letter that he sent, along with the three documents in question, to the editors of the Poughkeepsie newspaper.

"Being in company the other day with some acquaintance, the conversation turned on the prosecutions commenced against me, by John Callanan and Lanah Sawyer, the first for a Rape; and secondly for Seduction," his letter began, "one of the company observed, that he had heard it mentioned in this place, that the papers I had in my possession developing one of the most abominable plots to rob a man of life, character & money that ever disgraced any age, was a forgery and that I had obtained them to answer my own purposes. I enclose them to you for publication, and challenge the authors of this *base insinuation* to a refutation of them."

Explaining the origins of these documents, Bedlow wrote that soon after he received Sawyer's July 13, 1796, letter, his attorney Alexander Hamilton confronted her stepfather with it—only to have him reject it as not in her handwriting. According to Bedlow, he then informed Lanah of her stepfather's response—and she sent a second letter, dated September 12, 1796, accompanied by a sworn affidavit retracting her charge of rape and admitting to perjury. Seeing these two documents, according to Bedlow, Callanan cursed Lanah as a "damned bitch" and begged Bedlow's attorneys to come to a financial settlement that would cover his expenses.

Yet as any reader could see, Bedlow's narrative included obvious omissions. The July 13 letter got Lanah's name wrong in two ways: her first name had never been Helenah and, as John Callanan no doubt informed Alexander Hamilton, her last name, at that point, was no longer Sawyer. The second two documents accordingly referred to "Lanah Stymets." Moreover, the financial settlement Bedlow's family reached with Callanan did not come immediately on the heels of these second two documents but more than two months later. In his account, Bedlow made no effort to explain these discrepancies. Instead, he closed by heaping abuse on John Callanan and offering gratuitous allegations about Lanah's life as a married woman.

"The reader will be shocked at this unequaled instance of *human depravity*, a father compelling his daughter to *perjury*, and then receiving the money so *diabolically obtained*, I shall leave John Callanan firmly fixed on the pinnacle of *villainy*, and turn to that *non-pareil of virtue*, Mrs. Stymets, formerly Lanah Sawyer, who six months after marriage left her husband to pursue an occupation more congenial to her inclinations, *that of a common prostitute*, in this honorable way she had lived in for three years."

Bedlow ended by challenging anyone who could dispute his account to come forward, calling out by name Callanan's longtime attorney Nicholas Evertson, whose family had a large estate in Poughkeepsie.

And just as Hamilton had done, he claimed that he had left the original documents with the newspaper's printer so that they would be available for public review.

Then he published the three documents in question.

The first was the disputed "Helenah Sawyer" letter dated July 13, 1796.

Then there was the second letter:

> *Philadelphia, Sept. 12, 1796*
>
> DEAR BEDLOW,
>
>   *I Received yours dated the 6th inst. intimating Mr. Callanan's avowed disbelief, and supposed forgery of my letter to counteract which I have taken the precaution of going before John Jennings, Esq. one of the Aldermen of the city of Philadelphia, and availed myself of every measure necessary to convince the world of my sentiments, I here repeat to you as I have done before in my former letters, that had it not been for Mr. Callanan, this unfortunate business would never have gone so far—I now solemnly declare that I was as willing to go to Mrs. Carey's as you were; and what has been done was by compulsion, as he forced me to do that which heaven be my witness, my heart secretly revolted against—that which I have before write to you and to Col. Hamilton, has been sufficient proof that you never compelled me to go, it was with my own free will and consent. I now repeat to you that the letters Mr. Callanan supposes to be forged is genuine.*
>
>   *I am affectionately your's,*
>
>   LANAH STYMETS.

This letter was then followed by a formal affidavit, attributed to "LANAH STYMETS, formerly LANAH SAWYER," stating that her stepfather had forced her to perjure herself during the rape trial, that she had gone to Mother Carey's on her own accord, and "that it was with her own free will and consent that she became corporeally connected with the said Harry Bedlow."

The affidavit was attested on September 10 in Philadelphia, by John Jennings, who was described as one of the city's aldermen.

This, at least, was true. An insurance company clerk, Jennings had won his first public office during a special election six months earlier. That summer, his office was just four blocks north of Mrs. Carey's house.

Bedlow's letter and the appended documents were published in the next issue of the *Poughkeepsie Journal*, on October 2, 1798.

By publishing in Poughkeepsie—during a yellow fever outbreak that disrupted life in both New York and Philadelphia—Bedlow ensured that few readers would be able to fully evaluate his narrative and the documents he attributed to Lanah Sawyer. In the weeks to come, brief accounts of Bedlow's self-justificatory publication appeared in the New York newspapers. But neither his letter nor the documents in question were reprinted. No reference to the matter appeared beyond New York.

John Callanan and Nicholas Evertson did not rise to Bedlow's bait. And like Maria Reynolds a year earlier, Lanah Sawyer herself never took any public notice of the matter.

While those in New York had little basis for judgment, those who read the full version in the *Poughkeepsie Journal* may well have had questions. If Bedlow had all three documents two years earlier, while still in debtors' prison, why hadn't he made more effective use of them then? If Lanah had actually produced these documents to vindicate his honor, why in his own letter did he accuse her of the worst kind of impropriety? And what could explain the decidedly affectionate tone of the two letters attributed to Sawyer?

For anyone inclined to take up Bedlow's challenge, there were grounds for skepticism. The two letters attributed to Lanah seem to echo the style of his own letter—with long, convoluted sentences, flowery pretensions, and imperfect grammar. And both Bedlow's own letter and the "Lanah Sawyer" letter of September 12 employ an anomalous spelling of "yours"— with an apostrophe. (A search of all books published in the United States between 1795 and 1800 returned 17,885 texts that employed "yours" and only 565 that employed "your's.") And why would the July 1796 letter be signed "Helenah" and use the initial "H" if her name was actually Lanah? Why did two letters supposedly written in the summer of 1796 use two different last names—Sawyer in the first and Stymets in the second? Any reader could count back through three years of alleged prostitution and six months of alleged marriage to arrive at the conclusion that the marriage Bedlow described would have taken place sometime around April 1795, more than a year before either letter was written.

If Harry Bedlow had hoped that his publication in the *Poughkeepsie Journal* would finally put his troubles to rest, he was disappointed. The purported retraction did not end the long-running legal disputes stemming from his interaction with Lanah Sawyer five years earlier. And its success in reframing his reputation was, at best, limited.

By the time news of the supposed "retraction" reached Bedlow's parents in New York, during the first week of October 1798, his sixty-seven-year-old mother had already been bitten by the mosquito that would soon kill her.

Yellow fever, like ebola, is a hemorrhagic fever; the jaundiced skin that gives the disease its name is a consequence of internal bleeding—which causes intense pain, bleeding from the nose and eyes, and black vomit. After several days of suffering, Catharine Bedlow, like most patients, probably began to feel better for a day or so. For most people, as many as nine in ten, the recovery is permanent. But for others, the remission is just the eye of the storm; the infection returns more ferociously than before, and many succumb.

That, evidently, was the fate of Harry Bedlow's parents. His mother died in mid-October, his father four weeks later. Both were remembered with respectful newspaper notices and buried in her family vault at the Dutch Church.

For John Callanan, their passing required an adjustment to his legal strategy. The man now responsible for the late William Bedlow's debt was his original antagonist's uncle Henry Rutgers.

Harry Bedlow's publication that fall does not seem to have swayed his uncle's opinion of him. That winter, even before he instructed his attorney to deal with John Callanan's claim, Rutgers filed suit against his nephew for debts totaling $5,000. While his sister Catharine Bedlow was alive,

Rutgers may have indulged his errant nephew. But now his patience had worn through—and he saw their relationship as little more than a catalog of unpaid debts.

As for Callanan, he pressed on. At that point, the name of his pilot boat was *Perseverance*.

※

Lanah Sawyer came of age in a world fascinated by automatons—marvels of clockwork that could make inanimate models come to life, acting out complex movements and even making appropriate sounds. At the press of a button, the figure of a woman seated at a piano might begin to play, turning her head to acknowledge her audience's anticipated applause. Napoléon Bonaparte might be sent, over and over, through the choreography of signing a momentous treaty. In 1798, one of the most popular automatons in New York was a birdcage holding a canary—which, when activated, would adjust its wings, cock its head, open and shut its beak in the most lifelike manner, and produce one of six different songs.

What did it mean for Lanah to be turned into a kind of automaton herself—a figure on ink and paper sent, on demand, through endless performances of contrition and recrimination, pouring forth tears from her eyes and absolution from her heart? Contrition for having the courage to stand up against the man who raped her, recrimination against her most steadfast ally, absolution for the man who had called this version of her into being?

For Lanah Sawyer, the documents Harry Bedlow procured and eventually published must have come as a shock—first in the summer of 1796, when her parents, presumably, alerted her to their existence and the uses to which Bedlow and his attorneys were trying to put them, and then again, two years later, when news of their publication began to circulate in New York. Did someone send clippings to her—wherever she was living that fall? In any case, the letters and the affidavit were an attack: on the experiences she had recounted in court, on her most important relationships—with her parents, her family, her husband, her friends, and her neighbors. On her public reputation, and on her sense of reality itself.

Once again, Lanah Sawyer had been erased and overwritten, her true self replaced with a fantasy, an invention, a literary figment. Five years after her original ordeal—five years after she had been pulled back from the brink of despair—what feelings came to the fore? Anger? Fear? Humiliation? Disgust? Self-doubt?

Why didn't she respond?

Perhaps it was simply because she was too tired of being dragged down by a man who, from the start, had seen her as little more—maybe never anything more—than an object of dominion. Perhaps it was because she just wanted to be left alone, to put all that behind her.

That seems to be how Maria Reynolds felt. In the aftermath of the congressional investigation into Alexander Hamilton, she left her husband and returned to New York. With help from Aaron Burr, she eventually obtained a divorce, and then quickly remarried. When the public scandal broke in 1797, she kept quiet—and soon she and her husband moved across the Atlantic, seeking a fresh start in northern England. Later, she returned to Philadelphia and contemplated the possibility of publishing her own account of her story. But then she thought better of it. Presumably, like her, Lanah Sawyer decided it was better to focus on living her new life.

Ironically, the trumped-up documents Harry Bedlow published offer some of the only surviving clues about what that new life looked like. After the 1794 seduction trial, the flesh-and-blood Lanah Sawyer disappears from the historical record. This is not unusual. Most women at the time, especially women from poor, enslaved, and working families, left only scattered traces—if any—of their lives. But there are two claims that Harry Bedlow made about her in his 1798 publication that seem reliable: that, by the summer of 1796, she had married a man named Stymets and that she had moved to Philadelphia.

Presumably John Callanan had said as much when he rejected the "Helenah Sawyer" letter as a fraud. Neither claim can be verified now. But their validity would have been obvious, or at least easy enough to confirm, to those who knew her then.

If Lanah Sawyer did indeed get married, it was probably before she moved. Stymets was a rare name, of Dutch origin. The 1790 census of the United States listed fewer than a dozen Stymets households, almost all of them in and around New York. The man she married might have been Frederick Stymets: he was baptized in the city's Dutch Church a year before Lanah was born; his father was a carpenter; he was a mariner. Or, perhaps, he was George Stymets—whose first appearance in the historical record was as a grocer on Greenwich Street in a 1796 city directory; he then dropped out of view for a couple of years, reappeared in 1799 as a shoemaker on Barclay Street in 1799, was listed on the 1800 federal census with what appears to be a wife and at least one child, and then disappeared.

If nothing else, what marriage meant to Lanah Sawyer was that, despite all that people had said, she wasn't ruined. Marriage restored her sexual honor. It proved that a man, a man who presumably knew her story, was willing to join his life with hers. Her journey through the customary phases of a woman's life in that era was interrupted, but then it continued.

For anyone who wanted to leave New York but didn't want to head into the country, Philadelphia was the obvious place to go. It was the nation's second-largest city and only about a day's journey away. A change of place is always a chance to begin anew; sometimes it is an opportunity for discovery, exploration, reinvention. If Lanah felt trapped at home— mired in her past, caught up in all the stories other people thought they knew about her, caught up in her own stories about herself—making a break, moving away, was a chance to move on. To start fresh, to begin a new life. To reinvent herself. Or simply to discover what it felt like, after so long, to see a new version of herself reflected in the eyes of strangers.

In any case, these clues—her relocation; her marriage, happy or not— serve as reminders of her reality. As the last winter of the eighteenth century melted into spring, Lanah Sawyer was more than a victim, a survivor, a prosecutrix, more than a figment drawn in fugitive ink, more than an object in the battles of men. She was her own person. She was, to the extent she could be, the agent of her own destiny.

She was twenty-two.

Epilogue

Around the time Lanah Sawyer first encountered "lawyer Smith," a sewing teacher took a perfectly good piece of white linen and cut a series of holes in it, five across, five down. Some young woman was then to demonstrate her skill by taking her needle and thread and repairing the damage in the style of twenty-five different fabrics—from simple plain weaves, twills, herringbones, and knits to intricate textured patterns, stripes, and checks in red, white, and blue. Lanah's half sister worked elaborate embroidered pictures, but this was a more practical kind of needlework, intended not so much to show off genteel accomplishments as to hone useful skills. The sampler shows its age. It is yellowed and, in places, stained. But it endures: a silent testament to one generation preparing the next for a lifetime of damage, endurance, and repair.

A skilled needle can disguise and fortify, but however expertly mended, the original damage remains. The challenge of a mending sampler is not just to mimic specific patterns, but also to reestablish the fabric's tension and balance, so the finished repair will lie flat and smooth. Still, under the newly sewn threads lie spots worn thin or torn open—fibers weakened, severed, and frayed. So it is with other kinds of damage. Almost two hundred years after Lanah Sawyer told her mother that she had been raped, and the news began to spread, another young woman, Alice Sebold, described how that moment felt: "My life was over; my life had just begun."

When she first encountered "lawyer Smith," Lanah Sawyer was a young woman who both shrank from street harassment and embraced the possibility of a different future. Perhaps the gallant gentleman *was* interested in her. Perhaps the spark that flashed between them *was* powerful enough to transcend their social differences and transport her into a new kind of life. "Was it probable that lawyer Smith had any honorable designs in his connection with a sewing girl?" her scornful neighbor John Cozine later demanded. Was Lanah naïve, ambitious, discontented? Perhaps. But why not focus instead on the fact that all of these labels for female ambition demean and disparage? Why not honor this young woman's faith in herself? Even if others couldn't see past her social station, her work as a sewing girl, Lanah Sawyer could. She felt she had a right to a revolutionary dream of human equality. Other dreamers, too, were crushed in these years. Some of them, like her, had the courage to fight back. The assertion by women like Mary Wollstonecraft that they, like men, had basic rights was powerful, resonant, and controversial—and it, too, provoked a powerful backlash. "We hear no more," the historian Hannah Adams wrote in 1832, the "alarming" clamor for the "rights of women." Those who would pick up that fight would, like Lanah Sawyer, have to begin anew.

The story of her new life is largely lost to us. What's remarkable about Lanah Sawyer's story is not that so little of it is known but that we know as much as we do. Like many lower-class or enslaved women, she entered the historical record as a result of damage done to her by a man—a man she resisted and stood up against. There may not be a single written trace of Lanah Sawyer unrelated to her prosecution of Harry Bedlow for rape, the seduction suit, and his efforts to vindicate himself at her expense. Even some documents that used to exist are now missing: one of the file papers relating to the seduction suit was catalogued decades ago but cannot be found now. Two centuries earlier, the record of Lanah's christening at Trinity Church was lost to the ecclesiastical politics of the war into which she was born; the record book itself left the city with a Loyalist cleric— and vanished without a trace. Perhaps there is some record of her that I've failed to find because I didn't know where to look—a record of her marriage in some obscure church, a record of her family in the census tally of someone else's household, a record of her death on a stone long since knocked over and now buried under a blanket of grass.

No trace of Lanah appears in her stepfather's will. John Callanan died in 1805, at age fifty-two. He was remembered in the newspapers as the city's oldest branch pilot; the masters of vessels were asked to honor his passing by lowering their flags to half-mast. But his will makes no mention of his stepchildren. The will Lanah's mother wrote in 1821, two years before her death, is even more tantalizing. A long list of bequests itemizes her furniture: a looking glass, a large Bible, a bed with hangings, pieces of silver marked

"S" for "Sawyer" and "JJC" for "John and Jane Callanan." She remembered many of her surviving children and grandchildren—but not all of them. Lanah's brother, who was alive and living nearby, was not mentioned, though his daughter was. So the fact of Lanah's absence from her will is impossible to interpret. Had she already died? Or received her share of the estate? Or become estranged? Even in her mother's last testament there is no resolution to Lanah's story.

Some sense of the possibilities Lanah may have faced are suggested by the lives of her siblings, most of whom followed John Callanan's wake into the world of branch pilots. Her younger sister married one. Her brother Peter became a pilot, as did his own son and one of their two surviving half brothers. Her half sister Jane Callanan married an army officer who rose to the rank of colonel and is buried under an elaborate monument in Windham, Connecticut. Meanwhile, Lanah's younger sister Catharine Sawyer, who started out as a seamstress, followed a very different path. In 1799, she married the widowed keeper of a brothel—a business they operated together for the next decade, in an emerging center of prostitution on the old Rutgers farm, on a stretch of Market Street around the cross streets Henry and Bedlow. Shortly after her marriage, she was sentenced to six months in prison for keeping a disorderly house that allowed "whoring" and one month for assault and battery. A long series of legal scrapes ensued. In 1808, she and her husband responded to a new complaint about their business with a furious campaign for vengeance. He filed an extraordinary complaint of his own against seven women he claimed worked as prostitutes and no fewer than twenty-six neighboring brothel keepers. Catharine threatened to kill one man, telling him that she would get her revenge even at the cost of her life.

In the fictional narratives of Lanah Sawyer's day, the inevitable consequence of a woman's lost sexual innocence was an early and ignominious death, but the real lives of supposedly ruined women varied widely. Elizabeth Keteltas, who charged Edmund Ludlow with rape in early 1793, went on to a life of affluence and prestige, marrying ten years later and raising a family. Margaret Miller, a thirteen-year-old servant girl who was raped in 1800 and then slandered as a "whore" by a man who asked her to scrub his floors, went on to a life of continued brutality. When she was seventeen, she married a man who turned abusive; ten months later, he took his razor and slit her throat. At the same time, women at the center of seduction suits also commonly went on to marry. And Eliza Bowen Jumel was hardly the only woman whose work as a prostitute at one point in her life did not preclude remarkable social mobility. In August 1809, Philadelphia was atwitter with the news that, a day after his parents set sail for England, the great-grandson of Pennsylvania's founder had married a common prostitute. By that time, Maria Reynolds Clingman had left her second husband in England and returned to Philadelphia, where she kept quiet about her past, worked for a time as a housekeeper, married a respected physician, and developed a reputation for sober Christian piety. Once again, she had reinvented herself.

And what was the afterlife of Lanah Sawyer's cases against Harry Bedlow in the history of the law? In two sensational criminal trials in 1800, defense attorneys pointedly invoked the Bedlow case and Sawyer's supposed retraction to caution the jurors against a rush to judgment. In the first, a man was accused of murdering the woman he had been courting, twenty-two-year-old Gulielma Sands. His defense team included Brockholst Livingston, Alexander Hamilton, and Aaron Burr—and it was the latter who invoked Bedlow's rape prosecution, the subsequent riots and outrage, the seduction suit, his long imprisonment, and the supposed revelation that the original accusation had been false. Perhaps emboldened by the accused murderer's acquittal, Brockholst Livingston made the same argument a few months later during the trial of the man accused of raping Margaret Miller. In that case, the defendant was convicted and sentenced to life in prison—only to be pardoned by the governor a few years later. And this was hardly the only such case: two of the other three men convicted of sexual assaults in the city since the revolution had also been effectively pardoned.

Nonetheless, the myth of white men's supposed vulnerability to false allegations of rape by vengeful acquaintances continued to flourish. As recently as a few years ago, the arguments Burr and Livingston made about Bedlow's narrow escape from a false rape charge were repeated in the *Washington Times.*

There was, in fact, an early New York rape case that prompted not just insinuations about false testimony but actual charges of perjury. But the charges were against the man on trial, not his accuser. In 1810, immediately after the gentleman Charles Wakely was acquitted of rape, he was indicted for suborning five witnesses to lie on his behalf. In the end, only one was found guilty and sent to jail—a Black woman who worked as a domestic servant.

The notion that women reporting sexual assaults were the real aggressors—and that the men accused were the real victims—contributed to a narrowing of rape law. Cases involving acquaintances became especially hard to prosecute. Part of how that happened can be seen in the way that Brockholst Livingston refined and strengthened arguments he had made in the Bedlow case when he defended Margaret Miller's rapist, seven years later. Men feel an almost "uncontrollable" urge to "avenge the injury" of "one who is entitled to our protection," Livingston told the jurors in the Miller case, cautioning them to take care to "protect the life of a citizen." In fact, no part of that statement was true: the defendant was a British subject, not an American citizen; the worst punishment he faced was a prison sentence; and jurors repeatedly showed that they were perfectly capable of resisting the urge to convict rapists. But Livingston's assertions did not have to be literally true to serve his purpose: encouraging the jurors to feel what the philosopher Kate Manne has recently called "himpathy" for the defendant and the opposite for his accuser. Just as Livingston had smeared Lanah Sawyer, despite her spotless reputation, for potentially harboring secret desires, so he insinuated in the case of thirteen-year-old Margaret Miller that "the passions may be as warm in a girl of her years as in one of more advanced years." While shaming young women for their hypothetical lust, Livingston normalized men's predatory sexual behavior. "What is more common than for young men at a certain age," he asked the jurors, than "to single out some female, to whom they pay their temporary addresses, merely with a view of present gratification?" On the other hand, Livingston argued, the stigma attached to a "female" known to have had a "criminal connection" with a man, consensual or otherwise, creates such a strong incentive to cry rape "that it is hardly possible for a girl so situated to tell the truth." Supposedly chaste but secretly lusty, any woman who accused an acquaintance of rape, in Livingston's estimation, was literally unbelievable.

William Wyche's *Report of the Trial of Henry Bedlow, for Committing a Rape on Lanah Sawyer* (1793) was part of a broader trend toward sensationalizing crimes involving the rape, murder, or seduction of young women. By 1800, Wyche had moved away from New York. But others in the city followed his example, publishing reports of a 1797 rape trial and a

1798 seduction suit. The trial of Margaret Miller's rapist prompted another report, and the trial of the man accused of killing Gulielma Sands was followed by two brief, highly colored accounts and a quasi-official report taken in shorthand by the court clerk. Meanwhile, newspapers began to offer extensive, often lurid, coverage of such trials. While these accounts valorized female purity, their appeal was also prurient. Readers loved to be shocked by the exposure of sexual underworlds—the harsh realities and the dangerous desires that shaped the lives of real women.

It was this gap between the ideal and the real that allowed middle-class white women to claim a privileged status in the nineteenth century, launching public campaigns against vice in the forms of prostitution, intemperance, and slavery. The poor, working, enslaved, Black, and immigrant women these middle-class reformers targeted didn't always want their help or share their values. Often, instead of easing the burdens of other women, the standard of female sexual innocence championed by moral reformers added shame and stigma.

And what about Harry Bedlow? Leafing through a newspaper late in the summer of 1838, Philip Hone—the younger brother of the baker who lived across the street from Lanah—spotted a brief notice of Henry Bedlow's death and paused to reflect on the "old Beau, who at one time made a great noise in New York and 'frighted the Isle from her propriety.'" He remembered Lanah Sawyer, the rape trial, and the ensuing eruption of outrage. He looked back indulgently on the righteous indignation and boyish glee with which he had watched the riots. Since then, he had enjoyed a kind of social mobility only a few men could achieve—and the fortune he had made in the auction business and the term he had served as New York's mayor colored his memories. He recalled Mother Carey's "famous brothel," where "the libertine had decoyed his Victim," as the "very spot" on which he had subsequently built a luxurious hotel. Of Bedlow's life after the riots, Hone remembered nothing—not the seduction trial, not his imprisonment for debt, not his publication of the purported retraction. As for what Bedlow had done after the fall of 1793, Hone concluded, "history is silent."

Bedlow didn't live out the life of wealth and prominence he had anticipated. Even before publishing his September 1798 attack on Lanah Sawyer's sexual morality, he had already struck up a relationship with a woman he never married but with whom he had at least six children. Their last child, Caroline, was born in early 1808—within months of the time he married another woman, the adopted daughter of a South Carolina planter, with whom he lived on a farm in Belleville, New Jersey, and had eight more children. The published notice of the marriage identified him as "Henry Bedlow, Esq., only nephew of Col. Henry Rutgers"—effectively laying claim to his uncle's vast fortune. But if Rutgers pitied Bedlow, he considered him too "broken" to ever make much of himself. Indeed, Bedlow never learned to manage the property he inherited from his parents, quarreled with his sister's husband, was plagued by lawsuits, begged old family friends for loans, spent another long stretch imprisoned for debt in Newark, moved back to New York, and filed, once again, for bankruptcy, all the while dreaming of a windfall stemming from his ancestor's support for England's Glorious Revolution in 1688.

When Henry Rutgers died in 1830, Bedlow was shocked to find that far from receiving the lion's share of his uncle's vast estate—one of the first in American history to total almost a million dollars—he had been carefully cut out of it. Rutgers left Bedlow the insulting sum of $50 and stipulated that he be excluded from direct benefit or control of the almost $200,000 trust established for the benefit of Bedlow's surviving children—both those born to his wife and those from his previous relationship. Bedlow did not take this indignity gracefully. His sons by his paramour had all died young—one, a mariner, at sea; another, a cabinet maker, just before the Rutgers estate was settled. And when his only surviving child from that relationship, a daughter in her mid-twenties named Caroline Amelia Bedlow, requested an advance settlement from the Rutgers estate, he argued (unsuccessfully) that she should receive nothing, on the grounds that she had defied his wishes and married a disreputable man. Estranged from her father, she eventually moved away to make a new life for herself in a small town upstate, though she brought with her a singular memento: the tiny portrait that captured an image of him in the years before he met Lanah Sawyer, a young gentleman with an elaborate coiffeur and a sly smile.

Mother Carey, too, wanted to be remembered. In her will she stipulated that her body should be "decently interred" and that a "Marble Tomb Stone with my Name &c. engraved thereon shall be placed over my Grave." Accordingly, she was buried in the Christ Church graveyard in center city Philadelphia, alongside luminaries of the nation's founding, under an unusually large slab of white marble laid flat and inscribed:

IN MEMORY OF

ANN CAREY

WIFE OF JAMES CAREY

WHO DEPARTED THIS LIFE

OCTOBER 19TH 1796

AGED 57 YEARS.

Nothing could be more conventional: the story of a woman's life told in a handful of facts—her name, the name of her husband, the date of her death, her age. The memory she constructed for herself offers little sense of the kind of life she led; like a blank form populated with interchangeable details, it is at once personal and anonymous. There is nothing to suggest that she had at one point been married to another man, that she built a successful business as a bawdy-house keeper, that her role in a client's rape of a young sewing girl and her testimony in his trial led to the destruction of her home and the life she had made for herself, that she had been driven out of New York, that she had come to Philadelphia for a new start in her old age.

The stone is still there. Broken in half, its once-polished surface dulled, pitted, and blackened, it still dominates its section of one of the nation's most heavily visited burial grounds—across an expanse of grass from Independence Hall, the symbolic birthplace of the American republic. Like so many other marble stones—chosen originally for their brilliance, purity, and ease of carving—its surface has been eaten away by long years of exposure to rain and the acidic smoke of burned coal and oil. By the time of the Civil War, the erosion of the cemetery's inscriptions prompted the church warden to have them all transcribed. Now the letters and numbers Mother Carey wanted to mark her grave are unreadable. She had wanted to be wrapped up in the symbolism of this stone—respectable, Christian, prosperous—but now all the connections to her are gone without a trace, and all that remains is the symbolism of the big, expensive stone itself, the same size, shape, and material as Benjamin Franklin's. There is nothing to tell a passing tourist that it is anything other than a marker for some founding father. Her memorial is now anonymous, her life a blank slate.

Today, there is no way to visit the graves of Lanah Sawyer or even Harry Bedlow. His body was probably interred in his family's vault at the Dutch Church just north of Wall Street, but that block has long since been redeveloped and the remains moved—or buried under what is now the plaza in front of the Federal Reserve building.

As for Lanah Sawyer, or Lanah Stymets, we don't know where she was buried or even if her grave was ever marked. Her stepfather, whose burial does appear in the Trinity Church registers, has no surviving stone—unlike Charlotte Temple, the fictional victim of seduction, whose name, inscribed on a large ledger stone near the Broadway sidewalk, has attracted generations of teary-eyed devotees. Tucked in a quiet corner on the south side of the church stands a handsome brownstone marker for Lanah's half brother Owen Callanan, who was baptized the year she was raped and died four years later. Partly obscured by grass is a sentimental inscription: "Weep not for me my parents dear, I am not dead but sleeping here." Another member of her family was buried in a neighboring grave, though only the jagged bottom half of his broken marker remains. Further down the same row, in the shade of a blue-green cedar, is a small, brown, flaking footstone marked only with the initials "L.S."

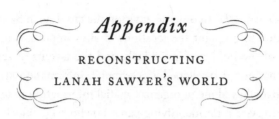

Appendix

RECONSTRUCTING
LANAH SAWYER'S WORLD

When I set out to explore Lanah Sawyer's story, I began with William Wyche's *Report of the Trial of Henry Bedlow*, the explosion of public outrage after the jury's not-guilty verdict, and the purported retraction published five years later. Early on, I decided that the most promising way to develop new insights about this story would be to research not just the specific people at its center but also their broader social and cultural contexts. I wanted to know everything I could about Lanah herself, her background, and her family; about her stepfather and his work as a branch pilot; about Henry Bedlow; and about Mother Carey and her business as a bawdy-house keeper. I also wanted to better understand the dynamic world of the emerging American republic: the social history of the rapidly expanding, economically stratified, racially divided, and politically tense city; the cultural history of an era preoccupied with the dangers and attractions of romantic love, sexual double standards, and public battles over honor and the nature of truth; and the legal history of sexual harms at a time when rape was becoming harder to prosecute and suits over seduction were becoming more common.

Most of this exploration involved the basic work of social and cultural historians—reading diaries, letters, newspapers, novels, court records, tax lists, wills, and inventories, and examining material remains, such as paintings, sewing tools, and clothes, in light of relevant scholarship. Throughout the project I was assisted by Nancy Gray Schoonmaker, PhD, whose help compiling data and searching out demographic and genealogical information was invaluable. Here, I want to explain how we went about developing and analyzing several distinct bodies of evidence.

❧

The New York 1793 GIS. In order to envision the city Lanah Sawyer inhabited, I wanted to pinpoint the locations of sites important to the story,
the homes of several dozen individuals, and the layouts of several large
tracts. To that end, I developed a geographic information system, *New
York 1793*, that allowed me to organize spatial information in terms of the
city's modern system for identifying parcels by borough, block, and lot—
and to visualize evidence from a variety of sources, including published
city directories, historic and modern maps, deeds, surveys, tax assessments,
censuses, and newspapers.

In the text, I generally use modern street addresses, though some streets
have been renamed, numbering schemes have changed repeatedly, and
a few blocks have been so dramatically redeveloped that modern street
numbers must be regarded as approximations. For example, at the site
of Mother Carey's home, 80 Beekman Street in 1793, there is no modern
lot; around 1795, that parcel was incorporated into Theatre Alley, between
what are now numbers 1 and 5 Beekman.

The published directories were crucial resources, but they generally
listed only household heads and often provided ambiguous addresses. In
1793, some streets were not numbered at all, other streets were numbered
but not in any immediately obvious order, and some addresses ("at the
corner" of Broadway and Liberty) were only so much help (*which* corner?).
In some cases, it helped to track individuals through multiple directories
as numbering schemes developed. The city's tax-assessment records identified not just owners but also tenants, making it possible in some cases to
track down deeds for the properties of renters like Lanah's stepfather. The
1793 Tax Records at the New-York Historical Society (NYHS) proved so
useful that we ended up transcribing the whole thing. Also helpful were
the early federal censuses and other tax lists, including Edmund P. Willis's
digital spreadsheets of New York City's tax assessments and census enumerations for 1789, 1800, and 1810 (Inter-University Consortium for Political and Social Research, #2863) and the 1796 Tax Records at the NYHS.

Magnificent tools are available for tracking the history of early Manhattan real estate. Deeds and mortgages for early Manhattan are held by Office
of the City Register (Manhattan) in the Department of Finance, which listed
deeds by grantor and grantee in a multivolume *Index of Conveyances Recorded*

in the Office of the Register of the City and County of New York (New York, 1858). Beginning in 1891, the Office of the City Register produced an extraordinary Block Index of Reindexed Conveyances Prior to 1917, bound in more than 230 volumes, which organizes some half a million early Manhattan deeds by their modern block and lot numbers; there is also an equivalent series for mortgages. While this project was underway, I. N. Phelps Stokes initiated his six-volume *Iconography of Manhattan Island, 1498–1909* (New York: Robert H. Dodd, 1915–1928), which includes not only useful discussions of early views and maps of the city but also detailed chronologies and meticulously researched histories of individual properties and landmarks.

To understand the city's development and street layouts in the years around 1793, I relied on the McComb (1789) and Taylor (1797) plans of the city, as well as earlier maps by John Montressor, Benard Ratzer, and John Hill. Several later maps overlaying old farm tracts on the emerging city grid were especially helpful, including George Heywood's "Map of the City of New York shewing . . . the location of the different Farms and Estates," published in D. T. Valentine's *History of the City of New York* (New York: G. P. Putnam's and Co., 1853) and J. B. Holmes's large-scale *Map of the Rutger's Farm As it existed in 1784* (1874).

For locating specific parcels in 1793, William Perris's *Maps of the City of New York* (New York, 1852) was useful because it showed the layout of lots on each block as well as street numbers—which in many cases were the same as those given in the *Directory for 1794.* The manuscript surveys produced by Evert Bancker during the 1780s and 1790s also proved crucial. Those at the NYHS (NYC Street Collection) included plans of individual properties (like Richard Varick's home) and a series of evocative appraisals of houses—noting, for example, whether the walls in different areas were finished with paneling, plaster, or just plain boards. Those at the NYPL (Bancker Plans, Mss Col. 193) included surveys of the Dyckman farm and of the Vineyard Tract (including modern block 90) that made it possible to locate Mother Carey's house.

❧

The New York City Sexual Assault Prosecutions Database. In order to analyze Lanah Sawyer's prosecution of Henry Bedlow, I developed a database of eighty-one sexual assault prosecutions in the city and county of New York (modern Manhattan) between 1730 and 1820. I began with a list of cases shared by Sharon Block and with those discussed by Julius Goebel Jr. and T. Raymond Naughton in *Law Enforcement in Colonial New York: A Study in Criminal Procedure (1664–1776)* (Montclair, NJ: Patterson Smith, 1970); by Thelma Foote, Douglas Greenberg, and Serena Zabin for the colonial period; and by Marybeth Hamilton Arnold, Timothy J. Gilfoyle, and Christine Stansell for the period after the revolution. From 1776 to 1784, civilian courts did not operate in Manhattan.

Starting in 1784, a crucial resource was a tabulation of criminal prosecutions, including names, charges, and outcomes, apparently compiled around 1822 by the city's high constable Jacob Hays: "A General List of All Persons Indicted and Convicted in the City and County of New York from the End of the American Revolution to the Year 1820." The "General List," as well as five volumes of minutes of the Manhattan proceedings of the Court of Oyer and Terminer (a criminal branch of the Supreme Court of Judicature), went missing long ago, but these documents are preserved on microfilm at the Queens Public Library archives. I also canvassed other surviving minute books and case files of the Court of Oyer and Terminer, the Supreme Court of Judicature, and the Court of General Sessions at the New York County Clerk's Division of Old Records. In 2017, the early records of the Supreme Court of Judicature (and the Court of Chancery) were transferred to the New York State Archives.

For the minutes of the Court of General Sessions, a useful guide is Kenneth Scott's series of careful abstracts published by the National Genealogical Society: *New York City Court Records, 1684–1760* (Washington, DC, 1982), *New York City Court Records, 1760–1797* (Washington, DC, 1983), *New York City Court Records, 1797–1801* (Arlington, VA, 1988), and *New York City Court Records, 1801–1804* (Arlington, VA, 1988). Official minute book entries from this period are typically sparse, and New York's courts were long ago permitted to destroy most of their early case files. On the state's early court records, see James D. Folts, *"Duely & Constantly Kept": A History of the New York Supreme Court, 1691–1847 and An Inventory of Its Records* (Albany: New York State Court of Appeals, 1991).

Some of the richest evidence of early criminal cases survives in two sets of prosecutors' papers. For the period between 1752 and 1776, the records of New York's attorneys general are held in the John Tabor Kempe Papers (NYHS). For the period after 1790, a voluminous series of District Attorney Indictment Records ("DA Indictments") for New York County (i.e., Manhattan) are held by the New York Municipal Archives. Over time, the advent of published trial reports and modern court reporting, as well as newspaper accounts, provided increasingly rich information about sexual assault trials. The first criminal court reports in New York were Daniel Rogers's *New-York City-Hall Recorder* (1816–1822), David Bacon's *New-York Judicial Repository* (September 1818–March 1819), and Jacob D. Wheeler's *Reports of Criminal Law Cases*, 3 vols. (New York, 1823–1825), which included a few earlier cases.

One trend that became clear through this work was that men accused of sexual assault were often accused of other crimes as well, ranging from other sexual and nonsexual assaults to breaking and entering, perjury, and attempted murder. The resulting impression that sexual assaults were often perpetrated by serial offenders is consistent with the modern research (see, for example, David Lisak, "Understanding the Predatory Nature of Sexual Violence," *Sexual Assault Report* 14, no. 4 [April 2011]: 49–57).

The Seduction Suits Database. Developing a robust sample of early seduction suits and, to a lesser extent, suits for breach of promise to marry is generally difficult because they are hard to distinguish in most court records from other kinds of suits. For New York, I developed a list of cases discussed in modern scholarship (such as Lea VanderVelde, "The Legal Ways of Seduction," *Stanford Law Review*, 48, no. 4 [April 1996]: 817–901). I also canvassed contemporary newspaper accounts, published trial reports, and reported legal cases. A few cases from as early as 1796 were included in the reports published by George Caines, who became the nation's first official court reporter in 1804; he was succeeded by a variety of official and unofficial reporters. For a handy guide to these works, see Charles C. Soule, *The Lawyer's Reference Manual of Law Books and Citations* (Boston: C. C. Soule, 1883), 38–45. When possible, I also examined the original court minutes and surviving file papers at the New York County Clerk's Division of Old Records in Manhattan and the New York State Archives in Albany.

For New Jersey, a more systematic approach was possible. The New Jersey State Archives has made available a comprehensive index to its collection of more than fifty thousand supreme court case files, 1704–1844 (online via its webpage for "Searchable Databases and Records Request

Forms"; https://wwwnet-dos.state.nj.us/DOS_ArchivesDBPortal/index
.aspx). This allowed me to develop a set of file papers for thirty-three
seduction suits between 1746 and 1841, as well as four related and three
unrelated breach-of-promise-to-marry suits. As in New York, the first
New Jersey court reports date to the early nineteenth century, but Richard
S. Coxe, *Reports of Cases Argued and Determined in the Supreme Court of
New Jersey* (Burlington, NJ: David Allinson, 1816), retrospectively covered
cases from 1790–1795 (see Soule, *Lawyer's Manual* [1883], 36–38). By convention, these reports are known collectively as *New Jersey Law Reports*
and identified by volume numbers organized by dates of coverage.

The Seduction Suits Database was designed to collect basic information from each case file including the names of the parties, the date and
jurisdiction of the suit, the damages claimed, the outcome (if available),
and information about the seduced woman herself—her relation to the
plaintiff, whether she filed a related breach-of-promise suit, and whether
it was claimed that the seduction had left her pregnant.

To explore how the experience of seduction affected these women's later
lives, we then undertook the painstaking task of tracing the marital history
of the seduced woman in each case—using a variety of resources including various census enumerations, church registers, tax rolls, vital records,
newspapers, books, and collections online available through FamilySearch
.org., Ancestry.com, GenealogyBank.com, FindaGrave.com, etc. Our basic
question was: Did the woman in question (generally young, seduced, abandoned, and impregnated) end up getting married? It wasn't always possible
to tell—generally because she wasn't named in the file papers or, more
often, because it was too difficult to distinguish among different individuals with the same names.

⌘

The Branch Pilots Database. To better understand the circumstances of
Lanah Sawyer's family and her stepfather's social networks, I developed
a database of all of the state-appointed branch pilots for Sandy Hook
from 1730 through 1833 (a smaller corps of Hell's Gate pilots operated
separately). I gleaned appointments (as well as disciplinary actions, sus-
pensions, and reinstatements) after 1710 from E. B. O'Callaghan, ed., *Calendar of Historical Manuscripts in the Office of the Secretary of State*, 1664–1776
(Albany: Weed, Parsons, and Co., 1865); Berthold Fernlow and Arnold J.

F. Van Laer, eds., *Calendar of Council Minutes 1668–1783* (Albany: University of the State of New York, 1902); E. B. O'Callaghan and Dorothy C. Barck, eds., *Calendar of New York Colonial Commissions, 1680–1770* (New York: New-York Historical Society, 1929); and Kenneth Scott, ed., *Calendar of New York Colonial Commissions, 1770–1776* (New York: National Society of Colonial Dames in the State of New York, 1972). Appointments from 1777 on were found in the records of the Council of Appointment at the New York State Archives (Index to the Minutes, 1777–1786, A1846; Minutes, 1786–1822, A1845). To get a better sense of how long each pilot served and how their deputies progressed through the ranks, we tracked them through the various lists published in annual editions of *Gaine's New-York Pocket Almanack* (beginning in 1772) and in the published city directories starting in 1787. The first listings of the various pilot companies and their members came in a series of notices published in New York newspapers in the summer of 1794: Morris's company (*Daily Advertiser*, 17 September 1794), Daniels's company (*Diary*, 18 September 1794); Gray's company (*Daily Gazette*, 23 September 1794), Buffelere's company (*Diary*, 24 September 1795). Comprehensive lists of branch pilots, organized by boat number, were published in 1818 (*National Advocate*, 21 March 1818) and 1833 (Edwin Williams, ed., *New York As It Is* [New York: J. Disturnell, 1833], 151–52).

With a list of Sandy Hook pilots, dates of appointment, and approximate dates of service, we set about collecting information that might illuminate their working lives, their economic standing, their family lives, and their social networks. Scattered evidence was gleaned from newspaper accounts and from mentions of pilots in publications such as *Naval Documents of the American Revolution*, 13 vols. to date (Washington, DC: Department of the Navy, 1964–), and the published minutes of New York's Committee of Safety (Albany: Thurlow Weed, 1842). We also surveyed church registers and other genealogical resources for records of pilots' births and marriages and their children's baptisms. It quickly became clear the world of the pilots was densely interconnected: positions were often handed down from father to son; they regularly served long apprenticeships through their teens, often married around the time they became deputy pilots in their early twenties, and typically received their branches in their thirties. Baptism records showed that pilots and their wives regularly served as sponsors at the baptisms of their colleagues' children. For pilots active in the late

1780s and early 1790s, we also identified information about their homes, wealth, and families from city directories, census enumerations, and tax lists. This revealed that most pilots were of middling social standing and were increasingly able to buy their own houses in the 1790s, and that several kept Black workers enslaved in their households. By 1794, most pilots lived in a small area of the city near John Callanan's house.

For more information, including a link to the New York 1793 GIS, a spreadsheet of the 1793 Tax Record for New York City, and the tables "New York City Sexual Assault Prosecutions, 1734–1820" and "New Jersey Seduction Suits, 1746–1841," see https://www.johnwoodsweet.com.

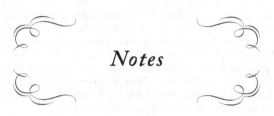

Notes

LIST OF ABBREVIATIONS

BIRC Block Index of Reindexed Conveyances Prior to 1917, Office of the City Register (Manhattan), NYC Department of Finance. More than 230 volumes, organized by block and lot.

CGS MB Court of General Sessions of the Peace (New York City and County), Minute Book, 1684–1839, New York County Clerk, Department of Old Records. Volumes identified by dates of coverage and "E" (for "Engrossed") or "R" (for "Rough").

CO&T MB Court of Oyer and Terminer (New York City and County terms), Minute Book, 1784–1826, the Archives at Queens Library. Volumes identified by dates of coverage or number (9–13).

DA Indictments Indictment Papers, 1790–1879, New York County District Attorney Records, 1790–1984, New York Municipal Archives. Identified by filing date.

Directory New York city directories identified by date in title and, in years when more than one was published, by publisher.

Hays, "General List" [Jacob Hays], "A General List Of all persons Indicted and Convicted in the City and County of New York, from the end of the American Revolution to the Year 1820," CMS#5 (microfilm), Historic Documents Collection, the Archives at Queens Library.

MC Judgments Judgments, 1786–1895, Mayor's Court, New York County Clerk, Department of Old Records.

MCC Minutes of the Common Council of the City of New York, 1675–1776, 8 vols. (New York, 1905), and *1784–1831,* 19 vols. (New York, 1919).

MC MB Mayor's Court (Court of Common Pleas for New York City and County), Minute Books, 1674–1821, New York County Clerk, Department of Old Records. Volumes identified by dates of coverage; some marked "E" (for "Engrossed") or "R" (for "Rough").

NARA National Archives and Records Administration.

NJSCCF New Jersey Supreme Court Case Files, 1704–1844, New Jersey State Archives. Identified by file number.

NYC Conveyances Office of the City Register (Manhattan), NYC Department of Finance.

NYCC-DOR New York County Clerk, Department of Old Records.

NYGB New York Genealogical & Biographical (Society and *Record*).

NYHS New-York Historical Society.

NYMA New York Municipal Archives.

NYPL New York Public Library.

NYSA New York State Archives.

NYSL New York State Library.

Pilmore marriage register The Rev. Joseph Pilmore, marriage register, 1786–1794 and 1804–1813 (St. Paul's Church, Philadelphia), 1794–1804 (Christ Church, New York), available via *Philadelphia Congregations Early Records*, https://philadelphiacongregations.org.

Report [William Wyche], *Report of the Trial of Henry Bedlow, for Committing a Rape on Lanah Sawyer* (New York, 1793). Passages identified by page number and speaker.

SCJ CC MB Circuit Court Minute Books, 1748–1842 (formerly "Nissi Prius Minute Books"), Supreme Court of Judicature, JN518, New York State Archives. Volumes identified by dates of coverage and "E" (for "Engrossed") or "R" (for "Rough").

SCJ Docket Judgment Dockets, 1785–1846, Supreme Court of Judicature, JN527, New York State Archives. Volumes identified by dates of coverage.

SCJ LJ Judgment Rolls, 1781–1847 (formerly "Law Judgments"), Supreme Court of Judicature, JN529, New York State Archives.

SCJ MB Minute Books, 1691–1847, Supreme Court of Judicature, JN531, New York State Archives. Volumes identified by dates of coverage; some labeled "Engrossed" ("E") or "Rough" ("R").

SCJ PL Court Papers (Misc.), 1754–1837 (formerly "Pleadings 1754–1837"), Supreme Court of Judicature, JN532, New York State Archives.

SCJ PR Civil and Criminal Parchments, 1684–1848 (formerly "Parchment Rolls"), Supreme Court of Judicature and Court of Chancery, JN519, New York State Archives.

Trinity Church registers Parish records, Archives, Trinity Church, Wall Street. Marriage, baptism, and burial registers cited by date. Databases of the Registers, the Trinity Churchyard, and the St. Paul's Churchyard: https://trinitywallstreet.org/history-archives.

PROLOGUE

1 **Beekman Street:** James Carey, 80 Beekman Street: *Directory for 1793*. The lot is now part of Theatre Alley; the closest modern address is 3 Beekman (part of 5 Beekman). See discussion of the Vineyard tract (Block 90) in chapter 2.

1 **late-summer morning:** *Gaine's New-York Pocket Almanack . . . for 1793* (New York, 1792), predicted, "September 5th sun eclipsed, partly visible at New-York." Fred Espenak, "Annular Solar Eclipse of 1793 Sep 05," last updated March 22, 2019, http://eclipsewise.com/solar/SEprime/1701–1800/SE1793Sep05Aprime.html.

1 **broad daylight:** *Report*, 6 and 8 (Sawyer).

1 **trouble she was in:** *Report*, 5 (Sawyer).

2 **breakfast time:** *Report*, 8 (Sawyer), 12–13 (Carey).

2 **kind of refuge:** *Report*, 8 (Sawyer).

3 **two hours passed:** *Report*, 8 (Sawyer).

3 **"in the street":** *Report*, 6 (Sawyer).

CHAPTER 1: RESCUE

5 **air felt raw:** *Report*, 3 (Sawyer). Weather: John Pintard, 25 Aug. 1793, Diary and Garden Calendar, Newark, 1793–1794, box 4, fol. 9, Pintard Papers, MS490, NYHS.

5 **had ventured out:** *Report*, 22 (Livingston).

5 **"*Vouz etes chagrinée*":** Catcalls: List of French phrases and English translations, ca. 1760, Nathaniel Minor Papers, Stonington (CT) Historical Society. See also: *Independent Mechanic*, 18 May 1811, NYHS. On street harassment: Christine Stansell, *City of Women: Sex and Class in New York, 1798–1860* (New York: Alfred A. Knopf, 1986), 27.

6 **St. Paul's Chapel:** *Moreau de St. Méry's American Journey, 1793–1798*, ed. and trans. Kenneth Roberts and Anna M. Roberts (Garden City, NY: Doubleday, 1947), 153.

6 **some prayed:** *Diary of Elizabeth Drinker*, ed. Elaine Forman Crane (Boston: Northeastern University Press, 1991), 1:899 (25 August 1793, Philadelphia).

6 **"too prevailing":** *New-York Journal* (New York), 22 September 1785.

6 **respectable connections:** *Diary* (New York), 11 July 1793.

7 **"a delicate foot":** Royall Tyler, *The Contrast*, ed. Cynthia A. Kierner (New York: New York University Press, 2007), 1.1.

7 **sexual aggression:** Marybeth Hamilton Arnold, "'The Life of a Citizen in the Hands of a Woman': Sexual Assault in New York City, 1790–1820," in *Passion and Power: Sexuality in History*, ed. Kathy Peiss and Christina Simmons (Philadelphia: Temple University Press, 1989), 35–56; Stansell, *City of Women*, 20–37.

8 **balmy 82 degrees:** Pintard, 31 August–1 September 1793, Diary and Garden Calendar.

8 **an alluring figure:** A 1794 example of a young man spotting a woman on Broadway and returning repeatedly to reconnect: Grant Thorburn, *Fifty Years' Reminiscences of New-York* (New York: Daniel Fanshaw, 1845), 19.

8 **all of fifteen:** Lanah's mother: Jane Outen Bogert, b. 1755 (*Baptisms from 1731 to 1800 in the Reformed Dutch Church, New York* [New York: NYGB Society, 1902], 200) married Francis Sawyer on 12 April 1772 (*Marriages from 1639 to 1801 in the Reformed Dutch Church . . . New York City* [New York: NYGB Society, 1940], 239). Lucretia Smith, b. 1762 (*Boston Transcript*, 162:250), married Peter Murphey (marriage bond 24:157, 4 October 1777, *New York Marriages Previous to 1784* [Baltimore: Genealogical Publishing Co., 1968], 276). Lanah's siblings: Peter, b. 1778 (Trinity Church registers) m. Christiana Henderson, b. ca.1782 (death notice, *New York Evening Post*, 1 December 1840), in 1799 (Pilmore marriage register); Mary, b. 1780 (Trinity Church registers) m. Robert Hewitt in 1798 (Pilmore marriage register); Catharine, b. 1782 (Trinity Church registers) m. William Macklin in 1799 (Pilmore marriage records).

9 **fetching water:** Gloria L. Main, "Women on the Edge: Life at Street Level in the Early Republic," *Journal of the Early Republic* 32, no. 3 (2012): 331–47; Seth Rockman, *Scraping By: Wage Labor, Slavery, and Survival in Early Baltimore* (Baltimore: Johns Hopkins University Press, 2009), ch. 6.

9 **two houses:** Deed of a house and lot from John Dyckman, his wife Rebecca, and Peter Sawyer, to Francis Cooly, 29 May 1759, NYC Conveyances 35:163; BIRC block 94, lot 14 (part of 13). Deed of two houses and lots from Christiana Bogert (widow of Martin) and her surviving children to William Moore, 31 July 1772, NYC Conveyances 38:402; BIRC block 95, lots 46–47.

9 **a decent living:** Jane Outen Bogert Sawyer m. John Callanan on 26 September 1783 (Trinity Church registers).

10 **around the corner:** Peter Sawyer was apprenticed to Robert Eaton (*John Callanan, guardian of Peter Sawyer, v. Robert Eaton*, MC Judgments 1794#172, filed 20 September 1794, NYCC-DOR), a branch pilot who lived at "40 Fair" (now Fulton) Street (*Directory for 1793*).

10 **for anything else:** Stansell, *City of Women*, 15–16; Marla R. Miller, *The Needle's Eye: Women and Work in the Age of Revolution* (Amherst: University of Massachusetts Press, 2006).

10 **"in the world":** *Diary* (New York), 8 July 1793, 11 July 1793.

11 **backyard pens:** On the Battery in the summer of 1793: John Drayton, *Letters written during a tour through the northern and eastern states of America* (Charleston, SC: Harrison and Bowen, 1794), 8–9, 20–21. Hogs, goats, and pigs: 20 September 1786, *MCC 1784–1831*, 1:250–51; hog hunt in the city: *Diary* (New York), 1 December 1792.

11 **his legs outstretched:** *Daily Advertiser* (New York), 4 September 1793. Alexander Anderson attended a 5:00 p.m. performance on 6 February 1793, *Alexander Anderson's New York City Diary, 1793–1799*, ed. Jane R. Pomeroy, 2 vols. (New Castle, DE: Oak Knoll Press, 2014), is a reliable edition of the manuscript at the Rare Book and Special Collections Library at Columbia University; cited hereafter as *Anderson's Diary*.

12 **flowers and tears:** Cathy N. Davidson, "Introduction," in Susanna Rowson, *Charlotte Temple* (New York: Oxford University Press, 1986), xiii–xv; C. J. Hughes, "Buried

in the Churchyard: A Good Story, at Least," *New York Times*, December 12, 2008, https://www.nytimes.com/2008/12/13/nyregion/13trinity.html.

12 **"venerable edifice":** Alvin F. Harlow, *Old Bowery Days* (New York: D. Appleton, 1931), 136–38.

12 **their families:** Stephanie Coontz, *Marriage, a History: How Love Conquered Marriage* (New York: Penguin Books, 2006).

12 **speak with Lanah:** William Wyche gives his name as "Joel Hone" (*Report*, 16), but he was correctly identifed in the official trial minutes: CO&T MB9 (1784–1796): 316–17.

13 **a growing family:** Samuel Hone (1766–1816) was the brother of John Hone (1764–1832) and Philip Hone (1780–1851), the mayor and diarist; "Notice of the death of Samuel Hone," *Evening Post* (New York), 5 February 1816. He married Hannah Quereau (1765–1812) on 8 January 1786; their son Philip was born 25 August 1786 (Trinity Church registers).

13 **for long periods:** Quote: Advertisement for sale of Dyckman house and bake house at Beekman and Gold Streets, *Daily Advertiser*, 19 June 1793. BIRC block 93, lot 36. Hone remained at that address through at least the summer of 1794 (*Directory for 1794*). 1793 Tax Records (BV New York City, NYHS) ward 3, p. 29: Widow [Rebecca] Dyckman rented a house, valued at $240, to Stephen Rudd ($30 personal estate) and the "bake house," valued at $160, to Samuel Hone ($20 personal estate).

13 **and one enslaved person:** Household members: 1790 NYC census.

13 **just a block away:** In 1769, Hannah's father, Benjamin Quereau, sold a parcel on Gold Street (50 Gold Street after 1793), near the corner of Fair (now Fulton) Street (NYC Conveyances 38:357) that was later owned by Lanah Sawyer's cousin Lucretia Harper (NYC Conveyance 76:448 [1807]). BIRC block 76, lot 29.

13 **"a very great rake":** *Report*, 4 (Sawyer), 16–17 (Hone). At the trial, Lanah Sawyer and Samuel Hone agreed on the substance of the exchange, but Hone denied saying that Bedlow was "a very great rake" to Sawyer; the prosecution attorney James Kent explained this as Sawyer's own thought (47).

14 **"entice from duty, debauch":** Noah Webster, *A Compendious Dictionary of the English Language* (Hartford: Sidney, 1806), 246 (rakehell, rakish), 271 (seduce).

14 **"reformed Rake" Royall Tyler:** Woody Holton, *Abigail Adams* (New York: Free Press, 2009), 180. Tyler, *The Contrast*.

15 *name was lawyer Smith*: *Report*, 4 (Sawyer).

15 **their better nature:** James Vernon, *Distant Strangers: How Britain Became Modern* (Berkeley: University of California Press, 2014), 18 (on Smith). Karen Halttunen, *Confidence Men and Painted Women: A Study of Middle-Class Culture in America, 1830–1870* (New Haven, CT: Yale University Press, 1983).

15 **characters of strangers:** Margaret Beekman Livingston to Edward Livingston, 13 December 1795, box 54, fol. 1, Edward Livingston Papers, CO280, Rare Books and Special Collections, Princeton University; "dissapation" in original.

15 **the book *First Impressions*:** See the editor's introduction in Jane Austen, *Pride and Prejudice*, the Cambridge Edition of the Works of Jane Austen, ed. Pat Rogers (New York: Cambridge University Press, 2006), xxiii–xxx.

16 **62 Gold Street:** Lanah Sawyer's family lived at 34 Gold Street (62 Gold Street after 1793): *Directory for 1793* and *Directory for 1794*, s.v. John Callanan. He was the tenant of John Conrey: 1793 Tax Records, ward 3, p. 20. William Perris, *Maps of the City of New York* (New York, 1852), plate 5, shows 62 Gold Street as BIRC block 94, lot 17. See NYC Conveyances: 314:594 (1795), Ruth Prince to Daniel Lawrence (lot 18, with John Cozine to the east, John Conrey to the west); 323:479 (1835), Lawrence et al. to Howe, with Daniel Lawrence to the east: 21'7" front, 19'9" rear, 47'5" east, 47'8–1/2" west. the parcel described as previously owned by Jonathan Conrey.

16 **by a cold snap:** Pintard, 4 September 1793, Diary and Garden Calendar.

17 **"for morning dress"**: *Grandmother Tyler's Book: The Recollections of Mary Palmer Tyler (Mrs. Royall Tyler)*, ed. Frederick Tupper and Helen Tyler Brown (New York: G.P. Putnam's Sons, 1925) 121–22.

17 **sporting long feathers:** Lanah Sawyer describes her gown and petticoats and their fastenings, and mentions her gloves and hat, in *Report*, 6, 8. For additional information and interpretation I'm indebted to Linda Baumgarten, meeting, November 29, 2016, and subsequent emails, and to Kimberly Alexander, conversation, August 26, 2019, and subsequent emails. Both agreed that in 1793, Sawyer was likely wearing a "round gown" with pins holding the bodice together and strings securing a fall-front at the waist (necessary to get the gown on and off) and, perhaps, additional strings at the neckline.

17 **into the street:** *Report*, 13 (Ann McFall); Wyche spells her name "M'Faul," but "McFall" was more standard.

17 **eyes of those inside:** Benches: Moreau, *American Journey*, 146.

18 **"old-fashioned, and utilitarian":** Jane Callanan described some of her possessions in her will, dated 4 January 1821, New York County Surrogate's Court, 58:252 (old liber 58:285–88), proved 23 September 1823. The 1793 Tax Records appraised John Callanan's personal property at £50—a modest sum, though more than that of most taxpayers.

18 **and another gentleman:** Walking stick: *Report*, 4 (Sawyer).

18 **on John Street:** *Directory for 1793*: "Steddiford, Gerard, vendue and commission-store, 34 Wall-street, and house—John do."

19 **at the rear:** A plan of the properties of Richard Varick and his neighbor is mislabeled as "Diagram of house and lot of Joseph de la Croix," n.d., New York City, Surveys of Streets, 1784–1797, box 33, fol. 12, NYHS.

19 **lower Broadway remained vacant:** For a map of lots listed as vacant on the 1789 New York City Tax Assessment List (NYMA), see Herbert S. Klein and Edmund Philip Willis, "The Distribution of Wealth in Late Eighteenth-Century New York City," *Histoire sociale—Social History* 18, no. 36 (1985): 259–83 (map: 263). See also 1789 Tax Records, electronic database, published by Willis in 2000: ICPSR 2863. The diminished number of vacant lots west of Broadway in the 1793 Tax Records indicates that redevelopment was continuing.

19 **a few years later:** Gravestone of Owen Callanan (30 December 1792–19 July 1797), son of Jane and John Callanan, Trinity Churchyard, section S3.

19 **America's first ice cream:** Joseph Corré rented a property on Broadway from the Tammany Society (1793 Tax List), identified as 24 Broadway (*Directory for 1793*). The numbers changed in 1794; it seems to be the property at 69 Broadway (its current number) in the Perris *Atlas* (1852) and in the GSET as part of Block 21, lot 6.

20 **"included ice cream":** On Washington's purchases of ice cream from Joseph Corré, see: J. L. Bell, "A Presidential Ice Cream Order," *Boston 1775* (blog), July 21, 2013, https://boston1775.blogspot.com/2013/07/a-presidential-ice-cream-order.html. Advertisement for "Ice and Ice Cream" at Corré's Hotel, *Daily Advertiser*, 12 May 1792. Abigail Adams to Mary Cranch, 9 August 1789, Richmond Hill, *Adams Family Correspondence*, vol. 8 (Cambridge, MA: Belknap Press, 2007), 397–401.

20 **"on the same errand":** *Anderson's Diary*, 25 June 1794; "Ice" in the original.

20 **an hour and a half:** *Report*, 23 (Livingston).

20 **lost in each other's eyes:** John Drayton's July 1793 sketch "A View of the Battery . . ." was engraved and published in his *Letters*, 20–21.

21 **across the night sky:** Sun and moon: www.timeanddate.com/sun and ~/moon (New York, 4 September 1793), accessed 4 February 2021; these modern calculations are very close to those in contemporary almanacks like *Greenleaf's New-York . . . Almanack . . . for . . . 1793* (New York: Thomas Greenleaf, 1792).

21 **until ten o'clock:** *Diary* (New York), 11 July 1793.

22 **in the streets that night:** *Report*, 4, 8 (Sawyer).

22 **brothels and disorderly taverns:** On the Vineyard tract, BIRC block 90, see chapter 2.

CHAPTER 2: MOTHER CAREY

23 **About 1:30 a.m.:** In Wyche's *Report*, Sawyer testified that she and Bedlow left the Battery about 1:00 a.m. (4); the walk to Carey's would have taken at least fifteen minutes. The defense questioned her account of time (Livingston: 23–24, 27) and put the time as "sometime after 10 o'clock" (Carey, 12) or "nearly between 10 and 11" (Thompson, 10).

23 **her front door:** Wyche misidentified Ann Carey as "Mary Cary" (*Report*, 12); in quotations from his report I have corrected the spelling of her surname. The CO&T MB1784–96: 317 gives her name as "Ann Carey," as did other legal documents and her gravestone—which gives her age in late 1796 as fifty-seven. See Edward L. Clarke, *Inscriptions . . . in the Burial-Grounds of Christ Church, Philadelphia* (Philadelphia: Collins, 1864), 498. The first published reference to "Mother Carey" was in the *Diary* (New York), 15 October 1793.

23 **names and faces:** Hallie Rubenhold, *The Covent Garden Ladies: Pimp General Jack & the Extraordinary Story of Harris's List* (Stroud, UK: Tempus Publishing, 2005), 55–56.

23 **acquired a reputation:** *Report*, 20 (Livingston).

23 **to Mother Carey's before:** Bedlow's attorney acknowledged that "he was probably well known at the house," *Report*, 27 (Livingston).

24 **part of the job:** Rubenhold, *Covent Garden Ladies*, 55.

24 **Lanah Sawyer by sight:** *Report*, 13 (McFall).

24 **"frill round the neck":** *Report*, 13 (Carey).

26 **at least for a time:** *Alexander Anderson's New York City Diary, 1793–1799*, ed. Jane R. Pomeroy, 2 vols. (New Castle, DE: Oak Knoll Press, 2014) 17 January 1793. At 1:00 p.m., the temperature was 38 degrees Fahrenheit: Jotham Post, 17 January 1793, Diary, 1792–1793, Mss Coll. BV Post, NYHS.

26 **with the disorder:** *Anderson's Diary*, 26 September 1793.

26 **lose her position:** *Anderson's Diary*, 22 June 1793 ("W[illiam Debow]'s attempt on the Irish servant maid"; 27 August 1793 (violent quarrel); 31 August 1793 (servant girl "dismiss'd").

26 **"a very familiar manner":** *Anderson's Diary*, 3 October 1793 ("wanton"); 21 October 1793 ("familiar").

27 **fallen counterparts with disgust:** Back in 1776, a Continental Army officer, who considered sexual self-control a masculine virtue, was horrified when his men flocked to New York's prostitutes: "it seems Strange that any Man can so divest himself of Manhood as to desire an intimate Connxion with these worse than brutal Creatures"; *Journal of Lieutenant Isaac Bangs, April 1 to July 29, 1776*, ed. Edward Bangs (Cambridge, MA: Wilson and Son, 1890), 29–30.

27 **guarded their reputations:** For a subtle analysis of poor women and reputation, see Arlette Farge, *Fragile Lives: Violence, Power, and Solidarity in Eighteenth-Century Paris* (Cambridge, MA: Harvard University Press, 1993), 20.

27 **"plying of their profession":** *Moreau de St. Méry's American Journey, 1793–1798*, ed. and trans. Kenneth Roberts and Anna M. Roberts (Garden City, NY: Doubleday, 1947), 156.

27 **or a graveyard:** Clare A. Lyons, *Sex Among the Rabble: An Intimate History of Gender and Power in the Age of Revolution, Philadelphia, 1730–1830* (Chapel Hill: University of North Carolina Press, 2006), 278–79.

27 **"Holy Ground":** Moreau, *American Journey*, 156.

27 **two live-in women:** In the 1790 census, James Carey's household included an adult white man (himself) and three white women (his wife and, probably, two employees).

According to *Report*, Ann Carey (12–13) and two white women testified that they were in the house that night (Mary Franklin, 14; Elizabeth Smith, 14). Earlier, Carey had told the mayor that also present was a "negro wench" (Varick, 15), probably a live-in servant.

27 **acting on their own:** Timothy J. Gilfoyle's tabulations of New York brothel keepers shows 68 percent were single women, 9 percent married couples, and 22 percent men in the 1820s and similar numbers thereafter: *City of Eros: New York City, Prostitution, and the Commercialization of Sex, 1790–1920* (New York: W. W. Norton, 1992), 73, 351–52 n46.

28 **desirable commodity, a virgin:** Moreau, *American Journey*, 313–14. See also Rubenhold, *Covent Garden Ladies*, 46–47 (virgins) and 57–61 (procurement).

28 **running a bawdy house:** New York City Court of Aldermen records, 1797–1798, MssCol. 23772, NYPL: 16 (13 November 1797, Nice and Kane). On the law, see: Willoughby Cyrus Waterman, *Prostitution and Its Repression in New York City, 1900–1930* (New York: Columbia University Press, 1932), 1–40 (esp. 12, quoting from *Laws of 1860*, ch. 508); Marilynn Wood Hill, *Their Sisters' Keepers: Prostitution in New York City, 1830–1870* (Berkeley: University of California Press, 1993), 116–44. See also Barbara Meil Hobson, *Uneasy Virtue: The Politics of Prostitution and the American Reform Tradition* (Chicago: University of Chicago Press, 1990), 32–33, 36–39; Lyons, *Sex Among the Rabble*, 334–39.

29 **under control:** On the family and household governance, see Ann M. Little, "Building Colonies, Defining Families," in *A Companion to American Women's History*, ed. Nancy A. Hewitt (Hoboken, NJ: Wiley-Blackwell, 2005), esp. 50–51. In practice, the form of indictments for disorderly house keeping varied, with specific offenses such as "whoring" and "gambling" often omitted or crossed out, even after printed forms came into use around 1800; see, for example, Samuel Clark, DA Indictments, filed 3 February 1791 ("whoring" crossed out); Nathaniel Taff and Eleanor Taff, DA Indictments, filed 13 January 1800 (printed form).

29 **skipped town:** Murder: *Boston Evening Post*, 2 November 1767; sentencing of Catharine Caroe: *New-York Journal*, 5 November 1767; Catharine Crow's house: *New York Mercury*, 18 January 1768; "famous Katy Crow": *New-York Gazette*, 18 February 1768, supplement.

29 **made it past sixty:** In 1786, only about 3.7 percent of white men were sixty or older in the city and 4.3 percent statewide; comparable figures for white women and people of color were not collected. City figures calculated from New York [City] 1786 Census, Common Council Records, NYMA. Henry A. Gemery, "The White Population of the Colonial United States, 1607–1790," in *A Population History of North America*, ed. Michael R. Haines and Richard H. Steckel (New York: Cambridge University Press, 2000), 155 (NY state 1786 census totals), 163–64. See also Herbert S. Klein, *A Population History of the United States* (New York: Cambridge Univeristy Press, 2004), 103.

29 **of ten pounds:** *Hilliad Magna. Being the Life and Adventures of Moll Placket-Hole* ([Philadelphia]: Anthony Armbruster, 1765). Moll's story closely parallels the story of Charlotte Hayes's early years—both were raised in brothels, had their virginity sold by their mothers, and became bawds themselves. On Hayes: Rubenhold, *Covent Garden Ladies*, 42–51.

30 **poverty and death:** See, for example: "Fatal Effects of Seduction," *New-York Weekly Magazine*, 6 Feb. 1790, [1]. Recent work on seduction and ruin includes Ruth H. Block, "Changing Conceptions of Sexuality and Romance in Eighteenth-Century America," 60, no. 1 *WMQ* (Jan. 2003), 130–42; Rodney Hessinger, *Seduced, Abandoned, and Reborn* (Philadelphia: University of Pennsylvania Press, 2005); and Lyons, *Sex Among the Rabble*, esp. 316–17.

30 **"as *honest* Housekeepers"**: *Moll Placket-Hole*, 4–5. On Hayes: Rubenhold, *Covent Garden Ladies*, 194–99.

30 **solemnized their vows:** Marriage of Ann Glover and James Carey, 22 April 1783, Trinity Church registers. Marriage bond 38:109 (22 April 1783), microfilm roll 6, series A1893, NYSA. Ann Carey's husband signed this bond with a mark—and someone else erroneously wrote his name as "Stephen Carey." The original license at the NYHS gives his name correctly; see Robert H. Kelley, "New York Marriage Licenses," *New York Marriages Previous to 1784* (Baltimore: Genealogical Publishing Co., 1968), 531, 537.

30 **population of about 12,000:** Five hundred prostitutes: Patrick M'Roberts, *A Tour Through Part of the Northern Provinces of America . . . in the years 1774 & 1775* (Philadelphia: Historical Society of Pennsylvania, 1935), 5.

30 **a year later:** Franks, *Directory* (New York, 1786); Franks, *Directory* (New York, 1787).

31 **not to the Careys:** New York City Tavern Licenses, 1783–1797, 1862, MS443.28, NYHS. None of the four-hundred-odd licenses in this collection between 1783 and 1796 was issued to either Carey (though some may be missing).

31 **keeper of a "brothel":** John Isaac Greenwood, "Reminiscences," 1858, 16–17, BV Greenwood, NYHS.

31 **their landlady's tenants:** Sketch of the Vineyard, 12 July 1784, Bancker Plans, Mss-Col 193, Manuscripts and Archives, NYPL. The property was owned by the widow Ann White. The list of tenants along Beekman Street was apparently added around 1790; four of the five names (McKay, Mrs. Car[e]y, W. B. [Ryle]Post, Mr. Gould) correlate to households in the *Directory for 1791* and the 1793 Tax Records. Since the 1750s, the "Vineyard" tract had been rented out as parcels on long-term leases. On the Vineyard tract, see I. N. Phelps Stokes, *Iconography of Manhattan Island, 1498–1909* (New York: Robert H. Dodd, 1915–1928), 1: description of plate 72a; 4:704; 6:155–56. Example of a sublease: advertisement for lease of lot 35 in the Vineyard, *New-York Gazette*, 28 January 1771. The Careys were evidently long-term lessors or sublessors (not short-term renters), because they were assessed for the value of the property in 1789 Tax Records (Willis) and 1793 Tax Records.

31 **a "boarding house":** *Directory for 1791* (James Carey); *Directory for 1792* (James Carey, Peter Gould); *Directory for 1793* (Hannah Gould).

31 **down by the Battery:** Joseph Corré was convicted at the August 1786 CGS (Hays, "General List"). In 1791, Corré was issued tavern license #131, Tavern Licenses, 1783–1796, 1862, NYHS.

31 **or her husband:** Disorderly house prosecutions, 1784–1819, from Hays, "General List."

32 **their earlier haunt:** In 1783, James Carey gave his address as "79 Beekman-Street, New-York": *Royal Gazette* (New York), 12 July 1783. Franks, *Directory* (1786): James "Ceary," 66 Broadway. From 1787 to 1793, city directories listed him at 80 Beekman.

32 **owned by Trinity Church:** On the Trinity Church tract, see Elizabeth Blackmar, *Manhattan for Rent, 1785–1830* (Ithaca: Cornell University Press, 1989), 30–33, 68–69, 89–93, 210.

32 **six bawdy houses:** In the four months from August to November 1793, at least six disorderly houses on Mother Carey's block (Manhattan block 90) came to public attention. 1) Bridget Parks, tavern keeper, 14 Chatham (now Park) Row (*Directory for 1793*), was convicted and fined for keeping a disorderly house (CGS MB1790–1797: 164 [12 August 1793], 167 [13 August 1793]); 2) John McGowan, tavern keeper, corner of Chatham Row and Beekman Street (1793 Tax Records, ward 4, p. 14), was prosecuted for keeping a disorderly house (CGS MB1790–1797: 188 [9 November 1793, indicted], 201 [8 February 1794, tried], and "whoring," DA Indictments, filed 6 February 1794); 3) Andrew Menzies, a shoemaker (4 Ann Street, *Directory for 1793*) who leased two adjacent houses on Ann Street (1793 Tax Records: ward 4, p. 26–27), was indicted for keeping a disorderly house (CGS MB1790–1797: 187 [9 November 1793]), no further record found. After the Bedlow trial, rioters attacked at least three brothels; 4) Car-

ey's; 5) that of Molly Frazier, tavern keeper, 3 Chatham Row (*Directory for 1793*), who prosecuted one rioter (Anthony Clawson, filed 8 November 1793, DA Indictments); and 6) "Mother Gibbons's" (*Anderson's Diary*, 15 October 1793; she is not listed in the *Directory for 1793*, but the *Directory for 1792* listed her as a tavern keeper at 3 Chatham Row). All of the above were likely brothels, as was the "tavern" kept by "Sally Morgan" at 2 Ann Street (*Directory for 1793*), or "Jane Morgan" (*Directory for 1792*); informal nicknames like "Sally" were rarely used in public documents for adult white women deemed respectable. In addition, there were other brothels nearby: Alexander Anderson reported that the post-trial riots also attacked the house of "Mother Giles"—likely Hannah Giles, "washer," at 23 Warren Street, just across the Fields (*Directory for 1793*). Meanwhile, Andrew Johnson, tavern keeper, Chatham Row (1793 Tax Records, ward 4, p. 3; *Directory for 1794*), was prosecuted for keeping a disorderly (not necessarily bawdy) house: CGC MB1790–1797: 168 (13 August 1793, pleads guilty to "keeping a Shuffle Board" and not guilty to an assault charge).

32 **"taverns and dram shops":** *Columbian Centinel* (New York), 19 February 1791 (excerpt from the *Pennsylvania Mercury* [Philadelphia], 17 February 1789).

32 **city's finer town houses:** In the 1793 Tax Records (ward 4, p. 3), James Carey's real estate was valued at £260 (about average) and his personal property at £200 (much higher than most people in modest houses). In the 1789 Tax Assessment (ward 5, p. 18), Carey's property was valued at £300 (significantly above average) and his personal property at £200 (far above average); Herbert S. Klein and Edmund Philip Willis, "The Distribution of Wealth in Late Eighteenth-Century New York City," *Histoire sociale—Social History* 18, no. 36 (1985): 259–83.

33 **a large garret:** Construction date, room for dancing, second floor, garret: *New-York Journal*, 14 May 1767. Wood-board walls, layout in 1793: *Report*, 15 (McReady). In a series of individual house "surveys," Evert Bancker often distinguished areas with paneling, plaster, and board walls: NYC Surveys of Streets, fol. 3 (1788), NYHS; paneling and plaster were most common in lower floors and public rooms, but many houses had plastered walls even in garrets.

33 **costly feather mattresses:** *Anderson's Diary*, 14 October 1793.

34 **negotiating business:** Carey's furnishings: Philip Hone, 8 August 1838, Diaries, 1826–1851, 14:287, Mss. Col. BV Hone, Philip, NYHS.

34 **looking for his wife:** A husband looking for his wife in a brothel: Francis Burdett Personel, *An authentic and particular account of the life of Francis Burdett Personel* (New-York, 1773), 9; a wife looking for her husband in a brothel: Lyons, *Sex Among the Rabble*, 255–56.

34 **no-longer-so-innocent daughter:** For example, see "Is that my daughter Ann," engraving (London, 1774), Lewis Walpole Library, Yale University.

34 **return on his own:** Moreau, *American Journey*, 313.

34 **fathers and sons:** *Independent Chronicle* (Boston), 1 November 1792.

34 **to keep quiet:** Moreau, *American Journey*, 312–13 (horse in Philadelphia), 315 (Frenchman in New York).

35 **"unloaded their freights":** *Moll Placket-Hole*, 4.

35 **old bawd's punchbowl:** Greenwood, "Reminiscences," 17. Greenwood, who was born in 1795, clearly heard this story secondhand; his sister, Jane Weaver Greenwood, was baptized on 20 December 1789 (Register of Baptisms, 1728–1790, p. 289, First Presbyterian Church, New York, Presbyterian Historical Society, Philadelphia).

36 **through the door:** Bedlow's reply is from the opening statement of his attorney: *Report*, 10 (Thompson).

36 **"and went away":** Except as noted above, this episode is reconstructed from the testimony of Sawyer, (*Report*, 5), Carey, (*Report*, 12), and Franklin (*Report*, 14).

38 **one way or another, seduced:** Rubenhold, *Covent Garden Ladies*, 126.

38 **"a novice at love":** Moreau, *American Journey*, 313–14.

38 **"as good a Virgin as ever":** Rubenhold, *Covent Garden Ladies*, 46–47, 219–21 (Hayes quotes, 220).

39 **still available to her:** Rubenhold, 57–61, 125–27, 210–12.

39 **deception or force:** Rubenhold, 125–26. On the evolving tone of Harris's Lists, see Elizabeth Campbell Denlinger, "The Garment and the Man: Masculine Desire in 'Harris's Lists of Covent-Garden Ladies,' 1764–1793," *Journal of the History of Sexuality* 11, no. 3 (2002), 357–94.

39 **always in demand:** Prostitution in eighteenth-century England was mostly a young women's trade: Randolph Trumbach, *Sex and the Gender Revolution*, vol. 1 (Chicago: University of Chicago Press, 1998), 116–18.

39 **attempted murder:** For criminal prosecutions, 1784–1819, see Hayes, "General List."

39 **across the color line was common:** Christine Stansell, *City of Women: Sex and Class in New York, 1798–1860* (New York: Alfred A. Knopf, 1986), 15 and 234 n33 (citing *Independent Mechanic*, 27 July 1811).

39 **a good number of them:** Shane White, *Somewhat More Independent: The End of Slavery in New York, 1770–1810* (Athens: University of Georgia Press, 1991), 165.

40 **"Black and white patrons":** Gilfoyle, *City of Eros*, 48. Dinah (aka Diana) "Sheffe," disorderly house, filed 5 April 1798, DA Indictments; CGS MB1797–1801: 107 (10 April 1798, indicted, disorderly house), 137 (8 June 1798, pleads not guilty), 138 (8 June 1798, convicted). *Longworth Directory 1798*: "Scheffee, Diana, 51 Warren." See also Betsey, "a black" (disorderly house), filed 9 August 1798, DA Indictments.

40 **"in bed with two Black Women":** White, *Somewhat More Independent*, 165. Statement of Amos Curtis, Nancy Cobus (disorderly house), filed August 6, 1802, DA Indictments; *Longworth Directory 1802*: Curtis, Amos M., grocer, 83 Chamber.

40 **of their subsistence:** Seth Rockman, "Women's Labor, Gender Ideology, and Working-Class Households in Early Republic Baltimore," *Pennsylvania History* 66, no. 5 (1999): 174–200; Rockman, *Scraping By*, 100–130.

40 **one-dollar cut:** Moreau, *American Journey*, 157 (sailor, laborer), 160 (laundress), 314 (prostitute).

40 **male protection rackets:** On the modern pimp system: Hill, *Their Sisters' Keepers*, 267–68, 392 n41. Stansell, *City of Women*, 174, dates the rise of pimps to after 1900. Gilfoyle, *City of Eros*, 88–89, 291, dates the start of this shift to the 1830s.

41 **her own bawdy house:** Lyons, *Sex Among the Rabble*, 31–33, 284–85 (quote, 285), 320–21. Companionship and camaraderie: Rubenhold, *Covent Garden Ladies*, 293.

41 **prosecuted for theft:** Rubenhold, *Covent Garden Ladies*, 44–45, 212.

42 **looking to turn tricks:** Margaret A. Oppenheimer, *The Remarkable Rise of Eliza Jumel: A Story of Money and Marriage in the Early Republic* (Chicago: Chicago Review Press, 2015), 1–16 (early years), 245–46 (1795 debt case), 234–35 (1802 bawdy house prosecution). Ruth Wallis Herndon, *Unwelcome Americans: Living on the Margin in Early New England* (Philadelphia: University of Pennsylvania Press, 2001), 145–48 (Margaret Fairchild Bowler).

42 **by getting married:** Lyons, *Sex Among the Rabble*, 284–87, 328–29. Rubenhold, *Covent Garden Ladies*, 287.

42 **eighteenth-century landmarks:** Oppenheimer, *The Remarkable Rise of Eliza Jumel*.

42 **a stone's throw:** Personel, *An authentic and particular account*. Francis "Personnel," gunsmith, married Mary Burties (also spelled Burtis), 4 April 1773, "Lutheran Church Marriages in New York City," *NYGB Record* 73, no. 4 (1942): 270.

43 **toddler out of trouble:** *Report*, 13 (McFall). Ann McFall described herself as the child's mother and as "a relation" of Mother Carey. Both had been married to members of the Glover family. "Agness" Clark married James Glover, 7 July 1787 (*Marriages from 1639 to 1801 in the Reformed Dutch Church . . . New York City* [New York: NYGB Society, 1940], 261). Their second son, Thomas Glover, was born 28 January 1790, which is consistent with Thompson's estimate of the "child's" age in the trial (*Record,*

11); the record of his baptism, 12 April 1790, gives her name as "Nancy Glover" and lists "Agness" Carey as godmother (*Baptisms from 1731 to 1800 in the Reformed Dutch Church, New York* [New York: NYGB Society, 1902], 404). In the early 1790s, she was listed at 18 George Street (now Spruce Street), probably just up Nassau Street from Mrs. Carey's (modern blocks 101 or 102); the *Directory for 1791* identified her as a widow, the *Directory for 1792* as a "washer." "Ann Glover" married "James McFall," 4 May 1792, Trinity Church registers. The *Directory for 1793* lists him as a house carpenter at 18 George Street.

44 **destroyed her belongings:** *Moll Placket-Hole*, 5–6.

44 **"put a seal upon his lips":** Moreau, *American Journey*, 315.

44 **simply disappeared:** People v. Bridget Parks, CGS MB1790–1797: 164 (12 August 1793, indicted, disorderly house); 167 (13 August 1793, convicted, fined £12). People v. Deborah Santie, CGC MB1790–1797: 164 (12 August 1793, indicted, disorderly house); no further record found. *Directory for 1793*: Park, Bridget, tavern-keeper, 14 Chatham-row (now Park Row); "Santore, Deborah, boarding house, 9 Roosevelt." Neither appeared in the *Directory for 1794*.

45 **those run by women:** Paul A. Gilje, *The Road to Mobocracy: Popular Disorder in New York City, 1763–1834* (Chapel Hill: University of North Carolina Press, 1987), 85–92; Gilfoyle, *City of Eros*, 76–91; Lyons, *Sex Among the Rabble*, 340–42. On white supremacy and brothel riots: John Wood Sweet, *Bodies Politic: Negotiating Race in the American North, 1730–1830* (Baltimore: Johns Hopkins University Press, 2003), 374–78.

45 **stop for breakfast:** Workers paid by the day worked from six to eight, nine to noon, and two to six; Moreau, *American Journey*, 157.

45 **size of their protuberances:** *Diary* (New York), 30 August 1793.

46 **the young woman to leave:** *Report*, 8 (Sawyer), 14 (Franklin). I find these accounts more credible than a defense lawyer's claim that the child got up unassisted around 7:00 a.m. (*Report*, 11 [Thompson]).

46 **husband, who had not:** *Report*, 12 (Carey).

47 ***some relation or acquaintance*:** *Report*, 6 (Sawyer), 12 (Carey); Carey accepted Sawyer's account except for the comment about her father.

CHAPTER 3: DAYLIGHT

48 **bravado had evaporated:** *Report*, 12 (Carey). Pintard, 5 September 1793, Diary and Garden Calendar, Newark, 1793–1794, box 4, fol. 9, Pintard Papers, MS490, NYHS: 72 1/2 "Milder."

48 **on its towering steeple:** *Report*, 42 (Cozine).

48 **craggy old buttonwood tree:** Hone, 8 August 1838, Diaries, 1826–1851, 14:287, Mss. Col. BV Hone, Philip, NYHS.

49 **hand along its roof:** John Isaac Greenwood, "Reminiscences," 1858, 22, BV Greenwood, NYHS. Greenwood described, and drew, two "shanties" at the corner of modern Park Row and Ann Street (BIRC block 90, lot 1)—3 Chatham Row (now Park Row) in the 1790s. This was the address of Mary Frazier, also spelled Fraser (*Directory for 1793*), and Ann Gibbons (*Directory for 1792*). For their status as bawdy-house keepers, see chapter 2.

50 **Passing by her:** *Report*, 6 (Sawyer).

50 **"before he heard her story":** *Report*, 6–7 (Sawyer).

50 **propensity for violence:** *Report*, 6–7 (Sawyer). On the process of disclosure in this period, see Sharon Block, "Bringing Rapes to Court," *Common-Place* 3, no. 3 (April 2003), http://commonplace.online/article/bringing-rapes-to-court/; and Block, *Rape and Sexual Power in Early America* (Chapel Hill: University of North Carolina Press, 2003), ch. 3.

51 **"Four Shillings each time":** *Royal Gazette*, 3 August 1782. Four shillings per person was also the price in 1793 when another bathing house opened on the East River: *Daily*

Advertiser, 5 June 1793. Henry Ludlam's bathing house was on North River at "the end" of Cedar (formerly Crown) Street (*Directory for 1793*; 1793 Tax List, ward 4, p. 15), abutting the open area shown south of the Paulus Hook ferry landing on McComb's 1789 *Plan of the City of New York*. After 1793, the bathing house changed ownership and the riverfront was reconfigured (Taylor, *New & Accurate Plan of the City of New York*, 1797).

51 **a kind of sponge bath:** Kathleen M. Brown, *Foul Bodies: Cleanliness in Early America* (New Haven, CT: Yale University Press, 2009), 26–32 (linens and laundry), 200–211 (bathing).

51 **within thirty minutes:** *New-York Packet*, 30 August 1784, supplement; *New-York Packet*, 3 July 1787; *Daily Advertiser*, 20 July 1790.

52 **or a sailor:** Four shillings New York currency was about $0.35. Moreau, *American Journey*, 157 (workman), 160 (laundress); Estelle M. Stewart and J. C. Bowen, *History of wages in the United States from colonial times to 1928*, Bulletin of the United States Bureau of Labor Statistics (Washington, DC, 1929), 97–98 (sailor).

52 **the violation, the trauma:** Christal L. Badour, Matthew T. Feldner, Kimberly A. Babson, Heidemarie Blumenthal, and Courtney E. Dutton, "Disgust, Mental Contamination, and Posttraumatic Stress: Unique Relations following Sexual versus Non-Sexual Assault," *Journal of Anxiety Disorders* 27, no. 1 (January 2013), 155–62.

52 **it promotes depression:** An early effort to analyze the range of responses among sexual assault survivors: Sally K. Bowie, Daniel C. Silverman, S. Michael Kalick, and Susan D. Edbril, "Blitz Rape and Confidence Rape: Implications for Clinical Intervention," *American Journal of Psychotherapy* 44, no. 2 (1990), 180–88.

52 **"she sat down by the Riverside":** *Report*, 7 (Sawyer).

52 **just over 72 degrees:** Pintard, 5 September 1793, Diary and Garden Calendar.

52 **until its arrival:** Mail stage schedule: *Daily Advertiser*, 17 August 1793.

53 **fragile wooden ships:** Robert Greemhalgh Albion, *The Rise of New York Port, 1815–1860* (New York: Charles Scribner's Sons, 1939), 20, 30.

53 **the river flowed calmly:** "A Tide Table," *Gaines's Almanack for 1793*: high tide at New York on 5 September 1793 came at 9:13 a.m. Low tide would have been about six hours later.

53 **a hopeless dream:** "The Repentant Prostitute," *Weekly Museum* (New York), 6 April 1796.

53 **"The Dying Prostitute":** Many variations on this theme appeared in American newspapers during the 1780s and 1790s, including a number of poems and prose fragments called "The Dying Prostitute."

54 **gave up and went away:** *Report*, 7 (Sawyer).

55 **on her body:** Bloody linens and "evident marks": *Report*, 17 (Jane Callanan), and 17 (Harper).

55 **"her aged aunt":** *Report*, 7 (Sawyer).

55 **of the Bowling Green:** 1793 Tax Records, ward 1, p. 23: "Widow Judah Bruce," house, £450 real estate, £100 personal estate. In 1793, about 5,200 properties were appraised: about 66 percent at less than Bruce's, about 30 percent at more.

55 **seem like a "threat":** James Barron, "Wounded by 'Fearless Girl,' Creator of 'Charging Bull' Wants Her to Move," *New York Times*, 12 April 2017, https://www.nytimes.com /2017/04/12/nyregion/charging-bull-sculpture-wall-street-fearless-girl.html.

56 **respectable female companion:** Judith Bayard, daughter of Nicholas Bayard and Elizabeth Rynders, was baptized on 29 February 1740 (*Baptisms from 1731 to 1800 in the Reformed Dutch Church, New York* [New York: NYGB Society, 1902], 78) and died in 1817, in her "80th year," (*Evening Post* [New York], 17 September 1817). Guest list: Rufus W. Griswold, *The Republican Court*, new ed. (New York: Appleton and Co., 1868), 98. Mrs. Bruce on a Hamilton guest list: Bushrod Washington to Alexander Hamilton, 15 April 1802, *Papers of Alexander Hamilton*, vol. 25 (New York: Columbia University Press, 1977), 602–5. The 1800 federal census for New York City lists two

enslaved people in Bruce's household (ward 1, p. 4); her 1813 will freed a woman named "Hall" and left her a modest annuity.

57 **Lanah's grandfather Peter Sawyer:** George (Joris) Dyckman, will, 8 December 1752, proved 29 March 1753, Will Libers 18:263, New York County Surrogate's Court, mentioned his son John and his daughter Mary, wife of Peter Sawyer. Among other property, Dyckman left a house on Gold Street that went to his children John and Maria; she died in 1755: "Wife of Peter Sawyer," 23 August 1755, "Record of Burials in the Dutch Church, New York [1727–1803] *Year Book of the Holland Society of New York* (1899), 189. Deed from John Dyckman, his wife Rebecca Dyckman, and Peter Sawyer to Francis Cooly, 29 May 1749, recorded 9 June 1759, NYC Conveyances 35:163. See BIRC block 94, lot 14 (part of 13) at corner of Gold and Fulton.

57 **Samuel Hone now rented:** "To be Sold, or Let, A Dwelling, Bake, and Bolt House . . . ," *New-York Packet*, 5 February 1784.

57 **growing family moved there:** Advertisement of the farm of the late Robert Benson, *New-York Gazette*, 1764. On the "John Dyckman Farm," see I. N. Phelps Stokes, *Iconography of Manhattan Island, 1498–1909* (New York: Robert H. Dodd, 1915–1928), vol. 1, plates 41, 42 and 6:100–101. "Alderman Dyckman's land between Bowery Lane and Great George Street," survey (blocks 507–510, 521, 522), 13 October 1780, Bancker Plans, NYPL.

57 **were repeatedly reelected:** The 1769 election returns include, for the first time, John Dyckman, Alderman, Out ward, for the Bowery Division, along with Matthew Buys as his assistant—perhaps a relation of his wife, Rebecca Buys; *MCC 1675–1776*, 7:184 (election), 7:185 (contested by the defeated incumbent Cornelius Roosevelt), 7:187 (confirmed), 7:189 (sworn). His reelection in 1770 was also contested by Roosevelt and confirmed; 7:231, 7:232, 7:235, 7:237. He was reelected in 1771 (7:318), 1772 (7:379), 1773 (7:447), and 1774 (8:57). In 1775, Nicholas Bayard, Mrs. Bruce's brother, was elected alderman, with Anthony Rutgers as assistant and Henry Rutgers Jr. as assessor (8:108).

58 **after her husband's death:** In 1790, before she moved in with Mrs. Bruce, Rebecca Dyckman's household included seven enslaved workers ("Widow Dyckman," Federal Census, 1790, Ward 7, p. 131). On people enslaved by Judith Bruce, see below.

58 **"a whore and strumpet":** Nicole Saffold Maskiell, "Bound by Bondage: Slavery Among Elites in Colonial Massachusetts and New York" (PhD. diss, Cornell University, May 2013), 42–45.

60 **Mrs. Bruce's brother:** Nicholas Bayard, alderman: *Directory for 1793*, 201. The Bayard and Dyckman ("Duycking") farms are shown on Bernard Ratzer, *Plan of the City of New York*, engraved by Thomas Kitchin, 58.4 x 88.5 cm (London, 12 January 1776), NYPL, https://digitalcollections.nypl.org/items/510d47da-f072-a3d9-e040-e00a18064a99.

60 **left their marital assets:** John Dyckman, will, 23 May 1786, proved 18 July 1793, Wills Liber 41:188–191, New York County Surrogate's Court.

60 **"Mother of Tunes Dickman":** 8 February 1799, "Burials in the Dutch Church, New York," 161 ("Dickma" in original).

60 **his poor health:** "Jeremiah Van Rensselaer," in James McLachlan, ed., *Princetonians, 1748–1768: A Biographical Dictionary* (Princeton, NJ: Princeton University Press, 1976), 252–53. "Beatific": Katherine D. Alcauska, "Painting and Frame," *Art Conservator* 3, no. 1 (Spring 2008), referring to: Thomas McIlworth, *Jeremias Van Rensselaer*, 1763, 30 x 25 in, Albany Institute of Art and History, #2007.020.

60 **manor would pass, in trust:** John Van Rensselaer, Esq., of Greenbush, will, 25 May 1782, proved 24 March 1783, Wills Liber 36:58–64 (old liber 36:48–52), New York County Surrogate's Court.

60 **aristocratic and undemocratic:** On entail: Holly Brewer, *By Birth or Consent: Children, Law, and the Anglo-American Revolution in Authority* (Chapel Hill: University of North Carolina Press, 2005), 37–39.

60 **and ultimately prevailed:** Julius Goebel and Joseph H. Smith, eds., *The Law Practice of Alexander Hamilton*, vol. 3 (New York: Columbia University Press, 1980), 308–51.

61 **found in each other:** In her will, Judith Bruce remembered a subsequent companion, Elizabeth Albright ("who for many years has and at present does live with me"), with gifts of personal property and a modest annuity; Judith Bruce, will, 9 January 1813, proved 19 December 1817, Wills Liber 54:229–35, New York County Surrogate's Court. Bruce's son also remembered Albright: Archibald Bruce, will, 11 November 1817, proved 26 March 1818, Wills Liber 54:327–29, New York County Surrogate's Court.

61 **months of marriage:** Patricia Cline Cohen, "Public and Print Cultures of Sex in the Long Nineteenth Century," in *The Oxford Handbook of American Women's and Gender History*, ed. Ellen Hartigan-O'Connor and Lisa G. Materson (New York: Oxford University Press, 2018), 195–216 (premarital pregnancy: 96–98).

61 **an advanced courtship:** See, for example, Arlette Farge, *Fragile Lives: Violence, Power, and Solidarity in Eighteenth-Century Paris* (Cambridge, MA: Harvard University Press, 1993), ch. 3.

61 **family's honor is preserved:** On 4 June 1822, a New York minister included a telling affidavit in his marriage record ("We the subscribers do hereby certify that there is a necessity and propriety in William Ross James and Matilda Carman being joined in marriage union"), "The Reverend Edward Mitchell and His Marriages," *NYGB Record* 93, no. 3 (1962): 136.

62 **(or simply precoital) promises:** Cohen, "Public and Print Cultures of Sex," 98–202; and email to author, 18 September 2020 ("power play").

63 **marry another woman:** John D'Emilio and Estelle B. Freedman, *Intimate Matters: A History of Sexuality in America*, 3rd. ed. (Chicago: University of Chicago Press, 2012), 26 (quote). Cornelia Dayton, "Taking the Trade: Abortion and Gender Relations in an Eighteenth-Century New England Village," *William and Mary Quarterly* 48, no. 1 (January 1991), 19–49; Clare A. Lyons, *Sex Among the Rabble: An Intimate History of Gender and Power in the Age of Revolution, Philadelphia, 1730–1830* (Chapel Hill: University of North Carolina Press, 2006), 97–98. Janet Farrell Brodie, *Contraception and Abortion in Nineteenth-Century America* (Ithaca, NY: Cornell University Press, 1994), ch. 2; Joanna N. Lahey, "Birthing a Nation: The Effect of Fertility Control Access on the Nineteenth-Century Demographic Transition," *Journal of Economic History* 74, no. 2 (June 2014), 482–508.

63 **"down and dejected":** *Report*, 7 (Sawyer), 18 ("Another witness"). Wyche identified two prosecution witnesses only as "another witness." According to the CO&T MB9: 317, they were Mary Caswell and Elizabeth "Aulbry" (probably Aubick). Caswell was probably the one testifying about Mrs. Bruce.

65 **twilight had faded:** Sunset: www.timeanddate.com/sun (New York, 5 September 1793), accessed 4 Februrary 2021.

65 **stone sidewalk of Broadway:** *Report*, 7 (Sawyer, referring to the first time she left Mrs. Bruce's); "Another witness" confirmed that Lanah left "between 6 and 7—nearer 7" (18).

65 **Dock Street:** Great Dock Street is now a portion of Pearl Street between Broad Street and Hanover Square.

66 **approached her mother:** Block, *Rape and Sexual Power*, 88–125. Dayton describes similar dynamics in "Taking the Trade."

66 **make ends meet:** Miss Pine was likely the daughter of Elizabeth Pine (ca. 1757–1826), the widow of William Pine who died in 1790 (death notice, *New York Post*, 29 November 1826). Until 1790, the Pines were close neighbors of the Callanans: William Pine was listed as a "painter" at 33 Gold Street in the *Directory for 1789* and the *Directory for 1790*; see also 1789 Tax List, ward 4, p. 31. Elizabeth Pine was listed as the head of a household with four white females in 1790 (Federal Census, Montgomery Ward, p. 82), but she moved repeatedly after that; the *Directory for 1791* lists

her as a "seamstress" at 5 Frankfort Street, the *Directory for 1793* lists her at 55 Dey Street. By then, her daughters, "Miss Pine" and "her sister" (*Report*, 7 [Sawyer]), were apparently living separately, perhaps as a domestic servant in a George (now Spruce) Street household. One of her daughters was evidently named Margaret; they were listed at the same address in the 1812 *Elliott Double Directory*.

66 **and they spoke:** *Report*, 7 (Sawyer), 18 (Robert Towt, who observed that Miss Pine was "then looking over her door").

67 **already dealt with:** The *Directory for 1793* listed Robert Towt, "inspector of leather," 26 George (now Spruce) Street. The 1793 Tax Records show Towt with £100 personal estate and renting a £400 house on George Street from George Peeks; see NYC Conveyances 84:514; BIRC block 101, lot 8. Towt's real estate included a £900 house on Beaver Street and a £400 house on New Street (1793 Tax Records, ward 1, p. 10, 12). By 1796, he also owned a house at 18 George Street (1796 Tax Records, NYHS, ward 3, p. 25) and a fourth house on Broadway (ward 1, p. 29). Even before the revolution, Towt had accumulated enough property to be an elector: see *A Copy of the Poll List . . . for the City and County of New-York (1768)* (New York: F. Hart & Co., 1880), 37. The 1790 federal census (North Ward, p. 49) listed the Towt household as including one adult white man, seven white females, and one enslaved worker.

    Sarah Burdett married Robert Towt in New York (marriage bond 10:96, 15 September 1766, *New York Marriages Previous to 1784* [Baltimore: Genealogical Publishing Co.], 55); both had had previous marriages and each had one daughter (Robert Towt, will, probated 18 March 1799, Wills Liber 43:40–45, New York County Surrogate's Court). Their children together included Sarah Towt, baptized 10 November 1793 ("Records of the First Presbyterian Church, New York," *NYGB Record* 10, no. 2 [1879]: 94), and Cornelia Hardecker Towt, born 26 December 1777 (*The Record*, First Presbyterian Church, Morristown, NJ, vol. 2, no. 10: 175).

67 **to escort them:** *Report*, 18 (Robert Towt).

67 **"afraid of going home":** *Report*, 18–19 (Robert Towt).

68 **looking for her:** *Report*, 7 (Sawyer).

CHAPTER 4: THE RAKE

69 **crashed into the stoop:** John Isaac Greenwood, "Reminiscences," 1858, 25, BV Greenwood, NYHS.

69 **"absence of his daughter":** *Report*, 15 (John Callanan). He testified that he was alarmed about Lanah's absence in the "evening"—perhaps after returning home from work. The sun set at 6:24 p.m., the moon at 6:37 p.m: www.timeanddate.com/sun and ~/moon (New York, 5 September 1793), accessed 16 February 2021. The weather was mild: Pintard, 5 September 1793, Diary and Garden Calendar, Newark, 1793–1794, box 4, fol. 9, Pintard Papers, MS490, NYHS.

69 **how they were perceived:** A subtle reading of honor as control of public perceptions: Kenneth S. Greenberg, *Honor and Slavery* (Princeton, NJ: Princeton University Press, 1996); Joanne B. Freeman, *Affairs of Honor: National Politics in the New Republic* (New Haven, CT: Yale University Press, 2001), 170–71.

71 **long, sharp pin:** Henry Bedlow portrait miniature, unidentified artist, n.d., watercolor on ivory, 1–5/8 x 1–1/4 in, object no. 1928.6, NYHS. The hairstyle and the turned-up collar suggest a date between 1785–1795; see a similar portrait miniature of George Henry Remsen, 1790–1795, watercolor on ivory, 1–11/16 x 1–5/16 in, object no. 1954.178, NYHS. For analysis of the Bedlow portrait, I'm indebted to René Chartrand, email to author, 12 May 2016; Linda Baumgarten, consultation, 29 November 2016, and subsequent emails; and Kimberly Alexander, conversation, 26 August 2019, and subsequent emails.

71 **daily house calls:** Hairdressing: Obrien Brown ad, *New-York Daily Gazette*, 28 March 1792, 4; Thomas Warner ad, *New-York Morning Post*, 3 February 1792, 3.

72 **have his portrait painted:** Bedlow as a rake: *Report*, 4 (Sawyer), 47 (Kent). As a man of "gallantry" who would go to "considerable lengths" to seduce women: *Report*, 20 (Livingston). Bedlow and George Henry Remsen were appointed ensigns in the same militia company in October 1786: Minutes of the Council of Appointment, 4 October 1786, 1:68–75, A1845, NYSA. Unlike Remen, Bedlow does not appear in subsequent lists of militia officers; see, for example, *Directory for 1789*, 127–30; *Directory for 1791*, 20–25 (25: George H. Remsen, captain); *Directory for 1793*, 205–209 (206, 209: George H. Remsen, captain).

72 **at least one infant:** A typical colonial woman gave birth about eight times, and out of every 1,000 live births an estimated 114 to 158 infants died (more in cities); Gemery, "White Population in the Colonial United States," 152–54, 160–61. The 2018 US infant mortality rate was 5.7; "Infant Mortality," Centers for Disease Control and Prevention, last reviewed 10 September 2020, https://www.cdc.gov/reproductivehealth/maternalinfanthealth/infantmortality.htm.

72 **"Knowledge & True Holyness":** William Bedlow, family record in *New Testament* (London, 1759), CS71.B4127 no. 1, NYHS. William Bedlow was born on 6 December 1722 and married to Catharina Rutgers on 12 August 1749.

72 **known as Bedlow's Island:** William S. Pelletreau, "The Family of Bedlow," in his *Historic Homes and Institutions and Genealogical and Family History of New York* (New York: Lewis Publishing Company, 1907), 111–19. In the 1850s, the old Dutch spelling ("Bedloe's Island") was revived; but the city's newspapers consistently referred to "Bedlow's Island" from at least 1760 (*New-York Gazette,* 21 April 1760) to about 1845 (*New York Herald*, 18 July 1845). On William of Orange: Henry Bedlow to Martin and Townsend, New York, 23 September 1821, Misc. MSS Bedlow, NYHS.

73 **slavery in the Americas:** William Bedlow, logbook, 1759–1773, BV Bedlow, William, NYHS.

73 **would fall ill:** For a summary of the history of the island: "Liberty Island Chronology," Statue of Liberty National Monument, New York, last updated 1 February 2018, https://www.nps.gov/stli/learn/historyculture/liberty-island-a-chronology.htm. "Price List," *The Collector: A Magazine for Autograph and Historical Collectors* 15, no. 162 (1902): 38, refers to a William Bedlow letter dated Bedlow Island, 1765.

73 **staunch Loyalists:** Judith L. Van Buskirk, *Generous Enemies: Patriots and Loyalists in Revolutionary New York* (Philadelphia: University of Pennsylavania Press, 2002); Ruma Chopra, *Unnatural Rebellion: Loyalists in New York City During the American Revolution* (Charlottesville: University of Virginia Press, 2011).

73 **"a post of infinite importance":** George Washington to Jonathan Trumbull, Sr., 14 March 1776, *Founders Online*, National Archives, accessed 29 August 2021, https://founders.archives.gov/documents/Washington/03-03-02-0345.

73 **took charge of the city:** Resolution of the Committee [of Safety], 5 July 1775, *New-York Gazette*, 10 July 1775; in the *London Chronicle*, 24 August 1775, this was called the Committee of Secrecy and Inspection. Bedlow also signed a petition supporting trade with Connecticut: *New-York Journal*, 13 July 1775.

73 **passage of British warships:** Bedlow's role as a commissioner for the fortification of the highlands is detailed in the *Journals of the Provincial Congress . . .* (Albany: Thurlow Weed, 1842), from his appointment on 22 August 1775 (1:113) to April 1777 (2:425), when the new state government supplanted the Provincial Congress. (In 1756, Bedlow had commanded a British navy vessel on Lake Ontario: editorial note 2, Alexander McDougall to George Washington, 19 January 1779, *Founders Online*, National Archives, accessed 29 August 2021, https://founders.archives.gov/documents/Washington/03-19-02-0030.)

74 **advantageous appointment:** For a summary of William Bedlow's wartime roles, see editorial note 6, Henry Beekman Livingston to George Washington, 11–14 June 1776, Fort Constitution, *Founders Online*, National Archives, accessed 29 August

2021, https://founders.archives.gov/documents/Washington/03–04–02–0393. The New York Provincial Congress appointed Bedlow a commissioner for fortifying the Highlands (22 August 1775) and, apparently, commissary of stores for the Highlands forts after December 1776; on Clinton's recommendation Bedlow became the Continental Army's deputy paymaster general at Fishkill (summer 1777); in 1779, he became one of the army's five auditors.

74 **strongholds in the Highlands:** For a vivid account of this phase of the war, see Nathaniel Philbrick, *Valiant Ambition: George Washington, Benedict Arnold, and the Fate of the American Revolution* (New York: Viking, 2016). A more detailed analysis is Robert K. Wright, "Too Little, Too Late: The Campaign of 1777 in the Hudson Highlands" (MA thesis, College of William and Mary, 1971), https://dx.doi.org/doi:10.21220/s2–36b0-g327.

74 **relieved of his position:** William Bedlow to Robert R. Livingston, 24 February 1778, offered for sale by Stuart Lutz Historic Documents, Inc., accessed 25 April 2015, http://www.historydocs.com/printinfo.asp?StockNo=2631.

74 **lack of consideration:** Bedlow to Livingston, 24 February 1778.

74 **army's five auditors:** Alexander McDougall to George Washington, 19 January 1779. Bedlow and four others appointed auditors of the army: *Journals of the Continental Congress, 1774–1789*, vol. 15 (Washington, DC: US Government Printing Office, 1909), 1252 (9 November 1779).

74 **a dour expression:** William Bedlow, sketch by Tadeusz Kościuszko (owned by Dr. Fenwick Beekman), reproduced in Philip L. White, *The Beekmans of New York in Politics and Commerce* (New York: New-York Historical Society, 1956), pl. 9.

74 **"injured by the times":** George Clinton to Nathaniel Sackett, 1 July 1781, *Public Papers of George Clinton* (Albany: Wynkoop Hallenbeck Crawford, 1900), 7:55. Even McDougall's letter to Washington, 19 January 1779, concluded "he has suffered greatly."

75 **long occupation of the city:** William Bedlow, account with Stephen McCrea, 28 March 1784 (payment 15 November 1783), box 13, fol. 1, Duyckinck Family Papers, MH15251, NYSL.

75 **a brilliant legal mind:** Peter Charles Hoffer, *Rutgers v. Waddington: Alexander Hamilton, the End of the War for Independence, and the Origins of Judicial Review* (Lawrence: University Press of Kansas, 2016).

75 **staggering sum of £80,000:** Estimate of the Value of the real Estates in the Out Ward of the City of New York belonging to Persons in Actual Rebellion, 1778 (Auckland Manuscripts at King's College Cambridge), *B. F. Stevens's Facsimiles of Manuscripts in European Archives Relating to America*, vol. 12 (London: Malby and Sons, 1892), doc. 1235.

76 **city's bustling waterfront:** "The Hendrick Rutgers Farm," I. N. Phelps Stokes, *Iconography of Manhattan Island, 1498–1909* (New York: Robert H. Dodd, 1915–1928), 6:134–36 (farm); see also 3:612 and plates 109a and 109b.

76 **cramped old city:** David J. Fowler, "Benevolent Patriot: The Life and Times of Henry Rutgers: Part One: 1636–1776," *Journal of the Rutgers University Libraries* 68, no. 1 (2016): 42–99 (on the farm, see notes 17 and 18). As Fowler notes (49), plans for subdividing the Rutgers farm were made about the same as time those for the DeLancey (after 1741) and Trinity Church farms (1762).

76 **a hundred building lots each:** Hendrick Rutgers, will, 28 August 1775, proved 15 November 1779, Wills Liber 33:306–11 (old liber 201–204), New York County Surrogate's Court. For the partition, see J. B. Holmes, *Map of the Rutger's Farm as It Existed in 1784* (New York: New York City Surveyor, 1874), NYPL.

77 **city's center of power:** Initially, deputy postmaster Bedlow rented the former Judge Daniel Horsmanden house at 38 Smith Street (*Independent New-York Gazette*, 6 December 1783; description in for-sale ad *Independent New-York Gazette*, 15 January

1784). He then settled at 8 Wall Street (*Directory for 1789*); see ad for the sale of the house "in the centre of Wall-Street, where Mr. Bedlow formerly kept the Post-Office" (*Daily Advertiser*, 7 February 1792).

77 **"nothing till next Spring":** William Bedlow to John Pierce, 10 January 1784, Manuscript File, RG93, NARA, Papers of the War Department Online, accessed 22 April 2016 via http://wardepartmentpapers.org (document 1784011060001).

77 **his uncle's heir:** In the notice of his marriage to Julia Halsey in 1808, he was described as "Henry Bedlow, esq., only nephew to Col Henry Rutgers," *Spectator* (New York), 7 April 1808.

77 **great real-estate fortunes:** On real-estate development and the Rutgers farm: Blackmar, *Manhattan for Rent*, 99–102, 176

77 **Dutch family crest:** Sugar tongs with Bedlow crest and motto, ca. 1800–1825, inventory no. 1939.320, NYHS; on the Bedlow crest and motto, see Bedlow to Martin and Townsend, 23 September 1821. See also the silver tea set engraved with the initials of Bedlow's sister, Mary E. G. B. Beekman, and the arms of her husband, John Beekman, made by William G. Forbes, ca. 1795–1797, inventory no. 1911.37a-e, NYHS.

77 **claiming his own freedom:** Flora and her daughters: William Bedlow family records, inventory of the estate of William Bedlow, 18 February 1799, box 12, fol. 2, Beekman Family Papers, NYHS. Mack: William Bedlow runaway advertisement, *Independent Journal* (New York), 19 January 1785.

78 **"manners and morals undepraved":** Thomas Jefferson, *Notes on the State of Virginia* (Philadelphia: Prichard and Hall, 1788), 172.

78 **in large letters: "Dominion":** William Bedlow, logbook, 1759–1773.

78 **the old Rutgers farm:** Catherine was the daughter of "Mr. James Van Horne of this city": *Independent Journal* (New York), 12 July 1786. James Van Horne (1745–1792) and Maayke (Mary) Lott obtained a marriage license on 2 December 1768 (bond 13:252: *Marriages Prior to 1784*, 238). Catherine's birth, of which I have found no record, apparently occurred soon after this marriage. She and Harry Bedlow were both great-grandchildren of Hermanus and Catharina (Meyer) Rutgers. James Van Horne owned a £285 house at the New Slip and no personal estate (1789 Tax Records [Willis], ward 7, p. 17). James Van Horne was not listed in the Franks *Directory* (1786); he was a "grocer" at Catharine Slip in the Franks *Directory* (1787); a "grocer" at 147 Front Street in the *Directory for 1789*; back on Catharine Slip in the *Directory for 1790*. In the 1790 federal census (New York, Out Ward, p. 116), his household included one enslaved person. He died in early 1792 (12 March 1792, "Record of Burials in the Dutch Church, New York [1727–1803]," *Year Book of the Holland Society of New York* [1899], 203) and left no will. His widow was back on Front Street (147 Front seems to have been at the corner of the Fly Market) in the 1793 and 1794 directories.

79 **marriage to Catherine Van Horne:** William Bedlow, family records. The original has been damaged and is partially illegible; for a seemingly complete transcription, see Jeannie F. J. Robinson and Henrietta C. Bartlett, eds., *Genealogical Records . . . Taken from Family Bibles, 1581–1917* (New York: Colonial Dames of the State of New York, 1917), 9–10.

80 **to their son alone:** Henry Rutgers to Henry Bedlow and Catherine, his wife, deed of Rutgers lot #193, NYC Conveyances 45:242, 28 November 1785, recorded 13 December 1788; William and Catharine Bedlow to Henry Bedlow, deed of Rutgers lot #295, NYC Conveyances 45:244, 28 November 1785, recorded 13 December 1788.

81 **"Dyed in Labor":** William Bedlow, family records.

81 **one woman in ten:** Susan Klepp, *Philadelphia in Transition: A Demographic History of the City and its Occupational Groups, 1720–1830* (New York: Garland, 1989) 189–91: 3.2 percent of elite women and 9.8 percent of poor women died during childbirth in post-revolution Philadelphia. Janet Golden, *A Social History of Wet Nursing in America: From Breast to Bottle* (New York: Cambridge University Press, 1996),

18–19, estimates the maternal death rate in early America as about 600 to 2,000 per 100,000 live births. By 1800, maternal mortality rates in England were around 500 to 1,000 per 100,000 live births. See Irvine Loudon, *Death in Childbirth: An International Study of Maternal Care and Maternal Mortality, 1800–1950* (New York: Ocford University Press, 1992), 158–63. In the United States in 2018, the figure was 17.4 maternal deaths per 100,000 live births: "Maternal Mortality," Centers for Disease Control and Prevention, last reviewed June 9, 2021, https://www.cdc.gov/nchs/maternal-mortality/index.htm.

81 **died soon after his birth:** 1790 Federal census (New York, Ward 4, p. 123) lists the Bedlow household with two white males over sixteen—Henry Bedlow and his father, William—but no white males under sixteen. I find no mention of the baby William Bedlow after the record of his birth in his grandfather's family records; I assume he died young and was buried, with his mother, in the Rutgers vault.

81 **New Dutch Church Yard:** Notice of the death of Catherine Van Horne Bedlow, *Independent Journal* (New York), 12 July 1786. Burial of "Wife of William [i.e., Henry] Bedlow," d. 7 July 1786, "Record of Burials in the Dutch Church, New York," *Year Book of the Holland Society of New York* (1899), 144.

82 **"kick up" new "capers":** Jules C. Ladenheim, "'The Doctor's Mob' of 1788," *Journal of the History of Medicine* 5, no. 1 (Winter 1950), 23–43. On Bedlow's role: "The Omnibus . . . by a Retired Physician," *Historical Magazine* 10, no. 2 (1868), 10–13 (quote, 12).

82 **pay a hairdresser:** *Daily Advertiser* (New York), 26 August 1789.

83 **difficult for the lender:** Bruce H. Mann, *Republic of Debtors: Bankruptcy in the Age of American Independence* (Cambridge, MA: Harvard University Press, 2002), 6–33. Toby L. Ditz, "Shipwrecked; or, Masculinity Imperiled: Mercantile Representations of Failure and the Gendered Self in Eighteenth-Century Philadelphia," *Journal of American History* 81, no. 1 (June 1994), 51–80.

83 **he sold his other lot:** At the time, his aunt was renting her properties in the Rutgers farm for about £5 per year: Mary Rutgers McCrea, Rent Book, 1785–1816, box 13, envelope 3, Duyckinck Family Papers, NYSL.

83 **sensed Bedlow's desperation:** Henry Bedlow to Benjamin Gatfield, Rutgers lot #295, 21 October 1788 (recorded 3 November 1788), NYC Conveyances 45:209 and Rutgers lot #193, 15 November 1788 (recorded 15 December 1788), NYC Conveyances 45:245.

83 **magnified by fees and court costs:** *John J. Remsen v. Henry Bedlow*, MC Judgments 1789#175, filed 12 February 1789: damages £15.6.6, costs £8.9.3; *John Harris v. Henry Bedlow*, MC Judgments 1789#97, filed 12 February 1789: damages £14.16.10, costs £8.9.3.

84 **Ebenezer Crosby:** *New-York Journal*, 18 July 1788; *Daily Advertiser* (New York), 18 July 1788; *Impartial Gazetteer*, 19 July 1788.

84 **a curious decision:** Her death: *New-York Packet*, 24 February 1789; *New-York Daily Gazette*, 23 February 1789; *Pennsylvania Mercury* (Philadelphia), 26 February 1789.

84 **"in the fear of God":** Mary Crosby, *Centennial anniversary of the birthday of William Bedlow Crosby, Feb'y 7th, 1866: a sketch of his life* (n.p., n.d.), 4.

84 **the nation's first president:** *Grandmother Tyler's Book: The Recollections of Mary Palmer Tyler (Mrs. Royall Tyler)*, ed. Frederick Tupper and Helen Tyler Brown (New York: G. P. Putnam's Sons, 1925), 119–21.

85 **an attached "store":** Advertisement for the sale of the house at 170 Queen Street tenanted by William Bedlow: *New-York Daily Gazette*, 24 January 1791.

85 **living in the Rutgers mansion:** Federal census for 1790: William Bedlow (ward 4, p. 123); Henry Rutgers (ward 7, p. 129); no listing for Henry Bedlow.

85 **Wall Street tailor Christian Baehr:** Christian Baehr, "merchant taylor, 49, Wall-street," *Directory for 1789*; same listing, *Directory for 1790*.

86 **"Deceive and defraud":** *Christian Baehr v. Henry Bedlow*, MC Judgments 1791#11, filed 12 September 1791; *Henry Bedlow & Stephen McCrea ads. Christian Baehr*, MC Judgment 1791#19, filed 9 August 1791.

86 **stoke up revolutionary fervor:** On Mary Rutgers and the McCreas: Mary de Peyster Rutgers McCrea Conger (Vanamee), *New York's Making: Seen through the Eyes of My Ancestors* (London; Methuen and Co., 1938), 63–88.

86 **the forfeited bond:** In addition to *Baehr v. Bedlow* and *McCrea and Bedlow ads. Baehr*, see: MC Docket of Judgments, 1786–1796, 13 (12 September 1791, "*Bedlow Henry ads. Christian Baehr* [£]43.13.10 Winter").

87 **disrupted his ability:** William Bedlow, ad for the sale of "several" lots in the Rutgers farm, *Daily Advertiser* (New York), 26 June 1790.

87 **was reduced to the role of messenger:** For the extensive correspondence and accounts exchanged by William Bedlow and Stephen McCrea between 14 October 1786 and July 1792, see box 13, fols. 1 and 11, Duyckinck Family Papers, SC15251. Stephen McCrea to Mrs. [Catharine] Bedlow, 20 March 1792 (box 13, fol. 11), was followed by the sharply worded "Mr Bedlow & Stephen McCrea Account, 1792" (box 13, fol. 1). The dispute carried on to McCrea's death: see The Estate of the Late Doctr. Stephen McCrea in Account with William Bedlow, 1795 (box 13, fol. 1).

87 **gone about his business:** Sawyer describes Bedlow leaving before she did when the household began to stir that morning (*Report*, 6); Carey testified that the family awoke and breakfasted at 8:00 a.m. and that Sawyer left around 10:00 (*Report*, 12); Franklin testified that the child sleeping in the back room got up around 8:00 a.m. (*Report*, 14).

87 **never held accountable:** For an influential analysis see Cathy N. Davidson, *The Revolution and the Word: The Rise of the Novel in America*, expanded ed. (New York: Oxford University Press, 2004), 176–82.

87 **no indication that he acknowledged:** *Report*, 6 (Sawyer).

88 **supervising some aspect:** *Report*, 15 (McCready).

89 **honor in his social inferiors:** On men "beneath" the code of honor: Freeman, *Affairs of Honor*, 172.

89 **Bedlow lied:** *Report*, 15–16 (Callanan). Samuel Hone confirmed Callanan's account of the search and confrontation (*Report*, 16–17); Mayor Richard Varick testified that Bedlow described the incident as "an assault" (*Report*, 15).

CHAPTER 5: THE PILOT

90 **criminal "assault"—broke out:** On Bedlow's complaint against Callanan for "an assault": *Report*, 15 (Varick).

91 **"say nothing to her":** *Report*, 15–16 (John Callanan), 16–17 (Samuel Hone).

91 **guide it up:** My account of this incident (including slightly adapted dialogue) is based on the examination of John Callanan ("Carleton"), corroborated by Benjamin Walker's testimony and Captain Kennedy's certificate, in *Journals of the Provincial Congress, Provincial Convention, Committee of Safety, and Council of Safety of the State of New-York* (Albany: Thurlow Weed, 1842), 288–89 (10 February 1776). The original minutes of the New York Committee of Safety (series A1814, NYSA) were damaged in a 1911 fire.

92 **a lookout perches precariously:** George Tobin, *Virginia Pilot boat, with a view of Cape Henry, at the entrance of the Chesapeake*, 1795 (probably January or February), watercolor drawing, 5 ⅞ x 9 ⅜ in, Mariner's Museum, Newport News, VA, http://catalogs .marinersmuseum.org/object/CL1088.

92 **other hidden dangers:** *Chart of the entrance of Hudson's River, from Sandy Hook to New York: with the banks, depths of water, sailing-marks, &ca.*, 69 x 52 cm (London: Robert Sawyer and John Bennett, 1776), NYPL, UUID 7e50a660-c5d5–012f-f71f-58d385a7bc34. See also *A chart of New York Harbour: with the soundings, views of land marks and nautical directions for the use of pilotage*, 80 x 55 cm (London: Joseph F. W. Des Barres, 1779), NYPL, UUID 012cbf70-c5ab-012f-e3bc-58d385a7bc34. On the

harbor and its approaches: Robert Greemhalgh Albion, *The Rise of New York Port, 1815–1860* (New York: Charles Scribner's Sons, 1939), 16–37.

93 **splintered by lightning:** Frostbite: *New-York Gazette*, 4 February 1782. Overset: *New-York Weekly Journal*, 11 December 1743; *American Weekly Mercury* (New York), 21 December 1743. Sails split: *Evening Post* (New York), 7 March 1810. Boom: *New-York Packet*, 12 December 1788; reprinted *Poughkeepsie Journal*, 16 December 1788. Run aground: *New-York Weekly Journal*, 14 November 1748. River ice: *New-York Journal*, 28 February 1771. Blown out to sea: *New-York Gazette*, 25 January 1762. Lightning: *New-York Weekly Journal*, 6 June 1748.

93 **report it immediately:** *Journals of the . . . Committee of Safety*, 195 (4 November 1775).

93 **stay away from the hook:** *Journals of the . . . Committee of Safety*, 249–50 (15 January 1776); 268 (25 January 1776).

93 **Two British warships had arrived:** *Journals of the . . . Committee of Safety*, 281 (3 February 1776).

93 **the city felt eerily deserted:** Martha J. Lamb, *History of the City of New York: Its Origin, Rise, and Progress* (New York: A. S. Barnes, 1877), 2:62–63; "Extract of a letter from New-York, Feb. 10," *Pennsylvania Packet* (Philadelphia), 19 Feb. 1776, [4].

93 **make its way to the hook:** A transport commanded by James Thompson, the *Kitty* was sent from Boston in convoy with another transport and HMS *Mercury* on 15 January 1776: *Naval Documents of the American Revolution*, vol. 3, ed. William Clark Bell (Washington, 1964), 795 and 993; for her arrival at New York, see 1217, 1231, 1302.

94 **hauled off to prison:** John Ethrington ("Atherton") imprisoned: *Journals of the . . . Committee of Safety*, 282 (4 February 1776).

94 **frozen to death :** *New York Mercury*, 21 December 1767; *New-York Journal*, 24 December 1767; *Boston Post-Boy*, 4 January 1768; *New-York Gazette*, 24 December 1767; *Boston Chronicle*, 4 January 1768. Later examples: *Diary* (New York), 29 October 1794; *American Minerva* (New York), 29 October 1794; *Daily Advertiser* (New York), 14 April 1795; *Weekly Museum* (New York), 18 April 1795.

94 **ended up beaten to death:** *Morning Chronicle* (New York), 18 October 1804.

95 **rigid hierarchies of rank:** Most guilds were regulated by the city; see Graham Russell Hodges, *New York City Cartmen, 1667–1850* (New York: New York University Press, 1986), 2–4. The branch pilots were regulated by the state: "Act to regulate the Pilots, and establish their pilotage between Sandy-Hook and the Port of New York," ch. 1215, passed 13 December 1763, *Laws of New-York, from . . . 1691 to 1773* (New York: Hugh Gaine, 1774), 1:433–36; "Act to regulate the Pilots and establish their Pilotage," passed 1 April 1775, *New York Session Laws. Seventh Session* (New York, 1775), ch. 69.

95 **trade often passed down:** For example, the fifteen branch pilots and twelve deputies listed in *Gaine's New-York Pocket Almanac for . . . 1776* (New York: Hugh Gaine, [1775]) included two father-son pairs: Francis James (appointed branch pilot 18 Janch 1769, *Calendar of Council Minutes*, 26:478) and his son Nicholas James (listed as branch pilot, but initial appointment not found)—and Joseph Price (appointed branch pilot 19 December 1757, *Calendar of Council Minutes* 25:437) and Michael Price (listed as a deputy).

95 **who his parents were:** Estimates of Callanan's age at his death in 1805 suggest he was born between 1752 and 1754. An obituary gave his age as fifty-three: *New-York Weekly Museum*, 30 November 1805; *New-York Gazette*, 25 November 1805. The burial record, 24 November 1805, Trinity Church registers, gave his age as fifty-one. He was probably twenty-one by the time he became a deputy pilot in 1774, suggesting a birthdate in 1752 or 1753.

95 **record a will:** For example, the carpenter Owen Callaghane (possibly the pilot's grandfather) became a freeman on 22 October 1723, Edward F. De Lancey, *The Burghers of New Amsterdam and the Freemen of New York, 1675–1866* (New York: New-York Historical Society, 1886), 104. Several Callahans/Callanans appear in the colonial parish

registers, Trinity Church Archives. My searches of NYC Conveyances and wills (New York County Surrogate's Court) did not turn up any Callanans before the revolution.

95 **bound to a deputy pilot:** Obituary of David Morris (in the fifty-ninth year of his age), *Daily Advertiser*, 6 March 1802.

95 **until his term ended:** Samuel McKee, *Labor in Colonial New York, 1664–1776* (New York: Columbia University Press, 1935), 71–76.

95 **decently fed and clothed:** Indenture of William Saunders (nineteen years old) to John Funk (Sandy Hook Pilot); for a term of one year and seven months, 18 February 1793, MS 1988, ser. 1, Boys Indentures, 1792–1794, NYHS. No provision for education was added to the preprinted form, as was usual in this series, probably because of Saunders's advanced age.

95 **advertised and hunted down:** Thomas Crookshanks (branch pilot) advertised runaway apprentice Benjamin Weatherly: *New-York Mercury*, 24 September 1759; William Minugh (branch pilot) advertised runaway apprentice "boy" Cornelius Kingston, *Mercantile Advertiser* (New York), 15 January 1806, 2.

96 **second British troop transport:** *Constitutional Gazette* (New York), 10 February 1776. See also *New-York Gazette*, 12 February 1776; *New-York Journal*, 15 February 1776.

96 **clearing his name:** *Journals of the . . . Committee of Safety*, 288–98 (10 February 1776).

96 **suspected of disloyalty:** Pilots imprisoned on HMS *Asia* in April 1776 included William Barwick and Jacob Germaine: *Naval Documents of the American Revolution*, 13 vols. to date (Washington, DC: Naval History and Heritage Command 1964–), 4:861–62. Pilots imprisoned by rebels in spring/summer 1776: *Calendar of Historical Manuscripts Relating to the War of the Revolution*, 2 vols. (Albany: Weed, Parsons & Co., 1868), 1:285, 293, 299, 373, 498 (Ryner Van Hoesen); 299, 314 (Henry Kilgrove).

96 **rocked at anchor:** A fleet of 110 British ships passed through the Narrows on 29 June 1776: Bruce Bliven Jr., *Under the Guns: New York:1775–1776* (New York: Harper & Row, 1972), 317–19. By mid-August the British navy had nearly 400 transports and 30 men-of-war at New York: Ira D. Gruber, *The Howe Brothers and the American Revolution* (New York: Athenaeum, 1972), 101.

97 **"melted majesty":** Alexander J. Wall, "The Equestrian Statue of George III and the Pedestrian Statue of William Pitt," *New-York Historical Society Quarterly Bulletin* 4 (July 1920), 36–57 (bullets: 52). Quote: Ebenezer Hazard to Horatio Gates,12 July 1776, Gates Papers, MS240, NYHS.

97 **rushed to escape:** Ruma Chopra, *Unnatural Rebellion: Loyalists in New York City During the Revolution* (Charlottesville: University of Virginia Press, 2011), 45–46.

97 **he and the city's other firefighters:** Firemen of the City of New York, June 1776, *Calendar of Historical Manuscripts Relating to the War of the Revolution*, 1:315–316.

97 **Firewood grew scarce:** Edwin G. Burrows and Mike Wallace, *Gotham: A History of New York City to 1898* (New York: Oxford University Press, 1999), 250–51 (fire), 251 (provisions), 255 (shade trees).

98 **foot of Bowery Lane:** Advertisement of property of James Delancey, *Royal Gazette* (New York), 20 July 1782. For "Love Lane," see John Montrésor, *A Plan of the City of New-York . . . Survey'd in the Winter, 1775* [i.e., 1766], engraving, 65 x 53 cm (London: Andrew Dury, 1775).

98 **tiny portion of the city's elite:** Pierre Eugene DuSimitière, "List of the names of the Families that Keep Coaches &c in New York 1770," DuSimitière Papers 964.F.70, Library Company of Philadelphia.

98 **nailed new metal tires:** Account of Humphrey Jones with Francis Sawyer, 15 January 1778, New York, Duane Family Papers, Series II: Legal and Business Papers, NYHS.

98 **of their newborn son:** Catharine Sawyer, baptism, 24 February 1782, Trinity Church registers.

98 **Lanah's baby sister:** Peter Sawyer, baptism (Cath[arine] Callenan, sponsor), 25 October 1778, Trinity Church registers. Catharine Sawyer, baptism, 24 February 1782, Trinity Church registers.

98 **she would be a helpmeet:** Breeching: Susan Burrows Swan, *Plain and Fancy: American Women and Their Needlework* (New York: Holt, Rinehart, and Winston, 1977), 34–35.

99 **taught "Needle-work":** Trinity charity school: *New-York Gazette*, 11 November 1782.

99 **technique and style:** Examples of sewing lessons on offer: *Royal Gazette* (New York), 17 May 1783; *Daily Advertiser* (New York), 25 December 1788; *Diary* (New York), 30 April 1793 ("finer branches").

99 **calling on his debtors:** *Royal Gazette* (New York), 30 July 1783.

100 **bound his fate:** "Calahan, Brodie & Jones," 26 September 1783, Andrew Elliot Papers, SC13349, box 3, fol 9, NYSL. John Callanan and Jane Sawyer married by Benjamin Moore, 26 September 1783, Trinity Church registers.

100 **prepared to return:** William Dobbs (whom George Washington repeatedly turned to for assistance during the war; see their correspondence at *Founders Online*) and James Hallett (who was imprisoned by the British and complained of mistreatment; see, for example, George Clinton to George Washington, 7 March 1779, *Founders Online*, National Archives, accessed 30 August 2021, https://founders.archives .gov/documents/Washington/03-19-02-0403) were among the active rebels who returned after the war. Among Loyalist evacuees in late 1783 were Henry Killgrove (David Bell, *American Loyalists to New Brunswick* [Halifax, NS: Formac, 2015], 134) and Francis James (Alexander Fraser, *United Empire Loyalists*, vol. 2 [Toronto: L. K. Cameron, 1905], 138), whose son Nicholas remained.

100 **embodiment of the patriarchal ideal:** Callanan was reappointed along with a new slate of pilots in spring 1784: Index to Council of Appointment Minutes, 1777–1786, fol. 7, A1846, NYSA: 290–91 (22 April 1784, twelve branch pilots), 294 (12 May 1783, three branch pilots). A surviving branch pilot certificate: Nathaniel Funk, 1 May 1784, Funk Family Documents, NYHS.

101 **a role to play:** This account is based on the most complete reports: *New-York Packet*, 5 August 1788.

102 **delight of spectators:** *New-York Packet*, 5 August 1788.

102 **puffed up with pride:** William Dunlap, *Diary of William Dunlap (1766–1839)*, 3 vols. (New York: New-York Historical Society, 1929), 1:14. See also Whitfield J. Bell, Jr., "The Federal Processions of 1788," *New-York Historical Society Quarterly* 46, no. 1 (January 1962): 5–39.

102 **tensions and resentments:** Paul A. Gilje, "The Common People and the Constitution: Popular Culture in New York City in the Late Eighteenth Century," in *New York in the Age of the Constitution, 1775–1800*, eds. Paul A. Gilje and William Pencak (Cranbury, NJ: Fairleigh Dickinson University Press, 1992), 48–73.

102 **higher offices:** Alfred F. Young, *The Democratic Republicans of New York: The Origins, 1763–1797* (Chapel Hill: University of North Carolina Press, 1967), 84–85. Nationwide, about 60 percent of adult white men could vote; Alexander Keyssar, *The Right to Vote: The Contested History of Democracy in the United States* (New York: Basic Books, 2000), 20, 24–25.

102 **Lanah's father had been:** De Lancey, *Burghers and Freemen*, 166 (Peter Sawyer, laborer, 11 April 1749), 236 (Francis Sawyer, wheelwright, 11 May 1773).

103 **modest, rented house:** 1789 Tax Assessment Data (Willis). Callanan's house at 34 (later 62) Gold Street was valued at £200 (the median, and most common, real estate assessment), his personal property at £50. Five of the sixteen branch pilots working in 1789 do not appear on the assessment: Thomas Gray, Isaac Simonson, Peter Parker, Charles Penny, and James Wilkie.

103 **tax assessors:** Herbert S. Klein and Edmund Philip Willis, "The Distribution of Wealth in Late Eighteenth-Century New York City," *Histoire sociale—Social History* 18, no. 36 (1985), 259–83; Klein and Willis estimate (265) that about 49 percent of all households were among the nonassessed "propertyless poor."

103 **"to keep men steady":** Alexander Hamilton to John Jay, 26 November 1775, *Founders Online*, National Archives, accessed August 31, 2021, https://founders.archives.gov /documents/Hamilton/01–01–02–0060.

103 **was out by the hook:** The *Fortune* was described as "the property of Messrs. [Matthew] Daniel, [John] Callahan, and [Zachariah] Russel" in the *Daily Advertiser* (New York), 2 September 1788, and most subsequent reports.

103 **"accommodations far superior":** *Independent Journal*, 22 March 1786; reprinted: *New-York Packet*, 23 March 1786. On the development of the New York pilot schooner: Tom Cunliffe, *Pilots: The World of Pilotage Under Sail and Oar*, vol. 1: *Pilot Schooners of North America and Great Britain* (Douarnenez, France: Wooden Boat Publications, 2001), 68–86.

103 **a single oar:** "New-York, Sept. 4," *Pennsylvania Packet* (Philadelphia), 8 September 1788; *Poughkeepsie* (NY) *Journal*, 9 September 1788; *New-Haven* (CT) *Gazette*, 11 September 1788; *Massachusetts Gazette* (Boston), 12 September 1788; *Providence Gazette*, 13 September 1788; *Litchfield* (CT) *Monitor*, 15 September 1788.

103 **"a negro man":** *Daily Advertiser* (New York), 2 September 1788. Similar examples: *New-York Journal*, 4 September 1788; *Impartial Gazetteer*, 6 September 1788.

103 **pilots' all-white ranks:** The 1790 census listed four pilots whose households included enslaved people: William Vandrun, Matthew Daniels, David Morris, and Edward Wilkie. See also Matthew Daniel advertisement for "negro boy" Duff, *New-York Gazette*, 21 April 1783; William Vandrun (Fundrun) advertisement for "Negroes" James Smith and Mary, *Newport* (RI) *Herald*, 12 February 1789.

104 **bound by complex webs:** In Philadelphia in 1790, there were reportedly sixty-six master pilots "in active service" and thirty-three apprentices operating twenty-three boats—about three "master" pilots per boat: *Daily Advertiser* (New York), 3 April 1790. An 1818 New York list shows a similar ratio of twenty-five branch pilots to seven boats; *National Advocate* (New York), 21 March 1818.

104 **borrowed the purchase price:** Letter on the business of piloting in Philadelphia: *Daily Advertiser* (New York), 3 April 1790.

104 **signed a receipt:** John Callanan, receipt for pilotage, 27 June 1789, New York, Receipt Book, 1787–1790, MSS BV Gouverneur, Kemble & Co., NYHS. For the schooner *Maria's* clearance: *New York Daily Gazette*, 23 June 1789. Address: *Directory for 1789*.

104 **clerk's 3 percent fee:** This provision was continued in postwar legal updates: Act for the regulation of pilots and pilotage in the Port of New York, ch. 31, passed 14 April 1784, *Laws of the state of New-York* (New York, 1789), 1:120–25.

104 **raised their fees:** *Daily Advertiser* (New York), 27 February 1788; *Daily Advertiser* (New York), 8 March 1790; *Daily Advertiser* (New York), 25 February 1794.

104 **Philadelphia pilots:** Kenneth W. Keller, "The Philadelphia Pilot's Strike of 1792," *Labor History* 18, no. 1 (Winter 1977), 36–38.

104 **"maintain a Family":** Quote: *New-York Gazette*, 30 January 1764. On the strike: *New-York Gazette*, 23 January 1764, reprinted *Pennsylvania Gazette* (Philadelphia), 2 February 1764; *Providence Gazette*, 4 February 1764; *New-York Gazette*, 30 January 1764. *Calendar of Council Minutes, 1668–1783*, 25:462 (20 January 1764, suspending pilots); 25:463 (8 February 1764, restoring pilots); 26:468 (27 March 1765, restoring William Hibbin).

105 **animated with new construction:** Pilot boat *New-York* launched (*Daily Advertiser* [New York], 22 December 1788); raced by Callanan's former co-owner Matthew Daniel (*New-York Gazette*, 15 August 1789). Paul M. O'Grady, "Vital Arteries: A History of the Streets of New York, 1783–1863" (PhD diss., Emory University, 2006), ch. 1.

105 **most elegant building:** Louis Torres, "Federal Hall Revisited," *Journal of the Society of Architectural Historians* 29, no. 4 (December 1970), 327–38.

105 **unity, pride, and hope:** *Daily Advertiser* (New York), 24 April 1789.

106 **French frigate *Embuscade*:** William R. Casto, "'We Are Armed for the Defense of the Rights of Man': The French Revolution Comes to America," *American Neptune* 61, no. 3 (2001), 263–81.

106 **Aristocracy and Democracy:** *Alexander Anderson's New York City Diary, 1793–1799,* ed. Jane R. Pomeroy, 2 vols. (New Castle, DE: Oak Knoll Press, 2014), 11 June 1793. See also *General Advertiser* (Philadelphia), 13 June 1793.

106 **"spirit of seventy-six":** Casto, "'We are Armed,'" 266 (quoting Edward Livingston).

106 **"the Rich & the Poor":** Alexander Hamilton to Rufus King, 4 May 1796, *Founders Online,* National Archives, accessed August 31, 2021. For context, see Alfred Young, "The Mechanics and the Jeffersonians, 1789–1801," *Labor History* 5, no. 3 (1964), 261–62; Paul A. Gilje, *The Road to Mobocracy: Popular Disorder in New York City, 1763–1834* (Chapel Hill: University of North Carolina Press), 100–112; and Howard B. Rock, "The Artisans and the State: A Comparison of New York and London," in Gilje and Pencak, eds., *New York in the Age of the Constitution,* 74–97 (esp. 85–93).

106 **rented out to spectators:** Governor Clinton, proclamation about foreign vessels, *Daily Advertiser* (New York), 14 May 1793.

106 **give me my bread:** *Diary* (New York), 1 August 1793 (in the original: "the pilot replied, he could not help it, that those merchants were his employers and gave him his bread"); reprinted *New-York Journal,* 3 August 1793.

106 **welcomed back in triumph:** Casto, "'We Are Armed,'" 275.

107 **across the nation:** Complaints about the pilots: *Diary* (New York), 31 July 1793; *Weekly Museum* (New York), 3 August 1793; *Independent Gazetteer* (Philadelphia), 3 August 1793; *Albany Register,* 5 August 1793; *Connecticut Gazette* (New London), 8 August 1793; *General Advertiser* (Philadelphia), 8 August 1793; *Apollo* (Chestertown, MD), 9 August 1793. Complaints specifically about pilots betraying French vessels (including the privateer *Republican*): *Diary* (New York), 6 August 1793; *Catskill* (NY) *Packet,* 13 August 1793.

107 **began to rebel:** Alfred Young, "The Mechanics and the Jeffersonians," 247–76.

107 **"British mercantile interest":** *Apollo* (Chestertown, MD), 9 August 1793; reprinted *Farmer's Register* (Kingston, NY), 17 August 1793.

107 **"Down with King Washington!":** Harlow Giles Unger, *Noah Webster: The Life and Times of an American Patriot* (New York: John Wiley and Sons, 1998), 186.

108 **near the groin:** The merchant Samuel Curzon was accused by Walter Burling (of Baltimore) of seducing and abandoning his sister Betsey Burling, who then bore an illegitimate son. Curzon's dueling death was widely lamented in the local papers: *New-York Journal,* 27 April 1786; *Daily Advertiser* (New York), 24 April 1786; *New-York Gazetteer,* 25 April 1786; *New-York Packet,* 27 April 1786; *Independent Journal,* 26 April 1786. On the duel: J. Hall Pleasants, *The Curzon Family of New York and Baltimore* (Baltimore, 1919), 41–45 (citing correspondence now in the J. H. Pleasants Papers, MS 194, Maryland Historical Society).

108 **"a great passion":** *Report,* 7 (Sawyer).

108 **"extremely angry at her":** *Report,* 17 (Jane Callanan, quote), 17 (Hannah Hone).

109 **to tell Lanah's mother:** *Report,* 17–19 (Harper).

CHAPTER 6: GATEKEEPERS

110 **50 Gold Street:** Lucretia Smith Murphey Harper and her second husband, Gideon Harper, lived at 41 Gold Street (after 1793, 50 Gold), which was part of the estate of her first husband: Executors of Peter Murphey, deed to Richard Thomas and George Henry (1807), NYC Conveyances 76:448; BIRC block 76, lot 29 (part).

110 **heavy with rain:** Pintard, 6 September 1793, Diary and Garden Calendar, Newark, 1793–1794, box 4, fol. 9, Pintard Papers, MS490, NYHS.

110 **brood of stepchildren:** *Directory for 1793*: Gideon Harper, "cooper and culler," 41 Gold Street. 1793 Tax List, ward 3, p. 20: Gideon Harper, 41 Gold St., $270 real estate, no personal estate.

110 **night soil:** "A Law to regulate . . . the Streets," sect. 8, *Laws and Ordinances . . . of the City of New-York* (New York, 1793), 15–16.

111 **"examined her linen":** *Report*, 18 (Harper).

111 **"could no longer be a virgin":** *Report*, 17 (Jane Callanan).

111 **with her mother:** Sawyer testified that she had been "desirous of acquainting her mother" with what had happened "first," *Report*, 6–7.

111 **"the whole affair":** *Report*, 7 (Sawyer).

112 **afraid of further violence:** A girl reports first to her mother: Case of John Hay (rape of Elizabeth Kidney), January 1766, box 11, fol. 19, John Tabor Kempe Papers, NYHS. Eight-year-old Catharine Larkings "afraid to tell her father" of her rape, which was interrupted by her mother: Case of John Domine, SJC, October 1766, box 1, fol. 3, Kempe Papers. A nine-year-old worried her mother would beat her: Sharon Block, *Rape and Sexual Power in Early America* (Chapel Hill: University of North Carolina Press, 2003), 93 (court martial of John Fisher, 1778, New York).

112 **too traumatized to respond:** Petition of Katerein Corgal to the Mayor of Albany, 29 August 1768, box 12, fol. 5, Kempe Papers.

112 **his family's public face:** Block, *Rape and Sexual Power*, 119–25.

113 **he would be angry:** *Report*, 7 (Sawyer), 17 (Jane Callanan).

113 **at the Harpers' house:** *Report*, 7 (Sawyer), 16 (John Callanan).

115 **her pleas for help:** Block, *Rape and Sexual Power*, 119–20, 132.

115 **"made her go with him":** *Report*, 7 (Sawyer), 16 (John Callanan).

115 **go in first:** *Report*, 8 (Sawyer).

115 **confronted Mrs. Carey:** *Report*, 16 (John Callanan).

116 **"the night-before-last":** *Report*, 8 (Sawyer).

116 **Mrs. Carey refused:** *Report*, 7–8 (Sawyer). Her account was corroborated by John Callanan (16) and Samuel Hone (17).

117 **144 Broadway:** *Directory for 1793*: Evertson, Nicholas, and Caleb S. Riggs, attorneys at law, corner of Crown-street (later Liberty Street) and Broadway. Correlating tax lists, city directories, and the BIRC indicates that this was block 48, lot 4 (part)—which would now be 144 Broadway.

117 **Monday, September 9:** When this consultation took place is unclear, but it must have been after Sawyer spoke with her parents on Friday morning and before the mayor arrested Bedlow on Tuesday. Conducting business was generally prohibited on Sundays. Given timing of the mayor's actions, this consultation was likely on Monday.

117 **"her own will":** *Report*, 16 (John Callanan).

118 **sent him to Yale:** Evertson: 1790 Federal census (Clinton, Dutchess County, 117 [Jacob Evertson]); Franklin Bowditch Dexter, *Biographical Sketches of the Graduates of Yale*, vol. 4 (New York: Henry Holt, 1907), 543 (Nicholas Evertson, 1787).

118 **his persistence legendary:** Riggs: John Greenwood, "Personal Recollections of Aaron Burr, and Some of his Contemporaries of the New York Bar," *Historical Magazine* 7, no. 11 (November 1863): 338–39; Charles Edwards, *Pleasantries about Courts and Laywers in the State of New York* (New York: Richardson & Co., 1867), 339–40.

118 **the penalty was death:** William Blackstone, *Commentaries on the Laws of England* (London, 1786), vol. 4, ch 15, pt. 3 (quote, 210). Riggs's copy is in the possession of the author.

118 **odds of prevailing:** Sharon Block, "Bringing Rapes to Court," *Common-Place* 3, no. 3 (April 2003), http://commonplace.online/article/bringing-rapes-to-court/.

118 **taken to trial:** Sofi Sinozich and Lynn Langton, *Rape and Sexual Assault Among College-Age Females, 1995–2013*, NCJ 24847, Bureau of Justice Statistics (Decem-

ber 2014), https://bjs.ojp.gov/library/publications/rape-and-sexual-assault-among
-college-age-females-1995-2013.

118 **more than five years:** Hays, "General List": the most recent prosecution had been
against Lewis D. Flynn, for attempted rape, in January 1787 (15).

118 **pursue the matter:** *The King v. John Hay, assault with intent to ravish Elizabeth Kidney,*
January 1766, box 11, vol. 19, John Tabor Kempe Papers; *The King v. John Hay,* SCJ
MB1764–66: 373, 376.

118 **better of people like you:** Katerien Corgall to mayor of Albany, 29 August 1768 (and
letter to same, 19 September 1768), box 12, fol. 5, Kempe Papers; in original: "Such
men Sum times Gets Better of poor pepel Before the Case his trayed."

119 **"leave this Country":** The Rev. T. T. Brown to John Tabor Kempe, 21 July 1762,
Sedgewick II, Massachusetts Historical Society. In 1762, Thomas Brown (1731–
1781), an Oxford graduate, was a British army chaplain at Albany: Frederick Lewis
Weiss, "Colonial Clergy of the Middle Colonies," *Proceedings of the American Anti-
quarian Society* 66, pt. 2 (1956): 189.

119 **if he was a man of color:** Block, *Rape and Sexual Power*, ch. 5; Cornelia Hughes Dayton, *Women Before the Bar: Gender, Law, and Society in Connecticut, 1636–1789* (Chapel
Hill: University of North Carolina Press, 1995), 246–74; Barbara Lindemann, "'To
Ravish and Carnally Know': Rape in Eighteenth-Century Massachusetts," *Signs* 10,
no. 1 (Autumn 1984): 64.

119 **changed her mind:** *The King v. Henry Vlock,* SCJ MB1766–69E: 315 (28 October 1767,
plead not guilty of rape); 326 and 327 (31 October 1767, prosecution defaulted); 382 (22
January 1768, discharged). On the accuser's identity and move to Philadelphia: *The King
v. Henry Vlock,* presentment for rape of Rosina Berkenmeyer, October term 1767, box 11,
fol. 2, Kempe Papers. See also Julius Goebel Jr. and T. Raymond Naughton (who refer
to him as Henry Klock), *Law Enforcement in Colonial New York: A Study in Criminal
Procedure (1664–1776)* (Montclair, NJ: Patterson Smith, 1970), 483 n447, 501 n59.

120 **receive harsh sentences:** Block, *Rape and Sexual Power*, 172–80 (charges); 189–99
(convictions).

120 **cut the man's body down:** On Cato: *New-York Weekly Journal*, 28 January 1734.
Embattled newspaper editor John Peter Zenger was rebuked for reporting the girl's
attempted rape as a rape: *New York Gazette*, 4 February 1734, 18 February 1734. On
Tom: *Newport* (RI) *Mercury*, 5 December 1763.

120 **ripe old age:** CO&T MB1784–1796: 101 (Eleazer Tennery arraigned), 104 (trial),
123 ("No judgment rendered"). Trial reported: *New-York Packet*, 13 June 1785, and
many reprints. Family: William Andrews Tennery, baptism, 6 May 1787, Trinity
Church registers. Death at eighty: E. M. Tennery, 5 January 1840, Cemetery Returns,
Board of Health, RG37.17, Philadelphia City Archives.

120 **the age of nine:** *New-York Journal*, 19 October 1786.

120 **at city expense:** *MCC 1784–1831*, 1:263 (9 November 1786, demanding that Lewis
Flynn pay his venereal disease treatment).

120 **A £2 fine:** *The People v. Lewis D. Flynn* (assault and battery with intent to rape), CGS
MB1762–1790, 333 (9 November 1786), 334 (10 November 1786), 341 (13 Novem-
ber 1786). Flynn was twice prosecuted for disorderly house keeping: Hays, "General
List": 12 (CGS, August 1786, acquitted), 135 (CGS, December 1803, convicted). He
was regularly listed in city directories as a "grocer"—in 1794 at 110 Water Street. In
1796, he owned a £500 house he rented out (1796 Tax Records, ward 1, p. 33). Lewis
D. Flynn m. Sarah Crawford, 26 April 1795, Trinity Church registers.

121 **"disposed to injure them":** Jotham Post (1771–1817), 7–9 January 1793, Diary, 1792–
1793, Mss Col. BV Post, NYHS; he gives the bail as £4,000; his spelling "Ketteltass"
standardized.

121 **a sugar plantation:** Bail (£2,000) and skipped 24 September 1793 court appearance:
Henry Onderdonk, *Queens County in Olden Times: Being a Supplement to the Several*

Histories Thereof (Jamaica, NY: Charles Welling, 1865), 82. See also "One of the People, To John Lansing and John Sloss Hobart, Esquires," *Herald* (New York), 3 June 1795. Memorial of Elizabeth Kettletas: *Albany Centinel*, 4 March 1798. Plantation: "George Duncan Ludlow (Jr.)," Centre for the Study of the Legacies of British Slavery, University College London, accessed 22 February 2021 http://wwwdepts-live.ucl.ac.uk/lbs/person/view/2146644037.

122 **Tuesday, September 10:** As noted above, the timing of this sequence of events is uncertain. This interview happened by the end of Tuesday, September 10, and, given the speed of justice in this period, likely earlier that day.

122 **Mayor Richard Varick:** The mayor, the recorder, and the aldermen each held all the powers of justices of the peace; James Kent, ed., *The Charter of the City of New York* (New York: McSpedon & Baker, 1854), 116–20 (1730 Charter, sect. 26), 270–73 (note xl).

122 **"his disposition and conduct":** Paul Cushman, *Richard Varick: A Forgotten Founding Father* (Amherst, Mass.: Modern Memoirs Publishing, 2010), 102 ("severe" quote from William A, Duer). James Sharples, Portraits of Col. and Mrs. Richard Varick, 1797–1811, pastel on paper, 13.5 x 11 in, Christies, Live Auction 2133, lot 231 (2009), accessed 1 February 2021, https://www.christies.com/en/lot/lot-5173354.

122 **private rank and public authority:** Diagram of a house and lot . . . signed by Richard Varick, n.d., NYC box 33, fol. 12, Surveys of Street 1784–1797, NYHS.

122 **"ready to be sworn":** *Report*, 15 (Varick).

123 **with her signature:** *Report*, 15 (Varick). Lanah's mother and stepfather could both sign their names, as could her father.

123 **in a small elite:** William Bedlow to Richard Varick, 5 September 1780, ser. 4, George Washington Papers, Library of Congress; Bedlow to Varick, 7 October 1780, box 1, fol. 1, Richard Varick Papers, NYHS.

124 **"nobody in her house":** *Report*, 15 (Varick), 27 (Livingston, acknowledged Carey was lying).

124 **circulating through the city:** Pintard, 10 September 1793, Diary and Garden Calendar.

124 **demand justice:** *Report*, 30: Livingston implied that Bedlow went to the mayor *knowing* that a warrant had been issued, but there is no evidence to that effect in the *Report*.

125 **he wasn't going to pursue:** There is no record of any criminal prosecution against Callanan in the 1790s: Hays, "General List"; DA Indictments.

125 **"he must commit his son":** *Report*, 15 (Varick).

126 **released on bail:** Bail could be, and was, given in rape cases (Goebel and Naughton, *Law Enforcement in Colonial New York*, 501). Edmund Ludlow was released on bail within days of his arrest in early 1793 (Post, diary, 9 January 1793).

126 **of obscure origins:** Since the war, there had been two sexual assault prosecutions in the city, as discussed above (case of Lewis D. Flynn; case of Eleazer M. Tennery), and both came to trial. In the decade before the war, there were six sexual assault prosecutions: one resulted in a conviction (Domine), one was dismissed (Vlock), and four may never have come to trial.

Case of John Domine, "Labourer" (reportedly from Philadelphia), for attempted rape of eight-year-old Catharine Larkins, SCJ, 30 October 1766, box 1, fol. 3, Kempe Papers; SCJ MB1766–1769R: 26 (indictment, 20 October 1766); 27 (found guilty, 31 October 1766); 31 (sentenced to be whipped, 1 November 1766).

Case of Henry Vlock (rape of Rosina Berkenmeyer, spinster), October 1767, box 11, fol. 2, Kempe Papers; SCJ MB1766–1769E: 315 (indictment for rape, 28 October 1767), 326 (released on bail, 31 October 1767), 327 (Berkenmeyer called and defaulted, 31 October 1767), 382 (discharged, 22 January 1768).

Case of William Territ, leather breeches maker, for attempted rape of Anne Lashier (seamstress), SCJ, July 1771, box 2, fol. 3, Kempe Papers. SCJ MB1769–1772E: 398–99 (2 August 1771, indicted for attempted rape), 400 (2 August 1771, bailed, order to plead in twenty days), 433 (15 October 1771, respited to last day of term); no further record found.

Case of Michael Corbet for rape: SCJ MB1769–1772E: 472 (23 January 1772, indicted for rape); no further record found.

Case of William Creighan for rape of Elizabeth Emmerson, spinster: CGS MB1760–1772: unnumbered (9 August 1771, indicted, referred to SCJ); no further record (see Goebel and Naughton, *Law Enforcement in Colonial New York*, 149 n44). Report of indictment: *New-York Journal*, 15 August 1771.

Case of John Barwick: CGS MB1772–1789, 183 (11 May 1776, indicted for attempted rape); no further record (perhaps because the war interrupted the court's work). He was a "carman" (list of freemen, CGS MB1760–1772: 7 February 1769).

127 **convicted of receiving:** The best account of this case is Serena R. Zabin, *Dangerous Economies: Status and Commerce in Imperial New York* (Philadelphia: University of Pennsylvania Press, 2009), 75–80; see also Block, *Rape and Sexual Power*, 122. Goebel and Naughton, *Law Enforcement in Colonial New York*, summarize the legal issues (262–63) and reprint the attorney general's brief (786–91).

Case of John Lawrence Jr., Charles Arding, Cornelius Livingston, and Hendrick Oudenard: SCJ PL K-501 (prosecution brief, 1 August 1754) and K-650. SCJ MB1754–57: 49 (1 August 1754, information against for assault of fourteen-year-old Mary Anderson), 53 (defendants ordered to plead within twenty days), 118 (25 January 1755, attorney general may collect testimony), 125 (January 1755, defendants to be brought to trial), 145–46 (18 April 1755, tried, found not guilty).

Case of King's Attorney William Kempe: SCJ MB1754–1757E: 82 (15 October 1754, Kempe indicted for maladministration), 116 (25 January 1755, Kempe requests indictment be quashed), 155 (19 April 1755, indictment quashed). See also William Livingston (defendants' attorney) to William Kempe, 26 August 1754, Livingston Papers, Vol. A., Massachusetts Historical Society. In a draft letter to Alderman Byvank, Kempe responded to a slur against Mary Anderson and insisted that he saw his role as an "equal and Impartial" administrator of justice for "the poor" and "the Rich" alike: box 16, fol. 2, Kempe Papers.

Mocking report of Elizabeth Anderson's whipping for receiving stolen goods: *New-York Mercury*, 19 August 1754.

Case of Elizabeth Anderson for keeping a disorderly house. SCJ MB1754–1757E: 47 (31 July 1754, indictment of Mary Anderson, disorderly house), 49 (1 August 1754, process ordered), 50 (2 August 1754, indicted again under the name Elizabeth Anderson, specifying "bawdry and tippling"), 86 (24 October 1754, Elizabeth Anderson, order to plea), 155 (19 April 1755, indictment quashed; her attorney is Mr. Nichol).

Kempe's attempted rape prosecution of James Mayne, Esq., in April 1754, had apparently gone nowhere: Complaint of Elizabeth Wright, April 1754, against James Mayne, Esq., for attempted rape (on herself, her twelve-year-old servant, and third woman), SCJ PL K-673. Indicted for attempted rape of Eleanor Murphy, SCJ MB1754–1757E: 16 (22 April 1754); no further record found. See also Complaint of Martin Blake against James Mayne, Esq., for breaking and entering and assault, n.d., SCJ PL K-675; related presentment, SCJ, April 1754, box 2, fol. 1, Kempe Papers; no further record found.

A year earlier, Kempe had attempted to prosecute another group of gentlemen for a sexual assault: Complaint of Abigail Cottrell against Philip Philipse (merchant), Robert Livingston (merchant), Captain Thomas French (mariner), and a man called Captain Johnson, 5 June 1753, SCJ PR 48-K-5; no further record found.

By contrast, Kempe's prosecution of the tailor James Gaines for the attempted rape of eight-year-old Margaret Bennet resulted in a quick conviction: SCJ MB1754–57E: 112 (23 January 1755, indicted), 115 (25 January 1755, found guilty), 116

(25 January 1755, sentenced), 200 (27 October 1755, released on recognizance). "James Gale, a Taylor," jailed for rape of six-year-old child: *New-York Mercury*, 2 December 1754, reprinted *Pennsylvania Gazette* (Philadelphia), 5 December 1754.

128 **seeking monetary damages:** Quote: *Henry Bedlow v. John Callanan*, MC Judgments 1793#21, filed 24 December1793.

128 **Callanan had turned to:** Bedlow's attorney, identified only as "Bogardus," was probably Robert Bogardus, admitted to the bar 26 April 1793, rather than William W. Bogardus, admitted to the bar 4 August 1792 (*Directory for 1793*, 226), since only Robert lived in the city (*Directory for 1794*: Robert Bogardus, attorney at law, 62 Cherry Street).

128 **a laborer's income:** Deborah A. Rosen, *Courts and Commerce: Gender, Law, and the Market Economy in Colonial New York* (Columbus: Ohio State University Press, 1997), 65 (majority of Mayor's Court cases settled out of court), 68–71 (costs and incomes of various occupations).

129 **withdraw the civil suit:** *Henry Bedlow v. John Callahan*, MC MB1793–1794: 208 (26 September 1793, Bogardus: Bedlow's motion to discontinue the case allowed).

129 **a formal declaration:** *John Callahan v. Henry Bedlow*, MC MB1793–1794: 218 (26 September 1793, Riggs: return on capias, Bedlow ordered to plea within seven days).

129 **financial compensation for it:** The sequence of events in these tangled proceedings is most clearly laid out in the judgment record prepared as the case unfolded by Callanan's attorney Caleb S. Riggs: *John Callanan ads. Henry Bedlow*, MC Judgments 1793#11, filed 24 December 1793.

129 **witnesses were summoned:** On the process of summoning jurors and giving notice to officials: James D. Folts, *"Duely & Constantly Kept": A History of the New York Supreme Court, 1691–1847, and an Inventory of Its Records* (Albany: New York State Court of Appeals, 1991), 95–96.

130 **room's massive windows:** The weather was unremarkable: Pintard, 30 September 1793, Diary and Garden Calendar, recorded only the high temperature of 68 degrees Fahrenheit; *Alexander Anderson's New York City Diary, 1793–1799*, ed. Jane R. Pomeroy, 2 vols. (New Castle, DE: Oak Knoll Press, 2014), 30 September 1793, did not describe the weather at all.

130 **the next act:** CO&T MB1784–1796: 301 (30 September 1793, grand jury impaneled).

131 **a fallback position:** On bringing charges in eighteenth-century Massachusetts: Lindemann, "'To Ravish and Carnally Know,'" 71–79. On the use of lesser charges to protect white men: Block, *Rape and Sexual Power*, 152–61.

131 **would not have met:** On the requirement that jurors have freehold status: Folts, *"Duely & Constantly Kept,"* 86 (citing Laws of 1786, ch. 41).

132 **Society of Saint Patrick:** On Daniel McCormick (1740–1834): J. A. Scoville, *The Old Merchants of New York City*, ser. 2 (New York: Carleton, 1864), 251–53, 257, 264, 282. 1790 Federal Census: ward 3, p. 118, two white men over sixteen, one white woman, four enslaved people.

132 **were also merchants:** Thirteen of the grand jurors can be confidently identified in the *Directory for 1793*: Daniel McCormick (merchant), David M. Clarkson (merchant), Nicholas Gouverneur (merchant), Francis Atkinson (merchant), Leonard Lespinard Jr. (brewer), Gilbert C. Willet (brewer and merchant), George Scriba (merchant), James Constable (merchant), John H. Thompson (merchant), Josiah Adams (merchant), Horace Johnson (merchant), Nathaniel Barrett (merchant), John P. Mumford (merchant). The remaining grand jurors were Charles Smith, Samuel McEvers, and James Roosevelt.

132 **stack of indictments:** CO&T MB1784–1796: 305 (3 October 1793, Henry Bedlow indicted for rape).

133 **Not guilty:** Indictment of Henry Bedlow, "late" of the fifth ward (i.e., now in custody), "Gentleman," for a rape on 5 September 1793 on the body of Lanah Sawyer, "Spinster," filed 3 October 1793, DA Indictments.

CHAPTER 7: THE PROSECUTRIX

135 **crush of others:** *Alexander Anderson's New York City Diary, 1793–1799*, ed. Jane R. Pomeroy, 2 vols. (New Castle, DE: Oak Knoll Press, 2014), 7–9 October 1793.

136 **"box" for witnesses:** Neither William Wyche nor any official source indicated which room the court used. But a letter about the trial referred to galleries—a feature of the former House chamber on the first floor: Charles Adams to John Adams, New York, 6 December 1793, *Founders Online*, National Archives, accessed 1 September 2021, https://founders.archives.gov/documents/Adams/04-09-02-0269. Moreau later confirmed that the "room for the Court of Justice" was "Below": *Moreau de St. Méry's American Journey, 1793–1798*, ed. and trans. Kenneth Roberts and Anna M. Roberts (Garden City, NY: Doubleday, 1947), 154.

136 **At ten o'clock:** CO&T MB1784–1796: 315 (8 October 1793).

136 **John Sloss Hobart:** On Hobart (1738–1805), see Franklin Bowditch Dexter, *Biographical Sketches of the Graduates of Yale* (New York: Henry Holt, 1896), 2:465–67.

136 **Samuel Jones:** On Jones (1734–1819), see Samuel Seabury, "Samuel Jones, New York's First Comptroller," *New York History* 28, no. 4 (October 1947): 397–403. He lived in an expensive house at the southeastern corner of Broadway and Liberty (*Directory for 1793*: 24 Broadway [now Zuccotti Park, about 141 Broadway]; 1793 Tax Records [ward 4, p. 6], Broadway, house £1,200, personal estate £800). GSET: block 50, lot 5; NYC Conveyances 43:348 (1786).

136 **John Campbell:** Campbell was the alderman for the sixth ward (*Directory for 1793*, 201). Seemingly a man of modest means, he lived at the corner of Barley and Great George (now Broadway). 1793 Tax Records (ward 6, p. 12): John Campbell, 100 Great George Street, house and pottery, £400; no personal estate.

136 **his accuser:** CO&T MB1784–1796: 308 (4 October 1793, indictment of John George Hobbolt), 312 (7 October 1793, motion to put the trial off), 316–17 (8 October 1793, trial).

136 **Bedlow's father had also hired:** Richard Harison to William Bedlow, New York, 2 December 1793, Letterbooks and catalogue, BV Harison, Richard, NYHS.

137 **James Kent:** John H. Langbein, "Chancellor Kent and the History of Legal Literature," *Columbia Law Review* 93, no. 3 (April 1993), 547–94.

137 **unthinkable a century later:** Allen Steinberg, *The Transformation of Criminal Justice: Philadephia, 1800–1880* (Chapel Hill: University of North Carolina Press, 1989), argues that private prosecutors remained central to the criminal justice system in Philadelphia and retained considerable control over their cases until the emergence of the modern policing system in the late nineteenth century.

137 **the usual formalities:** Wyche passes quickly over these preliminaries (*Report*, 3); this account is based on the most authoritative of several reports of a trial in the same court seven years later: William Coleman, *Report of the trial of Levi Weeks, on an indictment for the murder of Gulielma Sands* (New-York: John Furman, 1800), 9–12.

138 **truthful testimony:** Mike McConfille and Chester Mirsky, *Jury Trials and Plea Bargaining: A True History* (Oxford: Oxford University Press, 2005), 107, cite an 1869 New York statute giving defendants the right to testify in their own cases. Earlier, English courts had excluded parties in civil and criminal matters from offering sworn testimony in their cases, but with little practical effect until defense attorneys became common; this silencing of criminal defendants was debated and eliminated in the nineteenth century, on the grounds that juries could weigh their testimony as they did that of other witnesses: Michael Jonathan Millender, "The Transformation of the American Criminal Trial, 1790–1875" (PhD diss., Princeton University, 1996), 353–71.

138 **legendary hotel:** The jurors listed in the CO&T MB1784–96: 316, with addresses from the *Directory for 1793* and property valuations from the 1793 Tax Records: Henry Wyckoff (not identified); Benjamin Seixas (merchant, 8 Hanover Square; ward 1, p. 14: 8 Hanover Square, house, unfinished: £400); William I. Vredenburg (46 Great Dock (now Pearl) Street; ward 2, p. 17: 46 Great Dock Street, tenant with £100 personal property in £320 house of Widow Vredenburgh); John Townsend (merchant, 55 Cherry Street; £2,600; ward 3, p. 12: Peck Slip, £700 store, £700 personal property); Thomas Salter (merchant, 34 Broadway; not found on tax list), John Gilbert ("conductor" of the powder magazine, 54 Queen (now Pearl) Street; ward 3, p. 35: 54 Queen Street, £800 house); Cornelius Van Allen (merchant, Maiden Lane; possibly ward 4, p. 30: Barclay Street, £180 house, £40 personal estate); James McIntosh (grocer, corner of Jacob and Ferry Streets; ward 5, p. 6: Ferry Street, £350 house, £200 personal estate); John Stake ("Capt.", 49 William Street; ward 5, p. 7: £100 house, £25 personal estate, plus several other rental houses totaling £1,190); Stephen Ward (Stephen Ward Jr., merchant, 13 Peck Slip; ward 5, 17: Stephen Ward Jr., renter with £200 personal estate); John Crolius (both John Crolius Jr. and Sr. were listed as "stone-ware manufacturer, Potter-baker's hill"; John Croleus/Crolius owned five houses); Michael Ritter (shopkeeper, 40 Golden Hill Street; hardware and jewelry store, 24 Fly Market; ward 2, p. 39: Fly Market, £800 house, £150 personal estate; ward 6, p. 17: 100 Chatham St., £150 rental house). On Seixas: Scoville, *Old Merchants of New York* (1885), 2:125.

139 **"affair of this kind":** *Report*, 3.

139 **"sufficient to ground":** *Report*, 3.

140 **potentially malicious:** Matthew Hale, *History of the Pleas of the Crown* (1736), 1:628–33. Published in 1736, the book was written in the 1670s.

140 **"against her will":** Hale, *Pleas of the Crown* (1736), 1:628. On the element of force, see chapter 8. William Hawkins, *A Treatise on the Pleas of the Crown* (London, E. and R. Nutt, 1716–17), ch. 41, sect. 1: this formulation echoes the First Statute of Westminster (1275), 3 Edw 1, ch. 13., and William Blackstone, *Commentaries on the Laws of England* (London, 1770), 4:210.

143 **"There is a room":** *Report*, 5 (Sawyer): quotation marks in original; "t" capitalized.

144 **as much force as necessary:** David Lisak, "Understanding the Predatory Nature of Sexual Violence," *Sexual Assault Report* 14, no. 4 (April 2011), 49–57; Block, *Rape and Sexual Power in Early America* (Chapel Hill: University of North Carolina Press, 2003), 24–27. See also Nina Burrowes, *Responding to the Challenge of Rape in Court: A Guide for Prosecutors* (London: NB Research, 2013), availalbe via https://www.ninaburrowes.com/research.

145 **"an evidence of penetration":** Hale, *Pleas of the Crown* (1736), 628 (ch. 58).

145 **"the material facts requisite":** Blackstone, *Commentaries* (Philadelphia: Robert Bell, 1772), 213 (ch. 15).

145 **"amounted to proof":** *Report*, 6 (Sawyer).

146 **Bedlow dozing:** *Report*, 6 (Sawyer).

147 **"drawn frill":** A "drawn frill" was a folded strip of cloth or ribbon gathered by drawing a thread through it. On the construction of round gowns: Meredith Wright, *Everyday Dress of Rural America, 1783–1800* (New York: Dover Publications, 1992), 38–42. For a round gown with the neckline gathered with a drawstring: Lydia Edwards, *How to Read a Dress: A Guide to Changing Fashion from the 16th to the 20th Century* (New York: Bloomsbury Academic, 2017), 61.

147 **the fabric itself:** *Report*, 8 (Sawyer).

149 **she had made their case:** *Report*, 8 (Sawyer).

150 **nervous exhaustion:** Dexter, *Graduates of Yale*, 4:238–40.

152 **"a scene of fraud":** *Report*, 9–10 (Thompson).

152 **his first witness:** Most of the witnesses described in Wyche's *Report* are the same as those listed in the CO&T MB1784–1796: 317 and appear in the same order. A few discrepancies are noted below.

152 **Mrs. Carey's testimony began:** *Report* 12–13 (Carey). Wyche gives her name as "Mary Cary," but the minutes correctly identify her as "Ann Carey." In quotations from Wyche's *Report*, I have corrected her name to "Carey."

153 **about five thirty:** Sun, moon, and light data (moonrise 5:36 a.m., illumination 0 percent; sunrise 5:31 a.m.): www.timeanddate.com/sun and ~/moon (New York, 5 September 1793), accessed 12 September 2014.

154 **twilight faded:** Sunset was 6:25 p.m., civil twilight ended at 6:53 p.m: www .timeanddate.com/sun (New York, 5 September 1793).

154 **"Give my love":** *Report*, 13 (Carey); "g" in "Give" capitalized.

155 **The first of these witnesses:** *Report*, 13 (Ann McFall). Wyche gives her name as "M'Foul," but the minutes correctly identify her as "McFall."

155 **Mary Franklin:** *Report*, 14 (Mary Franklin). I have been unable to identify her.

156 **Elizabeth Smith:** *Report*, 14 (Elizabeth Smith). I have been unable to identify her.

156 **Thomas McCready:** Wyche's *Report* (15) gives "Thomas M'Ready" as the fifth defense witness; he is not listed in the CO&T minutes—the only such oversight in this case by the court clerk. Other records indicate the correct spelling of his name. *Directory for 1793*: "McCready, Thomas, house carpenter and grocer, corner of Beaver and Broad streets." This was a modest house (1793 Tax Records, ward 1, p. 14: £300 house) on the same block as Mrs. Bruce's: BIRC block 24, lot 3; NYC Conveyances 55:283 (30 January 1797) and 54:420 (19 June 1797).

157 **The last witness called:** *Report*, 15 (Varick).

159 **Lanah's stepfather, John Callanan:** In Wyche's *Report* (15–16), Callanan's name is misspelled "Callahan" and he appears as the second prosecution witness (before Samuel Hone); in the minutes, Callanan appears after Hone. However, in the report Hone refers Callanan as the previous witness, so I take Wyche's order as correct here.

161 **next witness for the people:** *Report*, 16–17. Wyche gets Samuel Hone's name wrong ("Joel Hone") and presents him as the third prosecution witness, after John Callanan (as do I); the minutes give his name correctly and list him before John Callanan.

162 **"marks of violence":** *Report*, 15 (Lawrence).

162 **Sawyer's mother, Jane Callanan:** *Report* (17). Wyche presents Jane Callanan as the fourth prosecution witness (before Hannah Hone), as do I; the minutes list Jane Callanan fifth (after Hannah Hone).

162 **Mrs. Hannah Hone:** *Report*, 17. Wyche does not give her first name and presents her as the fifth prosecution witness (after Jane Callanan), as do I; the minutes give her full name and list her fourth, before Jane Callanan.

162 **Lucretia Harper, who testified next:** *Report*, 17–18. Both Wyche and the minutes list Harper as the sixth prosecution witness.

163 **Robert Dowle was an English-born:** *Report*, 18 (Dowle). Variant spellings of his name are given by Wyche ("Dow") and the minutes ("Down"). Robert Dowle, watchmaker, from England, was naturalized on 9 February 1795, CGS MB1790–1797, 286; one of his supporting witnesses was the painter Alexander Robertson, of Scotland. *Directory for 1793*: "Dowle, Robert, clock and watch-maker, 47 Maiden-lane." The 1793 Tax Records listed him (ward 2, p. 47) on Crown Street (now Liberty), with £30 personal property, in an £800 house owned by John Stevens and occupied by several others. He evidently lived at the merging of Maiden Lane and Liberty Street at Gold; the *Directory for 1796* lists Dowle at the "corner of Maiden lane and Gold"; the *Directory for 1797* at 84 Maiden Lane. See William Perris, *Maps of the City of New York* (New York, 1852), 4; BIRC block 42, lot 16.

164 **George Warner was a prosperous:** *Report*, 18 (Warner). Wyche lists Warner as the ninth prosecution witness (after McDonald); in the minutes he appears eighth (between Dowle and McDonald). The *Directory for 1793* lists Warner as a sailmaker, with a sail-loft on Murray's wharf and a residence at 13 Little-Queen Street (now 14 Cedar Street); he was also (178) foreman of fire company 15. The 1793 Tax Records show that he owned at least six houses, including his £600 home at 13 Little Queen Street; his mother owned the £600 house next door at 12 Little Queen Street (ward 2, p. 52). See NYC Conveyances 315:439–40 (to George Warner, 23 August 1781); BIRC block 45, lot 13 (George Warner); block 45, lot 14 (his mother). On Warner's religious meetings and reputation as a Patriot: *Anderson's Diary*, 129 n1.

164 **Isabella McDonald lived up near:** *Report*, 18. Wyche gives her name as "Mary Mac-Donald" and puts her testimony *before* George Warner's; in the CO&T MB (317), Isabella McDonald is listed as the ninth witness for the people, immediately *after* Warner. Isabella Gardner married Walter McDonald on 22 September 1782 (Trinity Church registers); *New York Marriages Previous to 1784* (Baltimore: Genealogical Publishing Co., 1968), 149 (marriage bond 37:8, 21 September 1782). The *Directory for 1793* lists McDonald, Walter, school-master, Harman St. (Bowery).

164 **Elizabeth Aubrick:** *Report*, 18. Confusingly, Wyche identified two different individuals only as "Another witness." One appears in his *Report* as the ninth defense witness (and testified about living in the Callanan house for two months); the other appears as the eleventh defense witness (and testified about events at Mrs. Bruce's). The minutes give their name as "Mary Caswell" (tenth prosecution witness) and "Elizabeth Aburey" (eleventh prosecution witness). I have not identified either woman definitively, but the *Directory for 1793* lists "Aubrick, Earnest, tanner and currier, 25 Gold-street"—just down the street from Lanah's home. So I have identified Elizabeth Aubrick as the witness who lived at the Callanan house and Mary Caswell as the one at Mrs. Bruce's.

164 **Mary Caswell—likely a servant:** *Report*, 18 (Caswell). As noted above, I have identified the second of Wyche's unidentified witnesses as Mary Caswell, who was listed in the minutes as the eleventh prosecution witness.

164 **Robert Towt, a prosperous shoemaker:** *Report*, 18–19 (Towt). Both Wyche and the minutes list Towt as the twelfth and final prosecution witness. George Street is now Spruce Street.

CHAPTER 8: CLOSING ARGUMENTS

168 **typically took notes:** An example of informal trial notes kept by city recorder Samuel Jones, including summaries of testimony and occasional legal references not included in the court's official minutes: New York City Mayor's Court trial minutes, 1789–1790, MssCol 2182, NYPL. Many records of the state Supreme Court before 1847, including witness statements, were deliberately destroyed: James D. Folts, *"Duely & Constantly Kept": A History of the New York Supreme Court, 1691–1847, and an Inventory of Its Records* (Albany: New York State Court of Appeals, 1991), 9. As early as 1789, proceedings of the US Congress in New York were being recorded in shorthand by a private citizen: Marion Tinling, "Thomas Lloyd's Reports of the First Federal Congress," *William and Mary Quarterly* 18, no. 4 (October 1961), 519–45. In 1793, a manual of Lloyd's method (*Daily Advertiser* [New York], 15 February 1793) and lessons in another method (*Diary* [New York], 12 December 1793) were advertised.

168 **first published report:** On the early history of North American trial reports following British models, see Daniel Cohen, *Pillars of Salt, Monuments of Grace: New England Crime Literature and the Origins of American Popular Culture* (New York: Oxford University Press, 1993), 14–32. Before Wyche's 1793 *Report*, only a handful of North American trial reports were published—most of which reflected the interests of imperial or local officials. In New York, the only example before the Bedlow trial was city recorder Daniel Horsmanden's self-justifying *Journal of the Proceedings in the Detection*

of Conspiracy (New York: James Parker, 1744), published after his 1741 investigation of a suspected conspiracy of enslaved Blacks and others led to the executions of dozens of people and was decried as an illegitimate witch hunt.

169 **Wyche had to flee**: Robert A. Emery, "William Wyche," *Law Library Journal* 93, no. 3 (Summer 2001): 469–77. Cary Ludlow, affidavit in favor of Wm. Wyche, filed 8 April 1794, bundle 1, no. 69, Mayor's Court, Petitions of Naturalization, 1792–1895, NYCC-DOR; naturalization of William Wyche, "Student at Law," 8 April 1794, MC MB1793–1794, 360. Wyche served his three-year clerkship with Ludlow: MC MB1795E: 49 (14 April 1795); admitted to bar 4 May 1795 (*Directory for 1795*, 306). Duel: *Evening Mail* (London), 28 March 1791.

169 **summations often consumed**: In subsequent published reports of criminal trials, closing arguments often constituted a third or more of the proceedings. *The Trial of Nathaniel Price* [for rape] (New York: Elijah Weedg, 1797): about four pages of evidence and three of closing arguments; *Report of the Trial of Richard D. Croucher* [for rape] (New York: George Forman, 1800): ten pages evidence, eleven pages closing arguments; *Report of the Trial of Alpheus Hitchcock* [for murder] (New York: Seward and Williams, 1807): twenty-eight pages evidence, fifteen pages closing arguments. William Coleman, *Report of the trial of Levi Weeks, on an indictment for the murder of Gulielma Sands* [for murder] (New York: John Furman, 1800), was the first New York trial report based on shorthand minutes kept by the court clerk—but in this case the judges prevented the delivery of closing arguments.

169 **torrent of talk**: On more subtle power effects, see Gregrory M. Matoesian, *Reproducing Rape: Domination through Talk in the Courtroom* (Chicago: University of Chicago, 1993).

170 **wide latitude**: Statute of Westminster I, 1275, 3 Edw. 1, c. 13; Statute of Westminster II, 1285, 3 Edw. 1, c. 34 (rape defined only in terms of consent); the Common Informers Act, 1576, 18 Eliz. c. 7 (defining age of consent as ten). See also Edward Coke, *Third Part of the Institutes of the Laws of England* (London: M. Flesher, 1644), c. 11 (60), and Matthew Hale, *History of the Pleas of the Crown* (1736), 628. More generally: Anna Clark, *Women's Silence, Men's Violence: Sexual Assault in England, 1770–1845* (New York: Pandora, 1987).

170 **modern compilation**: The first, which included only seven criminal matters, was William Coleman, *Cases of Practice, adjudged in the Supreme Court of New-York . . . From October Term 1791, to October Term 1800* (New York: Isaac Collins, 1801).

171 **"Fear of Death, or of Duress"**: William Hawkins, *A Treatise on the Pleas of the Crown*, vol. 1 (London: E. and R. Nutt, 1716), ch. 40 (108–9).

171 **narrowing the definition of rape**: Estelle Freedman, *Redefining Rape: Sexual Violence in the Era of Suffrage and Segregation* (Cambridge, MA: Harvard University Press, 2013), ch. 1.

172 **"*forcibly and* against her will"**: William Blackstone, *Commentaries on the Laws of England*, 4 vols. (1765–1770), 4:210–13. (ch. 15, part 3); italics added. "Force" was not included as an element of rape in the 1275 statute, though it was in earlier compilations and commentaries including Bracton, Glanville, and the Mirror. Coke's discussion of "force" in the context of rape is somewhat confused: Coke, in his discussion of criminal law in the *Third Part of the Institutes*, distinguished between two crimes described in the 1275 statute: rape (c. 11), defined in terms of consent for women of age, and bride kidnapping (c. 12), defined by force. In earlier discussions of the 1275 and 1285 statutes, Coke does include "force" in his discussion of rape: *Second Part of the Institutes of the Lawes of England* (London: M. Flesher and R. Young, 1642), c. 13 (180–82), and c. 34 (433–37). Matthew Hale, writing in the 1670s, followed Coke's primary discussion of rape and did not include "force" in his definition of the crime. The first modern English authority who did was William Hawkins: *Treatise*, vol. 1, c. 41.

172 **Brockholst Livingston rose**: "Brockholst Livingston," in *Princetonians, 1748–1768: A Biographical Dictionary*, ed. James McLachlan (Princeton, NJ: Princeton University

Press, 1976), 2:397–407. For a portrait of Brockholst Livingston (1757–1823), ca. 1790, as well as those of relatives, see Edwin Brockholst Livingston, *The Livingstons of Livingston Manor* (New York: The Knickerbocker Press, 1910). 1793 Tax Records (ward 1, p. 16): White Hall Street (not numbered), Brockholst Livingston, £3,000 house, £2,000 personal estate; he also owned other real estate. The *Directory for 1794* gives the number as 17 Whitehall. See William Perris, *Maps of the City of New York* (New York, 1852) and BIRC block 10, lot 23 (part). 1790 Federal Census (ward 6, p. 133): Brockholst Livingston's household included two white men sixteen and over, one white man under sixteen, seven white women, one free person of color, and four enslaved people.

172 **twelve-year-old Mary Anderson:** "William Livingston," in Franklin Bowditch Dexter, *Biographical Sketches of the Graduates of Yale*, vol. 1 (New York: Henry Holt, 1885), 682–86. Anderson case: William Livingston to William Kempe, New York, 26 August 1754, Letterbook, 1754–1770, William Livingston Papers, Massachusetts Historical Society. Livingston's closing: *Report*, 19–34.

173 **someone entirely different:** Here I draw on Chanel Miller's incisive account of her own rape-trial experience: *Know My Name: A Memoir* (New York: Viking, 2019), 174.

173 **"life of a fellow-citizen":** *Report*, 19 (Livingston).

175 **a stereotype of womanhood:** On this kind of abstraction, see Miller, *Know My Name*, 180.

175 **"meditated a rape":** *Report*, 19–23 (Livingston).

176 **"I demand redress":** *Report*, 28–31 (Livingston).

176 **"stop that ravisher":** *Report*, 28 (Livingston).

177 **"a poor decent woman":** *Report*, 28–29 (Livingston).

177 **"invents this rape":** *Report*, 29–30 (Livingston).

178 **"must become a burthen":** *Report*, 31 (Livingston).

178 **"meditated his destruction":** *Report*, 31–32 (Livingston); comma after "Sawyer" and question mark added for clarity.

178 **"*without leaving the bar*":** *Report*, 32–34 (Livingston).

178 **Lanah was powerless to object:** On this kind of disorientation, see Miller, *Know My Name*, 195.

178 **small, dark eyes:** Ralph Earl, portrait of Robert Troup, 1786, oil on canvas, 32 x 29 in, private collection. His portrait of John Cozine (private collection) is strikingly similar.

179 **"ardent & generous feelings":** Wendell Tripp, "Robert Troup," *American National Biography*, ed. John A. Garraty and Mark C. Carnes (New York: Oxford University Press, 1999), 21:845–46. Quote: Donald M. Roper, "The Elite of the New York Bar as Seen from the Bench: James Kent's Necrologies," *New-York Historical Society Quarterly* 56 (July 1972): 214–15. Troup lived on Cedar Street, between the Dutch Churchyard on Nassau and George Warner's widowed mother: BIRC block 45, lot 15; NYC Conveyances 47:408 (deed to Troup, 1792), 50:342 (deed from Troup, 1795). 1790 Census, ward 5, p. 124: Troup's household included two enslaved people. Troup's closing: *Report*, 34–40.

180 **"immediate complaint":** *Report*, 34–36 (Troup).

180 **"no character themselves":** *Report*, 36–37 (Troup).

180 **actually "impossible":** *Report*, 37–38 (Troup).

181 **two doors down from her:** *Directory for 1793*: "Cozine, John, counselor at law, 56 Beekman" (24); admitted to the bar, 1 May 1773 (222); board member, City Dispensary (230); trustee, New-York Society Library (231). 1793 Tax Records: John Cozine (ward 3, p. 29): "House Office" between 57 and 54 Beekman St., $700 real estate value, $200 personal estate value; Cozine also owned at least one rental property in Ward 1. The *Directory for 1794* locates Cozine at "corner of Gold and Beekman streets." See BIRC block 94, lot 19; and NYC Conveyances 314:594 (Price to Lawrence, 1795),

which shows abutting neighbors as John Conrey (Callanan's landlord) and John Cozine. 1790 Census, ward 4, p. 120: John Cosine.

181 **"indolence, corpulence, and high living":** Martha J. Lamb, *History of the City of New York: Its Origin, Rise, and Progress* (New York: A. S. Barnes, 1877), 2:299–300. Ralph Earl's portrait of John Cozine, 1787—strikingly similar to that of Robert Troup—is in a private collection; I am grateful to Robert C. Strang of Williamsburg, VA, for images. Cozine's closing: *Report*, 40–43.

181 **"illicit commerce":** *Report*, 40 (Cozine).

181 **sex acts with shame and sin:** On sex negativity: Gayle Rubin, "Thinking Sex: Notes for a Radical Theory of the Politics of Sexuality," in Henry Abelove, Michèle Aina Barale, and David M. Halperin, eds., *The Lesbian and Gay Studies Reader* (New York: Routledge, 1993), 3–44.

182 **"forfeiture of his life":** *Report*, 43 (Cozine).

182 **Richard Harison was one:** Richard Harison (1747–1829) graduated from King's College in 1764. *Directory for 1793*: 94 Broadway (later 68 Broadway). 1793 Tax Records, ward 1, p. 22: Broadway (not numbered): £1,900 house and stable; £1,000 personal estate. BIRC block 23, lots 11 and 11–1/2; NYC Conveyances 50:317 (sale by Harisons, 1795). Relationship to the indicted rapist: William Gordon, "Gabriel Ludlow and his Descendants," *NYGB Record* 50, no. 1 (1919): 1–8 (Frances Ludlow, Harison's wife), 29–31 (Edmund Ludlow). 1790 Census: ward 6, p. 133. Harison's closing: *Report*, 43–46.

182 **morally loose and sexually profligate:** On stereotypes of working women: Christine Stansell, *City of Women: Sex and Class in New York, 1798–1860* (New York: Alfred A. Knopf, 1986), 24–30.

182 **"to constitute a rape":** *Report*, 43–45 (Harison).

183 **"unwilling woman":** *Report*, 45 (Harison).

183 **signs of blood and injury:** *Report*, 46 (Harison). In the century before the 1275 statute, English legal treatises emphasized the importance in rape cases of physical evidence of injury, including "any effusion of blood there may be and any tearing of her clothing": H. D. G. Hall, ed. and trans., *The Treatise on the Laws and Customs of the Realm Commonly Called Glanville* (London: Nelson, 1965), 175–76; Henry de Bracton, *On the Laws and Customs of England*, ed. Samuel E. Thorn, trans. George E. Woodbine (Cambridge, MA: Belknap Press, 1968), 2:414–19.

184 **even flinty, gaze:** James Sharples, portrait of James Kent (1763–1847), 1798, pastel on paper, 22.5 x 17.6 cm, C000.730, Columbia University; Ralph Earl, portrait of James Kent, ca. 1812, oil on canvas, 1946.97.1, Albany Institute; Samuel F. B. Morse, *James Kent*, ca. 1823, oil on canvas, 76.2 x 63.5 cm., 33–2/2, Nelson-Atkins Museum of Art.

184 **Wracked by grief:** "James Kent," Dexter, *Graduates of Yale*, 4:189–94; Roper, "James Kent's Necrologies," 214–15 (Troup), 227 (Hoffman). *Memoirs and Letters of James Kent*, ed. William Kent (Boston: Little, Brown, 1898), includes no mention of the Bedlow trial but shows that he read Hale and Blackstone in 1780 (19), his response to his daughter's death (52, quote), and his state of mind in October 1793 (54–55). 1793 Tax Records, ward 1, p. 8: Marketfield Street, tenant in £700 house of Nicholas Cruger, £20 personal estate. BIRC block 11, probably part of lot 50 (Cruger owned several abutting properties on that block). Kent's closing: *Report*, 46–49.

184 **"flowed from her lips":** *Report*, 46–47 (Kent).

185 **"iniquity and guilt":** *Report*, 47–48 (Kent).

185 **"scruple at perjury":** *Report*, 48–49 (Kent).

186 **created the Roman republic:** Among the original versions of the story is Titus Livius, *Ab urbe condita*, book I, sections 57–60. In *Memoirs and Letters*, ed. William Kent, James Kent describes reading Livy in the original between October 1791 and July 1792 (26). An example of a reference to the story of Lucretia: "The Ravishers Punished," *Weekly Museum* (New York), 12 November 1791.

186 **hold the rapist to account:** *Report*, 49 (Kent).

186 **Josiah Ogden Hoffman:** John Ramage, *Josiah Ogden Hoffman* (1766–1837), ca. 1790, portrait miniature on ivory, 1–¾ x 1–½ in, NYHS.

186 **expensive house with stables:** 1793 Tax Records, ward 2, p. 2: Josiah O. Hoffman, 37 Broad Street (subsequently 89 Broad Street), in £1,700 house and stables owned by Dr. John Charleton; £400 personal estate. See BIRC block 29, lots 60 and 58; NYC Conveyances 89:406 (1801). On Hoffman's family, see Eugene A. Hoffman, *Genealogy of the Hoffman Family* (New York: Dodd, Mead & Co., 1899), 204–206.

187 **"acutely intelligent":** Roper, "Necrologies of James Kent," 227. Hoffman served as a member of the state assembly during the 1790s, as New York's attorney general from 1795 to 1802, and, eventually, as the city recorder and superior court justice.

187 **"management of juries":** Lamb, *History of the City of New York*, 2:300.

187 **appeared virtuous:** *Report*, 50–51 (Hoffman).

187 **"sensual desire":** *Report*, 52–53 (Hoffman).

188 **"diabolical scheme":** *Report*, 55 (Hoffman); "cloaths" in original.

188 **"adherence to truth":** *Report*, 56–57 (Hoffman).

188 **We have been told:** *Report*, 57 (Hoffman).

188 **innocent maiden celebrated:** An incisive discussion of class and gender ideologies: Marybeth Hamilton Arnold, "'The Life of a Citizen in the Hands of a Woman': Sexual Assault in New York City, 1790–1820," in *Passion and Power: Sexuality in History*, ed. Kathy Peiss and Christina Simmons (Philadelphia: Temple University Press, 1989), 35–56. See also Kelly A. Ryan, *Regulating Passion: Sexuality and Patriarchal Rule in Massachusetts, 1700–1830* (New York: Oxford University Press, 2014), 129–30.

189 **"injured innocence":** *Report*, 58–59 (Hoffman).

189 **"find him guilty":** *Report*, 59–60 (Hoffman).

189 **notorious prison hulks:** Portrait miniature of Nathaniel Lawrence (1761–1797), ca. 1790, 3–⅛ x 2–⅝ in, formerly in collection of Miss Carolina Harris Gallagher, Baltimore; Frick Art Reference Library online. "Nathaniel Lawrence," in McLachlan, *Princetonians*, 3:424–29.

190 **"justice for her wrongs":** *Report*, 60 (Lawrence).

191 **new compilation of the state's laws:** Seabury, "Samuel Jones," 399–402 (prior experience), 400 (*Laws of the State of New-York* [New York, 1788]). Jones's charge to the jury appears in the *Report*, 60–62.

191 **"clearly impeachable":** *Report*, 60–61 (Jones).

191 **rewrite the law of rape:** Like Matthew Hale and William Blackstone, William Hawkins (quoted above) framed the timing of a rape complaint as evidence of a woman's credibility, not a procedural requirement.

192 **"you will find him guilty":** *Report*, 61–62 (Jones).

192 **fifteen minutes:** Wyche, *Report*, 62, gives the length of the trial as fifteen hours, but it was actually a bit less than that (the court had convened at 10:00 a.m., but the Bedlow trial started only after the fraud case).

192 **jurors were called out:** This account is based on the description of "this established and important custom" in *A Brief narrative of the trial for the bloody and mysterious murder of the unfortunate young woman, in the famous Manhattan well*, (New York: David Longworth, 1800), 14.

192 **one o'clock in the morning:** John Barent Johnson, 8 October 1793, Diary, 1787–1803, vol. 7, Columbiana MS 42, Columbia University.

CHAPTER 9: OUTRAGE

193 **hundreds of men:** Previous accounts of this riot include Christine Stansell, *City of Women: Sex and Class in New York, 1798–1860* (New York: Alfred A. Knopf, 1986), 23–26; Paul A. Gilje, *The Road to Mobocracy: Popular Disorder in New York City, 1763–1834*

(Chapel Hill: University of North Carolina Press), 86–89, 90—92; and Timothy J. Gilfoyle, "Strumpets and Misogynists: Brothel 'Riots' and the Transformation of Prostitution in Antebellum New York City," *New York History* 68, no. 1 (January 1987), 45–65.

193 **soft glow of moonlight:** October 14, 1793, was a mild day: 65 degrees at 2:00 p.m., with a "fresh" breeze (Pintard, 14 October 1793, Diary and Garden Calendar, Newark, 1793–1794, box 4, fol. 9, Pintard Papers, MS490, NYHS). The sun set at 6:09 p.m., the moon rose at 2:41 p.m (illumination 76 percent): www.timeanddate.com (New York, 14 Oct. 1793), accessed 1 October 2021.

193 **"fir'd from the house":** *Alexander Anderson's New York City Diary, 1793–1799*, ed. Jane R. Pomeroy, 2 vols. (New Castle, DE: Oak Knoll Press, 2014), 14 October 1793 (riots), 21 August 1793 (begins French classes at Mr. Durand's). *Directory for 1794*: "Durand, Peter, school-master, 6 Barclay."

194 **"so many Lawyers among us":** Inquisitive, "QUERIES," *Weekly Museum* (New York), 12 October 1793. The next week's issue included, among other reports on the riots, a response to Inquisitive by "One of Mother Cary's Chickens": *Weekly Museum*, 19 October 1793.

195 **"licentious mob":** John Drayton, *Letters written during a tour through the northern and eastern states of America* (Charleston, SC: Harrison and Bowen, 1794), 113 (Letter X, 16 October 1793, New York).

195 **"fill'd with Feathers":** *Anderson's Diary*, 14 October 1793; Philip Hone, 8 August 1838, Diaries, 1826–1851, 14:287, Mss. Col. BV Hone, Philip, NYHS.

195 **For Mayor Richard Varick:** *MCC 1784–1831*, 2:44 (14 October 1793).

195 **kicks and bruises:** *Anderson's Diary*, 14 October 1793. Charles Adams to John Adams, New York, 6 December 1793, *Adams Family Correspondence* vol. 9 (Cambridge, MA: Belknap Press, 2009), 463.

196 **"operations of a Mob":** John Barent Johnson, 14 October 1793, Diary, 1787–1803, vol. 7, Columbiana MS 42, Columbia University.

196 **"carry'd off by the poor people":** *Anderson's Diary*, 15 October 1793.

196 **"how things are done in France":** C. Adams to J. Adams, New York, 6 December 1793. Threats against Bedlow's attorneys were also described by Aaron Burr in a later murder trial: William Coleman, *Report of the trial of Levi Weeks, on an indictment for the murder of Gulielma Sands* (New York: John Furman, 1800), 67.

196 **fled the city:** Armed guard: "Extract of a letter from Newyork, dated Oct. 27," *Vermont Gazette* (Bennington), 8 November 1793. Bedlow's flight: Drayton, *Letters*, 114; *Diary* (New York), 17 December 1793.

196 **forced to disperse:** On the sequence of events: "ASSAULT AND BATTERY!," *Columbian Gazetteer* (New York), 17 October 1793; reprinted *New-Jersey Journal* (Elizabethtown), 23 October 1793. On the militia and riots in this period: Gilje, *Road to Mobocracy*, 25, 81–82, 272–73. On the watchmen: *MCC 1784–1831*, 2:45 (21 October 1793), payments to the high constable of £38.17 (the watchmen's regular monthly expense) and £4.16 (for "extra Watchmen to quell a riot," roughly doubling the typical four-day cost). *MCC 1784–1831*, 2:51 (18 November 1793, payment to Lieutenant John Lovel for deployment of the dragoons). Rutgers and the "Light Dragoons": *Directory for 1793*, 208.

198 **"half the inhabitants murdered":** E. H. Smith to Mason Cogswell, 19 October 1793, New York, box 3, Mason Cogswell Papers, Beinecke Library, Yale University.

198 **John Callanan, had set them:** Philip Hone, diary, 9 August 1838 (14:287–89), explained the riots as a result of outrage at Bedlow's acquittal and the fact that Lanah's stepfather was "well known amongst the sea faring people."

198 **several men were wounded:** Smith to Cogswell, 19 October 1793.

199 **"licentious houses":** A Citizen to "Messrs. Printers," *Diary* (New York), 15 October 1793.

199 **highly disciplined crowd actions:** Pauline Maier, *From Resistance to Revolution: Colonial Radicals and the Development of American Opposition to Britain, 1765–1776* (New York: Alfred A. Knopf, 1973), 1–16, 35–38.

199 **New York's Tea Party:** *New-York Gazette*, 25 April 1774; Gilje, *Road to Mobocracy*, 58–59.

199 **city again exploded in fury:** Gilje, *Road to Mobocracy*, 85–92 (1793 and 1799 brothel riots), 78–83 (1788 Doctors' Riot), 83–85 (1792 Anti-Duer Riot). Brothel riot prompted by a murder: Edward Bangs, ed., *Journal of Lieutenant Isaac Bangs, 1776* (Cambridge, MA: J. Wilson and Son, 1890), 29–30.

199 **city's leaders struck back:** Whether Varick issued this notice alone or in consultation with others is unclear; there was no recorded meeting of the Common Council that week: *MCC 1784–1831*, 2:44–45 (14–21 October 1793).

200 **"all parents, masters and mistresses":** "NOTICE BY THE MAGISTRATES," *Diary* (New York), 16 October 1793.

200 **six hundred men:** "AN AIRING!," *New-York Journal*, 16 October 1793; reprinted (in part): *Essex Journal* (Newburyport, MA), 30 October 1793; *Columbian Herald* (Charleston, SC), 2 November 1793.

200 **to maintain a free government:** Gilje, *Road to Mobocracy*, 30–32, 82, 89–90. Gilje mistakenly reports that seven men were prosecuted for the 1793 riots; his reference (90 n41) is to similar prosecutions a year later: *People v. Burr et al.* and *People v. Moses Hunt et al.*, CGS MB1790–97E, 260 (7 November 1794).

201 **worshiped at Trinity Church:** One example of complex kinship ties among branch pilots in the early 1790s: Branch pilots John Funk (1758–1821; death notice, *New York Evening Post*, 21 November 1821) and Nathaniel Funk (1759–1814; death notice, *New York Evening Post*, 21 November 1821) were brothers; their older sister Elizabeth Funk (1754–1823) was married to another pilot, David Morris (marriage: 24 August 1774, Trinity Church registers; her death notice, *New York Evening Post*, 15 April 1823). In another set of examples from the Trinity Church registers, Matthew Daniel named three sons after fellow branch pilots who sponsored their christenings: John Daniel (baptized 14 November 1779; sponsor: John Callanan); Edward Daniel (baptized 7 March 1784, sponsor: Edward Wilkie); Zachariah Daniel (baptized 1 November 1789, sponsors: Zachariah Russler and Elizabeth Russler). Edward Wilkie, in turn, sponsored the baptism of John and Jane Callanan's son John (14 August 1785), and they sponsored his children Elizabeth Wilkie (26 February 1786, sponsor: Jane Callanan) and Edward Wilkie (23 January 1788, sponsor: John Callanan). Meanwhile, Matthew Daniels served as godparent for the Callanan's son Lewis (baptized 22 August 1787).

201 **clustering together:** The *Directory for 1794* listed the addresses of fourteen branch pilots, at least half of whom lived in a tight cluster near John Callanan's house at 62 Gold Street: Nathaniel Funk, 70 Gold Street; John Minugh, 91 Gold; Thomas Williams, 3 Cliff Street; Charles Swan, 16 Cliff; William Carroll, 18 Cliff; Robert Eaton, 43 Cliff. Addresses alone don't make it clear how far away four others lived: James Ogden, 95 Fair Street; John Funk, 74 Fair; Zachariah Russler, 15 Ferry Street; Thomas Gray, 172 William Street. Three branch pilots clearly did live more than three blocks away from Callanan: Matthew Daniel, 49 Beaver Street; David Morris, 167 Front Street; Edward Wilkie, corner of Greenwich and Chamber Streets. Three branch pilots were not individually listed in the *Directory for 1794*: Charles Penny, Isaac Thompson, and Daniel Towser. At least three deputy pilots also lived in the cluster near Callanan's house: James Lynch, 28 Cliff Street; Christopher Seaward, 57 Cliff; Jacob Bufflaree, 52 Fair Street.

201 **one of the founding members:** Martinus Bogert (cartman, Montgomerie Ward) and twenty-nine others appointed firemen, 12 September 1738, *MCC 1675–1776*, 4:436–40.

201 **her father had joined:** List of New York City firemen, 1772, *MCC 1675–1776*, 7:384–87 (Francis Sawyer, David Morris, George Warner); Firemen of the City of New

York, June 1776, *Calendar of Historical Manuscripts Relating to the War of the Revolution* (Albany: Weed, Parson, and Co., 1868), 1:315–16 (Francis Sawyer, David Morris, John Bogert [Lanah's uncle?], George Warner).

201 **One of them was George Warner:** 1788 Constitiutional Procession: *New-York Packet*, 5 August 1788. Foreman of engine company 15: *Directory for 1793*, 178. Fire department president: *New-York Journal*, 8 February 1792.

201 **to destroy a brothel in the dark:** Benjamin L. Carp, "Fire of Liberty: Firefighters, Urban Voluntary Culture, and the Revolutionary Movement," *William and Mary Quarterly* 58, no. 4 (October 2001): 781–818.

201 **Anthony Clawson was only one:** "Extract of a letter from Newyork, dated October 20," *Vermont Gazette* (Bennington), 25 October 1793. Anthony Clawson (attack on the home of Polly Frazier on 15 October 1793), filed 8 November 1793, DA Indictments. CGS MB1790–1797: 180 (8 November 1793, Clawson pleads not guilty to assault and to rioting), 181–82 (8 November 1793, Clawson tried on both charges), 186 (9 November 1793, Clawson sentenced on both charges), 190 (9 November 1793, two other men also "Committed for Riot" discharged: John Anderson and Richard Bartlet).

201 **Clawson was a cartman:** Clawson lived on the stretch of waterfront between Whitehall Street and Moore Street; his address was given variously as 3 Whitehall (*Directory for 1793*) and Whitehall Dock (*Directory for 1789, Directory for 1794*). 1793 Tax Records, Ward 1, p. 16: Anthony Clawson, £120 house, no personal estate; tenant, John Wessells, no personal estate. 1790 Census, South Ward, p. 7: Anthony Clawson, three white men, two white boys, one white female. Clawson married Mary Brewau: marriage bond 35:133, 23 April 1782, *New York Marriages Previous to 1784* (Baltimore: Genealogical Publishing Co., 1968). He was admitted a freeman on 25 March 1784, along with a group of cartmen: Edward F. De Lancey, *The Burghers of New Amsterdam and the Freemen of New York, 1675–1866* (New York: New-York Historical Society, 1886), 242. For residents of Whitehall Dock, see *Directory for 1794*.

202 **aristocratic sexual predator:** Stansell, *City of Women*, 25.

202 **Varick's political opponents:** Graham Russell Hodges, *New York City Cartmen, 1667–1850* (New York: New York University Press, 1986), 81–89.

203 **concentration of brothels:** William Duer, *Reminiscences of an Old Yorker* (New York: W. L. Andrews, 1867), 10.

203 **same group of eleven neighbors:** Indictment of William Board (laborer, South Ward; address not found), disorderly house keeping, filed 3 February 1791, DA Indictments; Indictment of Nancy Camp, alias Ann Crea (spinster, South Ward; address not found), disorderly house keeping, filed 3 February 1791, DA Indictments; Indictment of Samuel Clark (laborer, South Ward; *Directory for 1790*: boat man, Little Dock [now the southern end of Water Street]), disorderly house keeping, filed 3 February 1791, DA Indictments. In all three cases, the same group of eleven prosecution witnesses (clustered around Moore Street, on modern blocks 4 and 8) testified: Andrew Morris (*Directory for 1790*: soap boiler and tallow chandler, 48 Great Dock Street [now the southern end of Pearl Street] and 70 Little Dock [now the southern end of Water Street]); Joseph Pearson (*Directory for 1790*: possibly Joseph Pearsall, watchmaker, 36 Queen Street); Jno. Anderson (*Directory for 1790*: probably the grocer, corner of Little Dock and Broad); Jonathan Fister (address not found); David Walker (*Directory for 1791*: grocer, corner of Moore Street and Little Dock); Timothy Van Bueruen (*Directory for 1791*: possibly related to Beekman Van Beuren, shopkeeper, Little Dock); Sebastian Needham (*Directory for 1791*: house carpenter, Little Dock); Jonathan Penny (*Directory for 1791*: hairdresser, Broad Street, near the Exchange); Anthony Smith (*Directory for 1791*: tavern keeper, 26 Great George Street); Andrew Underwick (*Directory for 1791*: flour merchant, 167 Queen Street); Simon Nathan (*Directory for 1791*: no occupation given, Little Dock). Also indicted on the same day

for disorderly house keeping was Eleanor Ogden, alias Eleanor Leary (spinster, South Ward; *Directory for 1791*: Ogden, widow, boardinghouse, 21 Moore Street). Three of the eleven men listed above (Morris, Pearson, and Anderson) testified against her at her trial: CGS MB1790–1797: 51 (1 February 1791, indicted), 54 (4 February 1791, tried; sentenced to ten days in jail).

203 **red-light districts:** Barbara Meil Hobson, *Uneasy Virtue: The Politics of Prostitution and the American Reform Tradition* (Chicago: University of Chicago Press, 1990), 23–27. Clare A. Lyons argues that brothel riots were rare in eighteenth-century Philadelphia: *Sex Among the Rabble: An Intimate History of Gender and Power in the Age of Revolution, Philadelphia, 1730–1830* (Chapel Hill: University of North Carolina Press, 2006), 341–42. Timothy J. Gilfoyle argues that brothel riots in nineteenth-century New York manifested men's resentment of female brothel keepers: *City of Eros: New York City, Prostitution, and the Commercialization of Sex, 1790–1920* (New York: W. W. Norton, 1992), 76–91, 321–29.

203 **only a trivial conviction:** CGS MB1790–1797: William Broad (above) was indicted, but his prosecution was dropped without explanation (51, 1 February 1791); Samuel Clark (above) was indicted (51, 1 February 1791), but his prosecution was dropped because of the time he had spent imprisoned while awaiting trial (55, 4 February 1791); Nancy Camp (above) got her initial indictment dropped on the ground that it had her name wrong (51, 1 February 1791) but was indicted again (52, 2 February 1791) and sentenced to ten days in prison (56, 5 February 1791).

203 **kept at it doggedly:** Indictment of William Foster (mariner, South Ward; *Directory for 1791*: mariner, 18 Moore Street), disorderly house keeping, August 1791 (witnesses included John Sullivan, who also testified against Eleanor Ogden in August 1792), DA Indictments; CGS MB1790–1797: 70 (2 August 1791, indicted), 75 (9 August 1791, fined £4).

203 **When Mother Ogden emerged:** For her February 1791 conviction and address, see above. *Directory for 1792*: Ogden, widow, boardinghouse, 7 Moore Street. CGS MB1790–1797: 117 (14 August 1792, indicted for disorderly house keeping), 126 (9 November 1792, tried, fined £6), 134 (13 November 1792, indicted for disorderly house keeping, pleads guilty, fined £4).

203 **still working to clear Moore Street:** Indictment of William Mason (laborer, First Ward; *Directory for 1794*: boardinghouse, 10 Moore Street) for disorderly house keeping, including whoring, filed August 1794, DA Indictments; witnesses from the 1791 group included David Walker (*Directory for 1794*: grocer, corner of Water and Moore Streets). Indictment of Dyer Carew (innkeeper, First Ward; *Directory for 1795*, 10 Water, grocer) for disorderly house keeping, including whoring, filed 10 August 1795, DA Indictments; witnesses from the 1791 group included Joseph Pierson (*Directory for 1795*: wire manufacturer and state measurer of lumber, 93 Broad Street) and Andrew Morris (*Directory for 1795*: soap and candle maker, 20 Water Street, corner of Broad Street)—and, at trial, David Walker. See CGS MB1790–1797, 324 (5 November 1795).

204 **The magistrates' "Notice":** Reprints and excerpts: *Daily Advertiser* (New York), 17 October 1793; *Columbian Gazetteer* (New York), 17 October 1793; *Federal Gazette* (Philadelphia), 18 October 1793; *New-York Journal*, 19 October 1793.

204 **studiously neutral report:** "NEW-YORK. WEDNESDAY, October 16," *Daily Advertiser* (New York), 16 October 1793; reprinted: *Federal Gazette* (Philadelphia), 17 October 1793; *Connecticut Courant* (Hartford), 21 October 1793 (slight change in wording).

204 **"AN AIRING!":** *New-York Journal*, 16 October 1793; corrected spelling of "Rape-venger" from reprint in the *Albany Register*, 21 October 1793. Other partial reprints: "NEW-YORK, Oct. 16," *Essex Journal* (Newburyport, MA), 30 October 1793; *Columbian Herald* (Charleston, SC), 2 November 1793.

204 **"nest of CHICKENS":** *Oxford English Dictionary*, s.v. "Chicken," definition 4: "*Mother Cary's (or Carey's) chicken*, a name given by sailors to the Stormy Petrel (*Procellaria pelagica*)."

205 **welter of other pieces:** Sardonic accounts included "ASSAULT AND BATTERY!," *Columbian Gazetteer* (New York), 17 October 1793 (immediately followed by the opening of the Magistrates' Notice); reprinted in *New-Jersey Journal* (Elizabethtown), 23 October 1793. Two pieces in the next *Weekly Museum* (New York), 19 October 1793, picked up on the "chickens" theme: "A letter from One of Mother Cary's Chickens" and "NEW-YORK, October 19."

205 **"atrocious crime":** "Bennington, Oct. 25," *Vermont Gazette* (Bennington), 25 October 1793.

205 **Harison decamped for Albany:** Richard Harison to Frances Harison, Albany, 15 October 1793, Ms Coll Harison, Columbia Rare Book and Manuscript Library.

205 **uncharacteristically forceful letter:** Given the date of Richard Harison's response and the schedule of the mail stages, this letter must have been posted by Wednesday (16 October 1793) at 9:00 p.m., when the mail for Albany closed (*Directory for 1793*, 237).

205 **fashionable dresser:** Benjamin Trott, *Frances Duncan Ludlow Harison*, portrait miniature, ca. 1795–1797, Butler Library, Columbia University, 81.15.2 CU (Harison gift).

205 **"chattering about Furniture":** Ene Sirvet, "The District Attorney and His Family: The Harisons of New York in the Eighteenth Century," *Columbia Library Columns* 32, no. 3 (May 1983): 14–22.

206 **"which could possibly be avoided":** Richard Harison to Frances Ludlow Harison, Albany, 20 October 1793, Ms Coll Harison, Columbia Rare Book and Manuscript Library.

206 **to accept his wife's apology:** Richard Harison to Frances Ludlow Harison, Albany, 27 October 1793, Ms Coll Harison, Columbia Rare Book and Manuscript Library.

206 **"Despotism of the Petticoat":** John Adams to Abigail Adams, 14 April 1776, *Adams Family Correspondence*, vol. 1 (Cambridge, MA: Belknap Press, 1963), 382.

207 **vigilante attacks on brothels:** On a case of seduction: *The Diary of Hannah Callender Sansom: Sense and Sensibility in the Age of the American Revolution*, ed. Susan E. Klepp and Karin A. Wulf (Ithaca, NY: Cornell University Press, 2010), 276. On prostitution and brothel riots: *Diary of Elizabeth Drinker*, ed. Elaine Forman Crane (Boston: Northeastern University Press, 1991), 3:1334 (25 August 1800); Drinker also discusses the illegitimate pregnancy of her servant Sally Brant: 1:581 (11 August 1794), 1:584 (20 August 1794), 2:808 (2 June 1796).

207 **a pious warning:** A good introduction to scholarship on the sexual politics of seduction stories are Cathy N. Davidson's reflections in *Revolution and the Word: The Rise of the Novel in America*, expanded ed. (New York: Oxford University Press, 2004), 29–38.

207 **"rights of women":** Rosemarie Zagarri, *Revolutionary Backlash: Women and Politics in the Early American Republic* (Philadelphia: University of Pennsylvania Press, 2007), 1–7, 37–45. Advertisements: *New-York Daily Gazette*, 25 March 1793 (Berry, Rogers, and Berry); *Daily Advertiser*, 10 May 1793 (James Rivington).

207 **"right of scolding":** "Rights Of Women," *Diary* (New York), 13 February 1792.

207 **patriarchal household governance:** *Weekly Museum* (New York), 16 March 1793.

207 ***Wrongs of Woman*:** Mary Wollstonecraft, *Maria: or The Wrongs of Woman*, ed. Anne K. Mellor (New York: W. W. Norton & Company, 1975).

208 **"spotless reputation":** Justitia, "FOR THE DIARY," *Diary* (New York), 18 October 1793; reprinted *Federal Gazette* (Philadelphia), 22 October 1793.

208 **"tumult among the lower classes":** Candidus, "FOR THE DIARY," *Diary* (New York), 21 October 1793; Civis, "FOR THE DIARY," *Diary* (New York), 21 October 1793.

209 **"sufficient correction":** Justitia, "FOR THE DIARY," *Diary* (New York), 23 October 1793.

209 **rational thought and self-control:** Ruth R. Bloch, "The Gendered Meanings of Virtue in Revolutionary America," *Signs* 13, no. 1 (Autumn 1987), 37–58.

209 **sex and politics:** Justitius, "FOR THE DIARY," 22 October, *Diary* (New York), 24 October 1793.

209 **challenging Justitius to a duel:** R, "Citizen Printers," *Diary* (New York), 25 October 1793, 2 (critiquing Civis and Candidus). Unsigned note (clearly in the voice of Justitia) responding to Justitius: *Diary* (New York), 25 October 1793.

210 **"NO NATURAL DIFFERENCE":** "The Fragment," *Columbian Gazetteer* (New York), 4 November 1793; reprinted as "The Rights of Women, a Fragment": *American Apollo* (Boston), 15 November 1793; *Impartial Herald* (Newburyport, MA), 22 November 1793.

210 **Harry Bedlow himself:** Maria, "For the WEEKLY MUSEUM," 22 October 1793, *Weekly Museum* (NewYork), 26 October 1793.

211 **frightened into better behavior:** *American Mercury* (Hartford), 4 November 1793. A riff on Mother Carey's imagined exposé: *Columbian Gazetteer* (New York), 14 November 1793.

211 **fictional Moll Placket-Hole:** *Hilliad Magna. Being the Life and Adventures of Moll Placket-Hole* ([Philadelphia]: Anthony Armbruster, 1765), 7.

211 **"REPORT OF THE LATE TRIAL":** *Columbian Gazetteer* (New York), 4 November 1793.

212 **few accounts of criminal trials:** For a list of early American trial reports, see Wilfred J. Ritz, *American Judicial Proceedings First Printed before 1801: An Analytical Bibliography* (Westport, CT: Greenwood Press, 1984).

212 **Old Bailey, routinely produced them:** On American trial reports and English precedents: Daniel Cohen, *Pillars of Salt, Monuments of Grace: New England Crime Literature and the Origins of American Popular Culture* (New York: Oxford University Press, 1993), 26–31.

212 **"a fair and unbiased statement":** Wyche, *Report*, 62.

212 **come to their own conclusions:** Cohen, *Pillars of Salt*, 26–31.

212 **five other reports:** For an incisive analysis of this cluster of reports, see Daniel A. Cohen, "Pillars of Salt: The Transformation of New England Crime Literature, 1674–1860" (PhD diss., Brandeis University, 1988), 342–90.

212 **London's high court:** Anna Clark, *Women's Silence, Men's Violence: Sexual Assault in England, 1770–1845* (New York: Pandora, 1987), 75.

213 **"hadn't even been paid":** Richard Harison to William Bedlow, 2 December 1793, in Letterbooks and catalog, 1790–1835, Mss Col. BV Harison, Richard, NYHS.

213 **"all fudge":** Decus, "For the DIARY," *Diary* (New York), 11 November 1793.

213 **extended newspaper debate:** The theme of class resentment and hostility to lawyers was amplified in a follow-up to Inquisitive's "Querries": "*For the* WEEKLY MUSEUM," *Weekly Museum* (New York), 19 October 1793.

214 **some repetitive parts:** *Report*, 6 (Saywer testimony omitted), 46 (repetition in defense arguments omitted); 49 (Kent's rendering of the familiar story of Lucretia omitted).

214 **what can be verified:** The identities of the witnesses and the order in which they appeared are, for example, largely the same in the CO&T MB and Wyche's *Report*.

214 **"mature age of several":** Richard Harison, John Cozine, Robert Troup, and Brockholst Livingston, "FOR THE DIARY," *Diary* (New York), 7 November 1793; reprinted: *Daily Advertiser* (New York), 11 November 1793; *Columbian Gazetteer* (New York), 14 November 1793.

214 **"no character themselves":** ONE OF THE HIGHER CLASS, "FOR THE DIARY," *Diary* (New York), 9 November 1793; reprinted: *Columbian Gazetteer* (New York), 14 November 1793 (preceded by the reprint of the four lawyers' letter and followed by a reprint of the Justice piece cited below). The quoted statement does not appear in Wyche's account of Cozine's closing, but does echo language in Troup's—

either because Wyche omitted it as repetitious or because One of the Higher Class confused the two speakers.

215 **"extreme anger"**: Decus, "For the DIARY," *Diary* (New York), 11 November 1793.

215 **even more "indecent" in court:** Justice, "For the Diary," *Diary* (New York), 9 November 1793; reprinted: *Columbian Gazetteer* (New York), 14 November 1793.

216 **"against the conduct of Bedlow"**: A. R., "For the Diary," *Diary* (New York), 17 December 1793.

216 **"hell enflamed ravisher"**: "Bennington, October 25," *Vermont Gazette*; reprinted: *Farmer's Journal* (Rutland, VT), 4 November 1793. This sensational account was followed in same issue of the *Vermont Gazette* with a more accurate report: "Extract of a letter from Newyork, dated 20 October to the Editor."

216 **"it should by foul"**: "Extract of a letter from Newyork to the editor, dated October 27," *Vermont Gazette* (Bennington), 8 November 1793; reprinted: *Federal Spy* (Springfield, MA), 3 December 1793; *Spooner's Vermont Journal* (Windsor), 9 December 1793.

217 **"to advocate the cause of infamy"**: On his visit to New York: John Adams to Abigail Adams, New York, 28 November 1793, *Adams Family Correspondence*, 9:459. On the Bedlow trial and riots: Charles Adams to John Adams, New York, 6 December 1793, *Adams Family Correspondence*, 9:462–64; Charles Adams to John Adams, New York, 19 December 1793, *Adams Family Correspondence*, 9:475.

217 **"disorderly house"**: John Adams to Abigail Adams, 22 December 1793, Philadelphia, *Adams Family Correspondence*, 9:481–82.

217 **"Mother Cary the old Bedlam"**: John Adams to Abigail Adams, Philadelphia, 15 December 1793, *Adams Family Correspondence*, 9:472–73.

218 **rumbles of thunder:** Pintard, 20 October 1793, Diary and Garden Calendar. Neither Webster (Richard Rollins, ed., *The Autobiographies of Noah Webster: From the Letters and Essays, Memoir, and Diary* [Columbia, SC: University of South Carolina Press], 314) nor *Anderson's Diary* commented on the weather that day.

218 **hanged herself:** "Extract of a letter from Newyork, dated Oct. 27," *Vermont Gazette* (Bennington), 8 November 1793; reprinted: *Federal Spy* (Springfield, MA), 3 December 1793; *Spooner's Vermont Journal* (Windsor), 9 December 1793; *New Hampshire Journal* (Walpole), 22 November 1793. On the network that connected *Vermont Gazette* editor Anthony Haswell to these other these newspapers, see Joseph M. Adelman, *Revolutionary Networks: The Business and Politics of Printing the News, 1763–1789* (Baltimore: Johns Hopkins University Press, 2019), 177–80.

CHAPTER 10: SEDUCTION

219 **"all that can form her happiness"**: W[illiam] W[yche], "The Fragment," *Columbian Gazetteer* (New York), 19 December 1793.

219 **"grief and vexation"**: SCJ MB1797–1800E: 51 (25 July 1797).

219 **rarely mentioned in local newspapers:** On the cultural history of suicide, see Richard Bell, *We Shall Be No More: Suicide and Self-Government in the Newly United States* (Cambridge, MA: Harvard University Press, 2012), esp. 3–5 (on an increase in reporting of suicides in Early Republic newspapers). My less systematic review of New York newspapers in the early 1790s suggests that local suicides were rarely reported by name and that attempted suicides were reported even less frequently. For example, the *New-York Journal* (14 September 1793) named William Brown after he drowned himself in Charleston, South Carolina, but two days later the *Diary* (New York) (16 September 1793) did not name a local man who drowned himself (see also *Daily Advertiser* [New York], 17 September 1793).

219 **"Extract of a letter from Newyork"**: *Vermont Gazette*, 8 November 1793; reprinted: *New Hampshire Journal* (Walpole), 22 November 1793; *Federal Spy* (Springfield, MA), 3 December 1793; *Spooner's Vermont Journal* (Windsor), 9 December 1793.

220 **young lady's suicide attempt:** Editor Anthony Haswell published extracts of three letters from this correspondent, beginning with "Extract of a Letter from Newyork, dated October 3, to the editor," *Vermont Gazette* (Bennington), 11 October 1793. He also referred to a fourth letter "from Newyork," dated 1 November: *Vermont Gazette* (Bennington), 15 November 1793.

220 **one of the most lethal:** A useful introduction to recent scholarship on the suicide "gender paradox" is Aislinné Freeman et al., "A Cross-National Study on Gender Differences in Suicide Intent," *British Journal of Psychiatry* 17, 234 (2017). More broadly, see Thomas Joiner, *Why People Die by Suicide* (Cambridge, MA: Harvard University Press, 2005).

221 **dizzying, disorienting blow:** Judith Lewis Herman, *Trauma and Recovery: The Aftermath of Violence* (New York: Basic Books, 1992), 50 (rape and suicide risk), 51–52 (safety and self-doubt), 57–58 (physical, psychological, moral violation), 60–61 (adolescents). More recent studies include Craig J. Bryan, Mary McNaugton-Cassill, Augustine Osman, and Ann Marie Hernandez, "The Associations of Physical and Sexual Assault with Suicide Risk in Nonclinical Military and Undergraduate Samples," *Suicide and Life-Threatening Behavior* 43, no. 2 (April 2013): 223–34.

221 **"you don't want to be yourself":** Mary Ann Vecchio, quoted in Patricia McCormick, "The Girl in the Kent State Photo," *Washington Post Magazine*, 19 April 2021.

221 **two powerful emotions:** Herman's assessment of resilience among survivors of traumatic events (*Trauma and Recovery*, 58–59) is consistent with Joiner's argument that the key components of suicidality are "burdensomeness" and "nonbelongingness" (*Why People Die by Suicide*).

221 **Callanan pursued him doggedly:** MC MB1793–1794, 28 November 1793: 268 (Hughes: *Henry Bedlow ads. John Callanan*), 272 (Riggs: *John Callanan v. Henry Bedlow*), 273 (Riggs: *John Callanan ads. Henry Bedlow*).

222 **still had not returned:** A. R., "For the Diary," *Diary* (New York), 17 December 1793.

222 **which, at £3.15.3, represented:** *Henry Bedlow v. John Callahan*, MC Judgments 1793#21, filed 24 December 1793.

222 **what he was now owed:** MC MB1793–1794: 291 (19 December 1793, Riggs: *John Callanan ads. Henry Bedlow*), 291–292 (19 December 1793, Riggs: *Marinus Willett* [sheriff] *v. William Bedlow*).

222 **force Bedlow to pay:** MC MB1793–1794: 310 (16 January 1794, Riggs: *Marinus Willett v. Henry Bedlow*); 357 (20 March 1794, Riggs: *John Callanan (alias Callihan) ads. Henry Bedlow*).

222 **"seduction of the Prosecutrix":** *Report*, 45 (Harison), 28 (Livingston), 36 (Troup).

223 **complex legal maneuver:** SCJ MB1794E: 44 (25 January 1794, Riggs: *John Callanan v. Henry Bedlow*). The mayor, recorder, and aldermen returned a writ of habeus corpus; SCJ authorized a writ of procedendo transferring the case to their jurisdiction.

223 **unspecified "irregularity":** MC MB1793–1794: 268 (28 November 1793, Hughes: *Henry Bedlow ads. John Callanan*).

223 **formal requirements and legal fictions:** On the legal history of seduction suits in the Early Republic and the limits of civil recourse for rape survivors, see Lea VanderVelde, "The Legal Ways of Seduction," *Stanford Law Review* 48, no. 4 (April 1996): 817–901; and Estelle Freedman, *Redefining Rape: Sexual Violence in the Era of Suffrage and Segregation* (Cambridge, MA: Harvard University Press, 2013), 33–51. For a trenchant analysis of seduction suits in light of broader cultural changes, see Patricia Cline Cohen, "Public and Print Cultures of Sex in the Long Nineteenth Century," in *The Oxford Handbook of American Women's and Gender History*, ed. Ellen Hartigan-O'Connor and Lisa G. Materson (New York: Oxford University Press, 2018) 195–216.

224 **meaningful restitution:** VanderVelde, "Legal Ways of Seduction," emphasizes the lack of established legal traditions to support civil claims by rape survivors against their assailants in this period.

224 **was also prosecuted for rape:** For New York cases, I cross-checked the names of defendants and survivors in my database of New York Sexual Assault Prosecutions, 1734–1820, against the names of parties to civil suits in the card files and electronic indices of file papers at the NYCC-DOR (now at the NYSA). For New Jersey, I used the NJSCCF collection to cross-check those involved in seduction and breach-of-promise suits against accused sexual assailants; see Appendix for details. VanderVelde, "Legal Ways of Seduction," 842, notes that the earliest New York case she was able to identify in which a woman recovered damages against her assailant in a rape-like attack was in 1859.

224 **"five thousand Pounds":** *John Callanan v. Henry Bedlow*, SCJ PR P-101-A-1, filed 13 January 1795.

225 **mothers or brothers:** VanderVelde, "Legal Ways of Seduction," 879–83.

226 *Treatise on the Practice:* On Wyche's treatise, see Robert A. Emery, "William Wyche," *Law Library Journal* 93, no. 3 (Summer 2001): 469, 471–73.

226 **"her consent is as nothing":** William Wyche, *A treatise on the practice of the Supreme Court of Judicature of the State of New-York in civil actions* (New York: T. and J. Swords, 1794), 24–25.

226 **became pregnant and gave birth:** Except for Anne VanHorn, all New Jersey seduction cases involved women impregnated by their seducers; see Appendix, Table 2.

227 **Sylvia Patterson:** *The Trial of Captain James Dunn, for an Assault with Intent to Seduce Sylvia Patterson, A Black Woman* (New York, 1809). For analysis of this case, see Sharon Block, *Rape and Sexual Power in Early America* (Chapel Hill: University of North Carolina Press, 2003), 178–79, 183.

227 **a fictive sexual assault:** *William VanHorn v. Alpheus Freeman*, 1794–1798, NJSCCF #42684. For analysis of this case, see VanderVelde, "Legal Ways of Seduction," 840–42.

227 **elude responsibility altogether:** On the "rape defense against seduction," see VanderVelde, "Legal Ways of Seduction," 862–84.

228 **"would otherwise be remediless":** For analysis of this case, see VanderVelde, "Legal Ways of Seduction," 840–42; quote, 841. A detailed report of *Vanhorn v. Freeman* (1794): William Halsted, *Reports of Cases Argued and Determined in the Supreme Court of Judicature of the State of New Jersey*, 3rd ed. (Jersey City: Frederick D. Linn, 1886), 1:325–330.

228 **only £60 plus costs:** *Thomas Atkinson v. Reuben Hains*, 1746, NJSCCF #598 (claim £200, award £60). In my review of seduction suits in NJSCCF prior to 1789, claims ranged from £100 to £500; half of them were for £200. Most of these records do not indicate verdicts or awards. Note that figures in New Jersey cases are given in local currency; around 1790, New Jersey pounds were worth about 9 percent more than New York pounds.

228 **The Coryells won both cases:** *Cornelius Coryell v. John Coolback* (seduction of his daughter Eleanor, who became pregnant). ca. 1789–91, NJSCCF #6250 (award £75); *Eleanor Coryell v. John Coolback* (breach of promise to marry) ca. 1789, NJSCCF #6397 (claim £1,000, award £77).

229 **followed the same pattern:** *Cornelius Stout v. Thomas Prall*, 1789–1790, NJSCCF #3744 (claim £300, award £100); his daughter filed her own suit, presumably for breach of promise, *Joanna Stout v. Thomas Prall* (unspecified trespass), ca. 1790, NJSCCF #37446 (claim and award not indicated). See also *William Lawrence v. Samuel Holmes*, 1791–1793, NJSCCF #22507 (claim £500, award not indicated); and *Joseph Baker v. Jacob Hutchinson*, 1792–1793, NJSCCF #3223 (claim £300, including childbirth-related expenses of £100; award not indicated).

229 **until the VanHorn case:** *William VanHorn v. Alpheus Freeman*, 1792–1798, NJSCCF #42684.

229 **horror of injured innocence:** VanderVelde makes a related argument about the new emphasis on chastity and "skyrocketing" damage awards in the mid-nineteenth century: "Legal Ways of Seduction," 883–91.

229 **merger doctrine provided:** VanderVelde, "Legal Ways of Seduction," 848–50.

230 **Around noon:** SCJ MB1794: 244–46 (23 April 1794); the court convened at 11 a.m. and the Callanan lawsuit was the eighth matter heard.

230 **was "not Guilty":** *Henry Bedlow ads. John Callanan*, plea of James Hughes, attorney for the defendant, filed 14 April 1794, SCJ PL C-246.

230 **ten days to prepare:** *John Callanan v. Henry Bedlow*, judgment roll, filed 13 January 1795, SCJ PR P-101-A-1.

231 **to have the trial delayed:** Notice of James M. Hughes to Caleb S. Riggs, 21 Apr. 1794; affidavit of Henry Bedlow, 21 Apr. 1794; deposition of Robert Bogardus, 23 Apr. 1794; in *Henry Bedlow ads. John Callanan*, SCJ PL C-246.

231 **John Beekman:** William Prowse Allsee, baptism, 16 May 1750, Melcomb-Regis (England), Composite Register, 1750–1775, PE-MCR/RE/1/7, Dorset History Center, UK. Allsee's naturalization: MC MB1793–1794: 185 (3 September 1793); Affidavit of John Beekman, druggist, filed 3 September 1793, no. 12, Naturalization Petitions, 1792–1794, microfilm roll 198, NYCC-DOR. On Allsee's family life, see the records of his divorce case: *William Allsee v. Elizabeth Allsee, action for divorce*, New York Court of Chancery, filed 13 February 1798, NYSA; reproduced in Mary-Jo Kline, ed., *The Papers of Aaron Burr, 1756–1836*, microfilm ed. (Glen Rock, NJ, 1978), NYCh Case 181. *Directory for 1794*: "William Alsee, ship-carpenter, 133 Cherry-Street."

231 **Bunce Island:** Among vessels recently cleared from New York was "Sch[ooner] Esther & Eliza, [Captain] Alsee, [bound for the] Coast of Africa," *Daily Advertiser* (New York), 10 October 1793. See voyage 25555, The Trans-Atlantic Slave Trade Database, v. 2.2.13, www.slavevoyages.org/voyage/database.

231 **a handful of attempts:** A search of the Trans-Atlantic Slave Trade Database (www.slavevoyages.org) reveals a total of seven slaving voyages from New York between 1784 and 1800.

232 **put the trial off:** SCJ MB1794: 246 (23 April 1794, Hughes).

232 **Captain Allsee did not:** "William Alsee, schooner Esther, [arrived] from St. Kitts," *New-York Journal*, 25 June 1794.

232 **heard news of Mother Carey:** *Directory for 1794*: "Carey, widow, Corlaer's-Hook." By July, the Careys had moved to Philadelphia: *Hardie Directory of Philadelphia for 1794* (2d ed.), "Carey James, dealer, 46, George Street." According to his advertisements, Hardie collected names for this second edition of the directory between 24 July 1794 (*Philadelphia Gazette*, 28 July 1794) and the end of August (*Philadelphia Gazette*, 25 August 1794).

232 **a mere £2.10:** *Peter Sawyer, by his guardian John Callahan v. Robert Eaton*, MC Judgments 1794#172, filed 20 September 1794. *Directory for 1794*: Eaton, Robert, pilot, 43 Cliff Street.

233 **"a violent storm threatening":** *Alexander Anderson's New York City Diary, 1793–1799*, ed. Jane R. Pomeroy, 2 vols. (New Castle, DE: Oak Knoll Press, 2014), 20 September 1794.

233 **unaware of the seduction suit:** John Barent Johnson (who was friends with several of both Callanan's and Bedlow's attorneys) made no mention of the matter: 29 September 1794, Diary, 1787–1803, vol. 8, Columbiana MS 42, Columbia University Columbia University. Nor did *Anderson's Diary*, 29 September 1794.

233 **called the seduction suit to trial:** My account of this trial is based on the surviving judgment record for this case, *John Callanan v. Henry Bedlow*, filed 13 January 1795, SJC PR P-101-A-1, and records of subsequent seduction suits in New York City. Early seduction trial reports include: *The Trial of Captain James Dunn* (New York, 1809); *Report of the Trial of Ann Saffen versus Edward Seaman, for seduction* (New York: Grattan and Banks, 1818); *Important Trial for Seduction: In the Superior Court of N. York . . . Nancy Van Haun v. Silas E. Burrows, on Wednesday 27th and Thursday 28 November 1833* (New York, 1833); and William B. Chittenden and Henry Godfrey Wheeler, *Report on the Second Trial of Silas E. Burrows: for the alleged seduction of Mary Carew, in the Superior Court of the City of New York* (New York: J. W. Bell, 1834).

Early compilations of reported cases included more or less detailed summaries of evidence and arguments. In George Caines, *New-York Term Reports: Cases of that State*, 2nd. ed. (New York: Isaac Riley, 1814), see *Seagar v. Sligerland*, New York, November 1804, 2:219–20; and *Akerley v. Haines*, Albany, February 1805, 2:292–93. In William Johnson, *Reports of Cases Argued and Determined in the Supreme Court . . . of New York* (New York, 1807–1823), see *Foster v. Scoffield*, New York, May 1806, 1:297–99; *Martin v. Payne*, New York, October 1812, 9:387–91; *Nichelson v. Stryker*, Albany, January 1813, 10:115–17. In John Anthon, *The Law of Nisi Prius: Being Reports of Cases Determined . . . in the Supreme Court of . . . New York [1807–1816]*, 2nd ed. (New York, 1883), see *Fletcher v. Randall*, after October term 1816, 267–68; see also *Mary Fletcher v. George Randall*, SCJ LJ 1808-R-12. In Esek Cowan, *Report of Cases Argued and Determined in the Supreme Court . . . of New-York* (Albany, 1824–1830), see *Moran v. Dawes*, New York, May 1825, 4:412–15; and *Sargent v. _____*, Albany, October 1825, 5:106–23. In John L. Wendell, *Reports of Cases Argued and Determined in the Supreme Court . . . of New York* (Albany, 1828–1841), see *Millar ads. Thompson*, Albany, October 1828, 2:447–540; *Clark v. Fitch*, New York, May 1829, 2:459–61; *Gillet v. Mead*, New York, May 1831, 7:193–94; *Stiles v. Tilford*, New York, May 1833, 10:339–41; and *Hewit v. Prime*, New York, May 1839, 21:79–83.

233 **Lanah Sawyer knew:** In the New York cases cited above, testimony of the seduced woman was usually at the center of trial; for two exceptions, see *The hypocrite unmask'd. Trial and conviction of John Baker, a Methodist teacher, of this city, for seducing Miss Ann Burns, under a promise of marriage* (New York, 1798) and *The Trial of Captain James Dunn* (New York, 1809).

233 **court's archive:** The minutes for this trial are no longer extant. The surviving SJC CC MB1784–1796 is a copy made in February 1821—by which point all of the minutes for 1794 were already missing. Moreover, the NYCC-DOR's mid-twentieth-century card index for the SCJ PR collection (now record series JN120, NYSA) refers to a now-missing "Venire & jury panel" for this case, SCJ PR P-246-D-1.

234 **"too much affected":** *Report of the trial of Ann Saffen versus Edward Seaman, for seduction* (New-York: Grattan and Banks, 1818), 5 (editor's comment).

234 **"would do well by me":** *Ann Saffen versus Edward Seaman*, 5–12 (Catharine Saffen); quotes 5 ("honourable"), 6 ("do well").

234 **unmarried and ruined:** *Ann Saffen versus Edward Seaman*, 4 (Saffen's attorney).

234 **"would be too severe":** *Ann Saffen versus Edward Seaman*, 54 (judge's charge).

235 **aware of the relationship:** In two cases from the early 1790s, *Stout v. Prall* (37442 NJSCCF) and *Lawrence v. Holmes* (22507 NJSCCF), the father accused the defendant of having sex with his daughter, in his house, at various times over a period of many months.

236 **defendant almost always lost:** My samples of NJSCCF (which generally don't indicate outcomes) and reported New York cases (most often appeals) do not support a systematic analysis of patterns in outcomes, but do support VanderVelde's observation that "the reported cases suggest an overwhelming number of jury verdicts for the plaintiffs" ("Legal Ways of Seduction," 868 n246).

236 **"reasonable doubt" standard:** John H. Langbein, *Origins of Adversary Criminal Trial* (New York: Oxford University Press, 2003), 261–66.

236 **prone to acquit:** Block, *Rape and Sexual Power*, 143–44, finds that shifting to from capital punishment to prison terms did result in a somewhat higher rate of sexual assault convictions for white men (31 percent before 1800, 42 percent between 1800 and 1820), but that these rates remained about half the conviction rate for Black men (192 n39). See also Freedman, *Redefining Rape*, 12–32.

236 **"great Infamy and disgrace":** Declaration of William Lawrence, November Term 1792, in *Lawrence v. Holmes*, 22507, NJSCCF.

236 **woman's lost innocence:** VanderVelde, "Legal Ways of Seduction," 869–70.

236 **"lily of the valley"**: Cohen, "Public and Print Cultures of Sex," at note 14 ("lilly" in original).

237 **"avengers of violated chastity"**: *Ann Saffen versus Edward Seaman*, 4.

237 **"nocturnal Battery walks"**: A. R., "For the Diary," *Diary* (New York), 17 December 1793, 2 ("battery" capitalized).

238 **restitution and accountability:** Freedman, *Redefining Rape*, 33–51; Cohen, "Public and Print Cultures of Sex." VanderVelde, "Legal Ways of Seduction," 885, emphasizes a shift in the nineteenth century toward an emphasis on chastity rather than pregnancy.

238 **on their own:** Christine Stansell, *City of Women: Sex and Class in New York, 1798–1860* (New York: Alfred A. Knopf, 1986), 11–18, 20–30, 83–89; Marybeth Hamilton Arnold, "'The Life of a Citizen in the Hands of a Woman': Sexual Assault in New York City, 1790–1820," in *Passion and Power: Sexuality in History*, ed. Kathy Peiss and Christina Simmons (Philadelphia: Temple University Press, 1989).

238 **nurturing, maternal creatures:** On the idealization of (middle-class white) women in America, foundational studies include Nancy F. Cott, "Passionlessness: An Interpretation of Victorian Sexual Ideology, 1790–1850," *Signs* 4, no. 2 (Winter 1978): 219–36, and Linda K. Kerber, *Women of the Republic: Intellect and Ideology in Revolutionary America* (Chapel Hill: University of North Carolina Press, 1980).

239 **damages award of $9,000:** *Sarah Moran v. William Dawes* (for seduction of her daughter, Jane Moran), filed 21 May 1825, SCJ LJ 1825-D-46; for Moran's efforts to collect this judgment, see *Sarah Moran v. William Dawes*, filed 4 February 1825, Chancery Court files, BM-M-1950, both reviewed at NYCC-DOR. See also *Moran v. Dawes*, May 1825, in Cowan, *Report of Cases*, 4:412–15. For newspaper coverage of this case, see Cohen, "Public and Print Cultures of Sex," at note 14. There was also a parallel suit for breach of promise: *Jane Moran v. William Dawes*, October 1824, SCJ PL M-1705 and M-706 (neither found at the NYCC-DOR on May 25, 2015).

239 **any "real" service at all:** Quote: *Clark v. Fitch*, May 1829, in Wendell, *Reports*, 2:460–62. This case also resulted in a protracted battle to recover the judgment: *Ferdinand Clark and James Norman v. Thomas Fitch*, filed 10 July 1838, judgment record 1838-C-279, Superior Court, NYCC-DOR. On the underlying trend, see VanderVelde, "Legal Ways of Seduction," 883–91, and Freedman, *Redefining Rape*, 33–51.

239 **sum of "ONE dollar":** *The Trial of Captain James Dunn* (New York, 1809), 18.

239 **openly racist newspaper:** *National Advocate* (New York), 24 February 1825; *Daily Advertiser* (New York), 24 February 1825; *Statesman* (New York), 25 February 1825 ("*dingy* lass").

239 **not-guilty verdict:** *Ann Saffen versus Edward Seaman*, 54.

239 **calculations of a woman's worth:** On this issue, I'm indebted to conversations and correspondence with Kathleen M. Brown and Patricia Cline Cohen.

240 **standard was unrealistic:** For a revealing analysis of New York sexual assault indictment records, ca. 1790–1820, see Arnold, "'The Life of a Citizen in the Hands of a Woman.'"

240 **October 23, 1794:** SCJ MB1794E: 614 (23 October 1794, Riggs).

241 **marked it "filed":** *John Callanan v. Henry Bedlow*, judgment roll, filed 13 January 1795, SCJ PR P-101-A-1.

CHAPTER 11: RECOVERY

243 **"Your affectionate friend":** This letter was appended to Henry Bedlow to Messrs. Power and Southwick, Poughkeepsie, 27 September 1798, *Poughkeepsie* (New York) *Journal*, 2 October 1798.

243 **modern kitchen shears:** Two iron keys, ca. 1730–1780, the larger 8.5 x 2.5 in, reportedly used in "New Gaol" (debtors' prison), 1880.15ab, NYHS.

243 **an ignominious pauper's grave:** Bruce H. Mann's *Republic of Debtors: Bankruptcy in the Age of American Independence* (Cambridge, MA: Harvard University Press, 2002),

includes a brilliant analysis of New York's debtors' prison in the 1790s (78–107, 147–65). For New York laws, see: "An Act for the Relief of Debtors, with Respect to the Imprisonment of their Persons," 12th session, ch. 23, *Laws of the state of New-York*, 2 vols. (New York: 1789), 2:408–17; amended to allow debtors owing more than £1,000 to petition for release after a year, 14th session, ch. 29, *Laws of the State of New York. Fourteenth Session* (New York: 1791), 20.

243 **£1 a month:** *MCC 1784–1831*, 2:224 (14 March 1796, subsistence increased to 1s per day).

244 **elicited shock and horror:** Mann, *Republic of Debtors*, 87 (haunted rumor), 96–98 (1798 escape).

244 **half a dozen like it:** Callanan's house was assessed at £260 (1793 Tax Records, ward 3, page 20).

244 **surviving rent books:** Mary McCrea, Rent Book, 1785–1816, box 13, env. 3, Duyck-inck Family Papers, SC15251, NYSL.

244 **full amount he was owed:** Mann, *Republic of Debtors*, 18–33.

245 **execution of his office:** SCJ MB1795E: 100 (30 January 1795, *People v. John W. Jolson, Benjamin Haskins and John DeGruche, and Henry Bedlow* for an assault and battery on Henry Burstell, a constable in the execution of his duty), 172 (31 January 1795, under "Riggs," return of Callanan's writ of *capias ad satisfaciendum* against Bedlow). Hays, "General List," does not list an outcome for the assault prosecution against Bedlow, indicating that the charges were ultimately dropped.

245 **getting the suit quashed:** *John Callanan ads. Henry Bedlow*, MC Judgments 1795#11 (suit initiated 3 February 1795, judgment signed and filed 23 July 1795); MC Docket of Judgments, 1786–1796, 6: "Bedlow Henry ads. John Callanan, £4.2.9, Evertson" (23 July 1795).

245 **"well and truly paid":** John Young (saddler) and Margaret Young (his wife) to John Callanan (pilot), 2 February 1795, for £1,000 (NY) to them paid; recorded 28 March 1816, NYC Conveyances 115:95; BIRC block 76, lot 4. See also Jane Callanan to William and Gerardus Post, recorded 28 March 1816, NYC Conveyances 115:97.

246 **possibility of public disclosure:** Ron Chernow, *Alexander Hamilton* (New York: Penguin Books, 2004), 364–70.

246 **scarred by the experience:** Mann, *Republic of Debtors*, 78, 79–80 (quote); see also 286 n5.

247 **surmounted by a cupola:** Mann, *Republic of Debtors*, 86–89.

248 **including liquor and prostitutes:** Mann, *Republic of Debtors*, 90 (prostitutes and liquor in Philadelphia's debtors' prison); 99–102 (wealthy debtors).

248 **visitors required appointments:** Mann, *Republic of Debtors*, 101–2.

248 **improvised, or imagined, background:** Elizabeth Mankin Kornhauser, *Ralph Earl: The Face of the Young Republic* (New Haven, CT: Yale University Press, 1991). The portrait of John Cozine (ca. 1787) is in a private collection; I am grateful to its owner for sharing a photograph.

248 *Forlorn Hope*: Most surviving issues are held by the NYHS. James M. Morris, "Journalism Behind Bars," *The Quarterly Journal of the Library of Congress* 40, no. 2 (Spring 1983), 150–61.

248 **throw off the roof and climb down:** In Debtors' Prison Papers, William Duer Papers, NYHS: Charge against Timothy Wales, 18 May 1796, no. 32, fol. 39 (a case involving smuggled liquor); list of demands to be put to prison keeper Thomas Hazard and his responses, 7 March 1796, no. 72, fol. 39 (tools for escape).

249 **"York Castle":** For example, see election meeting minutes, Middle Hall, York Castle, 10 October 1796, fol. 39, Debtors' Prison Papers.

249 **high-ranking British nobleman:** Henry Bedlow was one of two judges in the first extant record of the debtors'-prison court: *Harman v. Jones*, Minutes of the Court, 17–18 July 1795, no. 2, fol. 39, Debtors' Prison Papers.

249 **"in every civilized Society"**: Complaint of Margaret Trean against Charles Ellison, preferred by Attorney General William Mumford, 15 August 1795, no. 33, fol. 39, Debtors' Prison Papers.

249 **with her assets intact**: Charges against Haskins (re: harms to Margaret Trean), 23–24 July 1795, no. 10, fol. 39, Debtors' Prison Papers; see also the subsequent document labeled "Sundry Charges against Haskins."

250 **"Conceive to be decreasing rapidly"**: "Judges Order for Calling a Court to Consult on the Means of regaining Lost Priviledges," 18 November 1795, no. 50, fol. 39, Debtors' Prison Papers.

250 **informers were anathema**: Charge against Timothy Wales, 18 May 1796, no. 32, fol. 39, Debtors' Prison Papers.

250 **his attorney Alexander Hamilton**: "An Act for giving Relief in Cases of Insolvency" (passed 21 March 1788), in *Laws of the state of New-York . . . from the first to the twelfth session, inclusive*, 2 vols. (New-York: Hugh Gaine, 1789), Session 11, chapter 92, 2: 375–83; "An ACT for the Relief of Debtors" (13 February 1789), in *Laws of the state of New-York*, Session 12, chapter 23, 2:408–17 and 1791 revision.

251 **published in the city's newspapers**: William Bedlow, petitioning creditor, Notice (insolvency of Henry Bedlow), *Argus* (New York), 28 December 1795. This notice, which was repeated for six weeks, refers to the "insolvent debtor's act" with the 3/4 clause (21 March 1788); not the "imprisonment" of debtors act (13 February 1789, amended 1791). See *Laws of the state of New-York*, Session 11, Ch. 92, section v. (377–78).

251 **"sufficient Cause"**: Quote is from the statute of 21 March 1788; there is no record of this proceeding but the judge's ruling is clear because Bedlow's insolvency did not proceed and he went back to prison.

251 **"upon insolvency Act"**: "The Cash Book of Alexander Hamilton, 1795–1804," in Julius Goebel and Joseph H. Smith, eds., *The Law Practice of Alexander Hamilton*, vol. 5 (New York: Columbia University Press, 1981), 403 (4 February 1796).

251 **gloomier than ever**: I am grateful to archivists Kenneth Cobb at the NYMA and James Folts at the NYSL for searching their collections for materials relating to Bedlow's insolvency, but none were found.

251 **"get[ting] his Liberty"**: List of demands to be put to prison keeper Thomas Hazard and his responses, 7 March 1796.

251 **perhaps a couple of weeks**: This appears to be the only surviving record, other than deeds, that Catharine Bedlow produced.

252 **"Honl. Alexr. Hamilton Esq."**: Catharine Bedlow to Alexander Hamilton, New York, 2 August 1796, Hamilton Papers, Library of Congress; his endorsement on the letter reads "with Helena Sawyers letter." This letter (without the greeting or salutation and misreading "Sayer" as "Soyer") was published in Harold C. Syrett, *The Papers of Alexander Hamilton*, vol. 20 (New York: Columbia University Press, 1974), 289.

253 **on the outskirts of the city**: John Smith Leister to James Carey ("merchant"), 24 July 1794 (recorded 27 September 1794), Deed Book D45:317–18, Philadelphia City Archives. This property was on the west side of George Street between Shippen and Plumb (now the west side of the 700 block of S. American Street).

253 **a narrow ribbon of land**: This property, later owned and occupied by Ann McFall, is listed in the returns for Southwark, West District, Philadelphia: "general list" (book 2, no. 366), "particular lists" (p. 19; "Martin/Morton" to north, "McGuinnes" to south); "Cadwallader Griffith's return of Property sold for the District Tax" (no. 367); 1798 US Direct Tax Lists for Pennsylvania, RG58, M372, NARA.

253 **for her to get by**: Ann Carey, will, 20 May 1796 (signed with mark), proved 19 October 1796, Wills Book 10:501–4, Philadelphia City Archives.

253 **a justice of the peace**: Ann Carey, will, 20 May 1796. Among her legatees were Ann McFall, several single women, her "brother" Richard Glover, and "Mr. [Donald] Frazier Schoolmaster of New York." On women's reading and writing skills, see E. Jenni-

fer Monaghan, *Learning to Read and Write in Colonial America* (Amherst: University of Massachusetts Press, 2005). Carey's executor, Ebenezer Ferguson, was a tradesman who lived on what is now the 200 block of Bainbridge Street (listed as a house carpenter, "61 Shippen St.," in Stephens, *Philadelphia Directory for 1796*): Record Book of Ebenezer Ferguson, Justice of the Peace, Philadelphia, 1799–1800, ID no. 155501037, Post Revolutionary War Papers, 1784–1815, RG 94, NARA.

254 **citizens of the Middle Hall:** Bedlow appeared on the list of voters in the election for judges around 11 October 1796, no. 20, fol. 39, Debtors' Prison Papers.

254 **original jury award: £1,800:** *John Callahan v. William Bedlow*, judgment roll, filed 7 August 1798, SCJ PR P-32-E-7. In his narrative, Callanan claimed that Bedlow owed him $1,200 (about £480 New York currency) in addition to the £450 represented by the note William Bedlow gave Callanan in November 1796, bringing the total debt at that point to about £930—equivalent to about half of the original debt plus accumulated interest.

254 **Bedlow claimed that the deal:** Henry Bedlow to Messrs. Power and Southwick, Poughkeepsie, 27 September 1798.

254 **pay John Callanan £450:** *John Callahan v. William Bedlow*, judgment roll, filed 7 August 1798. £450 was about $1,100. Henry Rutgers's role as a guarantor for the note is indicated by a later legal filing: Henry Rutgers, manucaptor of William Bedlow, ads. John Callanan, rejoinder, filed 10 January 1799, SCJ PL C-939 (microfilm reel 13).

254 **the deal worked:** Henry Bedlow's name does not appear in any of the Debtors' Prison Papers after October 1796.

255 **Mother Carey had died:** Burial of Ann Carey, 19 October 1796, Register of Burials, Christ Church and St. Peter's Church, 1763–1831, 196, in Philadelphia Congregations Early Records, accessed 19 April 2021, https://philadelphiacongregations.org /records/items/show/293.

255 **"for her own Use":** Ann Carey, will, 20 May 1796.

256 **political ally Edward Livingston:** Henry Rutgers to Edward Livingston, New York, 3 February 1797, fol. 13, box 3, Edward Livingston Papers, CO280, Rare Books and Special Collections, Princeton University Library. Later that month, Rutgers noted that he had repaid the money Livingston had advanced to "Mr. Bedlow" and thanked him for his help: Rutgers to Livingston, New York, 24 February 1797, fol. 13, box 3, Edward Livingston Papers.

256 **any more expenses:** Rutgers to Livingston, New York, 20 January 1797, fol. 13, box 3, Edward Livingston Papers.

256 **grand new house:** 1796 Tax Assessment, NYHS: ward 7, p. 3: William Bedlow, Cherry Street, £2,500 real estate, £400 personal estate. *Directory for 1796*: William Bedlow, corner of Cherry and Charlotte (now Pike) Streets. Tax and land records indicate that this was the property on the northwest corner of Cherry and Pike, now a park under the Manhattan Bridge roadway; see BIRC block 254, lots 20–25. In 1793, William Bedlow had been renting a house from Jacamiah Ackerly on the block to the east (BIRC block 255).

256 **at least $4,000:** See SCJ Writ Book, 1797–1799 (JN545, NYSA): 54 (October Term 1797, Cozine: Medcef Eden v. Henry Bedlow Pluras Capias 4000 Dollars) and the following, identical, entry. This dispute seems to have dated back to at least the summer of 1796, when Alexander Hamilton represented William Bedlow in a suit brought by Medcef Eden; see "Law Register of Alexander Hamilton, 1795–1804," in Goebel Jr. and Smith, eds., *Law Practice of Alexander Hamilton*, vol. 5, 62 and 64 n3, 69 and 71 n1. Eden lived on the same block as Lanah's cousin Lucretia Harper (*Directory for 1797*: Eden, Medcef, brewer, 38 Gold Street). This matter may have been settled out of court: Eden died in September 1798; his estate was apparently insolvent, and much litigation ensued.

256 **"solicitous to have your Advise":** William Bedlow to Edward Livingston, New York, 10 April 1797, fol. 13, box 3, Edward Livingston Papers.

256 **"laboured under for four Years":** William Bedlow to Edward Livingston, New York, 2 May 1797, fol. 14, box 3, Edward Livingston Papers.

257 **scandalmonger James Callender:** No copies of these two pamphlets are extant, but their contents were later published in Callender's *History of the United States for 1796* (Philadelphia: Snowden and McCorkle, 1797), ch. 6 and 7. For a useful summary of the Reynolds Affair and textual analysis of key documents, see Julian P. Boyd, "Appendix: The First Conflict in the Cabinet," *Papers of Thomas Jefferson*, vol. 18 (Princeton, NJ: Princeton University Press, 1971), 611–68. On Callender, including his source, see Michael Durey, *With the Hammer of Truth: James Thompson Callender and America's Early National Heroes* (Charlottesville: University of Virginia Press, 1990), 97–104. Among the best recent analyses is Jacob Katz Cogan, "The Reynolds Affair and the Politics of Character," *Journal of the Early Republic* 16, no. 3 (Autumn 1996): 389–417.

257 **Revolutionary War veteran:** *Jesse Seymour v. James Reynolds* (for fraud against Joseph Vincent, formerly a Continental Army soldier), 4 May 1790, New York City Mayor's Court Trial Minutes, NYPL. The plaintiff won.

257 **this was "absurd":** James Callender to Alexander Hamilton, *Diary* (New York), 13 July 1797.

257 **"bucket of chastity":** Callender, *History*, 222.

257 **"suspicions were removed":** Callender, *History*, document v. (16 December 1792): 217–18, 230.

258 **"fabrication of colonel Hamilton":** Callender, *History*, document v. (2 January 1793): 218.

258 **And rumors spread:** For an incisive analysis of the spread and political uses of gossip in this period, see Joanne B. Freeman, *Affairs of Honor: National Politics in the New Republic* (New Haven, CT: Yale University Press, 2001), 62–104; esp. 70–72, on the Reynolds Affair. Hamilton and the threat of exposure: Durey, *Hammer of Truth*, 98–99. A threat against Hamilton: *Aurora* (Philadelphia), 11 June 1796. Hamilton (writing as Phocion) obliquely threatens Jefferson: no. IV, *Gazette of the United States* (Philadelphia), 19 October 1796; see also Chernow, *Hamilton*, 511–14.

258 **get a divorce:** Nancy Isenberg, *Fallen Founder: The Life of Aaron Burr* (New York: Viking, 2007), 107; Cogan, "Reynolds Affair," 416.

258 **"I have doubts":** Boyd, "Appendix," in *Papers of Thomas Jefferson*, 18:666–73. "Certificate by James Monroe, [16 August 1797]," *Founders Online*, National Archives, accessed September 13, 2021, https://founders.archives.gov/documents/Hamilton /01-21-02-0134 (original source: *The Papers of Alexander Hamilton*, vol. 21, *April 1797–July 1798*, ed. Harold C. Syrett [New York: Columbia University Press, 1974], 211–12.; quote from Monroe's cover letter to Burr of the same date as quoted in note 1 at *Founders Online*).

258 **"more serious stain":** Alexander Hamilton, *Observations on certain documents contained in no. V. & VI of "The history of the United States for the year 1796* (Philadelphia, 1797), 9 ("blush"), 10 ("stain").

259 **the original letters:** In "Appendix," in *Papers of Thomas Jefferson*, 18:611–68, Julian P. Boyd makes a strong case that Maria Reynolds's letters were indeed forged. Subsequent historians have generally ignored or dismissed Boyd's argument; see, notably, Harold C. Syrett, "Introductory Note: From Oliver Wolcott, Junior [3 July 1797], *Papers of Alexander Hamilton*, vol. 21 (New York: Columbia University Press, 1974), 121–44. For a recent argument supporting Boyd's analysis, see Tilar J. Mazzeo, *Eliza Hamilton: The Extraordinary Life and Times of the Wife of Alexander Hamilton* (New York: Gallery Books, 2018). For Hamilton's promise to deposit the letters with William Bingham, Esq., for review, see *Observations*, 31, lviii (note).

259 **Hamilton was too angry:** James Callender to Alexander Hamilton, Philadelphia, 29 October 1797, Hamilton Papers, Library of Congress; Hamilton endorsed the letter with "Impudent Experiment NO NOTICE."

259 **"deposited with me"**: William Bingham to James McHenry, [Lansdown, PA, 18 November 1799], enclosure in McHenry to Alexander Hamilton, Philadelphia, 18 November 1799, Hamilton Papers, Library of Congress.

259 **indignation and fraudulent defense:** James Thomson Callender, *Sketches of the History of America* (Philadelphia: Snowden and M'Corkle, 1798), ch. 5.

259 **"cannot be a swindler"**: Callender, *Sketches*, 91 ("ninety-three pages"), 100 ("swindler").

259 **"what she has to say"**: Callender, *Sketches*, 92 ("love-sick"), 99–100 (textual analysis), 107 ("send for the lady").

259 **"done him incomparable injury"**: On the reception of Hamilton's *Observations*, see, among other works, Mazzeo, *Eliza Hamilton* (focussing on the distress of his wife and her family); Isenberg, *Fallen Founder*, 167 (surveying newspaper reactions); Cogan, "Reynolds Affair" (on the gender ideologies that encouraged sympathy with Maria Reynolds). Quote: Robert Troup to Rufus King, New York, 3 June 1798, in Charles R. King, ed., *Life and Correspondence of Rufus King*, vol. 2 (New York: G. P. Putnam's Sons, 1895), 330.

260 **incentives to leave town:** Boyd, *Appendix*, 635–36, 641–43.

260 **drag the proceedings out:** The suit was initiated in January 1798: *John Callanan v. William Bedlow*, judgment roll, filed 7 August 1798, SCJ PR P-32-E-7.

260 **a "concealed debtor"**: James Kent, notice regarding William Bedlow, 21 February 1798, *Commercial Advertiser* (New York), 22 February 1798; the notice appeared every day except Sundays until Friday, 2 March 1798.

260 **Bedlow was ordered to pay:** *John Callanan v. William Bedlow*, judgment roll, filed 7 August 1798, SCJ PR P-32-E-7. Bedlow ordered to plead: SCJ MB1797–1800R: 468 (3 March 1798, Evertson). Trial: SCJ CC MB1796–1799: 258 (26 July 1798). Judgment approved: SCJ MB1797–1800R: 470 (1 August 1798).

262 *The hypocrite unmask'd*: *The hypocrite unmask'd. Trial and conviction of John Baker, a Methodist teacher, of this city, for seducing Miss Ann Burns, under a promise of marriage* (New York, 1798).

262 **reportedly £4,000:** Memorial of Elizabeth Ketteltas, *Albany Centinel*, 3 April 1798 (read and referred); *Albany Centinel*, 17 August 1798 (to be approved).

262 **outbreak of yellow fever:** Early news of the outbreak in Philadelphia: *Commercial Advertiser* (New York), 9 August 1798; *Daily Advertiser* (New York), 10 August 1798. Panic and flight: *New-York Gazette*, 23 August 1798; *New-York Journal*, 8 September 1798.

262 **half a dozen affairs of honor:** Freeman, *Affairs of Honor*, 326–27 n13.

262 **William Allsee had used:** William Allsee, Notice, New York, 9 February 1798, *Commercial Advertiser* (New York), 12 February 1798. In *Sex Among the Rabble: An Intimate History of Gender and Power in the Age of Revolution, Philadelphia, 1730–1830* (Chapel Hill: University of North Carolina Press, 2006), Clare A. Lyons discusses "runaway wife" advertisements published by husbands (ch. 1) and emphasizes that women did sometimes respond with their own notices (178–80).

263 **Elizabeth Allsee did:** Elizabeth Allsee, Counter Notice, *Commercial Advertiser* (New York), 14 February 1798. See also their divorce records: *William Allsee v. Elizabeth Allsee, action for divorce*, New York Court of Chancery, filed 13 February 1798, NYSA; reproduced in Mary-Jo Kline, ed., *The Papers of Aaron Burr, 1756–1836*, microfilm ed. (Glen Rock, NJ, 1978), NYCh Case 181.

263 **Harry Bedlow wrote:** *Poughkeepsie Journal*, 2 October 1798.

265 **Mrs. Carey's house:** *Gazette of the United States* (Philadelphia), 6 April 1796 (Jennings elected); *Claypool's American Daily Advertiser* (Philadelphia), 28 June 1796 (office at 4th and Union).

265 **beyond New York:** Excerpts of the affidavit, with explanatory introduction, were printed in *New York-Gazette*, 5 October 1798; *Commercial Advertiser* (New York), 5 October 1798; *Spectator* (New York), 6 October 1798.

265 **rise to Bedlow's bait:** This is not entirely certain since surviving runs of the *Poughkeepsie Journal* for that fall are incomplete.

266 **that employed "your's":** American Historical Imprints, Readex, accessed June 26, 2015.

266 **bitten by the mosquito:** Notice of the death of Catharine Bedlow, *Daily Advertiser* (New York), 16 October 1798. According to the typical course of the disease, Catharine Bedlow was likely infected between September 20–27: "Yellow Fever" fact sheet, World Health Organization, May 7, 2019, http://www.who.int/mediacentre/factsheets/fs100/en/.

266 **Harry Bedlow's parents:** "Wife of William Bedlow," between 14–16 October 1798, William Bedlow, 9 November 1798, "Record of Burials in the Dutch Church, New York," *Year Book of the Holland Society of New York* (1899), 144. William Bedlow's death: *Daily Advertiser* (New York), 9 November 1798; *New-York Gazette*, 10 November 1798; *Weekly Museum* (New York), 10 November 1798.

267 **catalog of unpaid debts:** *Henry Rutgers v. Henry Bedlow*, judgment roll, filed 15 February 1799, SCJ PR P-173-H-5; SCJ Docket of Judgments No. 2, 1795–1803 (JN527, NYSA): under January Term 1799, Henry Bedlow, judgment debtor, Henry Rutgers, judgment creditor; that Bedlow eventually paid what he owed to his uncle was recorded on 16 June 1802.

267 **he pressed on:** SCJ MB1797–100R: 481 (22 November 1798, Evertson: *John Callanan v. Henry Rutgers*). Rutgers, through his attorney Robert Troup, challenged his responsibility for the debt: *Henry Rutgers, manucaptor of William Bedlow, ads. John Callanan*, rejoinder, filed 10 January 1799, SCJ PL C-939 (microfilm reel 13). It seems that Rutgers settled with Callanan by March 1799, since no further record was found.

267 **pilot boat was *Perseverance*:** The pilot boat *Perseverance* rescued the ship *Neptune* in 1799: *Spectator* (New York), 25 December 1799. Associated legal records made it clear that this was the boat of Callanan's company: *Callaghan and others v. Hallett & Bowne*, SCJ MB1801–1805: 177 (13 May 1805), reported as *Callagan and others v. Hallett & Bowne*, New York, Apr. term 1803 in George Caines, *New York term reports of cases argued and determined in the Supreme court of that State*, vol. 1 (New York: I. Riley, 1804), 104–7.

267 **birdcage holding a canary:** Adelheid Voskuhl, *Androids in the Enlightenment: Mechanics, Artisans, and Cultures of the Self* (Chicago: University of Chicago, 2013). Napoleon: *Daily Advertiser* (New York), 4 July 1798. Birdcage: *Minvera* (New York), 31 May 1797; *Time Piece* (New York), 2 February 1798.

268 **how Maria Reynolds felt:** A good summary of Maria Reynolds's life after 1792 is in Cogan, "Reynolds Affair," 416. On her unpublished memoir: W[illiam] D[uane], *Aurora* (Philadelphia), 18 September 1802.

268 **can be verified now :** I'm also grateful to Scott Wilds for his advice; to Clare Lyons, Jen Marion, and Billy Smith for checking their files of Philadelphians in the Early Republic for traces of Lanah Sawyer/Stymets; and to archivist Joshua K. Blay, at the Philadelphia City Archives, for laborious searches of records there.

268 **Stymets was a rare name:** The name was spelled in various ways—"Stimets," "Stymetz"—but seems distinct from the dozen or so Steintmetz families in Pennsylvania. For exhaustive efforts to track down Stymets men alive in the 1790s and trace their marital histories, I am deeply grateful to Nancy Gray Schoonmaker; out of dozens of possible men in the database she compiled, only a handful did not appear to have documented marriages.

EPILOGUE

270 **elaborate embroidered pictures:** Jane Callanan, will, 4 January 1821, proved 23 September 1823, Wills Liber 58:252–54 (new), 285–88 (old), New York County Surrogate's Court (leaves daughter Jane the "Pictures embroidered by her").

270 **damage, endurance, and repair:** Anna Hofmann (maker), darning sampler, 36 x 33 cm, 1790–1830, 1964.1792, bequest of Henry Francis du Pont, Winterthur Museum. My thanks to Marla Miller and Emily Whitted for sharing their insights on this sampler.

270 **"my life had just begun":** Alice Sebold, *Lucky* (New York: Charles Scribner's Sons, 1999), 30.

270 **"Was it probable":** *Report*, 40–41 (Cozine).

271 **for the "rights of women":** Rosemarie Zagarri, *Revolutionary Backlash: Women and Politics in the Early American Republic* (Philadelphia: University of Pennsylvania Press, 2007), 1 (quote). See also Christine Stansell, *City of Women: Sex and Class in New York, 1798–1860* (New York: Alfred A. Knopf, 1986), 22–23.

271 **by a man:** On the challenge of recovering stories of the lives of enslaved Black women made visible—and silenced—by records of their abuse by white men, see Saidiya Hartman, "Venus in Two Acts," *Small Axe* 12, no. 2 (June 2008): 1–14; Marisa J. Fuentes, *Dispossessed Lives: Enslaved Women, Violence, and the Archive* (Philadelphia: University of Pennsylvania Press, 2016); and Sharon Block, "Reconstituting Archives of Violence and Silence in Early American Women's History," *Journal of Women's History* 30, no. 1 (Spring 2018): 154–62.

271 **vanished without a trace:** The missing registers were reportedly taken with Rector Charles Inglis when he removed to Nova Scotia, where he later became a bishop, but they do not appear in the archives of the Diocese of Nova Scotia and Prince Edward Island (Lorraine Slopek to author, email, 29 March 2018).

271 **John Callanan died:** Death notice: *Commercial Advertiser* (New York), 23 November 1805, 3. Will: 22 November 1805, proved 3 January 1806, Wills Liber 46:153–55 (new), 168–71 (old), New York County Surrogate's Court.

271 **The will Lanah's mother wrote:** Jane Callanan, will, 4 January 1821.

272 **half sister Jane Callanan:** Mary Sawyer (1780–?) married deputy pilot Robert Hewitt, 13 December 1798, Pilmore marriage register. Hewitt on list of branch pilots: *Gaine's New York Almanack for 1799* (1798). Peter Sawyer (1778–1826) was appointed branch pilot on 30 March. 1803: Minutes of the Council of Appointment, 1786–1822, 4:176, A1845, NYSA. Peter's son Alexander Henderson Sawyer (1806–?) and Lanah's half brother Lewis Callanan (1798–1851) were both listed as pilots in *Longworth's Directory for 1829*. Jane Callanan (1789–1863) married David G. Patterson in 1806 (*Weekly Museum* [New York], 9 May 1806) and Lt. Thomas Staniford (1788–1855) ten years later (*Weekly Museum* [New York], 30 November 1816). Memorial for Jane Staniford, widow of Lt. Col. Thomas Staniford, Windham (CT) Center Cemetery.

272 **younger sister Catharine Sawyer:** Catharine Sawyer m. William Maclin, 21 March 1799 (marginal note: "Gave a Certificate 25 October 1808"), Pilmore marriage register. There are a host of indictments and complaints relating to the Macklins in the DA Indictments: Indictment of William Macklin (seventh ward, tavern keeper, disorderly house), filed 5 December 1796; Complaint of Abraham Stagg against James Flyn, John Roche, William Macklin, John Laughlin & John Bissett (all tavern keepers on George Street), disorderly house keeping and suspected "whoring," 8 August 1798; Indictment of Catharine Macklin (described by the victim as a "seamstress"), assault and battery, filed 4 April 1800 (see also *Mercantile Advertiser* [New York], 9 April 1800); Indictment of William Macklin and Catharine Macklin (disorderly house keeping), filed 10 October 1807. Catharine then filed complaints against five different men: Samuel Armstrong, 5 June 1807; Caleb Huntington, 24 June 1807; William Sherman, 9 July 1807; George Card, 28 July 1807; and John Perry, 28 July 1807; the grand jury turned a deaf ear to all of these. Complaint against neighbors: Affidavit of William Macklin, 21 July 1808; Affidavits of Lewis French and James Wright (Catharine Macklin's murder threat), 1 August 1808; Indictment of William Macklin and Catharine Macklin (disorderly house keeping and "whoring" in May 1808), 5 August

1808. For a more complete summary of prosecutions against the Macklins, including outcomes, see Hays, "General List." Note: Market Street was formerly George (or E. George); Madison Street was formerly Bedlow.

272 **Elizabeth Keteltas:** Elizabeth Kettletas married Melancthon Fleet on 31 July 1803: Herbert Furman Seversmith, Colonial Families of Long Island, New York, and Connecticut, mimeographed typescript, Washington, DC, 1939, 2:934, accessed via HathiTrust on September 13, 2021, https://catalog.hathitrust.org/Record/005756269. She is buried, along with her father and husband, in Prospect Cemetery, Jamaica, Queens County, New York: "Elizabeth Keteltas Fleet," Find a Grave, accessed September 13, 2021, https://www.findagrave.com/memorial/88022893/elizabeth-fleet.

272 **Margaret Miller, a thirteen-year-old:** *Report of the trial of Richard D. Croucher on an indictment for a rape on Margaret Miller* (New York, 1800), 11 (bad girl, whore); 13 (whore). *The Only Correct Account of the Life, Character, and Conduct of John Banks . . . To Which is Prefixed a Correct copy of his Trial & Condemnation*, 4th ed. (New York, 1806): 9 (marriage date), 11 (maiden name). See also *An Authentic account of the Trial of John Banks* (n.p., n.d.).

272 **women at the center:** Out of a sample of thirty-three women in seduction cases in the NJSCCF collection between 1746 and 1841 (see Appendix), the marital histories of eighteen could not be traced (she was not named, it was impossible to distinguish between individuals with the same name, or no matching record was found); ten married; and five seem to have remained single—including Ann VanHorn; see Elizabeth Collette, "Journey to the Promised Land," *Western Pennsylvania Historical Magazine* 22, no. 4 (December 1939), 245–62.

273 **common prostitute:** George W. Corner, ed., *The Autobiography of Benjamin Rush . . . Together with his Commonplace Book* (Philadelphia: Princeton University Press, 1948), 205 (8 August 1809, 13 August 1809).

273 **Maria Reynolds Clingman:** The basic details of Maria Reynolds's later life are summarized in Jacob Katz Cogan, "The Reynolds Affair and the Politics of Character," *Journal of the Early Republic* 16, no. 3 (Autumn 1996): 417.

273 **and Aaron Burr:** William Coleman, *Report of the trial of Levi Weeks, on an indictment for the murder of Gulielma Sands* (New York: John Furman, 1800), 67. A less complete and accurate report indicated that this speech, which opened the defense case, was given by Aaron Burr: James Hardie, *An impartial account of the trial of Mr. Levi Weeks, for the supposed murder of Miss Julianna Elmore Sands. At a court held in the city of New-York, March 31, 1800* (New York: M. M'Farlane, 1800), 24.

273 **raping Margaret Miller:** *Report of the trial of Richard D. Croucher* (New York, 1800), 18 (Bedlow case). Governor George Clinton, pardon of Richard D. Croucher for rape, 1 February 1803, B0042–78, vol. 1:173–74, NYSA.

273 **also been effectively pardoned:** In 1785, Mayor Varick refused to enter a sentence after Eleazer M. Tennery was convicted of rape. In December 1798, William Purvis was convicted of attempted rape and sentenced to a year in prison (Hays, "General List"), and then promptly ordered pardoned by Governor John Jay on the advice of Mayor Varick, who called it "a hard and doubtful Case" (John Jay to Daniel Hale, 17 December 1798, NYHS). The only other man convicted of attempted rape (rather than a lesser count of simple assault and battery) between 1784 and 1800 in either the DA Indictments records or Hays's "General List" was Polete Clement; he was charged with three attempted rapes and convicted of one attempted rape and two simple assaults (Polete Clement, three indictments for attempted rape, filed 9 June 1798, DA Indictments; Hays, "General List"). Sharon Block, *Rape and Sexual Power in Early America* (Chapel Hill: University of North Carolina Press, 2003), 134n, refers to a pardon request by convicted sexual assailant William Van Tassel, but I find no record of his conviction, and his indictment is marked "non cul." for "not guilty" (*The People v. William Van Tassell*, filed 8 February 1800, DA Indictments).

273 **in the *Washington Times*:** See Muriel Dobbin, *Washington Times*, July 11, 2013, reviewing Paul Collins, *Duel with the Devil: The True Story of How Alexander Hamilton and Aaron Burr Teamed up to Take on America's First Sensational Murder Mystery* (New York: Crown, 2013). Collins reads the retraction attributed to Lanah Sawyer as authentic (145–46, 157).

273 **gentleman Charles Wakely:** *Trial of Charles Wakely, for a rape on Mrs. Rebecca Fay* (New York: M'Carty & White, 1810). DA Indictments: filed 12 February 1810 (rape); filed 24 February 1810 (perjury). Hays, "List," 243 (rape), 245 (perjury). Trial: *Columbian* (New York), 20 February 1810; *New York Gazette*, 23 February 1810. Perjury charges: *Columbian*, 26 February 1810; *Evening Post* (New York), 5 March 1810. Objections to the published report: *American Citizen* (New York), 5 March 1810; *New York Gazette*, 5 March 1810; *Republican Watch-Tower* (New York), 6 March 1810.

274 **recently called "himpathy":** Kate Manne, *Down Girl: The Logic of Misogyny* (New York: Oxford University Press, 2018), 195–204.

274 **Just as Livingston had smeared:** *Report of the trial of Richard D. Croucher* (New York, 1800), 15 (life of a citizen, passions), 18 (Bedlow case), 16 (to tell the truth).

274 **Wyche had moved away:** By late 1796, Wyche had moved to Charlestown: ad for the sale of land, *City Gazette* (Charleston, SC), 22 October 1796. There, he continued to practice law; see, for example, notices in the *City Gazette*, 26 March 1798 and 8 August 1799.

275 **quasi-official report:** On this cluster of New York trial reports through 1800, see Daniel Cohen, "Pillars of Salt: The Transformation of New England Crime Literature, 1674–1860" (PhD diss., Brandeis University, 1988), 342–78. On the broader cultural trend, see Patricia Cline Cohen, *The Murder of Helen Jewett: The Life and Death of a Prostitute in Nineteenth Century New York* (New York: Alfred A. Knopf, 1998); Karen Halttunen, *Murder Most Foul: The Killer and the American Gothic Imagination* (Cambridge, MA: Harvard University Press, 1998).

275 **shame and stigma:** Influential analyses of the special virtue claimed by middle-class white women include Caroll Smith Rosenberg, "Beauty, the Beast, and the Militant Woman: A Case Study in Sex Roles and Social Stress in Jacksonian America," *American Quarterly* 23, no. 4 (October 1971), 563–84; Nancy F. Cott, "Passionlessness: An Interpretation of Victorian Sexual Ideology, 1790–1850," *Signs* 4, no. 2 (Winter 1978), 219–36; and Stansell, *City of Women*. For a trenchant analysis of the class and racial dynamics of efforts to reform rape law in the nineteenth century, see Estelle Freedman, *Redefining Rape: Sexual Violence in the Era of Suffrage and Segregation* (Cambridge, MA: Harvard University Press, 2013).

275 **history is silent:** Philip Hone, 8 August 1838, Diaries, 1826–1851, 14:287, Mss. Col. BV Hone, Philip, NYHS; "frighted the Isle" is a reference to Shakespeare's *Othello*, ii.3.

275 **at least six children:** Three of Henry Bedlow's children by Christiana Tippets are named in Mary McCrea, will, 8 March 1817, proved 27 March 1817, Wills Liber 53:456–58 (new), New York County Surrogate's Court: Henry Bedlow, William Prouse Alsey Bedlow, and Caroline Amelia Bedlow. Henry Bedlow Jr. was born about 1798, had a "light complexion," and stood five feet seven and a half inches tall, Certificate 719, 30 October 1816, Quarterly Abstracts of Seamen's Protection Certificates, New York District, 1815–1819, NARA. William Prouse Alsey Bedlow was likely born between 1799 and 1804 and was named after his father's friend Captain William Prouse Allsee; see Rutgers estate documents below. "Burials in the Dutch Church, New York City [1804–1807]," *NYGB Record* 75, no. 3 (1944) lists "Henry Bedlow's Child," 30 April 1805 (131); "Henry Bedlow's wife" [probably his daughter], 20 April 1806 (134); "Henry Bedlow's child," 16 January 1807 (136). The Trinity Church registers list the burial of "Bedlow's child," age four months, 28 August 1807 (Trinity Churchyard). Caroline Amelia Bedlow was born about 1808; the 1870 Federal Census

gives her age as sixty-two (return for Homer, Cortland County, NY, p. 752A, M593–922, NARA).

276 **considered him too "broken":** "Married," *New York Post*, 5 April 1808, 3. Henry Rutgers to William Bedlow Crosby, Albany, 30 March 1807, William Bedlow Crosby Papers, ca. 1686–1892, NYHS.

276 **plagued by lawsuits:** A search of surviving file papers in the NYCC-DOR's Historic Documents Indexes returns eight lawsuits against Henry Bedlow in 1805 alone in the Mayor's Court (Judgments 1805#228, 1805#322, 1805#327, 1805#368, 1805#373, 1805#443, 1805#498, 1805#506) and three in the superior court (two brought by his erstwhile attorney Peter Jay Munro, SCJ LJ 1805-B-3 and 1805-B-63; as well as SCJ PR P-117-F-3, filed 5 February 1805).

276 **old family friends:** Henry Bedlow to Henry Remsen, Newark, 4 January 1809, PBA Galleries, San Francisco, online catalogue for sale 511, lot 128 (2013), http://www.pbagalleries.com/view-auctions/catalog/id/12/lot/7134/Autograph-Letter-Signed-1809-New-York-Patrician-Rapist-seeks-Wall-Street-loan.

276 **imprisoned for debt:** New Jersey State Archives Supreme Court File Papers #203, *John Alling v. Henry Bedlow*, for debt (1812), Essex County, NJ. Bedlow was apparently imprisoned from the time the suit was initiated, in January 1812, until at least May; Bedlow's appeal came before the supreme court in September: Henry Bedlow, Newark Gaol, 28 September 1815, notice of hearing regarding his release from imprisonment as an insolvent debtor, *Centinel of Freedom* (Newark, NJ), 26 September 1815. Four years after Alling brought his claim, the sheriff sold two parcels of Bedlow's to satisfy that debt: Henry Bedlow (by the sherrif) to David D. Crane, 1816, A-2:230; Henry Bedlow (by the sherrif) to Nehamiah Tunis Jr., 1816, A-2:618; Essex County Deeds, (microfilm), New Jersey State Archives. See also Henry Rutgers, advertisement for the sale of all the stock on the farm where Henry Bedlow had been living, *Centinel of Freedom* (Newark, NJ), 16 April 1816, 3.

276 **once again, for bankruptcy:** Notice of absconding debtor Henry Bedlow of Belleville, NJ, *Commercial Advertiser* (New York), 21 September 1815. Notice of 26 July 1820 insolvency hearing for Henry Bedlow, New York, *Daily Advertiser* (New York), 26 June 1820.

276 **England's Glorious Revolution:** Henry Bedlow to F. Martin & Townsend, New York, 29 September 1821, Misc. MSS Bedlow, NYHS. Half a century later, Bedlow's son was still pressing this claim: "Summary of News," *Lowell* (MA) *Daily Citizen*, 8 November 1879.

276 **mariner, at sea:** Henry Bedlow Jr. was swept overboard: *New-York Gazette* (New York), 28 November 1818.

276 **a cabinet maker:** Cabinet maker: Petition of William Prouse Alsey Bedlow, Schedule A (1 Nov. 1831), in *William Prouse Alsey Bedlow v. Richard Riker and others* (trustees of estate of Henry Rutgers), filed 25 November 1831, BM-719-B, NYCC Chancery Court. Death: Petition of Anthony Carroll, Caroline Amelia Williams, and Thompson P. Williams, 9 March 1835, in the matter of the petition of Carolina Amelia Bedlow (Thompson), filed 16 March 1835, BM-W-1603, NYCC Chancery Court.

276 **married a disreputable man:** In the matter of the petition of Caroline Amelia Bedlow (Thompson), filed 16 March 1835, BM-W-1603, NYCC Chancery Court. Bedlow's claim that her husband was already married was correct; Thompson P. Williams was married to (though long separated from) a woman in Connecticut: Jean de Chantal Kennedy, *Frith of Bermuda, Gentleman Privateer: A Biography of Hezekiah Frith, 1763–1848* (Hamilton: Bermuda Bookstore, 1964), 99–107, 114–21, 141–52. Williams died in 1841: *Connecticut Courant* (Hartford), 10 April 1841.

276 **the tiny portrait:** After the death of her first husband, Thompson P. Williams (see above), Caroline Bedlow remarried, to Joseph Homer: *New York Evening Post*, 7 October 1846. The 1870 US Census lists her living with her husband's sister in Homer,

New York, where she died on 7 November 1871; she is buried in Glenwood Cemetery in Homer. *The Catalogue of the American Portraits in the New-York Historical Society* (New York, 1941), 20, gives the provenance of the ca. 1790 Bedlow portrait miniature as: "owned by Joseph Homer, second husband of Henry Bedlow's eldest daughter, whose sister, Mrs. Sprague (of Homer, N.Y.) presented it to Mary Ann Redfield of Rochester. Mrs. Redfield was the mother of Mrs. Mary Ely of Ithaca, N.Y., from whom the society acquired it in 1928."

276 **"Marble Tomb Stone"**: Ann Carey, will, 20 May 1796, proved 19 October 1796, Wills Book 10:503, Philadelphia City Archives. The location of her gravestone (section 0, plot LXXIV) and its inscription were recorded by Edward L. Clark, *Record of the Inscriptions on the Tablets and Gravestones in the Burial-Ground of Christ-Church, Philadelphia* (Philadelphia: Collins, 1864), 498.

277 **The stone is still there:** My thanks to Scott Wilds for tracking down this grave in April 2021 and for his detailed report.

278 **half brother Owen Callanan:** The burials of members of Lanah's family appear in Trinity Church registers: her stepfather John "Callahan," 24 November 1805, and her nephew Peter Sawyer, 6 February 1819, were both buried in the Trinity Churchyard but are not represented by surviving stones. In Section S3 of the churchyard (on the south side of the church) is the stone for Lanah's half brother Owen Callanan/ "Callanen" (1797), a broken stone for her nephew Lewis C. Hewitt (1807), and the separated footstone marked "L.S." The "Charlotte Temple" stone is in section 1a-b. Lanah's niece Jane Hewitt, d. 1805: St. Paul's Churchyard, Section C1 & C3; Lanah's brother Peter Sawyer, d. 1826: St. John's Churchyard; both from burial registers, Trinity Church Archives.

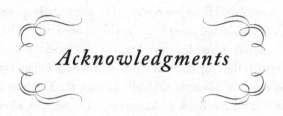

Acknowledgments

This book tells a story that, for many years, I thought I understood. Three decades ago, as a graduate student in a seminar led by the celebrated women's historian Christine Stansell, I was introduced to the *Report of the Trial of Henry Bedlow, for Committing a Rape on Lanah Sawyer* (New York, 1793). It was a gripping courtroom drama—by turns anguishing, exciting, and infuriating. And its parallels with the present were haunting. Two fellow graduate students, Marybeth Hamilton and Sharon Block, published brilliant studies of the case in light of broader historical patterns. So, when I began teaching, I often used it to help undergraduates and graduate students explore the historical roots of modern rape culture.

Then, about twelve years ago, one of my own graduate students, L. Maren Wood, shared a brief reference she had discovered in a New York City newspaper: five years after the trial, Lanah Sawyer had reportedly retracted her rape charge. Curious, I tracked down the original version of the supposed retraction in the *Poughkeepsie Journal*. It threw my assumptions about the case into doubt. Whatever had actually happened, the story had clearly not ended with the rape trial. It went on for years.

What really *was* Lanah Sawyer's story?

My long search for answers was made possible by archivists, curators, librarians, and collections at many repositories. Over the years, Joseph Van Nostrand and his staff have made work at the New York County Clerk's Division of Old Records pleasant and productive. Richard Tuske provided access to unique records at the New York City Bar library. Kenneth Cobb facilitated my work at New York City's Municipal Archives, and Robert Folts guided my way at the New York State Library and the New York State Archives. Microfilm copies of long-lost legal records, including the minutes of the rape trial, turned up in the archives at the Queens Public Library; I'm deeply grateful to Judith Todman for her help.

At the New-York Historical Society, I'm particularly grateful to Ted O'Reilly, Debra Bach, and Scott Wixon, who showed me the Bedlow portrait miniature and shared his thoughts. I'm also indebted to the interlibrary loan staff at the University of North Carolina at Chapel Hill, and to the professionals at the New York Public Library, the Museum of the City of New York, the Rare Book & Manuscript Library at Columbia University, the Archives at Trinity Church Wall Street, the Beinecke Library at Yale University, the Special Collections department of the Princeton University Libraries, the Massachusetts Historical Society, the New Jersey Historical Society, the New Jersey State Archives, the Historical Society of Pennsylvania, the Library Company of Philadelphia, the Pennsylvania State Archives, and the Philadelphia City Archives. While the Philadelphia City Archives was closed due to the pandemic, Joshua K. Blay doggedly searched for traces of Lanah Sawyer and Ann Carey. At the Library of Congress, Patrick Kerwin looked up the original manuscript of Catharine Bedlow's letter to Alexander Hamilton to see if the enclosed "Helenah Sawyer" letter was still there. It was not.

When I was obviously bewildered by the vast collection of property records at the New York City Department of Finance on John Street, a professional title searcher, "China" Williams, interrupted her own work to show me the way. For help harnessing the power of GIS mapping, I'm grateful to the UNC library's Digital Research Services team, especially Philip McDaniel.

Early on, Sharon Block generously shared her advice and her research files on New York sexual assault trials. Many others offered useful perspectives and insights, including Henry Abelove, Debby Applegate, Dick Brown, Melissa Bullard, Cornelia Dayton, Sheryl Kroen, Susan D. Pennybacker, Cara Robertson, and Lisa Wilson. Paul A. Gilje, Herbert S. Klein, and Edmund P. Willis shared the fruits of their work on postrevolutionary New York. Clare Lyons, Jen Manion, and Billy Smith all searched their Philadelphia research files for Lanah Sawyer and Ann Carey. Gracious guides to the history of the law included Holly Brewer, Douglass Greenberg, and Bruce Mann, who met with me at a busy time and answered my many questions with patience and deep expertise.

My thinking about this project has been expanded and enriched over the years by participants at a series of seminars and conferences. For invitations to present work in progress, I'm grateful to the organizers of the Omohundro Institute of Early American History and Culture Colloquium, College of William and Mary; the Washington Area Early American Seminar, University of Maryland at College Park; the Upstate Early American History Workshop, Binghamton University; the Boston Area Early American History Seminar, Massachusetts Historical Society; the "(En)gendering the Atlantic World" conference at New York University; and the "American Lives and American Studies" conference at the University of Connecticut. An Interdisciplinary Initiative grant from the College of Arts and Sciences at UNC supported a yearlong faculty-staff working group on "Rape: Realities, Perceptions, and Responses." I'm especially grateful to Christi Hurt, then director of the Carolina Women's Center; Ada Gregory, then director of the Duke Women's Center; and co-organizer Rachel F. Seidman. The activism of UNC graduates Annie E. Clark and Andrea Pino has been an inspiration.

During a meeting in Williamburg several years ago, Linda Baumgarten transformed my understanding of Lanah Sawyer's torn gown. I had read what I could about clothing of the period and came to her with questions about style and appearance—questions she answered with clarity, precision, and patience. Then she turned to the human meanings of the gown. Why, she asked, did Henry Bedlow pull it off? He could have just pulled up her skirts. His decision revealed something about his sexual aims. So, too, the damage sustained by the gown tells us something about Lanah: that she was struggling. Other leading experts on clothing and sewing in the Early Republic were extremely generous and helpful, especially Kimberly Alexander, Marla Miller, Emily Whitted, and Laura Johnson.

Former UNC undergraduates Justine Schnitzler, Victoria Hensley, and Nikita Shepard all provided meticulous research assistance—as did Christopher David Jillson, Alice Tessen, and Sarah Pearson Shapiro in New York and Paul Davis in Pennsylvania and New Jersey. Toward the end, Scott M. Wilds provided expert guidance—and located Mother Carey's grave.

At a crucial point, Kathleen M. Brown, Patricia Cline Cohen, Ann Little, and Katy Simpson Smith read the entire manuscript and offered trenchant critiques and generous help.

I think of a small group of friends and colleagues as this project's "long haulers." From start to finish, Mac Griswold and Lisa A. Lindsay read draft after draft and offered advice, reassurance, and the occasional kick in the pants. Anne Farrow read every word, more than once, with an eye for efficiency and focus. One of the great pleasures of this project has been the chance to work so closely for so long with two friends and colleagues, Nancy G. Schoonmaker and Randy M. Browne. Nancy provided expert assistance of all kinds, and the search for Lanah Sawyer and other figures in this book is deeply indebted to her research skills and tenacity. Randy has been an ideal work buddy—reading, talking, offering sage advice, and keeping me going day after day.

Chris Rogers first suggested I write this book and shepherded it through publication. Along the way, I benefited from Susan Rabiner's encouragement and advice and from the interest and insights generated by Susan Ferber, Kathleen McDermott, and Timothy Mennel. At Henry Holt and Co., I am grateful for the early enthusiasm of Barbara Jones, the sustained support of Sarah Crichton, and the swift, sure eye of my editor, Tim Duggan. The book was refined and enriched in countless ways by the work of Anita Sheih, Molly Pisani, Gene Thorp, Meryl Sussman Levavi, and Chris O'Connell.

Having spent years trying to follow Lanah Sawyer's trail only to lose sight of her in the end, I now hear echoes of her everywhere. I'm not going to name all the students, friends, neighbors, and members of my family— men and women, young and old—who have shared their stories. Each one comes as a shock, a revelation, a gift.

Over the past several years, when it seemed like I might get lost in Lanah Sawyer's world, friends and family brought me back. One of my grandmothers was a librarian; she lost her job to the male-breadwinner policies of the Great Depression but did not lose her love of reading. I think of her every time I hold a new book and spread back its pages the way she taught me. The lights of my life are the ones who wake me up every morning: my husband, Greg Fitch, and our children, Thomas and Betsey.

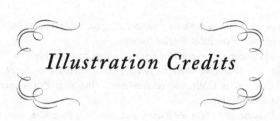

Illustration Credits

Fig. 2a. Portrait miniature of Henry Bedlow (1767–1838), ca. 1790, unidentified artist, watercolor on ivory, 4.1 x 3.2 cm, 1928.6, purchase, courtesy of the New-York Historical Society.

Fig. 2b. Portrait miniature of Susanna Rowson, ca. 1790, watercolor on paper, MSS 7379, courtesy of the University of Virginia Library.

Fig. 3a. Anne-Marguerite-Henriette Rouillé de Marigny, Baroness Hyde de Neuville (1771–1849), *Corner of Greenwich Street*, ca. January 1810, watercolor on paper, 18.6 x 33 cm, I. N. Phelps Stokes Collection of American Historical Prints, courtesy of the New York Public Library.

Fig. 3b. John Drayton, *A view of the Battery and harbour of New York, and the Ambuscade frigate*, engraving, 11.6 x 15.6 cm, in his *Letters written during a tour through the northern and eastern states of America* (Charleston, SC: Harrison and Bowen, 1794), courtesy of the John Carter Brown Library, Brown University.

Fig. 4. Charles B. J. F. de Saint-Mémin, *View of the City and Harbour of New York Taken from Mt. Pitt, New York, N.Y.*, 1796, hand-colored etching, 35.88 x 48.26 cm, 1973.6, courtesy of The Chipstone Foundation.

Fig. 5. The Beekman family coach, ca. 1770, wood, iron, paint, 98 x 161 x 52 in, 1911.25, gift of Gerald Beekman, courtesy of the New-York Historical Society.

Fig. 6a. George *Tobin, Virginia Pilot Boat, with a View of Cape Henry*, 1795, watercolor on paper, 14.9 x 23.8 cm, 1980.0018.000001, courtesy of the Mariner's Museum, Newport News, VA.

Fig. 6b. Archibald Robertson, *View up Wall Street with Federal Hall and Trinity Church*, ca. 1798, watercolor, black ink, and graphite on paper, 21.6 x 28.6 cm, 1864.14, courtesy of the New-York Historical Society.

Fig. 7a. Benjamin Trott, portrait miniature of Frances Duncan Ludlow Harison, ca. 1795–1797, watercolor on ivory, 5 x 6 cm, Richard Harison Papers, Rare Book and Manuscript Library, courtesy of Columbia University.

Fig. 7b. Keys used at New York's debtors' prison (the "New Gaol"), iron, ca. 1759–1783, larger: 21.6 x 6.4 cm, 1880.15ab, gift of A. P. M. Roome, courtesy of the New-York Historical Society.

Fig. 8. Darning sampler, Anna Hofmann, England or United States, 1790–1830, cotton thread on woven linen, 35.86 x 33.32 cm, 1964.1702, bequest of Henry Francis du Pont, courtesy of Winterthur Museum.

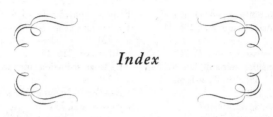

Index

Page numbers in *italics* refer to maps and illustrations.

About the Author

John Wood Sweet is a professor of history at the University of North Carolina at Chapel Hill and the former director of UNC's interdisciplinary Program in Sexuality Studies. His first book, *Bodies Politic: Negotiating Race in the American North, 1730–1830*, was a finalist for the Frederick Douglass Book Prize. He has served as a distinguished lecturer for the Organization of American Historians, and his work has been supported by fellowships from the National Endowment for the Humanities, the National Humanities Center, the Andrew W. Mellon Foundation, the Institute for the Arts and Humanities at UNC, the Gilder Lehrman Center at Yale, the McNeil Center at Penn, and the Institute for Global Studies in Culture, Power and History at Johns Hopkins. He lives in Chapel Hill with his husband, son, and daughter.